STANDING DOWN

SELECTED AND EDITED BY
Donald H. Whitfield

CONTRIBUTORS
Nancy Carr
Louise Galpine
Patrick Hurley
Kaara Kallen
Mary Klein
James Meredith
Dylan Nelson
Mary Williams

Cover graphic design: Gregory Borowski
Interior design: THINK Book Works

Standing Down: From Warrior to Civilian was made possible with generous financial support from the National Endowment for the Humanities and the Chicago Mercantile Exchange.

Any views, findings, conclusions, or recommendations expressed in this publication do not necessarily reflect those of the National Endowment for the Humanities.

STANDING
DOWN

FROM WARRIOR TO CIVILIAN

Foreword by Benjamin Busch

THE GREAT BOOKS FOUNDATION

A nonprofit educational organization

Published and distributed by

THE GREAT BOOKS FOUNDATION
A nonprofit educational organization

35 E. Wacker Drive, Suite 400
Chicago, IL 60601
www.greatbooks.org

First printing
9 8 7 6 5 4 3 2 1

Library of Congress Cataloging-in-Publication Data

Standing down : from warrior to civilian / selected and edited by
Donald H. Whitfield; contributors, Nancy Carr, Louise Galpine,
Patrick Hurley, Kaara Kallen, Mary Klein, James Meredith,
Dylan Nelson, Mary Williams.
      pages cm
   ISBN 978-1-939014-53-5 (pbk.)
   1. Soldiers--Literary collections. 2. Retired military personnel--
Literary collections. 3. Military art and science in literature.
I. Whitfield, Donald H., editor of compilation.
   PN6071.S55S73 2013
   808.8'0358--dc23
                                          2013019729

About the Great Books Foundation

The Great Books Foundation is an independent, nonprofit educational organization that provides opportunities for people of all ages to become more reflective, critical thinkers and readers through Shared Inquiry™ discussion of written works and ideas of enduring value.

The Great Books Foundation was established in 1947 to promote liberal education for the general public. In 1962, the Foundation extended its mission to children with the introduction of Junior Great Books.® Since its inception, the Foundation has helped thousands of people throughout the United States and in other countries begin their own discussion groups in schools, libraries, and community centers. Today, Foundation instructors conduct hundreds of workshops each year, in which educators and parents learn to lead Shared Inquiry discussion.

About Talking Service

Talking Service is an initiative to extend the Great Books Foundation's reading and discussion programs to current and former members of the United States Armed Forces. While Talking Service will emphasize discussion programs for veterans making the transition from military service back to civilian life, family members and friends of veterans, as well as all others interested in reflecting on the experiences of these men and women, will also be encouraged to participate. Complete information about Talking Service can be found at **talkingservice.greatbooks.org.**

Footnotes by the author are not bracketed; footnotes by the
Great Books Foundation, an editor, or a translator are [bracketed].

Spelling and punctuation have been modernized
and slightly altered for clarity.

Contents

Foreword

TO THE VETERAN

In French caves, painted in berry juice, are the first stories of humans as predators. These images are also the first evidence of a need to record our imagination, to identify the hunter and the hunted, and to use art to mark experience. These messages are still there, over seventeen thousand years old. We preyed on the animals and then we fought each other. When war became part of the human experience, it produced both casualties and survivors, the first veterans. Our stories of war became song, were carved into stone, with heroes rising and consuming most of the narrative, and foot soldiers mentioned only as masses, ranks, and lines. Loss and suffering were secondary experiences, and aftermath was rarely examined. It takes Odysseus ten years to journey home from the Trojan War, and he is so changed by hardship that he is unrecognized by his own wife. This one message ends the *Odyssey*. Homer knew there was transformation in a veteran's face and something larger at work within his head. The wars return with the warriors. In Latin, *veteranus* means nothing more than "old." It serves as the base for "veteran" and implies that you have been matured by your experience, aged beyond your years. Wounds, confusion, fear, savagery, boredom, hilarity, and ghosts are the unforgettable cost of your aging at arms.

The words "stand down" are in opposition to one another, an oxymoron like "good war" and "friendly fire." The term was first used as an order to the court witness who stood to give testimony and, when finished, would step down from the stand. It appeared in military commands during World War I, when troops in deep trenches ascended on fire steps to look out and engage charging Germans. They would "stand to" on alert and "stand down" to rest out of sight. Trench poet Wilfred Owen wrote while standing down. It is understood that warriors released from service have been ordered to stand down for the rest of their lives, but they cannot begin again as civilians as if just waking from a sleep. It is difficult for some of us veterans to remember what we were like before the wars. Our stories from the front echo in who we have become.

> *It is impossible to convey the life-sensation of any given epoch of one's existence—that which makes its truth, its meaning—its subtle and penetrating essence. It is impossible. We live, as we dream—alone. . . .*
> —Joseph Conrad, *Heart of Darkness*

It is into a certain solitude that a veteran returns home. I do not mean that we veterans are alone, but that there is a part of our lives separate from our families, our friends, and from the rest of our days. We have been away, have dug holes for protection, have carried everything we needed on our backs, and have been taught to be alert for our enemies. We have been trained to kill people like us. These are neither suburban activities nor the survival skills of people at peace. The cruel necessities of soldiering end with our enlistments and commissions, and we are returned to the people we left behind, those who gave us up for the singular purpose of bearing arms. "Terminal leave" concludes the period when our sense of purpose may have had the most clarity. It is at this moment that years of training and tension are expected to simply blow out of us—but I can tell you exactly how to assemble a pistol in the dark and that you shouldn't sit with your back to a doorway. How do we work this kind of knowledge into discussions about grocery lists and office politics? We have stories that stay in our other life.

Before we disperse into the entropy of our civilian afterlives as veterans, we belong to teams, sections, platoons, and companies. We share a collective witness to our military experience with those we serve beside. We all come from units as tight as families and then, all at once, we are blown apart with one word: discharge. It's a good word for how we can feel about our sudden severance. Weapons are discharged. The very word means to dismiss, to relieve of obligation and responsibility, but it does not address what becomes of the bullet. Out we go into the strange world we once knew, and now know differently. This idea of separation is one that runs throughout the readings in this anthology. We pack our stories, not realizing their weight, and walk away to find home. We don't recount how we sat and cleaned our rifles—for years—this repetitive act too unremarkable to find its way into small talk on the street, but it is heavy with muscle memory, and it was during this ritual that we knew we were foot soldiers of the nation. Then, one day, we turned in our weapons at the armory and never went back.

We are slow to return home sometimes, arriving later than our bodies to the place that is not war. We return to an environment where combat is little more than the subject of entertainment crafted to excite citizens who are safe. People might ask a veteran what it was like "over there," but get little more than, "You had to be there." Many veterans use this small response to dismiss stories of their service, or to say nothing instead of telling them at all. We often feel there is a certain authenticity lost somewhere, that language cannot completely express our experience to those who do not share it. "You wouldn't understand," we think to ourselves. We were there. In the jungles with the rain, insects, and primordial mud; in the deserts with the sun, dust, and goats. We were there with our fingers straight and off the trigger and we know these landscapes like the yards of our childhoods. We've been some places long and deep enough for them to be as clear in memory as home. To serve somewhere, anywhere, you have to be marooned there, touch the earth, smell the air. We have done this.

People go to the beach for vacation. They spread out blankets, take off their shoes, put their toes in the sand, and watch their children play. You, the veteran, have done this too. You know the beach like they do. This is a shared experience you can talk about with almost everyone. There is language for this. But how many people have patrolled deserts wearing their boots, weighed down with armor and bullets, their feet never touching the sand? How many people have attacked a beach from the sea? Sand is different to those who have. As veterans, we have all left home and have a new sense of the world because we have been thrown into the elements. We have been taught that we are in a contest with our environment, made to consider other people with armed suspicion, to endure exposure. We have suffered prolonged discomfort, privation, hopelessness, loss, and pain. Even if hardship never continued beyond basic training, there is that universal experience that implants a heightened sense of conflict with time, nature, and other people.

For thousands of years, soldiers have gone forth and returned with stories of where they went: some exultant, some so broken with laughter as to be incomprehensible, some coded with military dialect, and some quiet with sorrow or buried deep for shame. How do we know when one of our stories is true?

> *A true war story is never moral. It does not instruct, nor encourage virtue, nor suggest models of proper human behavior, nor restrain men from doing the things men have always done. If a story seems moral, do not believe it. If at the end of a war story you feel uplifted, or if you feel that some small bit of rectitude has been salvaged from the larger waste, then you have been made the victim of a very old and terrible lie.*
>
> —Tim O'Brien, *The Things They Carried*

There are stories by Tim O'Brien in this collection, and the works selected by the editors answer his warning. More important even than this, they prove that transference of experience is possible with language. In this collection, you will find yourself, fragments of your service struggled into sentences that seek to ring true with you more than any other reader. Are your feelings discovered in the spare sentences of Ernest Hemingway? The haunted poetry of Brian Turner? The confessional counsel of Karl Marlantes? The worried imagination of Siobhan Fallon? The angry outbursts of Michael Poggi? Literature has found the common soldier over time and has been trying to explain what we know. It has also finally reached the front line through the nurses, medics, corpsmen, and military families. Storytellers have learned that war is just the beginning of what war does to those who fight them.

So put these writers to the test. Search these sentences for a quiet path home. Use this language when it resonates to help others understand what it is to be gone to the wars. This is not a collection of stories crafted with any expectations. This is not a volume of judgments to bear out confessions, apologies, shame, or sympathy. This is a book of stories by and about men and women who went away, stories real and imagined, by writers trying to tell a truth about being there and standing to. You are now inseparable from military history, your place is now part of the narrative. You were there, a witness to your own life and to the lives of others.

> *He sat there on the porch reading a book on the war. It was a history and he was reading about all the engagements he had been in. It was the most interesting reading he had ever done. . . . Now he was really learning about the war.*
> —Ernest Hemingway, "Soldier's Home"

This is your book. Thank you for going forth, veteran. Welcome home. Stand down.

Benjamin Busch

Preface

Standing Down: From Warrior to Civilian was created for all readers who want to reflect on the experience of making the transition from private citizen to member of the armed forces and back again. Currently, many men and women in the United States are going through the difficult process of reentry into their circle of family and friends, their local communities, and the workforce while confronting the harsh aftermath of combat service. *Standing Down* is intended to help ease this transition by providing a collection of provocative readings that speak directly to many of the issues of concern to returning servicemen and servicewomen. It is also intended for family members, service providers, caretakers, and, indeed, all fellow citizens who would like to have a deeper understanding of what these men and women are facing.

But while what veterans are facing is very much of the present, it is also true that the experience of military service, combat, and homecoming has some constant characteristics that have not changed greatly through the centuries. With this in mind, *Standing Down* includes readings that span more than twenty-five hundred years, from the Trojan War to the recent operations in Iraq and Afghanistan. The authors, many of whom were in the military, speak in powerful voices, sometimes from long ago and far away, about matters that are perennial in human history. We invite the readers of *Standing Down* to enter into this age-old conversation about what it means to go to war.

However, *Standing Down* is more than an anthology to be read and put back on the shelf. It is conceived as an instrument to be used in discussion groups of veterans from all eras and others who would like to get together and talk about what the authors say and how it relates to their own lives. In keeping with the Great Books Foundation's mission of providing opportunities for people of all ages to learn together through group discussion, the Foundation has launched Talking Service, a multi-year, nationwide initiative to start reading and discussion groups focused on *Standing Down*. To advance this initiative, Foundation staff will work with an array of organizations and individuals to implement discussion groups in a variety of ways, including training in leading Shared Inquiry discussion. Complete information about Talking Service can be found at **talkingservice.greatbooks.org.**

The Great Books Foundation is committed to providing forums for the discussion of books and ideas that prompt us to examine our deepest assumptions about what it means to be a citizen of a free society. We hope that the Talking Service initiative and the discussion of the readings in *Standing Down* will contribute something of value to both public and private conversations about what we as a society value and are willing to protect with the lives of those who serve in the armed forces.

The Great Books Foundation would like to thank the National Endowment for the Humanities, the Wounded Warrior Project, the Chicago Mercantile Exchange, and the Plante Moran company for their generous support of *Standing Down* and Talking Service.

About Shared Inquiry

A Shared Inquiry™ discussion begins when the leader of the discussion group poses an interpretive question to participants about the meaning of a reading selection. The question is substantial enough that no single answer can resolve it. Instead, several answers—even answers that are in conflict—may be valid. In effect, the leader is telling the group: "Here is a problem of meaning that seems important. Let's try to resolve it."

From that moment on, participants are free to offer answers and opinions to the group, to request clarification of points, and to raise objections to the remarks of other participants. They also discuss specific passages in the selection that bear on the interpretive question and compare their differing ideas about what these passages mean. The leader, meanwhile, asks additional questions, clarifying and expanding the interpretive question and helping group members to arrive at more cogent answers. All participants don't have to agree with all of the answers—each person can decide which answer seems most convincing. This process is called Shared Inquiry.

In Shared Inquiry discussion, three kinds of questions can be raised about a reading selection: factual questions, interpretive questions, and evaluative questions. Interpretation is central to a Shared Inquiry discussion but factual questions can bring to light evidence in support of interpretations and can clear up misunderstandings. On the other hand, evaluative questions invite participants to compare the experiences and opinions of an author with their own and can introduce a personal dimension into the discussion.

The following guidelines will help keep the conversation focused on the text and assure all the participants a voice:

1. **Read the selection carefully before participating in the discussion.** This ensures that all participants are equally prepared to talk about the ideas in the reading.

2. **Discuss the ideas in the selection, and try to understand them fully.** Reflecting as individuals and as a group on what the author says makes the exploration of both the selection and related issues that will come up in the discussion more rewarding.

3. **Support interpretations of what the author says with evidence from the reading, along with insights from personal experience.** This provides focus for the group on the selection that everyone has read and builds a strong foundation for discussing related issues.

4. **Listen to other participants and respond to them directly.** Shared Inquiry is about the give and take of ideas, the willingness to listen to others and talk with them respectfully. Directing your comments and questions to other group members, not always to the leader, will make the discussion livelier and more dynamic.

5. **Expect the leader to mainly ask questions.** Effective leaders help participants develop their own ideas, with everyone gaining a new understanding in the process. When participants hang back and wait for the leader to suggest answers, discussion tends to falter.

How to Use This Book

The forty-four readings in *Standing Down: From Warrior to Civilian* were chosen for their ability to raise questions and provoke stimulating discussion about the experience of being in the military and returning home afterward. In order for discussions to be most rewarding, it is strongly recommended that a significant amount of time be spent coming to an understanding of what the author is saying by continually returning to the selection during the discussion. Doing so will provide a strong central focus for whatever personal accounts participants introduce into the conversation, as they evaluate the author's ideas in light of their own experiences.

To help prompt lively discussion, each selection is preceded by a brief introduction giving some background about the author's life and the historical context in which the selection was written. In addition, the introduction touches on a few general issues that the selection raises. Following each selection is a brief set of discussion questions to encourage exploration of the author's ideas. Some of the questions ask about something very specific in the selection, such as the meaning of a statement or the motivation of a character in a story. Others ask about more general issues related to the selection—these questions are broader and invite discussion of personal insights and opinions. Addressing both kinds of questions during a discussion, without tipping the balance heavily toward one or the other, will make for a more satisfying experience that not only engages with each author's distinctive voice, but also allows for participants in the group to contribute their insights in their own individual ways.

A thematic guide and a glossary of military acronyms are included to enrich the discussion of the selections.

Thematic Guide

The selections in *Standing Down* are ordered according to the birth dates of the authors, which in no way implies that they should be read in that order. Each reader and discussion group will have its own interests. In order to help easily identify some of the most prominent topics represented by the selections, the following thematic guide is provided. Many of the selections fall under a number of categories—an indication that they contain rich and complex levels of meaning to explore.

THEMES

Caretaking

Whitman	On Caregiving
Bein	A Journey Taken with My Son
Auger	A Piece of My Heart
Hrivnak	Medevac Missions

Civilians and War

Thucydides	The Melian Dialogue
O'Connor	Guests of the Nation
Atwood	It Is Dangerous to Read Newspapers
Berens	Reclamation
Busch	Dust to Dust
Gyokeres	The Hardest Letter to Write

Combat

Tennyson	The Charge of the Light Brigade
Tolstoy	War and Peace
Owen	Poems
Pyle	Reporting the War in Tunisia
Sherrod	Tarawa: The Story of a Battle
Portillo Trambley	Village
Caputo	A Rumor of War
McCary	To the Fallen

Confronting the Enemy

Homer	Iliad
Thucydides	The Melian Dialogue
Owen	Poems
Pyle	Reporting the War in Tunisia
O'Connor	Guests of the Nation
Portillo Trambley	Village
Caputo	A Rumor of War
Turner	Perimeter Watch
Gyokeres	The Hardest Letter to Write
McCary	To the Fallen

Family Relationships

Homer	Iliad
Shakespeare	Henry VI, Part I
Tolstoy	War and Peace
Hemingway	Soldier's Home
Marlantes	What It Is Like to Go to War
O'Brien	The Things They Carried
Bein	A Journey Taken with My Son
Finkel	The Good Soldiers
Busch	Dust to Dust
Fallon	You Know When the Men Are Gone

Grieving

Homer	Iliad
Lincoln	Gettysburg Address
Owen	Poems
O'Brien	The Things They Carried
Auger	A Piece of My Heart
Fallon	You Know When the Men Are Gone

Heroism

Homer	Iliad
Shakespeare	Henry VI, Part I
Lincoln	Gettysburg Address
Tennyson	The Charge of the Light Brigade
Yeats	An Irish Airman Foresees His Death
Crane	The Veteran
Read	To a Conscript of 1940
Pyle	Reporting the War in Tunisia

Homecoming

Homer	Iliad
Hemingway	Soldier's Home
Pyle	Reporting the War in Tunisia
Marlantes	What It Is Like to Go to War
Finkel	The Good Soldiers
Turner	Perimeter Watch
Humphreys	Veterans
Gyokeres	The Hardest Letter to Write
Fallon	You Know When the Men Are Gone

Honor and Memorializing

Homer	Iliad
Shakespeare	Henry VI, Part I
Lincoln	Gettysburg Address
Tennyson	The Charge of the Light Brigade

O'Brien	The Things They Carried
Komunyakaa	Facing It
Berens	Reclamation
McCary	To the Fallen

Nature of War

Tennyson	The Charge of the Light Brigade
James	The Moral Equivalent of War
Freud	Why War?
Sevareid	The Price We Pay in Italy

Patriotism

Washington	Letters
Tocqueville	On Discipline in Democratic Armies
Lincoln	Gettysburg Address
Yeats	An Irish Airman Foresees His Death
Owen	Poems
Read	To a Conscript of 1940
Redding	A Negro Looks at This War
Rodriguez	The Boy Without a Flag

Telling Stories

McCormick	Italian Ordeal Surprises Congress
Hemingway	Soldier's Home
Wolff	In Pharaoh's Army
O'Brien	The Things They Carried
Gyokeres	The Hardest Letter to Write

War in the Media

McCormick	Italian Ordeal Surprises Congress
Agee	These Terrible Records of War
Sherrod	Tarawa: The Story of a Battle
Atwood	It Is Dangerous to Read Newspapers

Women and War

Homer	Iliad
Bein	A Journey Taken with My Son
Auger	A Piece of My Heart
Fallon	You Know When the Men Are Gone
Gyokeres	The Hardest Letter to Write

Wounds

Whitman	On Caregiving
Wood	Revisiting My Memoir
Auger	A Piece of My Heart
Bein	A Journey Taken with My Son
Finkel	The Good Soldiers
Turner	Perimeter Watch
Busch	Dust to Dust
Hrivnak	Medevac Missions
Fallon	You Know When the Men Are Gone
Poggi	Shallow Hands

CONFLICTS

American Civil War

Lincoln	Gettysburg Address
Whitman	On Caregiving
Crane	The Veteran

World War I

Yeats	An Irish Airman Foresees His Death
Owen	Poems
Read	To a Conscript of 1940
Hemingway	Soldier's Home

World War II

McCormick	Italian Ordeal Surprises Congress
Read	To a Conscript of 1940
Pyle	Reporting the War in Tunisia
Redding	A Negro Looks at This War
Agee	These Terrible Records of War
Sherrod	Tarawa: The Story of a Battle
Sevareid	The Price We Pay in Italy
Wood	Revisiting My Memoir

Vietnam War

Portillo Trambley	Village
Atwood	It Is Dangerous to Read Newspapers
Caputo	A Rumor of War
Marlantes	What It Is Like to Go to War
Wolff	In Pharaoh's Army
O'Brien	The Things They Carried
Komunyakaa	Facing It
Auger	A Piece of My Heart

Wars in Iraq and Afghanistan

Bein	A Journey Taken with My Son
Berens	Reclamation
Finkel	The Good Soldiers
Turner	Perimeter Watch
Busch	Dust to Dust
Hrivnak	Medevac Missions
Fallon	You Know When the Men Are Gone
Humphreys	Veterans
Gyokeres	The Hardest Letter to Write
Poggi	Shallow Hands
McCary	To the Fallen

Homer

The epic war poem the *Iliad* was composed more than twenty-five hundred years ago in the Greek-speaking world of the eastern Mediterranean. Its author was said to be a poet named Homer, about whom nothing is now known for certain. Through the ages, the *Iliad* has inspired generations of warriors; it was rumored that Alexander the Great carried a copy on his campaigns of world conquest. Readers in all times and places have also discovered in the *Iliad* profound insights concerning the tragic consequences of war for both soldiers and civilians.

The *Iliad* tells the story of several key events during the legendary Trojan War. Helen, the beautiful wife of the Greek general Menelaus, has left her husband for Paris, a Trojan prince, and fled with him to the city of Troy, also known as Ilion. Outraged, the Greeks gather an army to sail to Troy and bring her home. The Greek siege of the city lasts ten years, but Homer's poem focuses on a short period toward the end of the conflict.

The *Iliad* highlights issues of heroism, honor, and duty that have confronted members of the military in every generation. When the Trojan prince Hector, chief defender of Troy, leaves the battlefield and visits briefly with his wife and son, he struggles to explain to them why he must return to his men. The bonds of family are tested by a competing sense of duty to his comrades. The Greek warrior Achilles struggles too, with how to be forceful and at the same time humane in his dealings with the elderly father of Hector, whom he has killed. Soldiers today face these same challenges of living between two worlds—home and the battlefront—and of negotiating fairly with their enemies. The questions with which these ancient heroes struggle are relevant even today to members of the armed forces.

ILIAD

(selection)

Book 6

After a period of fierce fighting, the Trojan army rallies and their Greek adversaries, led by Agamemnon, their king, pull back. Fearing another deadly assault, however, Hector withdraws to the city to ask the women to petition the gods to aid the Trojan cause.

The battle was left to rage on the level expanse
Between Troy's two rivers. Bronze spearheads
Drove past each other as the Greek and Trojan armies
Spread like a hemorrhage across the plain.

Telamonian Ajax, the Achaean wall,
Was the first Greek to break the Trojan line
And give his comrades some daylight.
He killed Thrace's best, Acamas,
Son of Eussorus, smashing through the horn
Of his plumed helmet with his spear
And driving through until the bronze tip
Pierced the forehead's bone. Acamas's eyes went dark.

Diomedes followed up by killing Axylus,
Teuthras's son, a most hospitable man.
His comfortable home was on the road to Arisbe,
And he entertained all travelers, but not one
Came by to meet the enemy before him
And save him from death. Diomedes killed

Not only Axylus but Calesius, his driver,
Two men who would now be covered by earth.

Then Euryalus killed Opheltius and Dresus
And went on after Aesepus and Pedasus,
Twins whom the naiad Abarbarea
Bore to Bucolion, Laomedon's eldest
Though bastard son. He was with his sheep
When he made love to the nymph. She conceived,
And bore him the twins whom Euryalus
Now undid. He left their bright bodies naked.

Then Polypoetes killed Astyalus;
Odysseus got Pidytes with his spear;
And Teucer took out Aretaon, a good man.
Nestor's son Antilochus killed Ablerus;
The warlord Agamemnon killed Elatus,
Who lived in steep Pedasus on the Satnioeis;
Leitus killed Phylacus as he fled;
And Eurypylus unmanned Melanthius.

But Menelaus took Adrastus alive.
Adrastus's terrified horses became entangled
In a tamarisk as they galloped across the plain,
And, breaking the pole near the car's rim,
Bolted toward the city with the others.
Their master rolled from the car by the wheel
And fell face first into the dust. Menelaus
Came up to him with his long-shadowed spear,
And Adrastus clasped his knees and prayed:

"Take me alive, son of Atreus, and accept
A worthy ransom from the treasure stored
In my father's palace, bronze, gold, wrought iron.
My father would lavish it all on you if he heard
I was still alive among the Achaean ships."

The speech had its intended effect.
Menelaus was about to hand him over
To be led back to the ships, but Agamemnon
Came running over to call him on it:

"Going soft, Menelaus? What does this man
Mean to you? Have the Trojans ever shown you
Any hospitality? Not one of them
Escapes sheer death at our hands, not even
The boy who is still in his mother's womb.
Every Trojan dies, unmourned and unmarked."

And so the hero changed his brother's mind
By reminding him of the ways of conduct and fate.
Menelaus shoved Adrastus aside,
And Agamemnon stabbed him in the flank.
He fell backward, and the son of Atreus
Braced his heel on his chest and pulled out the spear.

Then Nestor shouted and called to the Greeks:

"Soldiers of Greece, no lagging behind
To strip off armor from the enemy corpses
To see who comes back to the ships with the most.
Now we kill men! You will have plenty of time later
To despoil the Trojan dead on the plain."

Nestor's speech worked them up to a frenzy,
And the Trojans would have been beaten
Back to Ilion by superior force
Had not Helenus, Priam's son
And Troy's prophet, approached Aeneas and Hector:

"Aeneas and Hector, the Trojans and Lycians
Are counting on you. You two are the leaders
In every initiative in council and battle—

So make a stand here. Go through the ranks
And keep our men back from the gates,
Before they run through them and fall
Into their women's arms, making our enemies laugh.
Once you have bolstered our troops' morale,
We will stand our ground and fight the Danaans,
Tired as we are. We have our backs to the wall.
Hector, go into the city and find our mother.
Tell her to take a company of old women
To the temple of Athena on the acropolis
With the largest and loveliest robe in her house,
The one that is dearest of all to her,
And place it on the knees of braided Athena,
And promise twelve heifers to her in her temple,
Unblemished yearlings, if she will pity
The town of Troy, its wives and its children,
And if she will keep from holy Ilion
Wild Diomedes, who is raging with his spear.
I think he's the strongest of all the Achaeans.
We never even feared Achilles like this,
And they say he is half divine. But this man
Won't stop at anything. No one can match him."

Hector took his brother's advice.
He jumped down from his chariot with his gear
And toured the ranks, a spear in each hand.
He urged them on, and with a trembling roar
The Trojans turned to face the Achaeans.
The Greeks pulled back. It looked to them
As if some god had come from the starry sky
To help the Trojans. It had been a sudden rally.
Hector shouted and called to the Trojans:

"Soldiers of Troy, and illustrious allies,
Remember to fight like the men that you are,
While I go to the city and ask the elders

Who sit in council, and our wives, to pray
To the gods and promise bulls by the hundred."

And Hector left, helmet collecting light
Above the black-hide shield whose rim tapped
His ankles and neck with each step he took. . . .

When Hector reached the oak tree by the Western Gate,
Trojan wives and daughters ran up to him,
Asking about their children, their brothers,
Their kinsmen, their husbands. He told them all,
Each woman in turn, to pray to the gods.
Sorrow clung to their heads like mist.

Then he came to Priam's palace, a beautiful
Building made of polished stone with a central courtyard
Flanked by porticoes, upon which opened fifty
Adjoining rooms, where Priam's sons
Slept with their wives. Across the court
A suite of twelve more bedrooms housed
His modest daughters and their husbands.
It was here that Hector's mother met him,
A gracious woman, with Laodice,
Her most beautiful daughter, in tow.
Hecuba took his hand in hers and said:

"Hector, my son, why have you left the war
And come here? Are those abominable Greeks
Wearing you down in the fighting outside,
And does your heart lead you to our acropolis
To stretch your hands upward to Zeus?
But stay here while I get you
Some honey-sweet wine, so you can pour a libation
To Father Zeus first and the other immortals,
Then enjoy some yourself, if you will drink.
Wine greatly bolsters a weary man's spirits,

And you are weary from defending your kinsmen."

Sunlight shimmered on great Hector's helmet.

"Mother, don't offer me any wine.
It would drain the power out of my limbs.
I have too much reverence to pour a libation
With unwashed hands to Zeus almighty,
Or to pray to Cronion in the black cloud banks
Spattered with blood and the filth of battle.
But you must go to the war goddess's temple
To make sacrifice with a band of old women.
Choose the largest and loveliest robe in the house,
The one that is dearest of all to you,
And place it on the knees of braided Athena.
And promise twelve heifers to her in her temple,
Unblemished yearlings, if she will pity
The town of Troy, its wives, and its children,
And if she will keep from holy Ilion
Wild Diomedes, who's raging with his spear.
Go then to the temple of Athena the War Goddess,
And I will go over to summon Paris,
If he will listen to what I have to say.
I wish the earth would gape open beneath him.
Olympian Zeus has bred him as a curse
To Troy, to Priam, and all Priam's children.
If I could see him dead and gone to Hades,
I think my heart might be eased of its sorrow."

Thus Hector. Hecuba went to the great hall
And called to her handmaidens, and they
Gathered together the city's old women.
She went herself to a fragrant storeroom
Which held her robes, the exquisite work
Of Sidonian women whom godlike Paris
Brought from Phoenicia when he sailed the sea

On the voyage he made for high-born Helen.
Hecuba chose the robe that lay at the bottom,
The most beautiful of all, woven of starlight,
And bore it away as a gift for Athena.
A stream of old women followed behind.

They came to the temple of Pallas Athena
On the city's high rock, and the doors were opened
By fair-cheeked Theano, daughter of Cisseus
And wife of Antenor, breaker of horses.
The Trojans had made her Athena's priestess.
With ritual cries they all lifted their hands
To Pallas Athena. Theano took the robe
And laid it on the knees of the rich-haired goddess,
Then prayed in supplication to Zeus's daughter:

"Lady Athena who defends our city,
Brightest of goddesses, hear our prayer.
Break now the spear of Diomedes
And grant that he fall before the Western Gate,
That we may now offer twelve heifers in this temple,
Unblemished yearlings. Only do thou pity
The town of Troy, its wives, and its children."

But Pallas Athena denied her prayer.

While they prayed to great Zeus's daughter,
Hector came to Paris's beautiful house,
Which he had built himself with the aid
Of the best craftsmen in all wide Troy:
Sleeping quarters, a hall, and a central courtyard
Near to Priam's and Hector's on the city's high rock.
Hector entered, Zeus's light upon him,
A spear sixteen feet long cradled in his hand,
The bronze point gleaming, and the ferrule gold.
He found Paris in the bedroom, busy with his weapons,

Fondling his curved bow, his fine shield, and breastplate.
Helen of Argos sat with her household women
Directing their exquisite handicraft.

Hector meant to shame Paris and provoke him:

"This is a fine time to be nursing your anger,
You idiot! We're dying out there defending the walls.
It's because of you the city is in this hellish war.
If you saw someone else holding back from combat
You'd pick a fight with him yourself. Now get up
Before the whole city goes up in flames!"

And Paris, handsome as a god:

"That's no more than just, Hector,
But listen now to what I have to say.
It's not out of anger or spite toward the Trojans
I've been here in my room. I only wanted
To recover from my pain. My wife was just now
Encouraging me to get up and fight,
And that seems the better thing to do.
Victory takes turns with men. Wait for me
While I put on my armor, or go on ahead—
I'm pretty sure I'll catch up with you."

To which Hector said nothing.

But Helen said to him softly:

                    "Brother-in-law
Of a scheming, cold-blooded bitch,
I wish that on the day my mother bore me
A windstorm had swept me away to a mountain
Or into the waves of the restless sea,
Swept me away before all this could happen.

But since the gods have ordained these evils,
Why couldn't I be the wife of a better man,
One sensitive at least to repeated reproaches?
Paris has never had an ounce of good sense
And never will. He'll pay for it someday.
But come inside and sit down on this chair,
Dear brother-in-law. You bear such a burden
For my wanton ways and Paris's witlessness.
Zeus has placed this evil fate on us so that
In time to come poets will sing of us."

And Hector, in his burnished helmet:

"Don't ask me to sit, Helen, even though
You love me. You will never persuade me.
My heart is out there with our fighting men.
They already feel my absence from battle.
Just get Paris moving, and have him hurry
So he can catch up with me while I'm still
Inside the city. I'm going to my house now
To see my family, my wife, and my boy. I don't know
Whether I'll ever be back to see them again, or if
The gods will destroy me at the hands of the Greeks."

And Hector turned and left. He came to his house
But did not find white-armed Andromache there.
She had taken the child and a robed attendant
And stood on the tower, lamenting and weeping—
His blameless wife. When Hector didn't find her inside,
He paused on his way out and called to the servants:

"Can any of you women tell me exactly
Where Andromache went when she left the house?
To one of my sisters or one of my brothers' wives?
Or to the temple of Athena along with the other
Trojan women to beseech the dread goddess?"

The spry old housekeeper answered him:

"Hector, if you want the exact truth, she didn't go
To any of your sisters, or any of your brothers' wives,
Or to the temple of Athena along with the other
Trojan women to beseech the dread goddess.
She went to Ilion's great tower, because she heard
The Trojans were pressed and the Greeks were strong.
She ran off to the wall like a madwoman,
And the nurse went with her, carrying the child."

Thus the housekeeper, but Hector was gone,
Retracing his steps through the stone and tile streets
Of the great city, until he came to the Western Gate.
He was passing through it out onto the plain
When his wife came running up to meet him,
His beautiful wife, Andromache,
A gracious woman, daughter of great Eëtion,
Eëtion, who lived in the forests of Plakos
And ruled the Cilicians from Thebes-under-Plakos—
His daughter was wed to bronze-helmeted Hector.
She came up to him now, and the nurse with her
Held to her bosom their baby boy,
Hector's beloved son, beautiful as starlight,
Whom Hector had named Scamandrius
But everyone else called Astyanax, Lord of the City,
For Hector alone could save Ilion now.
He looked at his son and smiled in silence.
Andromache stood close to him, shedding tears,
Clinging to his arm as she spoke these words:

"Possessed is what you are, Hector. Your courage
Is going to kill you, and you have no feeling left
For your little boy or for me, the luckless woman
Who will soon be your widow. It won't be long
Before the whole Greek army swarms and kills you.

And when they do, it will be better for me
To sink into the earth. When I lose you, Hector,
There will be nothing left, no one to turn to,
Only pain. My father and mother are dead.
Achilles killed my father when he destroyed
Our city, Thebes with its high gates,
But had too much respect to despoil his body.
He burned it instead with all his armor
And heaped up a barrow. And the spirit women
Came down from the mountain, daughters
Of the storm god, and planted elm trees around it.
I had seven brothers once in that great house.
All seven went down to Hades on a single day,
Cut down by Achilles in one blinding sprint
Through their shambling cattle and silver sheep.
Mother, who was queen in the forests of Plakos,
He took back as prisoner, with all her possessions,
Then released her for a fortune in ransom.
She died in our house, shot by Artemis's arrows.
Hector, you are my father, you are my mother,
You are my brother and my blossoming husband.
But show some pity and stay here by the tower,
Don't make your child an orphan, your wife a widow.
Station your men here by the fig tree, where the city
Is weakest because the wall can be scaled.
Three times their elite have tried an attack here
Rallying around Ajax or glorious Idomeneus
Or Atreus's sons or mighty Diomedes,
Whether someone in on the prophecy told them
Or they are driven here by something in their heart."

And great Hector, helmet shining, answered her:

"Yes, Andromache, I worry about all this myself,
But my shame before the Trojans and their wives,
With their long robes trailing, would be too terrible

If I hung back from battle like a coward.
And my heart won't let me. I have learned to be
One of the best, to fight in Troy's first ranks,
Defending my father's honor and my own.
Deep in my heart I know too well
There will come a day when holy Ilion will perish,
And Priam and the people under Priam's ash spear.
But the pain I will feel for the Trojans then,
For Hecuba herself and for Priam king,
For my many fine brothers who will have by then
Fallen in the dust behind enemy lines—
All that pain is nothing to what I will feel
For you, when some bronze-armored Greek
Leads you away in tears, on your first day of slavery.
And you will work some other woman's loom
In Argos or carry water from a Spartan spring,
All against your will, under great duress.
And someone, seeing you crying, will say,
'That is the wife of Hector, the best of all
The Trojans when they fought around Ilion.'
Someday someone will say that, renewing your pain
At having lost such a man to fight off the day
Of your enslavement. But may I be dead
And the earth heaped up above me
Before I hear your cry as you are dragged away."

With these words, resplendent Hector
Reached for his child, who shrank back screaming
Into his nurse's bosom, terrified of his father's
Bronze-encased face and the horsehair plume
He saw nodding down from the helmet's crest.
This forced a laugh from his father and mother,
And Hector removed the helmet from his head
And set it on the ground all shimmering with light.
Then he kissed his dear son and swung him up gently
And said a prayer to Zeus and the other immortals:

"Zeus and all gods: grant that this my son
Become, as I am, foremost among Trojans,
Brave and strong, and ruling Ilion with might.
And may men say he is far better than his father
When he returns from war, bearing bloody spoils,
Having killed his man. And may his mother rejoice."

And he put his son in the arms of his wife,
And she enfolded him in her fragrant bosom
Laughing through her tears. Hector pitied her
And stroked her with his hand and said to her:

"You worry too much about me, Andromache.
No one is going to send me to Hades before my time,
And no man has ever escaped his fate, rich or poor,
Coward or hero, once born into this world.
Go back to the house now and take care of your work,
The loom and the shuttle, and tell the servants
To get on with their jobs. War is the work of men,
Of all the Trojan men, and mine especially."

With these words, Hector picked up
His plumed helmet, and his wife went back home,
Turning around often, her cheeks flowered with tears.
When she came to the house of man-slaying Hector,
She found a throng of servants inside,
And raised among these women the ritual lament.
And so they mourned for Hector in his house
Although he was still alive, for they did not think
He would ever come back from the war,
Or escape the murderous hands of the Greeks.

Paris meanwhile
Did not dally long in his high halls.
He put on his magnificent bronze-inlaid gear
And sprinted with assurance out through the city.

Picture a horse that has fed on barley in his stall
Breaking his halter and galloping across the plain,
Making for his accustomed swim in the river,
A glorious animal, head held high, mane streaming
Like wind on his shoulders. Sure of his splendor
He prances by the horse-runs and the mares in pasture.

That was how Paris, son of Priam, came down
From the high rock of Pergamum,
Gleaming like amber and laughing in his armor,
And his feet were fast.
                              He caught up quickly
With Hector just as he turned from the spot
Where he'd talked with his wife, and called out:

"Well, dear brother, have I delayed you too much?
Am I not here in time, just as you asked?"

Hector turned, his helmet flashing light:

"I don't understand you, Paris.
No one could slight your work in battle.
You're a strong fighter, but you slack off—
You don't have the will. It breaks my heart
To hear what the Trojans say about you.
It's on your account they have all this trouble.
Come on, let's go. We can settle this later,
If Zeus ever allows us to offer in our halls
The wine bowl of freedom to the gods above,
After we drive these bronze-kneed Greeks from Troy."

Book 24

Achilles has killed Hector and mutilated his corpse in retribution for Hector's having killed Achilles's friend Patroclus. Under cover of night, and led by the god Hermes, Hector's father, Priam, king of Troy, makes his way into the enemy Greek camp to persuade Achilles to return his son's body.

He found him inside. His companions sat
Apart from him, and a solitary pair,
Automedon and Alcimus, warriors both,
Were busy at his side. He had just finished
His evening meal. The table was still set up.
Great Priam entered unnoticed. He stood
Close to Achilles, and touching his knees,
He kissed the dread and murderous hands
That had killed so many of his sons.

Passion sometimes blinds a man so completely
That he kills one of his own countrymen.
In exile, he comes into a wealthy house,
And everybody stares at him with wonder.

So Achilles stared in wonder at Priam.
Was he a god?
                And the others there stared
And wondered and looked at each other.
But Priam spoke, a prayer of entreaty:

"Remember your father, godlike Achilles.
He and I both are on the doorstep
Of old age. He may well be now
Surrounded by enemies wearing him down
And have no one to protect him from harm.
But then he hears that you are still alive
And his heart rejoices, and he hopes all his days

To see his dear son come back from Troy.
But what is left for me? I had the finest sons
In all wide Troy, and not one of them is left.
Fifty I had when the Greeks came over,
Nineteen out of one belly, and the rest
The women in my house bore to me.
It doesn't matter how many they were,
The god of war has cut them down at the knees.
And the only one who could save the city
You've just now killed as he fought for his country,
My Hector. It is for him I have come to the Greek ships,
To get him back from you. I've brought
A fortune in ransom. Respect the gods, Achilles.
Think of your own father, and pity me.
I am more pitiable. I have borne what no man
Who has walked this earth has ever yet borne.
I have kissed the hand of the man who killed my son."

He spoke, and sorrow for his own father
Welled up in Achilles. He took Priam's hand
And gently pushed the old man away.
The two of them remembered. Priam,
Huddled in grief at Achilles's feet, cried
And moaned softly for his man-slaying Hector.
And Achilles cried for his father and
For Patroclus. The sound filled the room.

When Achilles had his fill of grief
And the aching sorrow left his heart,
He rose from his chair and lifted the old man
By his hand, pitying his white hair and beard.
And his words enfolded him like wings:

"Ah, the suffering you've had, and the courage.
To come here alone to the Greek ships
And meet my eye, the man who slaughtered

Your many fine sons! You have a heart of iron.
But come, sit on this chair. Let our pain
Lie at rest a while, no matter how much we hurt.
There's nothing to be gained from cold grief.
Yes, the gods have woven pain into mortal lives,
While they are free from care.
       Two jars
Sit at the doorstep of Zeus, filled with gifts
That he gives, one full of good things,
The other of evil. If Zeus gives a man
A mixture from both jars, sometimes
Life is good for him, sometimes not.
But if all he gives you is from the jar of woe,
You become a pariah, and hunger drives you
Over the bright earth, dishonored by gods and men.
Now take Peleus. The gods gave him splendid gifts
From the day he was born. He was the happiest
And richest man on earth, king of the Myrmidons,
And although he was a mortal, the gods gave him
An immortal goddess to be his wife.
But even to Peleus the god gave some evil:
He would not leave offspring to succeed him in power,
Just one child, all out of season. I can't be with him
To take care of him now that he's old, since I'm far
From my fatherland, squatting here in Troy,
Tormenting you and your children. And you, old sir,
We hear that you were prosperous once.
From Lesbos down south clear over to Phrygia
And up to the Hellespont's boundary,
No one could match you in wealth or in sons.
But then the gods have brought you trouble,
This constant fighting and killing around your town.
You must endure this grief and not constantly grieve.
You will not gain anything by torturing yourself
Over the good son you lost, not bring him back.
Sooner you will suffer some other sorrow."

And Priam, old and godlike, answered him:

"Don't sit me in a chair, prince, while Hector
Lies uncared for in your hut. Deliver him now
So I can see him with my own eyes, and you—
Take all this ransom we bring, take pleasure in it,
And go back home to your own fatherland,
Since you've taken this first step and allowed me
To live and see the light of day."

Achilles glowered at him and said:

"Don't provoke me, old man. It's my own decision
To release Hector to you. A messenger came to me
From Zeus—my own natural mother,
Daughter of the old sea god. And I know you,
Priam, inside out. You don't fool me one bit.
Some god escorted you to the Greek ships.
No mortal would have dared come into our camp,
Not even your best young hero. He couldn't have
Gotten past the guards or muscled open the gate.
So just stop stirring up grief in my heart,
Or I might not let you out of here alive, old man—
Suppliant though you are—and sin against Zeus."

The old man was afraid and did as he was told.

The son of Peleus leapt out the door like a lion,
Followed by Automedon and Alcimus, whom Achilles
Honored most now that Patroclus was dead.
They unyoked the horses and mules, and led
The old man's herald inside and seated him on a chair.
Then they unloaded from the strong-wheeled cart
The endless ransom that was Hector's blood price,
Leaving behind two robes and a fine-spun tunic
For the body to be wrapped in and brought inside.

Achilles called the women and ordered them
To wash the body well and anoint it with oil,
Removing it first for fear that Priam might see his son
And in his grief be unable to control his anger
At the sight of his child, and that this would arouse
Achilles's passion and he would kill the old man
And so sin against the commandments of Zeus.

After the female slaves had bathed Hector's body
And anointed it with olive, they wrapped it 'round
With a beautiful robe and tunic, and Achilles himself
Lifted him up and placed him on a pallet
And with his friends raised it onto the polished cart.
Then he groaned and called out to Patroclus:

"Don't be angry with me, dear friend, if somehow
You find out, even in Hades, that I have released
Hector to his father. He paid a handsome price,
And I will share it with you, as much as is right."

Achilles reentered his hut and sat down again
In his ornately decorated chair
Across the room from Priam, and said to him:

"Your son is released, sir, as you ordered.
He is lying on a pallet. At dawn's first light
You will go see him yourself.
Now let's think about supper.
Even Niobe remembered to eat
Although her twelve children were dead in her house,
Six daughters and six sturdy sons.
Apollo killed them with his silver bow,
And Artemis, showering arrows, angry with Niobe
Because she compared herself to beautiful Leto.
Leto, she said, had borne only two, while she
Had borne many. Well, these two killed them all.

Nine days they lay in their gore, with no one
To bury them, because Zeus had turned
The people to stone. On the tenth day
The gods buried them. But Niobe remembered
She had to eat, exhausted from weeping.
Now she is one of the rocks in the lonely hills
Somewhere in Sipylos, a place they say is haunted
By nymphs who dance on the Achelous's banks,
And although she is stone she broods on the sorrows
The gods gave her.
                          Well, so should we, old sir,
Remember to eat. You can mourn your son later
When you bring him to Troy. You owe him many tears."

A moment later Achilles was up and had slain
A silvery sheep. His companions flayed it
And prepared it for a meal, sliced it, spitted it,
Roasted the morsels and drew them off the spits.
Automedon set out bread in exquisite baskets
While Achilles served the meat. They helped themselves
And satisfied their desire for food and drink.
Then Priam, son of Dardanus, gazed for a while
At Achilles, so big, so much like one of the gods,
And Achilles returned his gaze, admiring
Priam's face, his words echoing in his mind.

When they had their fill of gazing at each other,
Priam, old and godlike, broke the silence:

"Show me to my bed now, prince, and quickly,
So that at long last I can have the pleasure of sleep.
My eyes have not closed since my son lost his life
Under your hands. I have done nothing but groan
And brood over my countless sorrows,
Rolling in the dung of my courtyard stables.

Finally I have tasted food and let flaming wine
Pass down my throat. I had eaten nothing till now."

Achilles ordered his companions and women
To set bedsteads on the porch and pad them
With fine, dyed rugs, spread blankets on top,
And cover them over with fleecy cloaks.
The women went out with torches in their hands
And quickly made up two beds. And Achilles,
The great sprinter, said in a bitter tone:

"You will have to sleep outside, dear Priam.
One of the Achaean counselors may come in,
As they always do, to sit and talk with me,
As well they should. If one of them saw you here
In the dead of night, he would tell Agamemnon,
And that would delay releasing the body.
But tell me this, as precisely as you can.
How many days do you need for the funeral?
I will wait that long and hold back the army."

And the old man, godlike Priam, answered:

"If you really want me to bury my Hector,
Then you could do this for me, Achilles.
You know how we are penned in the city,
Far from any timber, and the Trojans are afraid.
We would mourn him for nine days in our halls,
And bury him on the tenth, and feast the people.
On the eleventh we would heap a barrow over him,
And on the twelfth day fight, if fight we must."

And Achilles, strong, swift, and godlike:

"You will have your armistice."

And he clasped the old man's wrist
So he would not be afraid.
                              And so they slept,
Priam and his herald, in the covered courtyard,
Each with a wealth of thoughts in his breast.
But Achilles slept inside his well-built hut,
And by his side lay lovely Briseis.

Gods and heroes slept the night through,
Wrapped in soft slumber. Only Hermes
Lay awake in the dark, pondering how
To spirit King Priam away from the ships
And elude the strong watchmen at the camp's gates.
He hovered above Priam's head and spoke:

"Well, old man, you seem to think it's safe
To sleep on and on in the enemy camp
Since Achilles spared you. Think what it cost you
To ransom your son. Your own life will cost
Three times that much to the sons you have left
If Agamemnon and the Greeks know you are here."

Suddenly the old man was afraid. He woke up the herald.
Hermes harnessed the horses and mules
And drove them through the camp. No one noticed.
And when they reached the ford of the Xanthus,
The beautiful, swirling river that Zeus begot,
Hermes left for the long peaks of Olympus.

Questions

BOOK 6

1. After Menelaus has decided to spare Adrastus, why does Agamemnon's speech persuade him to change his mind?

2. Why do the Trojans send Hector, their greatest fighter, away from the battlefront where he is much needed and into the city to tell the women to pray to the gods?

3. Why does Hector first visit Paris and Helen and then start to leave the city without seeing his wife and son?

4. Why does Hector's wife call him "possessed"? (22)

5. Since Hector believes that Troy is doomed, why does he keep risking his life to defend it?

6. Is the belief that "no man has ever escaped his fate, rich or poor" compatible with a warrior's drive to perform heroic acts? (25)

BOOK 24

1. Why does Priam risk his life and go to his enemy, Achilles, in order to ransom Hector's body?

2. When Achilles tells Priam that "the gods have woven pain into mortal lives," is he implying that humans are not responsible for their own suffering and the suffering they cause others in war? (29)

3. When Priam says to Achilles, "you've taken this first step and allowed me / To live and see the light of day," why does this provoke Achilles's anger? (30)

4. Why does Achilles grant an armistice from the fighting for Hector's funeral?

5. Is shared grief able to forge a bond between people, even if they are enemies and have caused each other's suffering?

6. In war and its aftermath, what activities help survivors come to terms with grief for fallen comrades and family members and move on?

Thucydides

The *History of the Peloponnesian War,* by Thucydides (c. 460 BC–
c. 404 BC), is one of the earliest European accounts of war, military
operations, and the political situations in which they are carried
out. It is largely free from the bias and elements of legend and
hearsay that characterize other ancient histories. In his book,
Thucydides strove for a previously uncommon level of objectivity.

History of the Peloponnesian War describes the conflict between
the democratically governed city-state Athens and the military city-
state Sparta between 431 and 404 BC. At one time or another this
war involved almost every Greek city-state as an ally of one or the
other. Thucydides aimed for accuracy and impartiality in his history.
His narrative is based on personal observation—he participated
in many of the events himself—and eyewitness testimony from
Athenians and Spartans alike, and he cross-checked many different
accounts to produce his final version.

The following selection, "The Melian Dialogue," describes a
meeting between the powerful Athenians and the residents of
Melos, a small island off the southeastern coast of Greece. Melos
wished to remain neutral in the war, resisting the Athenians' first
attempt in 427 BC to force it under Athenian control. In 416 BC,
Athens sent a second expedition to the island to negotiate with the
Melians. The ensuing conversation highlights the Melians' dilemma:
either accept subjugation or enter a military conflict likely to lead
to disaster.

Thucydides's account raises issues of perpetual importance in
conflicts between nations. He asks us to consider such age-old
questions as whether might ever makes right and whether it is better to submit and compromise our principles in a hopeless situtation
than to risk almost certain destruction.

THE MELIAN DIALOGUE

The next summer the Athenians made an expedition against the isle of Melos. The Melians are a colony of Lacedaemon that would not submit to the Athenians like the other islanders and at first remained neutral and took no part in the struggle, but afterwards, upon the Athenians using violence and plundering their territory, assumed an attitude of open hostility. The Athenian generals encamped in their territory with their army, and before doing any harm to their land sent envoys to negotiate. These the Melians did not bring before the people, but told them to state the object of their mission to the magistrates and the council. The Athenian envoys then said:

ATHENIANS: As we are not to speak to the people, for fear that if we made a single speech without interruption we might deceive them with attractive arguments to which there was no chance of replying—we realize that this is the meaning of our being brought before your ruling body—we suggest that you who sit here should make security doubly sure. Let us have no long speeches from you either, but deal separately with each point, and take up at once any statement of which you disapprove, and criticize it.

MELIANS: We have no objection to your reasonable suggestion that we should put our respective points of view quietly to each other, but the military preparations which you have already made seem inconsistent with it. We see that you have come to be yourselves the judges of the debate, and that its natural conclusion for us will be slavery if you convince us, and war if we get the better of the argument and therefore refuse to submit.

ATHENIANS: If you have met us in order to make surmises about the future, or for any other purpose than to look existing facts in the face and to discuss the safety of your city on this basis, we will break off the conversations; otherwise, we are ready to speak.

MELIANS: In our position it is natural and excusable to explore many ideas and arguments. But the problem that has brought us here is our security, so, if you think fit, let the discussion follow the line you propose.

ATHENIANS: Then we will not make a long and unconvincing speech, full of fine phrases, to prove that our victory over Persia justifies our empire, or that we are now attacking you because you have wronged us, and we ask you not to expect to convince us by saying that you have not injured us, or that, though a colony of Lacedaemon, you did not join her. Let each of us say what we really think and reach a practical agreement. You know and we know, as practical men, that the question of justice arises only between parties equal in strength, and that the strong do what they can, and the weak submit.

MELIANS: As you ignore justice and have made self-interest the basis of discussion, we must take the same ground, and we say that in our opinion it is in your interest to maintain a principle which is for the good of all—that anyone in danger should have just and equitable treatment and any advantage, even if not strictly his due, which he can secure by persuasion. This is your interest as much as ours, for your fall would involve you in a crushing punishment that would be a lesson to the world.

ATHENIANS: We have no apprehensions about the fate of our empire, if it did fall; those who rule other peoples, like the Lacedaemonians, are not formidable to a defeated enemy. Nor is it the Lacedaemonians with whom we are now contending: the danger is from subjects who of themselves may attack and conquer their rulers. But leave that danger to us to face. At the moment we shall prove that we have come in the interest of our empire and that in what we shall say we are seeking the safety of your state; for we wish you to become our subjects with least trouble to ourselves, and we would like you to survive in our interests as well as your own.

MELIANS: It may be your interest to be our masters; how can it be ours to be your slaves?

ATHENIANS: By submitting you would avoid a terrible fate, and we should gain by not destroying you.

MELIANS: Would you not agree to an arrangement under which we should keep out of the war, and be your friends instead of your enemies, but neutral?

ATHENIANS: No; your hostility injures us less than your friendship. That, to our subjects, is an illustration of our weakness, while your hatred exhibits our power.

MELIANS: Is this the construction which your subjects put on it? Do they not distinguish between states in which you have no concern, and peoples who are most of them your colonies, and some conquered rebels?

ATHENIANS: They think that one nation has as good rights as another, but that some survive because they are strong and we are afraid to attack them. So, apart from the addition to our empire, your subjection would give us security: the fact that you are islanders (and weaker than others) makes it the more important that you should not get the better of the mistress of the sea.

MELIANS: But do you see no safety in our neutrality? You debar us from the plea of justice and press us to submit to your interests, so we must expound our own, and try to convince you, if the two happen to coincide. Will you not make enemies of all neutral powers when they see your conduct and reflect that some day you will attack them? Will not your action strengthen your existing opponents, and induce those who would otherwise never be your enemies to become so against their will?

ATHENIANS: No. The mainland states, secure in their freedom, will be slow to take defensive measures against us, and we do not consider them so formidable as independent island powers like yourselves, or subjects already smarting under our yoke. These are most likely to take a thoughtless step and bring themselves and us into obvious danger.

MELIANS: Surely then, if you are ready to risk so much to maintain your empire, and the enslaved peoples so much to escape from it, it would be criminal cowardice in us, who are still free, not to take any and every measure before submitting to slavery?

ATHENIANS: No, if you reflect calmly: for this is not a competition in heroism between equals, where your honor is at stake, but a question of self-preservation, to save you from a struggle with a far stronger power.

MELIANS: Still, we know that in war fortune is more impartial than the disproportion in numbers might lead one to expect. If we submit at once, our position is desperate; if we fight, there is still a hope that we shall stand secure.

ATHENIANS: Hope encourages men to take risks; men in a strong position may follow her without ruin, if not without loss. But when they stake all that they have to the last coin (for she is a spendthrift), she reveals her real self in the hour of failure, and when her nature is known she leaves them without means of self-protection. You are weak, your future hangs on a turn of the scales; avoid the mistake most men make, who might save themselves by human means, and then, when visible hopes desert them, in their extremity turn to the invisible—prophecies and oracles and all those things which delude men with hopes, to their destruction.

MELIANS: We too, you can be sure, realize the difficulty of struggling against your power and against fortune if she is not impartial. Still we trust that heaven will not allow us to be worsted by fortune, for in this quarrel we are right and you are wrong. Besides, we expect the support of Lacedaemon to supply the deficiencies in our strength, for she is bound to help us as her kinsmen, if for no other reason, and from a sense of honor. So our confidence is not entirely unreasonable.

ATHENIANS: As for divine favor, we think that we can count on it as much as you, for neither our claims nor our actions are inconsistent with what men believe about heaven or desire for themselves. We believe that heaven, and we know that men, by a natural law, always rule where they are stronger. We did not make that law nor were we the first to act on it; we found it existing, and it will exist forever, after we are gone; and we know that you and anyone else as strong as we are would do as we do. As to your expectations from Lacedaemon and your belief that she will help you from a sense of honor, we congratulate you on your innocence but we do not admire your folly. So far as they themselves and their national traditions are concerned, the Lacedaemonians are a highly virtuous people; as for their behavior to others, much might be said, but we can put it shortly by saying that, most obviously of all people we know, they identify their interests with justice and the pleasantest course with honor. Such principles do not favor your present irrational hopes of deliverance.

MELIANS: That is the chief reason why we have confidence in them now; in their own interest they will not wish to betray their own colonists and so help their enemies and destroy the confidence that their friends in Greece feel in them.

ATHENIANS: Apparently you do not realize that safety and self-interest go together, while the path of justice and honor is dangerous; and danger is a risk which the Lacedaemonians are little inclined to run.

MELIANS: Our view is that they would be more likely to run a risk in our case, and would regard it as less hazardous, because our nearness to Peloponnese makes it easier for them to act and our kinship gives them more confidence in us than in others.

ATHENIANS: Yes, but an intending ally looks not to the goodwill of those who invoke his aid but to marked superiority of real power, and of none is this truer than of the Lacedaemonians. They mistrust their own resources and attack their neighbors only when they have numerous allies, so it is not likely that, while we are masters of the sea, they would cross it to an island.

MELIANS: They might send others. The sea of Crete is large, and this will make it more difficult for its masters to capture hostile ships than for these to elude them safely. If they failed by sea, they would attack your country and those of your allies whom Brasidas did not reach; and then you will have to fight not against a country in which you have no concern, but for your own country and your allies' lands.

ATHENIANS: Here experience may teach you like others, and you will learn that Athens has never abandoned a siege from fear of another foe. You said that you proposed to discuss the safety of your city, but we observe that in all your speeches you have never said a word on which any reasonable expectation of it could be founded. Your strength lies in deferred hopes; in comparison with the forces now arrayed against you, your resources are too small for any hope of success. You will show a great want of judgment if you do not come to a more reasonable decision after we have withdrawn. Surely you will not fall back on the idea of honor, which has been the ruin of so many when danger and disgrace were staring them in the face. How often, when men have seen the fate to which they were tending, have they been enslaved by a phrase and drawn by the power of this seductive world to fall of their own free will into irreparable disaster, bringing on themselves by their folly a greater dishonor than fortune could inflict! If you are wise, you will avoid that fate. The greatest of cities makes you a fair offer, to keep your own land and become her tributary ally: there is no dishonor in that. The choice between war and safety is given you; do not obstinately take the worse alternative. The most successful people are those who stand up to their equals, behave properly to their superiors, and treat their inferiors fairly. Think it over when we withdraw, and reflect once and again that you have only one country, and that its prosperity or ruin depends on one decision.

The Athenians now withdrew from the conference; and the Melians, left to themselves, came to a decision corresponding with what they had maintained in the discussion, and answered, "Our resolution, Athenians, is unaltered. We will not in a moment deprive of freedom a city that has existed for seven hundred years; we put our trust in the fortune by which the gods have preserved it until now, and in the help of men, that is, of the Lacedaemonians; and so we will try and save ourselves. Meanwhile we invite you to allow us to be friends to you and foes to neither party, and to retire from our country after making such a treaty as shall seem fit to us both."

Such was the answer of the Melians. The Athenians broke up the conference saying, "To judge from your decision, you are unique in regarding the future as more certain than the present and in allowing your wishes to convert the unseen into reality; and as you have staked most on, and trusted most in, the Lacedaemonians, your fortune, and your hopes, so will you be most completely deceived."

The Athenian envoys now returned to the army; and as the Melians showed no signs of yielding, the generals at once began hostilities, and drew a line of circumvallation round the Melians, dividing the work among the different states. Subsequently the Athenians returned with most of their army, leaving behind them a certain number of their own citizens and of the allies to keep guard by land and sea. The force thus left stayed on and besieged the place.

Meanwhile the Athenians at Pylos took so much plunder from the Lacedaemonians that the latter, although they still refrained from breaking off the treaty and going to war with Athens, proclaimed that any of their people that chose might plunder the Athenians. The Corinthians also commenced hostilities with the Athenians for private quarrels of their own; but the rest of the Peloponnesians stayed quiet. Meanwhile the Melians in a night attack took the part of the Athenian lines opposite the market, killed some of its garrison, and brought in corn and as many useful stores as they could. Then, retiring, they remained inactive, while the Athenians took measures to keep better guard in future.

Summer was now over. The next winter the Lacedaemonians intended to invade the Argive territory, but on arriving at the frontier found the sacrifices for crossing unfavorable, and went back again. This intention of theirs made the Argives suspicious of certain of their fellow citizens, some of whom they arrested; others, however, escaped them. About the same time the Melians again took another part of the Athenian lines which were but feebly garrisoned. In consequence reinforcements were sent from Athens, and the siege was now pressed vigorously; there was some treachery in the town, and the Melians surrendered at discretion to the Athenians, who put to death all the grown men whom they took, and sold the women and children for slaves; subsequently they sent out five hundred settlers and colonized the island.

Questions

1. Why do the Athenians make it clear from the beginning that they do not want to speak of justice?

2. Why do the Melians think it would be "criminal cowardice" to submit to the great strength of the Athenians? (39)

3. Why do the Athenians try to convince the Melians to submit to them willingly instead of exercising their superior power to subjugate them?

4. Are the Melians or the Athenians more responsible for the fate of the Melians?

5. Were the Athenians justified in destroying the Melians after giving them the option of surrender?

6. Are the Melians fools or heroes for refusing the Athenian offer?

William Shakespeare

The plays of the great English writer William Shakespeare (1564–1616) range from comedies to dramatizations of historical events to tragedies that explore some of the deepest human concerns. His works are admired throughout the world by both playgoers and readers for their emotional power and their subtle depiction of the psychology of a vast array of characters representing almost every type of person.

Henry VI, Part I is the first in a trilogy of plays that tell the story of the English monarchy during the Hundred Years War (1337–1453) involving France, England, and their various allies.

In act 4, scenes 5 and 6, the English general Talbot is trapped by the French forces, and his son, John, has joined his father to learn the art of warfare. But Talbot now urges him to flee the batlefield, since John is certain to be killed if he stays. In act 4, scene 7, the French have won victory and John Talbot is dead. Dauphin Charles is France's heir to the throne. The character Pucelle (also known as Joan of Arc) has a leadership role among the French forces. Sir Lucy is an English messenger who has come to the French camp to learn the fate of any English prisoners.

In these scenes, Shakespeare shows both the private and the public aspects of war by contrasting the family drama of Talbot and his son with the spectacle of the victors' speeches over the bodies of the fallen heroes. At the same time, he raises the perennial question of how parents who have received military honors but are also concerned for their offspring's well-being should respond to their children's desire to achieve similar distinction for themselves.

HENRY VI, PART I (selection)

ACT 4, SCENE 5

Enter Talbot and his son [John].

TALBOT

O young John Talbot, I did send for thee
To tutor thee in stratagems of war,
That Talbot's name might be in thee reviv'd
When sapless age and weak unable limbs
Should bring thy father to his drooping chair.
But, O malignant and ill-boding stars!
Now thou art come unto a feast of death,
A terrible and unavoided danger.
Therefore, dear boy, mount on my swiftest horse,
And I'll direct thee how thou shalt escape
By sudden flight. Come, dally not, be gone.

JOHN

Is my name Talbot? And am I your son?
And shall I fly? O, if you love my mother,
Dishonor not her honorable name
To make a bastard and a slave of me!
The world will say he is not Talbot's blood,
That basely fled when noble Talbot stood.

TALBOT

Fly, to revenge my death, if I be slain.

JOHN

He that flies so will ne'er return again.

TALBOT

If we both stay, we both are sure to die.

JOHN

Then let me stay, and, father, do you fly.
Your loss is great, so your regard should be;
My worth unknown, no loss is known in me.
Upon my death the French can little boast;
In yours they will, in you all hopes are lost.
Flight cannot stain the honor you have won;
But mine it will, that no exploit have done.
You fled for vantage, every one will swear;
But, if I bow, they'll say it was for fear.
There is no hope that ever I will stay,
If the first hour I shrink and run away.
Here on my knee I beg mortality,
Rather than life preserv'd with infamy.

TALBOT

Shall all thy mother's hopes lie in one tomb?

JOHN

Ay, rather than I'll shame my mother's womb.

TALBOT

Upon my blessing, I command thee go.

JOHN

To fight I will, but not to fly the foe.

TALBOT

Part of thy father may be sav'd in thee.

JOHN

No part of him but will be shame in me.

TALBOT

Thou never hadst renown, nor canst not lose it.

JOHN

Yes, your renowned name. Shall flight abuse it?

TALBOT

Thy father's charge shall clear thee from that stain.

JOHN

You cannot witness for me, being slain.
If death be so apparent, then both fly.

TALBOT

And leave my followers here to fight and die?
My age was never tainted with such shame.

JOHN

And shall my youth be guilty of such blame?
No more can I be severed from your side
Than can yourself yourself in twain divide.
Stay, go, do what you will—the like do I;
For live I will not, if my father die.

TALBOT

Then here I take my leave of thee, fair son,
Born to eclipse thy life this afternoon.
Come, side by side together live and die,
And soul with soul from France to heaven fly.

Exeunt.

ACT 4, SCENE 6

*Alarum. Excursions, wherein Talbot's son is
hemmed about, and Talbot rescues him.*

TALBOT

Saint George and victory! Fight, soldiers, fight!
The Regent hath with Talbot broke his word
And left us to the rage of France his sword.
Where is John Talbot? Pause, and take thy breath.
I gave thee life and rescu'd thee from death.

JOHN

O, twice my father, twice am I thy son!
The life thou gav'st me first was lost and done,
Till with thy warlike sword, despite of fate,
To my determin'd time thou gav'st new date.

TALBOT

When from the Dauphin's crest thy sword struck
      fire,
It warm'd thy father's heart with proud desire
Of bold-fac'd victory. Then leaden age,
Quicken'd with youthful spleen and warlike rage,
Beat down Alençon, Orleans, Burgundy,
And from the pride of Gallia rescued thee.
The ireful bastard Orleans, that drew blood
From thee, my boy, and had the maidenhood
Of thy first fight, I soon encountered,
And interchanging blows I quickly shed
Some of his bastard blood; and in disgrace
Bespoke him thus: "Contaminated, base,
And misbegotten blood I spill of thine,
Mean and right poor, for that pure blood of mine
Which thou didst force from Talbot, my brave boy."
Here, purposing the Bastard to destroy,

Came in strong rescue. Speak, thy father's care.
Art thou not weary, John? How dost thou fare?
Wilt thou yet leave the battle, boy, and fly,
Now thou art seal'd the son of chivalry?
Fly, to revenge my death when I am dead.
The help of one stands me in little stead.
O, too much folly is it, well I wot,*
To hazard all our lives in one small boat!
If I today die not with Frenchmen's rage,
Tomorrow I shall die with mickle age.
By me they nothing gain and if I stay;
'Tis but the short'ning of my life one day.
In thee thy mother dies, our household's name,
My death's revenge, thy youth, and England's
    fame.
All these and more we hazard by thy stay;
All these are sav'd if thou wilt fly away.

JOHN

The sword of Orleans hath not made me smart;
These words of yours draw lifeblood from my
    heart.
On that advantage, bought with such a shame,
To save a paltry life and slay bright fame,
Before young Talbot from old Talbot fly,
The coward horse that bears me fall and die!
And like me to the peasant boys of France,
To be shame's scorn and subject of mischance!
Surely, by all the glory you have won,
And if I fly, I am not Talbot's son.
Then talk no more of flight. It is no boot.
If son to Talbot, die at Talbot's foot.

---

* [Know.]

TALBOT

Then follow thou thy desp'rate sire of Crete,
Thou Icarus. Thy life to me is sweet.
If thou wilt fight, fight by thy father's side;
And, commendable prov'd, let's die in pride.

Exeunt.

ACT 4, SCENE 7

Alarum. Excursions. Enter old Talbot led [by a servant].

TALBOT

Where is my other life? Mine own is gone.
O, where's young Talbot? Where is valiant John?
Triumphant Death, smear'd with captivity,
Young Talbot's valor makes me smile at thee.
When he perceiv'd me shrink and on my knee,
His bloody sword he brandish'd over me,
And like a hungry lion, did commence
Rough deeds of rage and stern impatience.
But when my angry guardant stood alone,
Tend'ring my ruin and assail'd of none,
Dizzy-ey'd fury and great rage of heart
Suddenly made him from my side to start
Into the clust'ring battle of the French;
And in that sea of blood my boy did drench
His over-mounting spirit; and there died
My Icarus, my blossom, in his pride.

Enter [soldiers], with John Talbot, borne.

SERVANT

O my dear lord, lo, where your son is borne!

TALBOT

Thou antic Death, which laugh'st us here to scorn,
Anon, from thy insulting tyranny,
Coupled in bonds of perpetuity,
Two Talbots, winged through the lither sky,
In thy despite shall scape mortality.
O thou, whose wounds become hard-favored Death,
Speak to thy father ere thou yield thy breath!
Brave Death by speaking, whether he will or no;
Imagine him a Frenchman and thy foe.
Poor boy! He smiles, methinks, as who should say,
Had Death been French, then Death had died today.
Come, come, and lay him in his father's arms.

[John is laid in his father's arms.]

My spirit can no longer bear these harms.
Soldiers, adieu! I have what I would have,
Now my old arms are young John Talbot's grave.

Dies.

*Enter Charles, Alençon, Burgundy, Bastard,
and Pucelle, [and forces].*

CHARLES

Had York and Somerset brought rescue in,
We should have found a bloody day of this.

BASTARD

How the young whelp of Talbot's, raging wood,
Did flesh his puny sword in Frenchmen's blood!

PUCELLE

Once I encount'red him, and thus I said:
"Thou maiden youth, be vanquish'd by a maid."
But, with a proud majestical high scorn,

He answer'd thus: "Young Talbot was not born
To be the pillage of a giglot wench."
So, rushing in the bowels of the French,
He left me proudly, as unworthy fight.

BURGUNDY

Doubtless he would have made a noble knight.
See where he lies inhearsed in the arms
Of the most bloody nurser of his harms!

BASTARD

Hew them to pieces, hack their bones asunder,
Whose life was England's glory, Gallia's wonder.

CHARLES

O, no, forbear! For that which we have fled
During the life, let us not wrong it dead.

Enter [Sir William] Lucy [attended;
Herald of the French preceding].

LUCY

Herald, conduct me to the Dauphin's tent,
To know who hath obtain'd the glory of the day.

CHARLES

On what submissive message art thou sent?

LUCY

Submission, Dauphin? 'Tis a mere French word.
We English warriors wot not what it means.
I come to know what prisoners thou hast ta'en
And to survey the bodies of the dead.

CHARLES

For prisoners ask'st thou? Hell our prison is.
But tell me whom thou seek'st.

LUCY

> But where's the great Alcides of the field,
> Valiant Lord Talbot, Earl of Shrewsbury,
> Created, for his rare success in arms,
> Great Earl of Washford, Waterford, and Valence,
> Lord Talbot of Goodrig and Urchinfield,
> Lord Strange of Blackmere, Lord Verdun of Alton,
> Lord Cromwell of Wingfield, Lord Furnival of
>   Sheffield,
> The thrice-victorious Lord of Falconbridge,
> Knight of the noble order of Saint George,
> Worthy Saint Michael, and the Golden Fleece,
> Great marshal to Henry the Sixth
> Of all his wars within the realm of France?

PUCELLE

> Here is a silly stately style indeed!
> The Turk, that two and fifty kingdoms hath,
> Writes not so tedious a style as this.
> Him that thou magnifi'st with all these titles
> Stinking and fly-blown lies here at our feet.

LUCY

> Is Talbot slain, the Frenchmen's only scourge,
> Your kingdom's terror and black Nemesis?
> O, were mine eyeballs into bullets turn'd,
> That I in rage might shoot them at your faces!
> O, that I could but call these dead to life!
> It were enough to fright the realm of France.
> Were but his picture left amongst you here,
> It would amaze the proudest of you all.
> Give me their bodies, that I may bear them hence
> And give them burial as beseems their worth.

PUCELLE

> I think this upstart is old Talbot's ghost,
> He speaks with such a proud commanding spirit.

For God's sake, let him have 'em! To keep them
    here,
They would but stink and putrefy the air.

CHARLES

Go, take their bodies hence.

LUCY

I'll bear them hence; but from their ashes shall be
    rear'd
A phoenix that shall make all France afeard.

CHARLES

So we be rid of them, do with 'em what thou wilt.
And now to Paris in this conquering vein.
All will be ours, now bloody Talbot's slain.   *Exeunt.*
                        [The bodies are borne out.]

Questions

1. Why does Talbot finally agree to fight side by side with his son, John?

2. After Talbot rescues his son, what does he mean when he tells him, "Now thou art seal'd the son of chivalry"? (51)

3. Why does Burgundy call Talbot "the most bloody nurser of his [son's] harms"? (54)

4. Was John Talbot courageous or foolish in rushing into the thick of combat?

5. Are there ever circumstances when it is honorable to flee from battle?

6. What challenges are faced by children in military families when they decide to make their own careers in the armed forces?

New York Legislature / George Washington

George Washington (1732–1799), the first president of the United States, was also the commander in chief of all the colonial military forces during the American Revolutionary War. Washington had earlier distinguished himself in the French and Indian War but had retired from his command in 1758 to manage his prosperous estates. As a major colonial landowner, he was involved in the years preceding the Revolutionary War in deliberations about how to deal with Britain's growing economic demands. Washington was a Virginia delegate in the first two Continental Congresses, conventions of representatives from the thirteen colonies which debated the issue of political independence from Britain.

After the clash between colonial and British forces at Lexington and Concord, Massachusetts, on April 19, 1775, the Second Continental Congress, convened in May, set about choosing someone to pull together the disorganized American militias into a unified army. Although Washington did not seek the appointment and declared his unfitness for the position, he accepted the commission with the understanding that he would receive payment only for expenses incurred in carrying out his duties. He went on to lead the all-volunteer Continental Army, often under the most unfavorable conditions, to victory over the British forces on October 19, 1781.

In 1775, when Washington accepted the commission to command the Continental Army, colonial leaders as well as the general public were apprehensive about creating a strong standing army that might, after victory, try to use its power to take over the functions of government. The following selection, an exchange of letters between the New York Legislature and Washington after his appointment as commander in chief, indirectly addresses this concern and raises questions about where the ultimate loyalties lie for citizens who assume the responsibilities of soldiers.

LETTERS

The following letter, written from the president of the New York Legislature to Washington, is dated June 26, 1775. Washington's response, written the same day, follows.

May it please Your Excellency—

At a time when the most loyal of his majesty's subjects, from a regard to the laws and constitution by which he sits on the throne, feel themselves reduced to the unhappy necessity of taking up arms to defend their dearest rights and privileges; while we deplore the calamities of this divided empire, we rejoice in the appointment of a gentleman from whose abilities and virtue we are taught to expect both security and peace.

Confiding in you, Sir, and in the worthy generals immediately under your command, we have the most flattering hopes of success in the glorious struggle for American liberty; and the fullest assurances that whenever this important contest shall be decided, by that fondest wish of each American soul; an accommodation with our mother country; you will cheerfully resign the important deposit committed unto your hands, and reassume the character of our worthiest citizen.

By Order—
C. V. B. Livingston, President

Gentlemen:

At the same time that with you I deplore the unhappy necessity of such an appointment, as that with which I am now honoured, I cannot but feel sentiments of the highest gratitude for this affecting instance of distinction and regard.

May your every wish be realized in the success of America, at this important and interesting period; and be assured that the every exertion of my worthy colleagues and myself will be equally extended to the re-establishment of peace and harmony between the mother country and the colonies, as to the fatal, but necessary, operations of war. When we assumed the soldier, we did not lay aside the citizen; and we shall most sincerely rejoice with you in that happy hour when the establishment of American liberty, upon the most firm and solid foundations, shall enable us to return to our private stations in the bosom of a free, peaceful, and happy country.

I am etc.
George Washington

Questions

1. In its letter to Washington congratulating him on his appointment, why does the New York Legislature end by expressing its assurance that he will "cheerfully resign" when the conflict with Britain has been resolved? (59)

2. What does the legislature mean when it refers to Washington as having "the character of our worthiest citizen"? (59)

3. When Washington speaks of both "the reestablishment of peace and harmony" as well as "the fatal, but necessary, operations of war," is he speaking as a citizen, a soldier, or some combination of the two? (60)

4. What does Washington mean when he says, "When we assumed the soldier, we did not lay aside the citizen"? Why does he include this remark in his response? (60)

5. What duties, responsibilities, and rights should a citizen retain as a soldier? When there is a conflict between these and the duties and responsibilities of a soldier, how should the conflict be resolved?

6. In a free, democratic nation, is it safer or more dangerous to maintain powerful, standing armed forces that are administered by a professional military class?

7. Is it good or bad for the military operations of the United States that the commander in chief of its armed forces—the president—is a civilian?

Alexis de Tocqueville

In 1831, the French nobleman Alexis de Tocqueville (1805–1859), working as a civil servant, traveled to the United States to study the American prison system and its possible application in France. Although he wrote about his findings on American prisons, the more significant result of his travels was his political and social study *Democracy in America* (1835–1840).

Tocqueville traveled across America, from Eastern cities to what was then considered the Western frontier, and as he compiled his research he talked with Americans of many social classes. In *Democracy in America*, Tocqueville considers how the structure of U.S. government contributes to the maintenance and evolution of democratic society, and how the ideal of equality influences all aspects of American society. *Democracy in America* is remarkable not only for Tocqueville's sharp observations, but also for his insights concerning the directions American government and society would take in the future.

Tocqueville was keenly aware of both the possibilities and the dangers of a transition to a government based on democratic principles. After the French Revolution and the overthrow of the monarchy in the late 1700s, his country suffered an extremely violent period before order was gradually restored. In his survey of democracy in the United States, Tocqueville aimed to profile a different, less volatile transition to successful democratic rule.

In the following selection from *Democracy in America*, "On Discipline in Democratic Armies," Tocqueville highlights a central problem for military discipline in a democracy: How can an obedient, hierarchically structured army be maintained in a society that encourages free thinking and equality?

ON DISCIPLINE IN DEMOCRATIC ARMIES

It is a very widespread opinion, above all among aristocratic peoples, that the great equality reigning within democracies makes the soldier, in the long term, independent of the officer and thus destroys the bond of discipline.

This is an error. There are, in fact, two kinds of discipline that must not be confused.

When the officer is a noble and the soldier a serf, the one rich and the other poor; when the first is enlightened and strong and the second, ignorant and weak, it is easy to establish the strictest bond of obedience between these two men. The soldier bows to military discipline, so to speak, before entering the army, or rather military discipline is only a perfecting of social servitude. In aristocratic armies, the soldier comes easily enough to be almost insensitive to all things except the orders of his chiefs. He acts without thinking, triumphs without ardor, and dies without complaining. In this state he is no longer a man, but he is still a very formidable animal trained for war.

Democratic peoples must despair of ever obtaining from their soldiers the blind, minute, resigned, and always equable obedience that aristocratic peoples impose on theirs without trouble. The state of society does not prepare it: they would risk losing their natural advantages if they wished to acquire that one artificially. In democratic peoples military discipline ought not to try to negate the free flight of souls; it can only aspire to direct it; the obedience that it creates is less exact, but more impetuous and more intelligent. Its root is in the very will of the one who obeys; it is supported not solely by his instinct, but by his reason; so it often tightens itself as danger renders it necessary. The discipline of an aristocratic army is easily relaxed in war because this discipline is founded on habits, and war disturbs these habits. The discipline of a democratic army is on the contrary steadied before the enemy, because then each soldier sees very clearly that he must be silent and obey in order to be able to win.

Peoples who have done the most considerable things by war have known no other discipline than the one I am speaking of. Among the ancients, only free men and citizens, who differed little from one another and were accustomed to treating each other as equals, were accepted in the armies. In this sense one can say that the armies of antiquity were democratic although they came from the heart of an aristocracy; so a sort of familiar fraternity between officer and soldier reigned within these armies. Of this one is convinced in reading Plutarch's *The Lives of the Great Captains*. In that, soldiers speak constantly and very freely to their generals, and the latter listen willingly to the discourse of their soldiers and respond to it. They lead them by words and examples much more than by constraint and chastisements. One would say they were as much companions as chiefs.

I do not know if Greek and Roman soldiers ever perfected the little details of military discipline to the same point as the Russians; but that did not prevent Alexander from conquering Asia, and Rome, the world.

Questions

1. According to Tocqueville, why would democratic societies "risk losing their natural advantages" if they tried to impose the kind of discipline used in aristocratic armies? (63)

2. What does Tocqueville mean when he says that discipline in a democratic army "ought not to try to negate the free flight of souls"? (63)

3. Why does Tocqueville think that obedience in a democratic army can be "more impetuous and more intelligent" than obedience in an aristocratic army? (63)

4. According to Tocqueville, why is the discipline of a democratic army "steadied before the enemy" while the discipline of an aristocratic army is "easily relaxed in war"? (63)

5. Why does Tocqueville believe that "the armies of antiquity were democratic although they came from the heart of an aristocracy"? (64)

6. To what extent can the principle of equality among all citizens in a democratic society carry over into military training and service?

Abraham Lincoln

Abraham Lincoln (1809–1865) served as president of the United States from 1861 to 1865, working to preserve the Union during the Civil War years and to end the institution of slavery in the United States. While Lincoln and many others had long disavowed slavery on moral grounds, the importance of slaves to the South's economy and social order became powerfully evident in the years leading up to the war. As the war progressed, Lincoln found both the moral and the military advantages of abolition to be compelling. He was assassinated in April 1865, shortly after the end of the war and his inauguration to a second term in office.

Lincoln's Gettysburg Address commemorates the Battle of Gettysburg, July 1–3, 1863, generally considered a turning point for ultimate Union victory in the war. The Union and Confederate armies together suffered an estimated fifty thousand casualties, including some eight thousand killed. In his November 1863 address dedicating Soldier's National Cemetery (now Gettysburg National Cemetery), Lincoln chose to reiterate the lofty goal he saw as the Union's cause—to ensure a nation of free people, by free people, and for free people.

Lincoln's desire that the nation should come through the war to "a new birth of freedom" reflects a struggle common in the aftermath of many conflicts. Lincoln challenges the people of his own time and all future American citizens to consider how to perpetuate and sustain the principles for which the soldiers at Gettysburg gave their lives. In doing so, he raises one of the most fundamental questions for a democratic republic founded on political revolution: How can each successive generation assure that the spirit that gave birth to the nation will remain a living principle?

GETTYSBURG ADDRESS

Fourscore and seven years ago our fathers brought forth on this continent a new nation, conceived in liberty, and dedicated to the proposition that all men are created equal.

Now we are engaged in a great civil war, testing whether that nation, or any nation so conceived and so dedicated, can long endure. We are met on a great battlefield of that war. We have come to dedicate a portion of that field as a final resting place for those who here gave their lives that that nation might live. It is altogether fitting and proper that we should do this.

But, in a larger sense, we cannot dedicate—we cannot consecrate—we cannot hallow—this ground. The brave men, living and dead, who struggled here, have consecrated it far above our poor power to add or detract. The world will little note nor long remember what we say here, but it can never forget what they did here. It is for us, the living, rather, to be dedicated here to the unfinished work which they who fought here have thus far so nobly advanced. It is rather for us to be here dedicated to the great task remaining before us—that from these honored dead we take increased devotion to that cause for which they gave the last full measure of devotion; that we here highly resolve that these dead shall not have died in vain; that this nation, under God, shall have a new birth of freedom; and that government of the people, by the people, for the people, shall not perish from the earth.

Questions

1. Why does Lincoln say that the war is not only testing whether the United States can survive, but whether "any nation so conceived and so dedicated" can survive?

2. Why does Lincoln tell his listeners that those who have fought on the battlefield have "consecrated it far above our poor power to add or detract"?

3. Why does Lincoln describe those who have died as giving "the last full measure of devotion"?

4. According to Lincoln, how can the living ensure "that these dead shall not have died in vain"?

5. What is the most "fitting and proper" way to honor soldiers who have died in battle?

6. Is a "new birth of freedom" something that was accomplished once and for all by the Civil War? Or is it something that citizens in a democracy must reestablish from generation to generation?

Alfred, Lord Tennyson

In 1850 the popular English poet Alfred, Lord Tennyson (1809–1892) was appointed Britain's Poet Laureate. One of the responsibilities of this position was to commemorate in verse events of national importance.

Tennyson's poem "The Charge of the Light Brigade" recounts the Battle of Balaclava, fought on October 25, 1854, between British and Russian forces during the Crimean War. Through an error of judgment, a British brigade of over six hundred men charged into a valley, where they were trapped and almost surrounded by enemy forces twenty-five thousand strong and positioned on higher ground. Despite the error, which led to heavy British losses, the charge was initially considered a success, and the British public drew on the episode as a symbol of pride and honor.

In his poem, Tennyson does not offer a searing critique of military incompetence, though he does allude to someone's "blunder." There is no doubt that the valor of the doomed men appealed to the Victorian public's imagination and was praised as heroic. However, when Tennyson later published a revised version of the poem with the line about the blunder removed and the last stanza rewritten in even more soaringly patriotic tones, his original version was still widely preferred, even by the survivors of the charge themselves.

Criticism of military command by civilians has always been a sensitive topic, especially when there are significant casualties. This is particularly true today, when writers, filmmakers, and the general public have become more outspoken in their views on the effectiveness of military operations. Tennyson's poem challenges us to think about the fine line between valid criticism of a flawed military action and loyalty to a national cause and the warriors who made a sacrifice in its service.

THE CHARGE OF THE LIGHT BRIGADE

1

Half a league, half a league,
Half a league onward,
All in the valley of Death
    Rode the six hundred.
"Forward the Light Brigade!
Charge for the guns!" he said.
Into the valley of Death
    Rode the six hundred.

2

"Forward, the Light Brigade!"
Was there a man dismay'd?
Not though the soldier knew
    Someone had blunder'd.
Theirs not to make reply,
Theirs not to reason why,
Theirs but to do and die.
Into the valley of Death
    Rode the six hundred.

3

Cannon to right of them,
Cannon to left of them,
Cannon in front of them
    Volley'd and thunder'd;
Storm'd at with shot and shell,
Boldly they rode and well,
Into the jaws of Death,

Into the mouth of hell
    Rode the six hundred.

4

Flash'd all their sabres bare,
Flash'd as they turn'd in air
Sabring the gunners there,
Charging an army, while
    All the world wonder'd.
Plunged in the battery-smoke
Right thro' the line they broke;
Cossack and Russian
Reel'd from the sabre-stroke
    Shatter'd and sunder'd.
Then they rode back, but not,
    Not the six hundred.

5

Cannon to right of them,
Cannon to left of them,
Cannon behind them
    Volley'd and thunder'd;
Storm'd at with shot and shell,
While horse and hero fell,
They that had fought so well
Came thro' the jaws of Death,
Back from the mouth of hell,
All that was left of them,
    Left of six hundred.

6

When can their glory fade?
O the wild charge they made!
    All the world wonder'd.
Honour the charge they made!
Honour the Light Brigade,
    Noble six hundred!

Questions

1. Why does Tennyson say that even though the soldiers knew that "Someone had blunder'd," they were not dismayed? (71)

2. Why does Tennyson keep repeating the phrase "the six hundred"? (71–72)

3. What does Tennyson mean when he says that "All the world wonder'd" at the charge of the Light Brigade? Why does he repeat these words at the end, just before telling us to honor the Light Brigade? (72)

4. Does Tennyson think that the charge was a military victory for the British?

5. Do you agree that a warrior should follow all orders unquestioningly?

6. Is the honor a soldier receives diminished in any way if the war in which he or she fought is conducted badly?

Walt Whitman

Walt Whitman (1819–1892), one of America's most important poets, created a new kind of poetry that he felt was closely attuned to the spirit and language of the United States, especially during the period of rapid, vibrant growth and turmoil before, during, and after the Civil War. His most important collection of poems, repeatedly revised during his lifetime, is *Leaves of Grass* (1855). In it, he echoed the rhythms and slang of American speech and celebrated the bonds among people from all walks of life, particularly the masses of workers who were building America.

After witnessing suffering at the front during the Civil War, Whitman volunteered as a nurse in military hospitals in Washington, D.C., and his 1865 poetry collection *Drum Taps*, from which "The Wound-Dresser" is taken, captures this experience of tending to sick and wounded soldiers. Whitman regards each instance of suffering as a unique tragedy and sees each wounded soldier as a being deserving of love and care, an outlook reflected in the following selections from his *Specimen Days* (1882–1883). After the war, Whitman's writing again re-affirmed the patriotic hopefulness of his earlier poetry, but he also criticized the young nation for failing to live up to its bold promise.

The work of comforting the wounded and dying is continued today by medical professionals and volunteers, who work with wounded veterans to help them overcome injuries and assimilate back into their communities. How society views the wounded is an issue as relevant today as it was in Whitman's time.

ON CAREGIVING

The Wound-Dresser

1

An old man bending I come among new faces,
Years looking backward resuming in answer to children,
Come tell us old man, as from young men and maidens that love
    me,
(Arous'd and angry, I'd thought to beat the alarum, and urge
    relentless war,
But soon my fingers fail'd me, my face droop'd and I resign'd
    myself,
To sit by the wounded and soothe them, or silently watch the
    dead;)
Years hence of these scenes, of these furious passions, these
    chances,
Of unsurpass'd heroes, (was one side so brave? the other was
    equally brave;)
Now be witness again, paint the mightiest armies of earth,
Of those armies so rapid so wondrous what saw you to tell us?
What stays with you latest and deepest? of curious panics,
Of hard-fought engagements or sieges tremendous what deepest
    remains?

2

O maidens and young men I love and that love me,
What you ask of my days those the strangest and sudden your
    talking recalls,
Soldier alert I arrive after a long march cover'd with sweat and
    dust,

In the nick of time I come, plunge in the fight, loudly shout in
    the rush of successful charge,
Enter the captur'd works—yet lo, like a swift-running river they
    fade,
Pass and are gone they fade—I dwell not on soldiers' perils or
    soldiers' joys,
(Both I remember well—many the hardships, few the joys, yet I
    was content.)

But in silence, in dreams' projections,
While the world of gain and appearance and mirth goes on,
So soon what is over forgotten, and waves wash the imprints off
    the sand,
With hinged knees returning I enter the doors, (while for you up
    there,
Whoever you are, follow without noise and be of strong heart.)

Bearing the bandages, water and sponge,
Straight and swift to my wounded I go,
Where they lie on the ground after the battle brought in,
Where their priceless blood reddens the grass the ground,
Or to the rows of the hospital tent, or under the roof'd hospital,
To the long rows of cots up and down each side I return,
To each and all one after another I draw near, not one do I miss,
An attendant follows holding a tray, he carries a refuse pail,
Soon to be fill'd with clotted rags and blood, emptied, and fill'd
    again.

I onward go, I stop,
With hinged knees and steady hand to dress wounds,
I am firm with each, the pangs are sharp yet unavoidable,
One turns to me his appealing eyes—poor boy! I never knew you,
Yet I think I could not refuse this moment to die for you, if that
    would save you.

3

On, on I go, (open doors of time! open hospital doors!)
The crush'd head I dress, (poor crazed hand tear not the bandage
    away,)
The neck of the cavalryman with the bullet through and through
    I examine,
Hard the breathing rattles, quite glazed already the eye, yet life
    struggles hard,
(Come sweet death! be persuaded O beautiful death!
In mercy come quickly.)

From the stump of the arm, the amputated hand,
I undo the clotted lint, remove the slough, wash off the matter
    and blood,
Back on his pillow the soldier bends with curv'd neck and side-
    falling head,
His eyes are closed, his face is pale, he dares not look on the
    bloody stump,
And has not yet look'd on it.

I dress a wound in the side, deep, deep,
But a day or two more, for see the frame all wasted and sinking,
And the yellow-blue countenance see.

I dress the perforated shoulder, the foot with the bullet-wound,
Cleanse the one with a gnawing and putrid gangrene, so
    sickening, so offensive,
While the attendant stands behind aside me holding the tray and
    pail.

I am faithful, I do not give out,
The fractur'd thigh, the knee, the wound in the abdomen,
These and more I dress with impassive hand, (yet deep in my
    breast a fire, a burning flame.)

4

Thus in silence in dreams' projections,
Returning, resuming, I thread my way through the hospitals,
The hurt and wounded I pacify with soothing hand,
I sit by the restless all the dark night, some are so young,
Some suffer so much, I recall the experience sweet and sad,
(Many a soldier's loving arms about this neck have cross'd and
    rested,
Many a soldier's kiss dwells on these bearded lips.)

Specimen Days (selection)

Some Specimen Cases

June 18th

In one of the hospitals I find Thomas Haley, Company M, Fourth New York Cavalry—a regular Irish boy, a fine specimen of youthful physical manliness—shot through the lungs—inevitably dying— came over to this country from Ireland to enlist—has not a single friend or acquaintance here—is sleeping soundly at this moment (but it is the sleep of death)—has a bullet hole straight through the lung. I saw Tom when first brought here, three days since, and didn't suppose he could live twelve hours (yet he looks well enough in the face to a casual observer). He lies there with his frame exposed above the waist, all naked, for coolness, a fine built man, the tan not bleach'd from his cheeks and neck. It is useless to talk to him, as with his sad hurt, and the stimulants they give him, and the utter strangeness of every object, face, furniture, etc., the poor fellow, even when awake, is like some frighten'd, shy animal. Much of the time he sleeps, or half sleeps. (Sometimes I thought he knew more than he show'd.) I often come and sit by him in perfect silence; he will breathe for ten minutes softly and evenly as a young babe asleep. Poor youth, so handsome, athletic, with profuse beautiful shining hair. One time as I sat looking at him while he lay asleep, he suddenly, without the least start, awaken'd, open'd his eyes, gave me a long steady look, turning his face very slightly to gaze easier—one long, clear, silent look— a slight sigh—then turn'd back and went into his doze again. Little he knew, poor death-stricken boy, the heart of the stranger that hover'd near.

W. H. E., Co. F., 2nd N.J.—His disease is pneumonia. He lay sick at the wretched hospital below Aquia Creek for seven or eight days before brought here. He was detail'd from his regiment to go there and help as nurse, but was soon taken down himself. Is an elderly, sallow-faced, rather gaunt, gray hair'd man, a widower, with children. He express'd a great desire for good, strong green tea. An excellent lady, Mrs. W., of Washington, soon sent him a package; also a small sum of money. The doctor said give him the tea at pleasure; it lay on the table by his side, and he used it every day. He slept a great deal; could not talk much, as he grew deaf. Occupied bed 15, ward I, Armory. (The same lady above, Mrs. W., sent the men a large package of tobacco.)

J. G. lies in bed 52, ward I; is of Company B, Seventh Pennsylvania. I gave him a small sum of money, some tobacco, and envelopes. To a man adjoining also gave twenty-five cents; he flush'd in the face when I offer'd it—refused at first, but as I found he had not a cent, and was very fond of having the daily papers to read, I prest it on him. He was evidently very grateful but said little.

J. T. L., of Company F., Ninth New Hampshire, lies in bed 37, ward I. Is very fond of tobacco. I furnish him some; also with a little money. Has gangrene of the feet; a pretty bad case; will surely have to lose three toes. Is a regular specimen of an old fashion'd, rude, hearty, New England countryman, impressing me with his likeness to that celebrated singed cat, who was better than she look'd.

Bed 3, ward E, Armory, has a great hankering for pickles, something pungent. After consulting the doctor, I gave him a small bottle of horse-radish; also some apples; also a book. Some of the nurses are excellent. The woman nurse in this ward I like very much. (Mrs. Wright—a year afterward I found her in Mansion House Hospital, Alexandria—she is a perfect nurse.)

In one bed a young man, Marcus Small, Company K, Seventh Maine—sick with dysentery and typhoid fever—pretty critical case—I talk with him often—he thinks he will die—looks like it indeed. I write a letter for him home to East Livermore, Maine—I let him talk to me a little, but not much, advise him to keep very quiet—do most of the talking myself—stay quite a while with him, as he holds on to my hand—talk to him in a cheering, but slow, low, and measured manner—talk about his furlough and going home as soon as he is able to travel.

Thomas Lindly, First Pennsylvania Cavalry, shot very badly through the foot—poor young man, he suffers horribly, has to be constantly dosed with morphine, his face ashy and glazed, bright young eyes—I give him a large handsome apple, lay it in sight, tell him to have it roasted in the morning, as he generally feels easier then, and can eat a little breakfast. I write two letters for him.

Opposite, an old Quaker lady is sitting by the side of her son, Amer Moore, Second U.S. Artillery—shot in the head two weeks since, very low, quite rational—from hips down paralyzed—he will surely die. I speak a very few words to him every day and evening—he answers pleasantly—wants nothing (he told me soon after he came about his home affairs, his mother had been an invalid, and he fear'd to let her know his condition). He died soon after she came.

Gifts—Money—Discrimination

As a very large proportion of the wounded came up from the front without a cent of money in their pockets, I soon discover'd that it was about the best thing I could do to raise their spirits and show them that somebody cared for them, and practically felt a fatherly or brotherly interest in them, to give them small sums in such cases, using tact and discretion about it. I am regularly supplied with funds for this purpose by good women and men in Boston, Salem, Providence, Brooklyn, and New York. I provide myself with a quantity of bright new ten-cent and five-cent bills, and, when I think it incumbent, I give twenty-five or thirty cents, or perhaps fifty cents, and occasionally a still-larger sum to some particular case. As I have started this subject, I take opportunity to ventilate the financial question. My supplies, altogether voluntary, mostly confidential, often seeming quite providential, were numerous and varied. For instance, there were two distant and wealthy ladies, sisters, who sent regularly, for two years, quite heavy sums, enjoying that their names should be kept secret. The same delicacy was indeed a frequent condition. From several I had carte blanche. Many were entire strangers. From these sources, during from two to three years, in the manner described, in the hospitals, I bestowed, as almoner for others, many, many thousands of dollars. I learn'd one thing conclusively—that beneath all the ostensible greed and heartlessness of our times there is no end to the generous benevolence of men and women in the United States, when once sure of its object. Another thing became clear to me—while *cash* is not amiss to bring up the rear, tact and magnetic sympathy and unction are, and ever will be, sovereign still.

Questions

"THE WOUND-DRESSER"

1. Why did the wound-dresser turn away from urging war to "sit by the wounded and soothe them"? (75)

2. When the young people ask the wound-dresser to tell them about what he remembers of "the mightiest armies of earth," why does he tell them about how he worked among the wounded? (75)

3. Why does the wound-dresser describe in detail all the types of bodily wounds he has tended?

4. Why does the wound-dresser's hand remain "impassive," even though he feels "deep in my breast a fire, a burning flame"? (77)

5. Why does the wound-dresser end his recollections with memories of being affectionately embraced by those he has tried to help?

6. Is it helpful or harmful for caregivers to think about the cause the wounded were fighting for when they were injured?

"SPECIMEN DAYS"

1. Why does Whitman call these injured soldiers "specimen cases"? (79)

2. What does Whitman mean when he says that the dying boy he visits does not know "the heart of the stranger that hover'd near"? (79)

3. What does Whitman think is the reason that "good women and men" send him money to distribute to strangers? (81) How would you compare the value of their contribution to that of Whitman's?

4. Why does Whitman make a point to "ventilate the financial question"? (81) Why is this topic a question?

5. Why does Whitman qualify his statement about the generosity of Americans by saying that they only give "when once sure of its object"? (81)

6. What is the "magnetic sympathy and unction" that Whitman says are "sovereign still"? (81) Over what are they sovereign?

Leo Tolstoy

During his long career, the Russian author Leo Tolstoy (1828–1910) produced novels, short stories, plays, and essays that reflect his deep understanding of human motivations and the workings of society. His books are full of memorable characters, incidents, and plots that entertain readers while challenging them to think about issues and ideas that people have been grappling with from the beginning of civilization up to the present day.

Tolstoy saw military service when he followed his older brother into the Russian army in 1852; he was involved in action during the Chechen insurgency and the Crimean War. He left the army shortly thereafter, traveled in Europe for several years, and returned to manage his family estate and write. During the next twenty years, Tolstoy produced the two highly popular novels that established his international reputation: *War and Peace* (in six volumes, 1868–1869) and *Anna Karenina* (serialized, 1875–1877). Later in life, Tolstoy became committed to a form of Christian belief that advocated a simple communal lifestyle and complete abstinence from violence of any kind. His pacifism was a direct inspiration to the Indian leader Mohandas Gandhi and, through him, an indirect influence on Martin Luther King Jr.

War and Peace, from which the following passages are taken, offers a panorama of life during the Napoleonic wars of 1805–1812 and focuses on the members of several interrelated families in the Russian aristocracy. The French, under their emperor Napoleon, invaded Russia and advanced deep into the country but were finally defeated by the Russians' defensive war of attrition and the brutal Russian winter. Alongside the story Tolstoy tells, he speculates about why individuals leave the comfort of their homes to follow leaders into war and the almost-certain suffering of combat. He concludes that leaders are as much pawns of impersonal historical forces as the lowest-ranking members of the infantry.

WAR AND PEACE

(selection)

In the following passage from War and Peace, *commanders of the Russian military debate battlefield tactics during their fight against the French. One of the young men under their command is Nicholas Rostóv, a member of one of the central families in* War and Peace, *experiencing combat for the first time.*

The attack of the Sixth Chasseurs secured the retreat of our right flank. In the center Túshin's forgotten battery, which had managed to set fire to the Schön Grabern village, delayed the French advance. The French were putting out the fire which the wind was spreading, and thus gave us time to retreat. The retirement of the center to the other side of the dip in the ground at the rear was hurried and noisy, but the different companies did not get mixed. But our left—which consisted of the Azóv and Podólsk infantry and the Pávlograd hussars—was simultaneously attacked and outflanked by superior French forces under Lannes and was thrown into confusion. Bagratión had sent Zherkóv to the general commanding that left flank with orders to retreat immediately.

Zherkóv, not removing his hand from his cap, turned his horse about and galloped off. But no sooner had he left Bagratión than his courage failed him. He was seized by panic and could not go where it was dangerous.

Having reached the left flank, instead of going to the front where the firing was, he began to look for the general and his staff where they could not possibly be, and so did not deliver the order.

The command of the left flank belonged by seniority to the commander of the regiment Kutúzov had reviewed at Braunau and in which Dólokhov was serving as private. But the command of the extreme left flank had been assigned to the commander of the Pávlograd regiment in which Rostóv was serving, and a misunderstanding arose. The two commanders were much exasperated with one another and long after the action had begun on the right flank and the French were already advancing were engaged in discussion with the sole object of offending one another. But the regiments, both cavalry and infantry, were by no means ready for the impending action. From privates to general they were not expecting a battle and were engaged in peaceful occupations, the cavalry feeding the horses and the infantry collecting wood.

"He higher iss dan I in rank," said the German colonel of the hussars, flushing and addressing an adjutant who had ridden up, "so let him do vhat he vill, but I cannot sacrifice my hussars . . . Bugler, sount ze retreat!"

But haste was becoming imperative. Cannon and musketry, mingling together, thundered on the right and in the center, while the capotes of Lannes's sharpshooters were already seen crossing the milldam and forming up within twice the range of a musket shot. The general in command of the infantry went toward his horse with jerky steps, and having mounted drew himself up very straight and tall and rode to the Pávlograd commander. The commanders met with polite bows but with secret malevolence in their hearts.

"Once again, Colonel," said the general, "I can't leave half my men in the wood. I beg of you, I beg of you," he repeated, "to occupy the position and prepare for an attack."

"I peg of you yourself not to mix in vot is not your pusiness!" suddenly replied the irate colonel. "If you vere in the cavalry . . ."

"I am not in the cavalry, Colonel, but I am a Russian general and if you are not aware of the fact . . ."

"Quite avare, your excellency," suddenly shouted the colonel, touching his horse and turning purple in the face. "Vill you be so goot to come to ze front and see dat zis position iss no goot? I don't vish to desstroy my men for your pleasure!"

"You forgot yourself, Colonel. I am not considering my own pleasure and I won't allow it to be said!"

Taking the colonel's outburst as a challenge to his courage, the general expanded his chest and rode, frowning, beside him to the front line, as if their differences would be settled there amongst the bullets. They reached the front, several bullets sped over them, and they halted in silence. There was nothing fresh to be seen from the line, for from where they had been before it had been evident that it was impossible for cavalry to act among the bushes and broken ground, as well as that the French were outflanking our left. The general and colonel looked sternly and significantly at one another like two fighting cocks preparing for battle, each vainly trying to detect signs of cowardice in the other. Both passed the examination successfully. As there was nothing to be said, and neither wished to give occasion for it to be alleged that he had been the first to leave the range of fire, they would have remained there for a long time testing each other's courage had it not been that just then they heard the rattle of musketry and a muffled shout almost behind them in the wood. The French had attacked the men collecting wood in the copse. It was no longer possible for the hussars to retreat with the infantry. They were cut off from the line of retreat on the left by the French. However inconvenient the position, it was now necessary to attack in order to cut a way through for themselves.

The squadron in which Rostóv was serving had scarcely time to mount before it was halted facing the enemy. Again, as at the Enns bridge, there was nothing between the squadron and the enemy, and again that terrible dividing line of uncertainty and fear—resembling the line separating the living from the dead—lay between them. All were conscious of this unseen line, and the question whether they would cross it or not, and how they would cross it, agitated them all.

The colonel rode to the front, angrily gave some reply to questions put to him by the officers, and, like a man desperately insisting on having his own way, gave an order. No one said anything definite, but the rumor of an attack spread through the squadron. The command to form up rang out and the sabers whizzed as they were drawn from their scabbards. Still no one moved. The troops of the left flank, infantry and hussars alike, felt that the commander did not himself know what to do, and this irresolution communicated itself to the men.

"If only they would be quick!" thought Rostóv, feeling that at last the time had come to experience the joy of an attack of which he had so often heard from his fellow hussars.

"Fo'ward, with God, lads!" rang out Denísov's voice. "At a twot fo'ward!"

The horses' croups began to sway in the front line. Rook pulled at the reins and started of his own accord.

Before him, on the right, Rostóv saw the front lines of his hussars and still farther ahead a dark line which he could not see distinctly but took to be the enemy. Shots could be heard, but some way off.

"Faster!" came the word of command, and Rostóv felt Rook's flanks drooping as he broke into a gallop.

Rostóv anticipated his horse's movements and became more and more elated. He had noticed a solitary tree ahead of him. This tree had been in the middle of the line that had seemed so terrible—and now he had crossed that line and not only was there nothing terrible, but everything was becoming more and more happy and animated. "Oh, how I will slash at him!" thought Rostóv, gripping the hilt of his saber.

"Hur-a-a-a-ah!" came a roar of voices. "Let anyone come my way now," thought Rostóv, driving his spurs into Rook and letting him go at a full gallop so that he outstripped the others. Ahead, the enemy was already visible. Suddenly something like a birch broom seemed to sweep over the squadron. Rostóv raised his saber, ready to strike, but at that instant the trooper Nikítenko, who was galloping ahead, shot away from him, and Rostóv felt as in a dream that he continued to be carried forward with unnatural speed but yet stayed on the same spot. From behind him Bondarchúk, a hussar he knew, jolted against him and looked angrily at him. Bondarchúk's horse swerved and galloped past.

"How is it I am not moving? I have fallen, I am killed!" Rostóv asked and answered at the same instant. He was alone in the middle of the field. Instead of the moving horses and hussars' backs, he saw nothing before him but the motionless earth and the stubble around him. There was warm blood under his arm. "No, I am wounded and the horse is killed." Rook tried to rise on his forelegs but fell back, pinning his rider's leg. Blood was flowing from his head; he struggled but could not rise. Rostóv also tried to rise but fell back, his sabretache having become entangled in the saddle. Where our men were, and where the French, he did not know. There was no one near.

Having disentangled his leg, he rose. "Where, on which side, was now the line that had so sharply divided the two armies?" he asked himself and could not answer. "Can something bad have happened to me?" he wondered as he got up: and at that moment he felt that something super-fluous was hanging on his benumbed left arm. The wrist felt as if it were not his. He examined his hand carefully, vainly trying to find blood on it. "Ah, here are people coming," he thought joyfully, seeing some men running toward him. "They will help me!" In front came a man wearing a strange shako and a blue cloak, swarthy, sunburned, and with a hooked nose. Then came two more, and many more running behind. One of them said something strange, not in Russian. In among the hindmost of these men wearing similar shakos was a Russian hussar. He was being held by the arms and his horse was being led behind him.

"It must be one of ours, a prisoner. Yes. Can it be that they will take me too? Who are these men?" thought Rostóv, scarcely believing his eyes. "Can they be French?" He looked at the approaching Frenchmen, and though but a moment before he had been galloping to get at them and hack them to pieces, their proximity now seemed so awful that he could not believe his eyes. "Who are they? Why are they running? Can they be coming at me? And why? To kill me? Me whom everyone is so fond of?" He remembered his mother's love for him, and his family's, and his friends', and the enemy's intention to kill him seemed impossible. "But perhaps they may do it!" For more than ten seconds he stood not moving from the spot or realizing the situation. The foremost Frenchman, the one with the hooked nose, was already so close that the expression of his face could be seen. And the excited, alien face of that man, his bayonet hang-ing down, holding his breath, and running so lightly, frightened Rostóv. He seized his pistol and, instead of firing it, flung it at the Frenchman and ran with all his might toward the bushes. He did not now run with the feeling of doubt and conflict with which he had trodden the Enns bridge, but with the feeling of a hare fleeing from the hounds. One sin-gle sentiment, that of fear for his young and happy life, possessed his whole being. Rapidly leaping the furrows, he fled across the field with the impetuosity he used to show at catchplay, now and then turning his good-natured, pale, young face to look back. A shudder of terror went through him: "No, better not look," he thought, but having reached the bushes he glanced round once more. The French had fallen behind, and just as he looked round the first man changed his run to a walk and, turning, shouted something loudly to a comrade farther back. Rostóv paused. "No, there's some mistake," thought he. "They can't have wanted to kill me." But at the same time, his left arm felt as heavy as if a seventy-pound weight were tied to it. He could run no more. The Frenchman also stopped and took aim. Rostóv closed his eyes and stooped down. One bullet and then another whistled past him. He mustered his last remaining strength, took hold of his left hand with his right, and reached the bushes. Behind these were some Russian sharpshooters. . . .

In this passage, Nicholas Rostóv's family in Moscow, far from the battlefield where he is serving, have heard nothing of him for months, a common situation before modern means of communication. The main characters in this scene are Nicholas's sisters, Natásha and Véra; his little brother, Pétya; his girlfriend, Sónya; his mother and father, the Count and Countess Rostóv; and a close family friend, Anna Mikháylovna.

It was long since the Rostóvs had news of Nicholas. Not till midwinter was the count at last handed a letter addressed in his son's handwriting. On receiving it, he ran on tiptoe to his study in alarm and haste, trying to escape notice, closed the door, and began to read the letter.

Anna Mikháylovna, who always knew everything that passed in the house, on hearing of the arrival of the letter went softly into the room and found the count with it in his hand, sobbing and laughing at the same time.

Anna Mikháylovna, though her circumstances had improved, was still living with the Rostóvs.

"My dear friend?" she said, in a tone of pathetic inquiry, prepared to sympathize in any way.

The count sobbed yet more.

"Nikólenka . . . a letter . . . wa . . . a . . . s . . . wounded . . . my darling boy . . . the countess . . . promoted to be an officer . . . thank God . . . How tell the little countess!"

Anna Mikháylovna sat down beside him, with her own handkerchief wiped the tears from his eyes and from the letter, then having dried her own eyes she comforted the count, and decided that at dinner and till teatime she would prepare the countess, and after tea, with God's help, would inform her.

At dinner Anna Mikháylovna talked the whole time about the war news and about Nikólenka, twice asked when the last letter had been received from him, though she knew that already, and remarked that they might very likely be getting a letter from him that day. Each time that these hints began to make the countess anxious and she glanced uneasily at the count and at Anna Mikháylovna, the latter very adroitly turned the conversation to insignificant matters. Natásha, who, of the whole family, was the most gifted with a capacity to feel any shades of intonation, look, and expression, pricked up her ears from the beginning of the meal and was certain that there was some secret between her father and Anna Mikháylovna, that it had something to do with her brother, and that Anna Mikháylovna was preparing them for it. Bold as she was, Natásha, who knew how sensitive her mother was to anything relating to Nikólenka, did not venture to ask any questions at dinner, but she was too excited to eat anything and kept wriggling about on her chair regardless of her governess's remarks. After dinner, she rushed headlong after Anna Mikháylovna and, dashing at her, flung herself on her neck as soon as she overtook her in the sitting room.

"Auntie, darling, do tell me what it is!"

"Nothing, my dear."

"No, dearest, sweet one, honey, I won't give up—I know you know something."

Anna Mikháylovna shook her head.

"You are a little slyboots," she said.

"A letter from Nikólenka! I'm sure of it!" exclaimed Natásha, reading confirmation in Anna Mikháylovna's face.

"But for God's sake, be careful, you know how it may affect your mamma."

"I will, I will, only tell me! You won't? Then I will go and tell at once."

Anna Mikháylovna, in a few words, told her the contents of the letter, on condition that she should tell no one.

"No, on my true word of honor," said Natásha, crossing herself, "I won't tell anyone!" and she ran off at once to Sónya.

"Nikólenka . . . wounded . . . a letter," she said in gleeful triumph.

"*Nicholas!*" was all Sónya said, instantly turning white.

Natásha, seeing the impression the news of her brother's wound produced in Sónya, felt for the first time the sorrowful side of the news.

She rushed to Sónya, hugged her, and began to cry.

"A little wound, but he has been made an officer; he is well now, he wrote himself," she said through her tears.

"There now! It's true that all you women are crybabies," remarked Pétya, pacing the room with large, resolute strides. "Now I'm very glad, very glad indeed, that my brother has distinguished himself so. You are all blubberers and understand nothing."

Natásha smiled through her tears.

"You haven't read the letter?" asked Sónya.

"No, but she said that it was all over and that he's now an officer."

"Thank God!" said Sónya, crossing herself. "But perhaps she deceived you. Let us go to Mamma."

Pétya paced the room in silence for a time.

"If I'd been in Nikólenka's place I would have killed even more of those Frenchmen," he said. "What nasty brutes they are! I'd have killed so many that there'd have been a heap of them."

"Hold your tongue, Pétya, what a goose you are!"

"I'm not a goose, but they are who cry about trifles," said Pétya.

"Do you remember him?" Natásha suddenly asked, after a moment's silence.

Sónya smiled.

"Do I remember *Nicholas*?"

"No, Sónya, but do you remember so that you remember him perfectly, remember everything?" said Natásha, with an expressive gesture, evidently wishing to give her words a very definite meaning. "I remember Nikólenka too, I remember him well," she said. "But I don't remember Borís. I don't remember him a bit."

"What! You don't remember Borís?" asked Sónya in surprise.

"It's not that I don't remember—I know what he is like, but not as I remember Nikólenka. Him—I just shut my eyes and remember, but Borís . . . No!" (She shut her eyes.) "No! there's nothing at all."

"Oh, Natásha!" said Sónya, looking ecstatically and earnestly at her friend as if she did not consider her worthy to hear what she meant to say and as if she were saying it to someone else, with whom joking was out of the question, "I am in love with your brother once for all and, whatever may happen to him or to me, shall never cease to love him as long as I live."

Natásha looked at Sónya with wondering and inquisitive eyes, and said nothing. She felt that Sónya was speaking the truth, that there was such love as Sónya was speaking of. But Natásha had not yet felt anything like it. She believed it could be, but did not understand it.

"Shall you write to him?" she asked.

Sónya became thoughtful. The question of how to write to *Nicholas*, and whether she ought to write, tormented her. Now that he was already an officer and a wounded hero, would it be right to remind him of herself and, as it might seem, of the obligations to her he had taken on himself?

"I don't know. I think if he writes, I will write too," she said, blushing.

"And you won't feel ashamed to write to him?"

Sónya smiled.

"No."

"And I should be ashamed to write to Boris. I'm not going to."

"Why should you be ashamed?"

"Well, I don't know. It's awkward and would make me ashamed."

"And I know why she'd be ashamed," said Pétya, offended by Natásha's previous remark. "It's because she was in love with that fat one in spectacles" (that was how Pétya described his namesake, the new Count Bezúkhov) "and now she's in love with that singer" (he meant Natásha's Italian singing master), "that's why she's ashamed!"

"Pétya, you're a stupid!" said Natásha.

"Not more stupid than you, madam," said the nine-year-old Pétya, with the air of an old brigadier.

The countess had been prepared by Anna Mikháylovna's hints at dinner. On retiring to her own room, she sat in an armchair, her eyes fixed on a miniature portrait of her son on the lid of a snuffbox, while the tears kept coming into her eyes. Anna Mikháylovna. with the letter, came on tiptoe to the countess's door and paused.

"Don't come in," she said to the old count, who was following her. "Come later." And she went in, closing the door behind her.

The count put his ear to the keyhole and listened.

At first he heard the sound of indifferent voices, then Anna Mikháylovna's voice alone in a long speech, then a cry, then silence, then both voices together with glad intonations, and then footsteps. Anna Mikháylovna opened the door. Her face wore the proud expression of a surgeon who has just performed a difficult operation and admits the public to appreciate his skill.

"It is done!" she said to the count, pointing triumphantly to the countess, who sat holding in one hand the snuffbox with its portrait and in the other the letter, and pressing them alternately to her lips.

When she saw the count, she stretched out her arms to him, embraced his bald head, over which she again looked at the letter and the portrait, and in order to press them again to her lips, she slightly pushed away the bald head. Véra, Natásha, Sónya, and Pétya now entered the room, and the reading of the letter began. After a brief description of the campaign and the two battles in which he had taken part, and his promotion, Nicholas said that he kissed his father's and mother's hands asking for their blessing, and that he kissed Véra, Natásha, and Pétya. Besides that, he sent greetings to Monsieur Schelling, Madame Schoss, and his old nurse, and asked them to kiss for him "dear Sónya, whom he loved and thought of just the same as ever." When she heard this Sónya blushed so that tears came into her eyes and, unable to bear the looks turned upon her, ran away into the dancing hall, whirled round it at full speed with her dress puffed out like a balloon, and, flushed and smiling, plumped down on the floor. The countess was crying.

"Why are you crying, Mamma?" asked Véra. "From all he says one should be glad and not cry."

This was quite true, but the count, the countess, and Natásha looked at her reproachfully. "And who is it she takes after?" thought the countess.

Nicholas's letter was read over hundreds of times, and those who were considered worthy to hear it had to come to the countess, for she did not let it out of her hands. The tutors came, and the nurses, and Dmítri, and several acquaintances, and the countess reread the letter each time with fresh pleasure and each time discovered in it fresh proofs of Nikólenka's virtues. How strange, how extraordinary, how joyful it seemed, that her son, the scarcely perceptible motion of whose tiny limbs she had felt twenty years ago within her, that son about whom she used to have quarrels with the too-indulgent count, that son who had first learned to say "pear" and then "granny," that this son should now be away in a foreign land amid strange surroundings, a manly warrior doing some kind of man's work of his own, without help or guidance. The universal experience of ages, showing that children do grow imperceptibly from the cradle to manhood, did not exist for the countess. Her son's growth toward manhood, at each of its stages, had seemed as extraordinary to her as if there had never existed the millions of human beings who grew up in the same way. As twenty years before, it seemed impossible that the little creature who lived somewhere under her heart would ever cry, suck her breast, and begin to speak, so now she could not believe that that little creature could be this strong, brave man, this model son and officer that, judging by this letter, he now was.

"What a *style*! How charmingly he describes!" said she, reading the descriptive part of the letter. "And what a soul! Not a word about himself . . . Not a word! About some Denísov or other, though he himself, I dare say, is braver than any of them. He says nothing about his sufferings. What a heart! How like him it is! And how he has remembered everybody! Not forgetting anyone. I always said when he was only so high—I always said . . ."

For more than a week preparations were being made, rough drafts of letters to Nicholas from all the household were written and copied out, while under the supervision of the countess and the solicitude of the count, money and all things necessary for the uniform and equipment of the newly commissioned officer were collected. Anna Mikháylovna, practical woman that she was, had even managed by favor with army authorities to secure advantageous means of communication for herself and her son. She had opportunities of sending her letters to the Grand Duke Constantine Pávlovich, who commanded the Guards. The Rostóvs supposed that "The Russian Guards, Abroad," was quite a definite address, and that if a letter reached the Grand Duke in command of the Guards there was no reason why it should not reach the Pávlograd regiment, which was presumably somewhere in the same neighborhood. And so it was decided to send the letters and money by the Grand Duke's courier to Borís and Borís was to forward them to Nicholas. The letters were from the old count, the countess, Pétya, Véra, Natásha, and Sónya, and finally there were six thousand rubles for his outfit and various other things the old count sent to his son.

Questions

1. How does Rostóv know when he has crossed the combat boundary that Tolstoy describes as the "terrible dividing line of uncertainty and fear"? (87) Once he has crossed it, why does everything become "more and more happy and animated" for him? (88)

2. Why is Rostóv astonished that the advancing French soldiers want to kill him, "whom everyone is so fond of"? (89)

3. Why do the count and Anna Mikháylovna delay telling the countess about her son's letter?

4. Why does Nicholas's letter make the countess feel that her son's status as a "manly warrior" is strange, extraordinary, and joyful? (95)

5. How is a warrior's actual experience of combat different from what he or she may have anticipated?

6. What can men and women who have joined the military do to help their parents understand their new status as warriors?

William James

William James (1842–1910) was an American philosopher and psychologist who published influential works across a wide range of disciplines. As a child, he traveled with his cosmopolitan, intellectual family between the United States and Europe, and received an unusually broad education. His rich background and boundless curiosity laid the foundation for his later vigorous investigation of social and moral issues.

In "The Moral Equivalent of War," James recognizes the moral and social value of war in building individual character and creating social cohesion. He wrote the essay at a time when President Theodore Roosevelt's concept of "the strenuous life" had gained popularity across the country. Roosevelt advocated individual and national success through vigorous effort, toil, and labor. He also supported U.S. expansionist military activity abroad. James understood the central position the military had come to occupy in the identity of the country in the early twentieth century, but suggests an alternative to the prevalent militaristic culture. He considers how nations might sustain civic strength without the binding focus of military action.

In supporting a future society without war, James outlines the basis of a national service program that could, in some ways, replace the role of warfare in society. Civic conscription programs can inspire discipline, empathy, civic bonding, fitness, and cooperation just as wars do, but within a peaceful, nonmilitary framework. James argues that although martial instincts will remain, they can be channeled through civic activities toward nonviolent purposes. From these collective efforts, social bonds can be maintained without the threat of violence. James proposes a new model whereby other forms of social service can achieve the same purposes as military activities.

THE MORAL EQUIVALENT OF WAR

The war against war is going to be no holiday excursion or camping party. The military feelings are too deeply grounded to abdicate their place among our ideals until better substitutes are offered than the glory and shame that come to nations as well as to individuals from the ups and downs of politics and the vicissitudes of trade. There is something highly paradoxical in the modern man's relation to war. Ask all our millions, north and south, whether they would vote now (were such a thing possible) to have our war for the Union expunged from history, and the record of a peaceful transition to the present time substituted for that of its marches and battles, and probably hardly a handful of eccentrics would say yes. Those ancestors, those efforts, those memories and legends, are the most ideal part of what we now own together, a sacred spiritual possession worth more than all the blood poured out. Yet ask those same people whether they would be willing in cold blood to start another civil war now to gain another similar possession, and not one man or woman would vote for the proposition. In modern eyes, precious though wars may be, they must not be waged solely for the sake of the ideal harvest. Only when forced upon one, only when an enemy's injustice leaves us no alternative, is a war now thought permissible.

It was not thus in ancient times. The earlier men were hunting men, and to hunt a neighboring tribe, kill the males, loot the village, and possess the females was the most profitable, as well as the most exciting, way of living. Thus were the more martial tribes selected, and in chiefs and peoples a pure pugnacity and love of glory came to mingle with the more fundamental appetite for plunder.

Modern war is so expensive that we feel trade to be a better avenue to plunder; but modern man inherits all the innate pugnacity and all the love of glory of his ancestors. Showing war's irrationality and horror is of no effect upon him. The horrors make the fascination. War is the *strong* life; it is life *in extremis*; war taxes are the only ones men never hesitate to pay, as the budgets of all nations show us.

History is a bath of blood. The *Iliad* is one long recital of how Diomedes and Ajax, Sarpedon and Hector *killed*. No detail of the wounds they made is spared us, and the Greek mind fed upon the story. Greek history is a panorama of jingoism and imperialism—war for war's sake, all the citizens being warriors. It is horrible reading, because of the irrationality of it all—save for the purpose of making "history"—and the history is that of the utter ruin of a civilization in intellectual respects perhaps the highest the earth has ever seen.

Those wars were purely piratical. Pride, gold, women, slaves, excitement, were their only motives. In the Peloponnesian war for example, the Athenians ask the inhabitants of Melos (the island where the Venus de Milo was found), hitherto neutral, to own their lordship. The envoys meet and hold a debate that Thucydides gives in full, and that, for sweet reasonableness of form, would have satisfied Matthew Arnold. "The powerful exact what they can," said the Athenians, "and the weak grant what they must." When the Melians say that sooner than be slaves they will appeal to the gods, the Athenians reply: "Of the gods we believe and of men we know that, by a law of their nature, wherever they can rule they will. This law was not made by us, and we are not the first to have acted upon it; we did but inherit it, and we know that you and all mankind, if you were as strong as we, would do as we do. So much for the gods; we have told you why we expect to stand as high in their good opinion as you." Well, the Melians still refused, and their town was taken. "The Athenians," Thucydides quietly says, "thereupon put to death all who were of military age and made slaves of the women and children. They then colonized the island, sending thither five hundred settlers of their own."

Alexander's career was piracy pure and simple, nothing but an orgy of power and plunder, made romantic by the character of the hero. There was no rational principle in it, and the moment he died his generals and governors attacked one another. The cruelty of those times is incredible. When Rome finally conquered Greece, Paulus Aemilius was told by the Roman Senate to reward his soldiers for their toil by "giving" them the old kingdom of Epirus. They sacked seventy cities and carried off a hundred and fifty thousand inhabitants as slaves. How many they killed I know not; but in Etolia they killed all the senators, five hundred and fifty in number. Brutus was "the noblest Roman of them all," but to reanimate his soldiers on the eve of Philippi he similarly promises to give them the cities of Sparta and Thessalonica to ravage, if they win the fight.

Such was the gory nurse that trained societies to cohesiveness. We inherit the warlike type; and for most of the capacities of heroism that the human race is full of, we have to thank this cruel history. Dead men tell no tales, and if there were any tribes of other type than this they have left no survivors. Our ancestors have bred pugnacity into our bone and marrow, and thousands of years of peace won't breed it out of us. The popular imagination fairly fattens on the thought of wars. Let public opinion once reach a certain fighting pitch, and no ruler can withstand it. In the Boer War both governments began with bluff but couldn't stay there; the military tension was too much for them. In 1898 our people had read the word "war" in letters three inches high for three months in every newspaper. The pliant politician McKinley was swept away by their eagerness, and our squalid war with Spain became a necessity.

At the present day, civilized opinion is a curious mental mixture. The military instincts and ideals are as strong as ever but are confronted by reflective criticisms that sorely curb their ancient freedom. Innumerable writers are showing up the bestial side of military service. Pure loot and mastery seem no longer morally avowable motives, and pretexts must be found for attributing them solely to the enemy. England and we, our army and navy authorities repeat without ceasing, arm solely for "peace," Germany and Japan it is who are bent on loot and glory. "Peace" in military mouths today is a synonym for "war expected." The word has become a pure provocative, and no government wishing peace sincerely should allow it ever to be printed in a newspaper. Every up-to-date dictionary should say that "peace" and "war" mean the same thing, now *in posse*, now *in actu*. It may even reasonably be said that the intensely sharp competitive *preparation* for war by the nations *is the real war*, permanent, unceasing; and that the battles are only a sort of public verification of the mastery gained during the "peace" interval.

It is plain that on this subject civilized man has developed a sort of double personality. If we take European nations, no legitimate interest of any one of them would seem to justify the tremendous destructions that a war to compass it would necessarily entail. It would seem as though common sense and reason ought to find a way to reach agreement in every conflict of honest interests. I myself think it our bounden duty to believe in such international rationality as possible. But, as things stand, I see how desperately hard it is to bring the peace party and the war party together, and I believe that the difficulty is due to certain deficiencies in the program of pacifism that set the militarist imagination strongly, and to a certain extent justifiably, against it. In the whole discussion both sides are on imaginative and sentimental ground. It is but one utopia against another, and everything one says must be abstract and hypothetical. Subject to this criticism and caution, I will try to characterize in abstract strokes the opposite imaginative forces and point out what to my own very fallible mind seems the best utopian hypothesis, the most promising line of conciliation.

In my remarks, pacifist though I am, I will refuse to speak of the bestial side of the war regime (already done justice to by many writers) and consider only the higher aspects of militaristic sentiment. Patriotism no one thinks discreditable; nor does anyone deny that war is the romance of history. But inordinate ambitions are the soul of every patriotism, and the possibility of violent death the soul of all romance. The military patriotic and romantic-minded everywhere, and especially the professional military class, refuse to admit for a moment that war may be a transitory phenomenon in social evolution. The notion of a sheep's paradise like that revolts, they say, our higher imagination. Where then would be the steeps of life? If war had ever stopped, we should have to reinvent it, on this view, to redeem life from flat degeneration.

Reflective apologists for war at the present day all take it religiously. It is a sort of sacrament. Its profits are to the vanquished as well as to the victor; and quite apart from any question of profit, it is an absolute good, we are told, for it is human nature at its highest dynamic. Its "horrors" are a cheap price to pay for rescue from the only alternative supposed, of a world of clerks and teachers, of coeducation and zoophily, of "consumer's leagues" and "associated charities," of industrialism unlimited, and feminism unabashed. No scorn, no hardness, no valor anymore! Fie upon such a cattle yard of a planet!

So far as the central essence of this feeling goes, no healthy-minded person, it seems to me, can help to some degree partaking of it. Militarism is the great preserver of our ideals of hardihood, and human life with no use for hardihood would be contemptible. Without risks or prizes for the darer, history would be insipid indeed; and there is a type of military character that everyone feels that the race should never cease to breed, for everyone is sensitive to its superiority. The duty is incumbent on mankind of keeping military characters in stock—of keeping them, if not for use, then as ends in themselves and as pure pieces of perfection— so that Roosevelt's weaklings and mollycoddles may not end by making everything else disappear from the face of nature.

This natural sort of feeling forms, I think, the innermost soul of army writings. Without any exception known to me, militarist authors take a highly mystical view of their subject and regard war as a biological or sociological necessity, uncontrolled by ordinary psychological checks and motives. When the time of development is ripe the war must come, reason or no reason, for the justifications pleaded are invariably fictitious. War is, in short, a permanent human *obligation*. General Homer Lea, in his recent book *The Valor of Ignorance*, plants himself squarely on this ground. Readiness for war is for him the essence of nationality, and ability in it the supreme measure of the health of nations.

Nations, General Lea says, are never stationary—they must necessarily expand or shrink, according to their vitality or decrepitude. Japan now is culminating; and by the fatal law in question it is impossible that her statesmen should not long since have entered, with extraordinary foresight, upon a vast policy of conquest—the game in which the first moves were her wars with China and Russia and her treaty with England, and of which the final objective is the capture of the Philippines, the Hawaiian Islands, Alaska, and the whole of our coast west of the Sierra passes. This will give Japan what her ineluctable vocation as a state absolutely forces her to claim, the possession of the entire Pacific Ocean; and to oppose these deep designs we Americans have, according to our author, nothing but our conceit, our ignorance, our commercialism, our corruption, and our feminism. General Lea makes a minute technical comparison of the military strength that we at present could oppose to the strength of Japan and concludes that the islands, Alaska, Oregon, and Southern California would fall almost without resistance, that San Francisco must surrender in a fortnight to a Japanese investment, that in three or four months the war would be over, and our republic, unable to regain what it had heedlessly neglected to protect sufficiently, would then "disintegrate," until perhaps some Caesar should arise to weld us again into a nation.

A dismal forecast indeed! Yet not unplausible, if the mentality of Japan's statesmen be of the Caesarian type of which history shows so many examples, and that is all that General Lea seems able to imagine. But there is no reason to think that women can no longer be the mothers of Napoleonic or Alexandrian characters; and if these come in Japan and find their opportunity, just such surprises as *The Valor of Ignorance* paints may lurk in ambush for us. Ignorant as we still are of the innermost recesses of Japanese mentality, we may be foolhardy to disregard such possibilities.

Other militarists are more complex and more moral in their considerations. The *Philosophie des Krieges*, by S. R. Steinmetz, is a good example. War, according to this author, is an ordeal instituted by God, who weighs the nations in its balance. It is the essential form of the state, and the only function in which peoples can employ all their powers at once and convergently. No victory is possible save as the resultant of a totality of virtues, no defeat for which some vice or weakness is not responsible. Fidelity, cohesiveness, tenacity, heroism, conscience, education, inventiveness, economy, wealth, physical health, and vigor—there isn't a moral or intellectual point of superiority that doesn't tell, when God holds his assizes and hurls the peoples upon one another. *Die Weltgeschichte ist das Weltgericht*; and Dr. Steinmetz does not believe that in the long run chance and luck play any part in apportioning the issues.

The virtues that prevail, it must be noted, are virtues anyhow, superiorities that count in peaceful as well as in military competition; but the strain on them, being infinitely intenser in the latter case, makes war infinitely more searching as a trial. No ordeal is comparable to its winnowings. Its dread hammer is the welder of men into cohesive states, and nowhere but in such states can human nature adequately develop its capacity. The only alternative is "degeneration."

Dr. Steinmetz is a conscientious thinker, and his book, short as it is, takes much into account. Its upshot can, it seems to me, be summed up in Simon Patten's words, that mankind was nursed in pain and fear, and that the transition to a "pleasure economy" may be fatal to a being wielding no powers of defense against its disintegrative influences. If we speak of the "fear of emancipation from the fear regime," we put the whole situation into a single phrase; fear regarding ourselves now taking the place of the ancient fear of the enemy.

Turn the fear over as I will in my mind, it all seems to lead back to two unwillingnesses of the imagination, one aesthetic, and the other moral; unwillingness, first, to envisage a future in which army life, with its many elements of charm, shall be forever impossible, and in which the destinies of peoples shall nevermore be decided quickly, thrillingly, and tragically, by force, but only gradually and insipidly by "evolution"; and, second, unwillingness to see the supreme theater of human strenuousness closed, and the splendid military aptitudes of men doomed to keep always in a state of latency and never show themselves in action. These insistent unwillingnesses, no less than other aesthetic and ethical insistencies, have, it seems to me, to be listened to and respected. One cannot meet them effectively by mere counterinsistency on war's expensiveness and horror. The horror makes the thrill; and when the question is of getting the extremest and supremest out of human nature, talk of expense sounds ignominious. The weakness of so much merely negative criticism is evident—pacificism makes no converts from the military party. The military party denies neither the bestiality nor the horror, nor the expense; it only says that these things tell but half the story. It only says that war is *worth* them; that, taking human nature as a whole, its wars are its best protection against its weaker and more cowardly self and that mankind cannot *afford* to adopt a peace economy.

Pacificists ought to enter more deeply into the aesthetical and ethical point of view of their opponents. Do that first in any controversy, says J. J. Chapman, *then move the point*, and your opponent will follow. So long as antimilitarists propose no substitute for war's disciplinary function, no *moral equivalent* of war, analogous, as one might say, to the mechanical equivalent of heat, so long as they fail to realize the full inwardness of the situation. And as a rule they do fail. The duties, penalties, and sanctions pictured in the utopias they paint are all too weak and tame to touch the military-minded. Tolstoy's pacificism is the only exception to this rule, for it is profoundly pessimistic as regards all this world's values and makes the fear of the Lord furnish the moral spur provided elsewhere by the fear of the enemy. But our socialistic peace advocates all believe absolutely in this world's values; and instead of the fear of the Lord and the fear of the enemy, the only fear they reckon with is the fear of poverty if one be lazy. This weakness pervades all the socialistic literature with which I am acquainted. Even in Lowes Dickinson's exquisite dialogue, high wages and short hours are the only forces invoked for overcoming man's distaste for repulsive kinds of labor. Meanwhile men at large still live as they always have lived, under a pain-and-fear economy—for those of us who live in an ease-economy are but an island in the stormy ocean—and the whole atmosphere of present-day utopian literature tastes mawkish and dishwatery to people who still keep a sense for life's more bitter flavors. It suggests, in truth, ubiquitous inferiority.

Inferiority is always with us, and merciless scorn of it is the keynote of the military temper. "Dogs, would you live forever?" shouted Frederick the Great. "Yes," say our utopians, "let us live forever, and raise our level gradually." The best thing about our "inferiors" today is that they are as tough as nails, and physically and morally almost as insensitive. Utopianism would see them soft and squeamish, while militarism would keep their callousness but transfigure it into a meritorious characteristic, needed by "the service," and redeemed by that from the suspicion of inferiority. All the qualities of a man acquire dignity when he knows that the service of the collectivity that owns him needs them. If proud of the collectivity, his own pride rises in proportion. No collectivity is like an army for nourishing such pride; but it has to be confessed that the only sentiment that the image of pacific cosmopolitan industrialism is capable of arousing in countless worthy breasts is shame at the idea of belonging to *such* a collectivity. It is obvious that the United States of America as they exist today impress a mind like General Lea's as so much human blubber. Where is the sharpness and precipitousness, the contempt for life, whether one's own or another's? Where is the savage "yes" and "no," the unconditional duty? Where is the conscription? Where is the blood tax? Where is anything that one feels honored by belonging to?

Having said thus much in preparation, I will now confess my own utopia. I devoutly believe in the reign of peace and in the gradual advent of some sort of a socialistic equilibrium. The fatalistic view of the war function is to me nonsense, for I know that war-making is due to definite motives and subject to prudential checks and reasonable criticisms, just like any other form of enterprise. And when whole nations are the armies, and the science of destruction vies in intellectual refinement with the sciences of production, I see that war becomes absurd and impossible from its own monstrosity. Extravagant ambitions will have to be replaced by reasonable claims, and nations must make common cause against them. I see no reason why all this should not apply to yellow as well as to white countries, and I look forward to a future when acts of war shall be formally outlawed between civilized peoples.

All these beliefs of mine put me squarely into the antimilitarist party. But I do not believe that peace either ought to be or will be permanent on this globe, unless the states pacifically organized preserve some of the old elements of army discipline. A permanently successful peace economy cannot be a simple pleasure economy. In the more or less socialistic future toward which mankind seems drifting we must still subject ourselves collectively to those severities that answer to our real position upon this only partly hospitable globe. We must make new energies and hardihoods continue the manliness to which the military mind so faithfully clings. Martial virtues must be the enduring cement; intrepidity, contempt of softness, surrender of private interest, obedience to command, must still remain the rock upon which states are built—unless, indeed, we wish for dangerous reactions against commonwealths fit only for contempt and liable to invite attack whenever a center of crystallization for military-minded enterprise gets formed anywhere in their neighborhood.

The war party is assuredly right in affirming and reaffirming that the martial virtues, although originally gained by the race through war, are absolute and permanent human goods. Patriotic pride and ambition in their military form are, after all, only specifications of a more general competitive passion. They are its first form, but that is no reason for supposing them to be its last form. Men now are proud of belonging to a conquering nation, and without a murmur they lay down their persons and their wealth, if by so doing they may fend off subjection. But who can be sure that *other aspects of one's country* may not, with time and education and suggestion enough, come to be regarded with similarly effective feelings of pride and shame? Why should men not some day feel that it is worth a blood tax to belong to a collectively superior in *any* ideal respect? Why should they not blush with indignant shame if the community that owns them is vile in any way whatsoever? Individuals, daily more numerous, now feel this civic passion. It is only a question of blowing on the spark till the whole population gets incandescent, and on the ruins of the old morals of military honor, a stable system of morals of civic honor builds itself up. What the whole community comes to believe in grasps the individual as in a vise. The war function has grasped us so far; but constructive interests may some day seem no less imperative and impose on the individual a hardly lighter burden.

Let me illustrate my idea more concretely. There is nothing to make one indignant in the mere fact that life is hard, that men should toil and suffer pain. The planetary conditions once for all are such, and we can stand it. But that so many men, by mere accidents of birth and opportunity, should have a life of *nothing else* but toil and pain and hardness and inferiority imposed upon them, should have *no* vacation, while others natively no more deserving never get any taste of this campaigning life at all—*this* is capable of arousing indignation in reflective minds. It may end by seeming shameful to all of us that some of us have nothing but campaigning, and others nothing but unmanly ease. If now—and this is my idea—there were, instead of military conscription, a conscription of the whole youthful population to form for a certain number of years a part of the army enlisted against nature, the injustice would tend to be evened out, and numerous other goods to the commonwealth would follow. The military ideals of hardihood and discipline would be wrought into the growing fiber of the people; no one would remain blind as the luxurious classes now are blind, to man's relations to the globe he lives on, and to the permanently sour and hard foundations of his higher life. To coal and iron mines; to freight trains; to fishing fleets in December; to dishwashing, clothes washing, and window washing; to road building and tunnel making; to foundries and stokeholes; and to the frames of skyscrapers, would our gilded youths be drafted off, according to their choice, to get the childishness knocked out of them, and to come back into society with healthier sympathies and soberer ideas. They would have paid their true blood tax, done their own part in the immemorial human warfare against nature; they would tread the earth more proudly, the women would value them more highly, they would be better fathers and teachers of the following generation.

Such a conscription, with the state of public opinion that would have required it, and the many moral fruits it would bear, would preserve in the midst of a pacific civilization the manly virtues that the military party is so afraid of seeing disappear in peace. We should get toughness without callousness, authority with as little criminal cruelty as possible, and painful work done cheerily because the duty is temporary, and threatens not, as now, to degrade the whole remainder of one's life. I spoke of the "moral equivalent" of war. So far, war has been the only force that can discipline a whole community, and until an equivalent discipline is organized, I believe that war must have its way. But I have no serious doubt that the ordinary prides and shames of social man, once developed to a certain intensity, are capable of organizing such a moral equivalent as I have sketched, or some other just as effective for preserving manliness of type. It is but a question of time, of skill propagandism, and of opinion-making men seizing historic opportunities.

The martial type of character can be bred without war. Strenuous honor and disinterestedness abound elsewhere. Priests and medical men are in a fashion educated to it, and we should all feel some degree of it imperative if we were conscious of our works as an obligatory service to the state. We should be *owned*, as soldiers are by the army, and our pride would rise accordingly. We could be poor, then, without humiliation, as army officers now are. The only thing needed henceforward is to inflame the civic temper as past history has inflamed the military temper. H. G. Wells, as usual, sees the center of the situation. "In many ways," he says,

> military organization is the most peaceful of activities. When the contemporary man steps from the street, of clamorous insincere advertisement, push, adulteration, underselling, and intermittent employment into the barrack yard, he steps on to a higher social plane, into an atmosphere of service and cooperation and of infinitely more honorable emulations. Here at least men are not flung out of employment to degenerate because there is no immediate work for them to do. They are fed and

drilled and trained for better services. Here at least a man is supposed to win promotion by self-forgetfulness and not by self-seeking. And beside the feeble and irregular endowment of research by commercialism, its little shortsighted snatches at profit by innovation and scientific economy, see how remarkable is the steady and rapid development of method and appliance in naval and military affairs! Nothing is more striking than to compare the progress of civil conveniences that has been left almost entirely to the trader, to the progress in military apparatus during the last few decades. The house appliances today, for example, are little better than they were fifty years ago. A house of today is still almost as ill ventilated, badly heated by wasteful fires, clumsily arranged and furnished as the house of 1858. Houses a couple of hundred years old are still satisfactory places of residence, so little have our standards risen. But the rifle or battleship of fifty years ago was beyond all comparison inferior to those we possess; in power, in speed, in convenience alike. No one has a use now for such superannuated things.

Wells adds that he thinks that the conceptions of order and discipline, the tradition of service and devotion, of physical fitness, unstinted exertion, and universal responsibility, which universal military duty is now teaching European nations, will remain a permanent acquisition, when the last ammunition has been used in the fireworks that celebrate the final peace. I believe as he does. It would be simply preposterous if the only force that could work ideals of honor and standards of efficiency into English or American natures should be the fear of being killed by the Germans or the Japanese. Great indeed is fear; but it is not, as our military enthusiasts believe and try to make us believe, the only stimulus known for awakening the higher ranges of men's spiritual energy. The amount of alteration in public opinion that my utopia postulates is vastly less than the difference between the mentality of those black warriors who pursued Stanley's party on the Congo with their cannibal war cry of "Meat! Meat!" and that of the "general staff" of any civilized nation. History has seen the latter interval bridged over: the former one can be bridged over much more easily.

Questions

1. According to James, what benefits does war offer?

2. What does James mean by the "martial virtues"? (107) Why does he insist on the importance of the martial type of character?

3. How does James think that the civic temper can be inflamed without also inflaming the military temper?

4. What does it mean for something to be "the moral equivalent of war"? (99)

5. Is James's proposal for reducing the possibility of war that of a pacifist?

6. Do you agree that the kind of national service James recommends is likely to have the effect he supposes?

Sigmund Freud

Sigmund Freud (1856–1939) is widely considered the father of psychoanalysis. His ideas, including the Oedipus complex and the link between dreams and the unconscious, have become central to our understanding of psychology and continue to influence art, literature, and the social sciences to this day.

Freud was born to a Jewish family in Moravia (now the Czech Republic), but he spent most of his life in Vienna, Austria, where he became internationally famous for his pioneering work in psychoanalysis. When Austria was annexed by the Nazis in 1938, Freud fled to London, where he died of cancer in 1939.

World War I led Freud to consider unsettling questions about mankind's innate aggression. The war's unprecedented destruction shocked Europe, and with three sons serving in the military, Freud directly confronted the effects of military service in his own family. Concerned for the safety of his sons and professionally interested in the "war neuroses" and "neurotic disturbances" that often accompanied physical injuries, Freud began to consider the effects of war upon individuals and, later, on society as a whole.

In the following letter, Freud replies to Albert Einstein's question about why war seems to be a constant in human history. Freud argues that the violent instincts of individuals may be constrained by social institutions, but can never be completely eliminated. He also raises the question of whether pacifist attempts to strengthen these social institutions can ever successfully end war.

WHY WAR?

Vienna, September, 1932

Dear Professor Einstein,

When I heard that you intended to invite me to an exchange of views on some subject that interested you and that seemed to deserve the interest of others besides yourself, I readily agreed. I expected you to choose a problem on the frontiers of what is knowable today, a problem to which each of us, a physicist and a psychologist, might have our own particular angle of approach and where we might come together from different directions upon the same ground. You have taken me by surprise, however, by posing the question of what can be done to protect mankind from the curse of war. I was scared at first by the thought of my—I had almost written "our"—incapacity for dealing with what seemed to be a practical problem, a concern for statesmen. But I then realized that you had raised the question not as a natural scientist and physicist but as a philanthropist: you were following the promptings of the League of Nations just as Fridtjof Nansen, the polar explorer, took on the work of bringing help to the starving and homeless victims of the World War. I reflected, moreover, that I was not being asked to make practical proposals but only to set out the problem of avoiding war as it appears to a psychological observer. Here again you yourself have said almost all there is to say on the subject. But though you have taken the wind out of my sails I shall be glad to follow in your wake and content myself with confirming all you have said by amplifying it to the best of my knowledge—or conjecture.

You begin with the relation between right and might. There can be no doubt that that is the correct starting point for our investigation. But may I replace the word "might" by the balder and harsher word "violence"?

Sigmund Freud

Today right and violence appear to us as antitheses. It can easily be shown, however, that the one has developed out of the other; and if we go back to the earliest beginnings and see how that first came about, the problem is easily solved. You must forgive me if in what follows I go over familiar and commonly accepted ground as though it were new, but the thread of my argument requires it.

It is a general principle, then, that conflicts of interest between men are settled by the use of violence. This is true of the whole animal kingdom, from which men have no business to exclude themselves. In the case of men, no doubt, conflicts of *opinion* occur as well which may reach the highest pitch of abstraction and which seem to demand some other technique for their settlement. That, however, is a later complication. To begin with, in a small human horde it was superior muscular strength which decided who owned things or whose will should prevail. Muscular strength was soon supplemented and replaced by the use of tools: the winner was the one who had the better weapons or who used them the more skillfully. From the moment at which weapons were introduced, intellectual superiority already began to replace brute muscular strength; but the final purpose of the fight remained the same—one side or the other was to be compelled to abandon his claim or his objection by the damage inflicted on him and by the crippling of his strength. That purpose was most completely achieved if the victor's violence eliminated his opponent permanently, that is to say, killed him. This had two advantages: he could not renew his opposition and his fate deterred others from following his example. In addition to this, killing an enemy satisfied an instinctual inclination which I shall have to mention later. The intention to kill might be countered by a reflection that the enemy could be employed in performing useful services if he were left alive in an intimidated condition. In that case the victor's violence was content to subjugate him instead of killing him. This was a first beginning of the idea of sparing an enemy's life, but thereafter the victor had to reckon with his defeated opponent's lurking thirst for revenge, and sacrificed some of his own security.

Such, then, was the original state of things: domination by whoever had the greater might—domination by brute violence or by violence supported by intellect. As we know, this régime was altered in the course of

114

fact that from its very beginning the community compromises elements of unequal strength—men and women, parents and children—and soon, as a result of war and conquest, it also comes to include victors and vanquished, who turn into masters and slaves. The justice of the community then becomes an expression of the unequal degrees of power obtaining within it; the laws are made by and for the ruling members and find little room for the rights of those in subjection. From that time forward there are two factors at work in the community which are sources of unrest over matters of law but tend at the same time to a further growth of law. First, attempts are made by certain of the rulers to set themselves above the prohibitions which apply to everyone—they seek, that is, to go back from a dominion of law to a dominion of violence. Secondly, the oppressed members of the group make constant efforts to obtain more power and to have any changes that are brought about in that direction recognized in the laws—they press forward, that is, from unequal justice to equal justice for all. This second tendency becomes especially important if a real shift of power occurs within a community, as may happen as a result of a number of historical factors. In that case right may gradually adapt itself to the new distribution of power, or, as is more frequent, the ruling class is unwilling to recognize the change, and rebellion and civil war follow, with a temporary suspension of law and new attempts at a solution by violence, ending in the establishment of a fresh rule of law. There is yet another source from which modifications of law may arise, and one of which the expression is invariably peaceful: it lies in the cultural transformation of the members of the community. This, however, belongs properly in another connection and must be considered later.

Thus we see that the violent solution of conflicts of interest is not avoided even inside a community. But the everyday necessities and common concerns that are inevitable where people live together in one place tend to bring such struggles to a swift conclusion and under such conditions there is an increasing probability that a peaceful solution will be found. But a glance at the history of the human race reveals an endless series of conflicts between one community and another or several others, between larger and smaller units—between cities, provinces, races, nations, empires—which have almost always been settled by force of arms. Wars of this kind end either in the spoliation or in the complete overthrow and conquest of one of the parties. It is impossible to make any sweeping judgement upon wars of conquest. Some, such as those waged by the Mongols and Turks, have brought nothing but evil. Others, on the contrary, have contributed to the transformation of violence into law by establishing larger units within which the use of violence was made impossible and in which a fresh system of law led to the solution of conflicts. In this way the conquests of the Romans gave the countries round the Mediterranean the priceless *Pax Romana*, and the greed of the French kings to extend their dominions created a peacefully united and flourishing France. Paradoxical as it may sound, it must be admitted that war might be a far from inappropriate means of establishing the eagerly desired reign of "everlasting" peace, since it is in a position to create the large units within which a powerful central government makes further wars impossible. Nevertheless it fails in this purpose, for the results of conquest are as a rule short-lived: the newly created units fall apart once again, usually owing to a lack of cohesion between the portions that have been united by violence. Hitherto, moreover, the unifications created by conquest, though of considerable extent, have only been *partial*, and the conflicts between these have cried out for violent solution. Thus the result of all these warlike efforts has only been that the human race has exchanged numerous, and indeed unending, minor wars for wars on a grand scale that are rare but all the more destructive.

If we turn to our own times, we arrive at the same conclusion which you have reached by a shorter path. Wars will only be prevented with certainty if mankind unites in setting up a central authority to which the right of giving judgement upon all conflicts of interest shall be handed over. There are clearly two separate requirements involved in this: the creation of a supreme authority and its endowment with the necessary power. One without the other would be useless. The League of Nations is designed as an authority of this kind, but the second condition has not been fulfilled: the League of Nations has no power of its own and can only acquire it if the members of the new union, the separate States, are ready to resign it. And at the moment there seems very little prospect of this. The institution of the League of Nations would, however, be wholly unintelligible if one ignored the fact that here was a bold attempt such as has seldom (perhaps, indeed, never on such a scale) been made before.

It is an attempt to base upon an appeal to certain idealistic attitudes of mind the authority (that is, the coercive influence) which otherwise rests on the possession of power. We have heard that a community is held together by two things: the compelling force of violence and the emotional ties (identifications is the technical name) between its members. If one of the factors is absent, the community may possibly be held together by the other. The ideas that are appealed to can, of course, only have any significance if they give expression to important concerns that are common to the members, and the question arises of how much strength they can exert. History teaches us that they have been to some extent effective. For instance, the Panhellenic idea, the sense of being superior to the surrounding barbarians—an idea which was so powerfully expressed in the Amphictyonies, the Oracles, and the Games—was sufficiently strong to mitigate the customs of war among Greeks, though evidently not sufficiently strong to prevent warlike disputes between different sections of the Greek nation or even to restrain a city or confederation of cities from allying itself with the Persian foe in order to gain an advantage over a rival. In the same way, the community of feeling among Christians, powerful though it was, was equally unable at the time of the Renaissance to deter Christian states, whether large or small, from seeking the Sultan's aid in their wars with one another. Nor does any idea exist today which could be expected to exert a unifying authority of the sort. Indeed it is all too clear that the national ideals by which nations are at present swayed operate in a contrary direction. Some people are inclined to prophesy that it will not be possible to make an end of war until Communist ways of thinking have found universal acceptance. But that aim is in any case a very remote one today, and perhaps it could only be reached after the most fearful civil wars. Thus the attempt to replace actual force by the force of ideas seems at present to be doomed to failure. We shall be making a false calculation if we disregard the fact that law was originally brute violence and that even today it cannot do without the support of violence.

I can now proceed to add a gloss to another of your remarks. You express astonishment at the fact that it is so easy to make men enthusiastic about a war and add your suspicion that there is something at work in them—an instinct for hatred and destruction—which goes halfway to meet the efforts of the warmongers. Once again, I can only express my entire agreement. We believe in the existence of an instinct of that kind and have in fact been occupied during the last few years in studying its manifestations. Will you allow me to take this opportunity of putting before you a portion of the theory of the instincts which, after much tentative groping and many fluctuations of opinion, has been reached by workers in the field of psychoanalysis?

According to our hypothesis human instincts are of only two kinds: those which seek to preserve and unite—which we call "erotic," exactly in the sense in which Plato uses the word "Eros" in his *Symposium*, or "sexual," with a deliberate extension of the popular conception of "sexuality"—and those which seek to destroy and kill and which we class together as the aggressive or destructive instinct. As you see, this is in fact no more than a theoretical clarification of the universally familiar opposition between love and hate which may perhaps have some fundamental relation to the polarity of attraction and repulsion that plays a part in your own field of knowledge. We must not be too hasty in introducing ethical judgements of good and evil. Neither of these instincts is any less essential than the other; the phenomena of life arise from the operation of both together, whether acting in concert or in opposition. It seems as though an instinct of the one sort can scarcely ever operate in isolation; it is always accompanied—or, as we say, alloyed—with an element from the other side, which modifies its aim or is, in some cases, what enables it to achieve that aim. Thus, for instance, the instinct of self-preservation is certainly of an erotic kind, but it must nevertheless have aggressiveness at its disposal if it is to fulfill its purpose. So, too, the instinct of love, when it is directed towards an object, stands in need of some contribution from the instinct of mastery if it is in any way to possess that object. The difficulty of isolating the two classes of instinct in their actual manifestations is indeed what has so long prevented us from recognizing them.

If you will follow me a little further, you will see that human actions are subject to another complication of a different kind. It is very rarely that an action is the work of a *single* instinctual impulse (which must in itself be compounded of Eros and destructiveness). In order to make an action possible there must be as a rule a *combination* of such compounded motives. This was perceived long ago by a specialist in your own subject, a Professor G. C. Lichtenberg who taught physics at Göttingen during our classical age—though perhaps he was even more remarkable as a psychologist than as a physicist. He invented a Compass of Motives, for he wrote: "The motives that lead us to do anything might be arranged like the thirty-two winds and might be given names on the same pattern: for instance, 'food-food-fame' or 'fame-fame-food.'" So that when human beings are incited to war they may have a whole number of motives for assenting—some noble and some base, some of which they speak openly and others on which they are silent. There is no need to enumerate them all. A lust for aggression and destruction is certainly among them: the countless cruelties in history and in our everyday lives vouch for its existence and its strength. The gratification of these destructive impulses is of course facilitated by their admixture with others of an erotic and idealistic kind. When we read of the atrocities of the past, it sometimes seems as though the idealistic motives served only as an excuse for the destructive appetites; and sometimes—in the case, for instance, of the cruelties of the Inquisition—it seems as though the idealistic motives had pushed themselves forward in consciousness, while the destructive ones lent them an unconscious reinforcement. Both may be true.

I fear I may be abusing your interest, which is after all concerned with the prevention of war and not with our theories. Nevertheless I should like to linger for a moment over our destructive instinct, whose popularity is by no means equal to its importance. As a result of a little speculation, we have come to suppose that this instinct is at work in every living being and is striving to bring it to ruin and to reduce life to its original condition of inanimate matter. Thus it quite seriously deserves to be called a death instinct, while the erotic instincts represent the effort to live. The death instinct turns into the destructive instinct if, with the help of special organs, it is directed outwards, on to objects. The living creature preserves its own life, so to say, by destroying an extraneous one. Some portion of the death instinct, however, remains operative *within* the living being, and we have sought to trace quite a number of normal and pathological phenomena to this internalization of the destructive instinct. We have even been guilty of the heresy of attributing the origin of conscience to this diversion inwards of aggressiveness. You will notice that it is by no means a trivial matter if this process is carried too far: it is positively unhealthy. On the other hand, if these forces are turned to destruction in the external world, the living creature will be relieved and the effect must be beneficial. This would serve as a biological justification for all the ugly and dangerous impulses against which we are struggling. It must be admitted that they stand nearer to nature than does our resistance to them, for which an explanation also needs to be found. It may perhaps seem to you as though our theories are a kind of mythology and, in the present case, not even an agreeable one. But does not every science come in the end to a kind of mythology like this? Cannot the same be said today of your own physics?

For our immediate purpose then, this much follows from what has been said: there is no use in trying to get rid of men's aggressive inclinations. We are told that in certain happy regions of the earth, where nature provides in abundance everything that man requires, there are races whose life is passed in tranquillity and who know neither compulsion nor aggressiveness. I can scarcely believe it and I should be glad to hear more of these fortunate beings. The Russian Communists, too, hope to be able to cause human aggressiveness to disappear by guaranteeing the satisfaction of all material needs and by establishing equality in other respects among all the members of the community. That, in my opinion, is an illusion. They themselves are armed today with the most scrupulous care and not the least important of the methods by which they keep their supporters together is hatred of everyone beyond their frontiers. In any case, as you yourself have remarked, there is no question of getting rid entirely of human aggressive impulses: it is enough to try to divert them to such an extent that they need not find expression in war.

Our mythological theory of instincts makes it easy for us to find a formula for *indirect* methods of combating war. If willingness to engage in war is an effect of the destructive instinct, the most obvious plan will be to bring Eros, its antagonist, into play against it. Anything that encourages the growth of emotional ties between men must operate against war. These ties may be of two kinds. In the first place they may be relations resembling those towards a loved object, though without having a sexual aim. There is no need for psychoanalysis to be ashamed to speak of love in this connection, for religion itself uses the same words: "Thou shalt love they neighbour as thyself." This, however, is more easily said than done. The second kind of emotional tie is by means of identification. Whatever leads men to share important interests produces this community of feeling, these identifications. And the structure of human society is to a large extent based on them.

A complaint which you make about the abuse of authority brings me to another suggestion for the indirect combating of the propensity to war. One instance of the innate and ineradicable inequality of men is their tendency to fall into the two classes of leaders and followers. The latter constitute the vast majority; they stand in need of an authority which will make decisions for them and to which they for the most part offer an unqualified submission. This suggests that more care should be taken than hitherto to educate an upper stratum of men with independent minds, not open to intimidation and eager in the pursuit of truth, whose business it would be to give direction to the dependent masses. It goes without saying that the encroachments made by the executive power of the state and the prohibition laid by the church upon freedom of thought are far from propitious for the production of a class of this kind. The ideal condition of things would of course be a community of men who had subordinated their instinctual life to the dictatorship of reason. Nothing else could unite men so completely and so tenaciously, even if there were no emotional ties between them. But in all probability that is a utopian expectation. No doubt the other indirect methods of preventing war are more practicable, though they promise no rapid success. An unpleasant picture comes to one's mind of mills that grind so slowly that people may starve before they get their flour.

The result, as you see, is not very fruitful when an unworldly theoretician is called in to advise on an urgent practical problem. It is a better plan to devote oneself in every particular case to meeting the danger with whatever weapons lie to hand. I should like, however, to discuss one more question, which you do not mention in your letter but which specially interests me. Why do you and I and so many other people rebel so violently against war? Why do we not accept it as another of the many painful calamities of life? After all, it seems quite a natural thing, no doubt it has a good biological basis and in practice it is scarcely avoidable. There is no need to be shocked at my raising this question. For the purpose of an investigation such as this, one may perhaps be allowed to wear a mask of assumed detachment. The answer to my question will be that we react to war in this way because everyone has a right to his own life, because war puts an end to human lives that are full of hope, because it brings individual men into humiliating situations, because it compels them against their will to murder other men, and because it destroys precious material objects which have been produced by the labours of humanity. Other reasons besides might be given, such as that in its present-day form war is no longer an opportunity for achieving the old ideals of heroism and that owing to the perfection of instruments of destruction a future war might involve the extermination of one or perhaps both of the antagonists. All this is true, and so incontestably true that one can only feel astonished that the waging of war has not yet been unanimously repudiated. No doubt debate is possible upon one or two of these points. It may be questioned whether a community ought not to have a right to dispose of individual lives; every war is not open to condemnation to an equal degree; so long as there exist countries and nations that are prepared for the ruthless destruction of others, those others must be armed for war. But I will not linger over any of these issues; they are not what you want to discuss with me, and I have something different in mind. It is my opinion that the main reason why we rebel against war is that we cannot help doing so. We are pacifists because we are obliged to be for organic reasons. And we then find no difficulty in producing arguments to justify our attitude.

No doubt this requires some explanation. My belief is this. For incalculable ages mankind has been passing through a process of evolution of culture. (Some people, I know, prefer to use the term "civilization.") We owe to that process the best of what we have become, as well as a good part of what we suffer from. Though its causes and beginnings are obscure and its outcome uncertain, some of its characteristics are easy to perceive. It may perhaps be leading to the extinction of the human race, for in more than one way it impairs the sexual function; uncultivated races and backward strata of the population are already multiplying more rapidly than highly cultivated ones. The process is perhaps comparable to the domestication of certain species of animals and it is undoubtedly accompanied by physical alterations; but we are still unfamiliar with the notion that the evolution of culture is an organic process of this kind. The psychical modifications that go along with the cultural process are striking and unambiguous. They consist in a progressive displacement of instinctual aims and a restriction of instinctual impulses. Sensations which were pleasurable to our ancestors have become indifferent or even intolerable to ourselves; there are organic grounds for the changes in our ethical and aesthetic ideals. Of the psychological characteristics of culture two appear to be the most important: a strengthening of the intellect, which is beginning to govern instinctual life, and an internalization of the aggressive impulses, with all its consequent advantages and perils. Now war is in the crassest opposition to the psychical attitude imposed on us by the cultural process, and for that reason we are bound to rebel against it; we simply cannot any longer put up with it. This is not merely an intellectual and emotional repudiation; we pacifists have a constitutional intolerance of war, an idiosyncrasy magnified, as it were, to the highest degree. It seems, indeed, as though the lowering of aesthetic standards in war plays a scarcely smaller part in our rebellion than do its cruelties.

And how long shall we have to wait before the rest of mankind become pacifists too? There is no telling. But it may not be utopian to hope that these two factors, the cultural attitude and the justified dread of the consequences of a future war, may result within a measurable time in putting an end to the waging of war. By what paths or by what side tracks this will come about we cannot guess. But one thing we *can* say: whatever fosters the growth of culture works at the same time against war.

I trust you will forgive me if what I have said has disappointed you, and I remain, with kindest regards,

Yours sincerely,
Sigm. Freud

Questions

1. Does Freud think that a rational solution to the problem of war is possible?

2. According to Freud, why must the instinct to wage war be countered by *"indirect* methods"? (121)

3. Why does Freud emphasize that an inclination toward violence for its own sake—rather than poverty or injustice—is the true cause of war?

4. Why does Freud say that love and hate rarely operate apart from one another?

5. Is Freud suggesting that people will have to find new outlets for their aggressive instincts if war is eliminated?

6. Do nonviolent political movements disprove Freud's belief that mankind has basic instincts for hatred, destruction, and war?

William Butler Yeats

One of the great poets of the twentieth century, Irish writer William Butler Yeats (1865–1939) was fascinated by Celtic history and led the Irish Literary Revival, a movement that renewed interest in traditional Irish literature and culture. This movement helped shape a sense of national identity for Ireland during the first decades of the century, a period of political turmoil marked by violent rebellion against British rule.

Yeats's friend and patron Lady Gregory was a generous supporter of Irish arts and culture. With Lady Gregory and others, Yeats helped found the Irish Literary Theatre, later famous as the Abbey Theatre. "An Irish Airman Foresees His Death" was written in response to the loss of Lady Gregory's son Robert during World War I. Robert Gregory was an outstanding artist, athlete, and pilot for the British Royal Flying Corps during the war. He was shot down and killed by friendly fire on the Italian front in January 1918.

Aerial warfare marked a new way of doing battle in World War I, and the pilots who mastered this type of combat were seen as heroic figures who operated in an entirely different realm from rank-and-file soldiers. Yeats, writing this poem in response to a mother's grief, focuses on the unique outlook and experience of Lady Gregory's son as Yeats imagines it, rather than on the numberless casualties on the ground. Through the voice of the pilot-narrator, Yeats challenges us to consider how those in active service might feel about joining the military and about their personal commitment to the causes for which they are fighting.

AN IRISH AIRMAN FORESEES HIS DEATH

I know that I shall meet my fate
Somewhere among the clouds above;
Those that I fight I do not hate,
Those that I guard I do not love;
My country is Kiltartan Cross,
My countrymen Kiltartan's poor,
No likely end could bring them loss
Or leave them happier than before.
Nor law, nor duty bade me fight,
Nor public men, nor cheering crowds,
A lonely impulse of delight
Drove to this tumult in the clouds;
A lonely impulse of delight
Drove to this tumult in the clouds;
I balanced all, brought all to mind,
The years to come seemed waste of breath,
A waste of breath the years behind
In balance with this life, this death.

Questions

1. Why is the airman convinced that he will die?

2. Why does the airman list all the things—law, duty, public men, cheering crowds—that did *not* motivate him to fight?

3. What does the airman mean by the "lonely impulse of delight" that led him to become a pilot?

4. Why do "the years to come" seem a waste to the airman when he compares them to his life and death as a pilot?

5. Is it necessary to hate the enemy in order to be effective in combat?

6. Is it honorable to serve in the military while feeling no allegiance to the country or cause for which one is fighting?

Stephen Crane

As a young man, Stephen Crane (1871–1900) lived in New York City and worked as a freelance journalist, writing fiction in his spare time. Crane wrote in a style called naturalism, vivid in realistic detail and often presenting harsh and unpleasant truths about human society. His Civil War novel, *The Red Badge of Courage* (1895), made him famous, and his unflinching portrayal of war landed him a job as a war correspondent. He survived a shipwreck on the way to Cuba to cover the Spanish-American War and later traveled to Greece to cover the Greco-Turkish War. Crane's promising literary career was cut short by tuberculosis at the age of twenty-eight.

The protagonist of Crane's short story "The Veteran" is an older Henry Fleming, the same man who had been the young hero of *The Red Badge of Courage*. "The Veteran" takes place years after the Civil War and Fleming is at ease with his earlier military experiences. The credibility of his war tales is brought into question through Fleming's own honesty, but his bravery is tested once again by a barn fire on his farm, an incident far removed from military daring but similarly fraught with danger.

Many potential forms of courage and heroism, bravado and cowardice, are hinted at in this story. Crane offers a vision of bravery, honor, and fulfillment that can exist for veterans, long after their return to home and family. Crane asks us to consider how the experience of combat, with its sacrifices and heroic deeds, may have a lifelong influence on how veterans respond to later calls to action as civilians.

THE VETERAN

Out of the low window could be seen three hickory trees placed irregularly in a meadow that was resplendent in springtime green. Farther away, the old, dismal belfry of the village church loomed over the pines. A horse meditating in the shade of one of the hickories lazily swished his tail. The warm sunshine made an oblong of vivid yellow on the floor of the grocery.

"Could you see the whites of their eyes?" said the man who was seated on a soapbox.

"Nothing of the kind," replied old Henry warmly. "Just a lot of flitting figures, and I let go at where they 'peared to be the thickest. Bang!"

"Mr. Fleming," said the grocer—his deferential voice expressed somehow the old man's exact social weight—"Mr. Fleming, you never was frightened much in them battles, was you?"

The veteran looked down and grinned. Observing his manner, the entire group tittered. "Well, I guess I was," he answered finally. "Pretty well scared, sometimes. Why, in my first battle I thought the sky was falling down. I thought the world was coming to an end. You bet I was scared."

Everyone laughed. Perhaps it seemed strange and rather wonderful to them that a man should admit the thing, and in a tone of their laughter there was probably more admiration than if old Fleming had declared that he had always been a lion. Moreover, they knew that he had ranked as an orderly sergeant, and so their opinion of his heroism was fixed. None, to be sure, knew how an orderly sergeant ranked, but then it was understood to be somewhere just shy of a major general's stars. So, when old Henry admitted that he had been frightened, there was a laugh.

"The trouble was," said the old man, "I thought they were all shooting at me. Yes, sir, I thought every man in the other army was aiming at me in particular, and only me. And it seemed so darned unreasonable, you know. I wanted to explain to 'em what an almighty good fellow I was, because I thought then they might quit all trying to hit me. But I couldn't explain, and they kept on being unreasonable—blim!—blam!—bang! So I run!"

Two little triangles of wrinkles appeared at the corners of his eyes. Evidently he appreciated some comedy in this recital. Down near his feet, however, little Jim, his grandson, was visibly horror-stricken. His hands were clasped nervously, and his eyes were wide with astonishment at this terrible scandal, his most magnificent grandfather telling such a thing.

"That was at Chancellorsville. Of course, afterward I got kind of used to it. A man does. Lots of men, though, seem to feel all right from the start. I did, as soon as I 'got on to it,' as they say now; but at first I was pretty well flustered. Now, there was young Jim Conklin, old Si Conklin's son—that used to keep the tannery—you none of you recollect him—well, he went into it from the start just as if he was born to it. But with me it was different. I had to get used to it."

When little Jim walked with his grandfather he was in the habit of skipping along on the stone pavement in front of the three stores and the hotel of the town and betting that he could avoid the cracks. But upon this day he walked soberly, with his hand gripping two of his grandfather's fingers. Sometimes he kicked abstractedly at dandelions that curved over the walk. Anyone could see that he was much troubled.

"There's Sickles's colt over in the medder, Jimmie," said the old man. "Don't you wish you owned one like him?"

"Um," said the boy, with a strange lack of interest. He continued his reflections. Then finally he ventured, "Grandpa—now—was that true what you was telling those men?"

"What?" asked the grandfather. "What was I telling them?"

"Oh, about your running."

"Why, yes, that was true enough, Jimmie. It was my first fight, and there was an awful lot of noise, you know."

Jimmie seemed dazed that this idol, of its own will, should so totter. His stout boyish idealism was injured.

Presently the grandfather said: "Sickles's colt is going for a drink. Don't you wish you owned Sickles's colt, Jimmie?"

The boy merely answered, "He ain't as nice as our'n." He lapsed then into another moody silence.

One of the hired men, a Swede, desired to drive to the county seat for purposes of his own. The old man loaned a horse and an unwashed buggy. It appeared later that one of the purposes of the Swede was to get drunk.

After quelling some boisterous frolic of the farm hands and boys in the garret, the old man had that night gone peacefully to sleep, when he was aroused by clamoring at the kitchen door. He grabbed his trousers, and they waved out behind as he dashed forward. He could hear the voice of the Swede, screaming and blubbering. He pushed the wooden button, and, as the door flew open, the Swede, a maniac, stumbled inward, chattering, weeping, still screaming: "De barn fire! Fire! Fire! De barn fire! Fire! Fire! Fire!"

There was a swift and indescribable change in the old man. His face ceased instantly to be a face; it became a mask, a gray thing, with horror written about the mouth and eyes. He hoarsely shouted at the foot of the little rickety stairs, and immediately, it seemed, there came down an avalanche of men. No one knew that during this time the old lady had been standing in her night clothes at the bedroom door, yelling: "What's th' matter? What's th' matter? What's th' matter?"

When they dashed toward the barn it presented to their eyes its usual appearance, solemn, rather mystic in the black night. The Swede's lantern was overturned at a point some yards in front of the barn doors. It contained a wild little conflagration of its own, and even in their excitement some of those who ran felt a gentle secondary vibration of the thrifty part of their minds at sight of this overturned lantern. Under ordinary circumstances it would have been a calamity.

But the cattle in the barn were trampling, trampling, trampling, and above this noise could be heard a humming like the song of innumerable bees. The old man hurled aside the great doors, and a yellow flame leaped out at one corner and sped and wavered frantically up the old gray wall. It was glad, terrible, this single flame, like the wild banner of deadly and triumphant foes.

The motley crowd from the garret had come with all the pails of the farm. They flung themselves upon the well. It was a leisurely old machine, long dwelling in indolence. It was in the habit of giving out water with a sort of reluctance. The men stormed at it, cursed it; but it continued to allow the buckets to be filled only after the wheezy windlass had howled many protests at the mad-handed men.

With his opened knife in his hand old Fleming himself had gone headlong into the barn, where the stifling smoke swirled with the air currents, and where could be heard in its fullness the terrible chorus of the flames, laden with tones of hate and death, a hymn of wonderful ferocity.

He flung a blanket over an old mare's head, cut the halter close to the manger, led the mare to the door, and fairly kicked her out to safety. He returned with the same blanket, and rescued one of the work horses. He took five horses out, and then came out himself, with his clothes bravely on fire. He had no whiskers, and very little hair on his head. They soused five pailfuls of water on him. His eldest son made a clean miss with the sixth pailful, because the old man had turned and was running down the decline and around to the basement of the barn, where were the stanchions of the cows. Someone noticed at the time that he ran very lamely, as if one of the frenzied horses had smashed his hip.

The cows, with their heads held in the heavy stanchions, had thrown themselves, strangled themselves, tangled themselves: done everything which the ingenuity of their exuberant fear could suggest to them.

Here, as at the well, the same thing happened to every man save one. Their hands went mad. They became incapable of everything save the power to rush into dangerous situations.

The old man released the cow nearest the door, and she, blind drunk with terror, crashed into the Swede. The Swede had been running to and fro babbling. He carried an empty milk pail, to which he clung with an unconscious, fierce enthusiasm. He shrieked like one lost as he went under the cow's hoofs, and the milk pail, rolling across the floor, made a flash of silver in the gloom.

Old Fleming took a fork, beat off the cow, and dragged the paralyzed Swede to the open air. When they had rescued all the cows save one, which had so fastened herself that she could not be moved an inch, they returned to the front of the barn and stood sadly, breathing like men who had reached the final point of human effort.

Many people had come running. Someone had even gone to the church, and now, from the distance, rang the tocsin note of the old bell. There was a long flare of crimson on the sky, which made remote people speculate as to the whereabouts of the fire.

The long flames sang their drumming chorus in voices of the heaviest bass. The wind whirled clouds of smoke and cinders into the faces of the spectators. The form of the old barn was outlined in black amid these masses of orange-hued flames.

And then came this Swede again, crying as one who is the weapon of the sinister fates. "De colts! De colts! You have forgot de colts!"

Old Fleming staggered. It was true; they had forgotten the two colts in the box stalls at the back of the barn. "Boys," he said, "I must try to get 'em out." They clamored about him then, afraid for him, afraid of what they should see. Then they talked wildly each to each. "Why, it's sure death!" "He would never get out!" "Why, it's suicide for a man to go in there!" Old Fleming stared absentmindedly at the open doors. "The poor little things!" he said. He rushed into the barn.

When the roof fell in, a great funnel of smoke swarmed toward the sky, as if the old man's mighty spirit, released from its body—a little bottle—had swelled like the genie of fable. The smoke was tinted rose-hue from the flames, and perhaps the unutterable midnights of the universe will have no power to daunt the color of this soul.

Questions

1. Why does Fleming admit that he was frightened during his first battle? Why does he seem amused as he tells the story?

2. Why do the men who are listening laugh at Fleming's admission of fear in his first battle?

3. When he arrives at the burning barn, why does Fleming go into it "headlong" and succeed in rescuing five horses? (134) Why aren't the other men capable of doing much to help?

4. Why does Fleming go back into the barn to save the colts, even though the men tell him it is "sure death" to do so? (135)

5. Was Fleming's behavior during his first battle cowardly?

6. Is it brave or foolish to risk one's own life when the risk seems to outweigh the benefit?

Anne O'Hare McCormick

As a European correspondent for the *New York Times*, Anne O'Hare McCormick (1882–1954) covered the rise of the dictator Benito Mussolini in Italy and interviewed many major figures of the day, including Adolf Hitler, Winston Churchill, Josef Stalin, and Neville Chamberlain. In 1937 she became the first woman to win a Pulitzer Prize for journalism, and she served as the first woman on the editorial board of the *New York Times*.

In her 1944 article "The Italian Ordeal Surprises Members of Congress," McCormick describes how members of a United States House of Representatives committee visit Italy and are shocked by the conditions in which the Allied Italian campaign against the Germans is being waged, resulting in some of the highest numbers of casualties of the war. The committee members claim not to have known the truth of conditions on the Italian front, and they ask why this information was not readily available. Yet McCormick notes that many journalists had been publishing detailed accounts of the struggles faced by the Allied soldiers in Italy and suggests that words may be inadequate to communicate their experiences.

McCormick raises the question of whether there is an inevitable gap, which no piece of writing can bridge, between the experiences of soldiers in combat and the understanding of readers on the home front. After such extreme experiences, how can veterans readjust to civilian life? Already, in 1944, such questions were a serious concern. The inability of soldiers and civilians to communicate fully with one another has the potential to create enormous problems on return, and servicemen still face this complex issue today, when war is over and they return to their families, friends, and communities.

ITALIAN ORDEAL SURPRISES CONGRESS

Rome, Dec. 22

Members of the House Military Affairs Committee who concluded their tour of European battlefields with a visit to the Italian front expressed shocked surprise at the rigors of the campaign in Italy. Nothing they had seen in France, they said, could compare with the terrible terrain of the Apennines, and nothing they had read at home prepared them for the inhuman conditions in which men of the Fifth Army have to fight. The burden of complaint was that they didn't know the Italian battlefield was one of the toughest in the world. They had no idea of the tremendous natural obstacles the GI's have to contend with in addition to the stubbornness of the enemy stand on the best defensive positions he holds in Europe.

The congressmen charged that the full story of this battlefield has not been told, and declared that the people in the United States should be given more realistic news. Evidently they hadn't a true picture themselves and they wanted to know who was to blame.

The trouble is not with the reporters. It is not at the home copy desk. In this case, at least so far as the terrain is concerned, it isn't even with the censors. Newsmen covering the campaign from Cassino to Bologna have described over and over again the murderous character of this battleground. Who has not heard a hundred times that Italy has been defended throughout history from invasion by her impassable mountains rising, wall after wall, from the toe of the boot to the Po Valley? Who does not know that fighting all the way up this rocky peninsula has never before been attempted?

As to the doughboys grinding their way up steep escarpments under enemy fire from on top, or slithering through muddy valleys in snow and rain, their grim endurance and casual courage have inspired countless newspaper epics. Nobody can do them justice, but the press men who have shared their hardships have tried their best to tell the tale of the heroic fight. "If you write stories we will print them," Representative Shafer of Michigan, a newspaper publisher, told the Rome correspondents.

Stories have been written and have been printed. They have even been overwritten and printed so many times that readers don't see the mud or blood anymore. They don't hear the scream of shells or the thunder of fallen rockets. They don't realize what happens when towns are blasted from the earth and human beings are either buried under debris or scattered like ants when somebody steps on an anthill. The boys they know sleep in wet holes, stand in water until their feet freeze, charge up slopes raked by machine guns, but words describing these things are not sensational enough to produce an answering sensation.

The trouble is with the congressmen. Either they didn't read the accounts of the Italian battle or they couldn't take in the meaning of what they read. They had to see war for themselves before it really registered. And this lack of realization is not their fault. It is because the thing is indescribable. To write about the front is to try in vain to translate one world into another. The United States is in the war as much as Europe, perhaps more, for over here ten miles behind the lines people try to forget it, and over there people try to remember it.

Soldiers from the front don't talk about battle to people in the rear. They can't. An officer just returned from a short leave in the United States says he couldn't discuss at home what he saw and felt in the war theater, because it didn't seem to fit into the context of normal life. He was desperately homesick after two years of overseas service, but when he got home he felt restless, alien, and eager to get back.

This problem of domestication and spiritual readjustment is going to be as difficult as the problem of reemployment and reconversion. There is no getting away from the fact that millions of men in battle zones are leading abnormal lives in an abnormal world that comes in time to seem more normal than the one they have left.

The plaint of the congressmen on the battlefront, "Why weren't we told about this?" underlines the gap between information and realization. It can be bridged, not wholly but in part, by continual effort at better translation of the abnormal to the normal world by bringing fresh eyes like the congressmen's to look at the war picture, and more imagination not so much to the reporting end—for no war was ever so fully reported—as to the receiving end.

Perhaps it is more important to bring the normal world closer to the abnormal by keeping soldiers in touch with what is going on at home. A service newspaper like the *Stars and Stripes* does an excellent job, especially in this theater, of relaying general home news to men in the battle areas; but several congressmen came back from the front convinced that overseas editions of home newspapers should be sent to troops. "Boys are dying to know what the people at home are doing and thinking," said one legislator. "They want to know how the war news is reported. They are too much out of contact with American life." This is a more serious gap than the other, for war is a long exile in a strange world, and the future of America depends on the mood and spirit in which the exiles return.

Questions

1. Does McCormick think anyone is to blame for the lack of understanding by the congressional committee of the terrible conditions in the Italian campaign?

2. Why does McCormick think that the United States is perhaps more in the war than Europe? What does she mean when, referring to the United States, she says, "over there people try to remember it"? (140)

3. Why does McCormick refer to the lives of men in battle zones as abnormal? What does she mean when she says that the abnormal world they live in "comes in time to seem more normal than the one they have left"? (140)

4. How important is it for soldiers in combat to be aware of how the war is being reported back home?

5. Have modern means of communication made it easier to follow McCormick's suggestion about making an effort to translate "the abnormal to the normal world"? (140)

6. How can soldiers, while they are still in combat, help prepare their families and friends for their eventual return home?

Wilfred Owen

Wilfred Owen (1893–1918) is the most celebrated English poet of World War I. Deeply troubled by the impact of war, he nevertheless left his teaching job in France and returned to England to enlist. Owen served in the infantry until June 1917, when he was diagnosed with shell shock and sent to Craiglockhart War Hospital in Scotland. At the hospital he met fellow poet and patient Siegfried Sassoon, who strongly encouraged Owen in his writing and influenced the direction of his later poetry.

Owen returned to the front in September 1918 and was soon awarded the Military Cross for his bravery. But on November 4, 1918, one week before the armistice, he was killed helping lead his men across a canal. A book of his poetry was published after his death in 1920 by Sassoon.

Owen was among the first poets to write about the horrors of war in a graphic, realistic way. His anger and his helplessness are vividly expressed in violent and unsettling language, shocking images, and unsentimental attitudes. The increasingly industrialized nature of warfare and its dehumanizing consequences were frequent concerns of Owen's. New technologies, such as mustard gas and tanks, along with the grinding misery of life in the trenches of the Western Front, were presented starkly for the first time in his poetry, with ghastly and horrifying clarity. Owen's approach to writing about war was entirely new, abandoning the romantic heroism of earlier writers. He specifically sought to undermine old motives of honor and bravery as encapsulated in the widely quoted Latin motto *Dulce et decorum est pro patria mori* (It is sweet and fitting to die for one's country). In Owen's view, such attitudes do not capture what it is like to go to war.

POEMS

Dulce et Decorum Est

Bent double, like old beggars under sacks,
Knock-kneed, coughing like hags, we cursed through sludge,
Till on the haunting flares we turned our backs
And towards our distant rest began to trudge.
Men marched asleep. Many had lost their boots
But limped on, blood-shod. All went lame; all blind;
Drunk with fatigue; deaf even to the hoots
Of tired, outstripped Five-Nines that dropped behind.

Gas! GAS! Quick, boys!—An ecstasy of fumbling,
Fitting the clumsy helmets just in time;
But someone still was yelling out and stumbling,
And flound'ring like a man in fire or lime . . .
Dim, through the misty panes and thick green light,
As under a green sea, I saw him drowning.

In all my dreams, before my helpless sight,
He plunges at me, guttering, choking, drowning.

If in some smothering dreams you too could pace
Behind the wagon that we flung him in,
And watch the white eyes writhing in his face,
His hanging face, like a devil's sick of sin;
If you could hear, at every jolt, the blood
Come gargling from the froth-corrupted lungs,
Obscene as cancer, bitter as the cud
Of vile, incurable sores on innocent tongues,—

My friend, you would not tell with such high zest
To children ardent for some desperate glory,
The old Lie: Dulce et decorum est
Pro patria mori.

Strange Meeting

It seemed that out of battle I escaped
Down some profound dull tunnel, long since scooped
Through granites which titanic wars had groined.

Yet also there encumbered sleepers groaned,
Too fast in thought or death to be bestirred.
Then, as I probed them, one sprang up, and stared
With piteous recognition in fixed eyes,
Lifting distressful hands, as if to bless.
And by his smile, I knew that sullen hall,—
By his dead smile I knew we stood in Hell.

With a thousand pains that vision's face was grained;
Yet no blood reached there from the upper ground,
And no guns thumped, or down the flues made moan.
"Strange friend," I said, "here is no cause to mourn."
"None," said that other, "save the undone years,
The hopelessness. Whatever hope is yours,
Was my life also; I went hunting wild
After the wildest beauty in the world,
Which lies not calm in eyes, or braided hair,
But mocks the steady running of the hour,
And if it grieves, grieves richlier than here.
For by my glee might many men have laughed,
And of my weeping something had been left,
Which must die now. I mean the truth untold,
The pity of war, the pity war distilled.
Now men will go content with what we spoiled,
Or, discontent, boil bloody, and be spilled.
They will be swift with swiftness of the tigress.
None will break ranks, though nations trek from progress.
Courage was mine, and I had mystery,
Wisdom was mine, and I had mastery:
To miss the march of this retreating world

Into vain citadels that are not walled.
Then, when much blood had clogged their chariot-wheels,
I would go up and wash them from sweet wells,
Even with truths that lie too deep for taint.
I would have poured my spirit without stint
But not through wounds; not on the cess of war.
Foreheads of men have bled where no wounds were.

"I am the enemy you killed, my friend.
I knew you in this dark: for so you frowned
Yesterday through me as you jabbed and killed.
I parried; but my hands were loath and cold.
Let us sleep now. . . ."

Questions

"DULCE ET DECORUM EST"

1. Why does the poet choose this episode—a comrade's gruesome death by gassing when the troops are trudging back to base camp—to highlight the realities of warfare?

2. Why does the poet say that reexperiencing his comrade's death in "smothering dreams," rather than just remembering it, is so disturbing? (145)

3. In the last stanza of the poem, whom is the poet addressing when he repeatedly says "you"? (145–146)

4. Why does the poet say that it is children who are "ardent for some desperate glory"? (146)

5. Why does the poet call the motto "It is sweet and fitting to die for one's country" an "old Lie"? If it is a lie, are there more truthful ways of talking about what it is like to die for your country? (146)

6. Is this poem un-patriotic?

"STRANGE MEETING"

1. Why does Owen have the speaker and the man he killed meet after death in hell?

2. Why doesn't the poet recognize the man he killed even though the man recognizes him?

3. Why does the poet say to the man he killed, "here is no cause to mourn"? Why does he respond, "Whatever hope is yours, / Was my life also"? (147)

4. What does the man who was killed mean by "the truth untold, / The pity of war, the pity war distilled"? Why does he think this truth dies with him? (147)

5. Why does the dead man address his killer as "my friend"? At the end of the poem, why does he say to the poet, "Let us sleep now. . . ."? (148)

6. Do you believe that enemies in combat can be fundamentally alike?

Herbert Read

Herbert Read (1893–1968) was a British art critic and poet. During World War I he served in the infantry, earning the Military Cross and membership in the Distinguished Service Order. After the war he was a prominent figure in artistic and literary circles and a strong influence on young artists of the 1920s.

"To a Conscript of 1940" appears in Read's collection of poetry, *A World Within a War* (1944). In 1940 British men were being conscripted into the army to serve in World War II. Many historians see World War II stemming directly from the mishandling of the peace after World War I. The Treaty of Versailles punished Germany in many ways, and the resulting poverty and anger in Germany is often cited as a factor in the rise of Hitler. Rather than being "the war to end all wars," the aftermath of World War I led directly to the next. As a veteran of World War I, more than twenty years earlier, Read sees parallels between the two conflicts and questions the goals and likely result of the new war. Read's soldier-ghost expresses the disillusionment of the soldiers who returned from World War I to find little change in the world. Now the veteran sees it happening all over again for a new generation of young men.

The experience and advice of one generation of combatants to the next has varied over the years. Some return with tales of glory, others are disheartened, and others cynical. But the need to pass on the experience represents a bond between all those who are serving now and have served before, drawing them together into a conversation about what they have endured in common.

TO A CONSCRIPT OF 1940

He who has not once despaired of honor, will never be a hero.
GEORGE BERNANOS

A soldier passed me in the freshly fallen snow
His footsteps muffled, his face unearthly grey;
And my heart gave a sudden leap
As I gazed on a ghost of five-and-twenty years ago.

I shouted Halt! and my voice had the old accustomed ring
And he obeyed it as it was obeyed
In the shrouded days when I too was one
Of an army of young men marching

Into the unknown. He turned towards me and I said:
"I am one of those who went before you
Five-and-twenty years ago: one of the many who never returned,
Of the many who returned and yet were dead.

"We went where you are going, into the rain and the mud;
We fought as you will fight
With death and darkness and despair;
We gave what you will give—our brains and our blood.

"We think we gave in vain. The world was not renewed.
There was hope in the homestead and anger in the streets
But the old world was restored and we returned
To the dreary field and workshop, and the immemorial feud

"Of rich and poor. Our victory was our defeat.
Power was retained where power had been misused
And youth was left to sweep away
The ashes that the fires had strewn beneath our feet.

"But one thing we learned: there is no glory in the deed
Until the soldier wears a badge of tarnished braid;
There are heroes who have heard the rally and have seen
The glitter of a garland round their head.

"Theirs is the hollow victory. They are deceived.
But you, my brother and my ghost, if you can go
Knowing that there is no reward, no certain use
In all your sacrifice, then honour is reprieved.

"To fight without hope is to fight with grace,
The self reconstructed, the false heart repaired."
Then I turned with a smile, and he answered my salute
As he stood against the fretted hedge, which was like white lace.

Questions

1. Why does the older veteran introduce himself to the young conscript as one of "the many who returned and yet were dead"? (152)

2. Even though the veteran fought in a different, earlier war, why does he tell the conscript, "We went where you are going"? (152)

3. Why does the veteran, speaking of his own generation of warriors, say to the conscript, "Our victory was our defeat"? (153) Do you think his judgment is correct?

4. What does the veteran mean when he says to the conscript, "if you can go / Knowing that there is no reward, no certain use / In all your sacrifice, then honour is reprieved"? (153) Do you think this is good advice to give to a soldier going off to war?

5. If you were the conscript, how would you respond to what the veteran says about war and honor?

6. How can those who served in the military during wartime decide if their sacrifices were in vain or made a difference in the world?

Ernest Hemingway

"Soldier's Home" is set in a small town in Oklahoma in 1919, the year after World War I ended. Its author, Ernest Hemingway (1899–1961), had served as an ambulance driver for the American Red Cross but was wounded in July 1918 and withdrew from active duty. Hemingway went on to become one of the twentieth century's most influential writers and in his early works drew on his own experiences to portray those of soldiers during the war. Through his powerful storytelling, he depicts the trauma of being wounded and how it affects every aspect of life, physically, emotionally, and socially.

The United States entered World War I in 1917, making Krebs, the main character in "Soldier's Home," one of the early enlistees. We are told that he had fought at Belleau Wood, Soissons, the Champagne, St. Mihiel, and the Argonne, sites of some of the worst battles of the war for American troops. The advent of rapid-firing artillery, the machine gun, poison gas, and airborne firepower marked a profound change in the nature of combat. Armies on both sides were forced to fight from deep trenches, resulting in bitter stalemates with extremely high casualty rates.

Although "Soldier's Home" tells the story of a World War I veteran, it reflects the difficulties that military personnel in other wars face as they return to civilian life from combat and try to reestablish relationships with their families, friends, and communities. One of the questions that this story challenges us to consider is how servicemen and servicewomen can communicate their experiences to those who have not shared them. Another is the flip side of the same coin: How can those who are closest to these servicemen and servicewomen make it easier for them to talk about what they have experienced?

SOLDIER'S HOME

K rebs went to the war from a Methodist college in Kansas. There is a picture which shows him among his fraternity brothers, all of them wearing exactly the same height and style collar. He enlisted in the Marines in 1917 and did not return to the United States until the second division returned from the Rhine in the summer of 1919.

There is a picture which shows him on the Rhine with two German girls and another corporal. Krebs and the corporal look too big for their uniforms. The German girls are not beautiful. The Rhine does not show in the picture.

By the time Krebs returned to his hometown in Oklahoma the greeting of heroes was over. He came back much too late. The men from the town who had been drafted had all been welcomed elaborately on their return. There had been a great deal of hysteria. Now the reaction had set in. People seemed to think it was rather ridiculous for Krebs to be getting back so late, years after the war was over.

At first Krebs, who had been at Belleau Wood, Soissons, the Champagne, St. Mihiel, and in the Argonne did not want to talk about the war at all. Later he felt the need to talk but no one wanted to hear about it. His town had heard too many atrocity stories to be thrilled by actualities. Krebs found that to be listened to at all he had to lie, and after he had done this twice he, too, had a reaction against the war and against talking about it. A distaste for everything that had happened to him in the war set in because of the lies he had told. All of the times that had been able to make him feel cool and clear inside himself when he thought of them; the times so long back when he had done the one thing, the only thing for a man to do, easily and naturally, when he might have done something else, now lost their cool, valuable quality and then were lost themselves.

His lies were quite unimportant lies and consisted in attributing to himself things other men had seen, done, or heard of, and stating as facts certain apocryphal incidents familiar to all soldiers. Even his lies were not sensational at the pool room. His acquaintances, who had heard detailed accounts of German women found chained to machine guns in the Argonne forest and who could not comprehend, or were barred by their patriotism from interest in, any German machine gunners who were not chained, were not thrilled by his stories.

Krebs acquired the nausea in regard to experience that is the result of untruth or exaggeration, and when he occasionally met another man who had really been a soldier and they talked a few minutes in the dressing room at a dance he fell into the easy pose of the old soldier among other soldiers: that he had been badly, sickeningly frightened all the time. In this way he lost everything.

During this time, it was late summer, he was sleeping late in bed, getting up to walk downtown to the library to get a book, eating lunch at home, reading on the front porch until he became bored, and then walking down through the town to spend the hottest hours of the day in the cool dark of the pool room. He loved to play pool.

In the evening he practiced on his clarinet, strolled downtown, read, and went to bed. He was still a hero to his two young sisters. His mother would have given him breakfast in bed if he had wanted it. She often came in when he was in bed and asked him to tell her about the war, but her attention always wandered. His father was noncommittal.

Before Krebs went away to the war he had never been allowed to drive the family motorcar. His father was in the real estate business and always wanted the car to be at his command when he required it to take clients out into the country to show them a piece of farm property. The car always stood outside the First National Bank building where his father had an office on the second floor. Now, after the war, it was still the same car.

Nothing was changed in the town except that the young girls had grown up. But they lived in such a complicated world of already defined alliances and shifting feuds that Krebs did not feel the energy or the courage to break into it. He liked to look at them, though. There were so many good-looking young girls. Most of them had their hair cut short. When he went away only little girls wore their hair like that or girls that were fast. They all wore sweaters and shirt waists with round Dutch collars. It was a pattern. He liked to look at them from the front porch as they walked on the other side of the street. He liked to watch them walking under the shade of the trees. He liked the round Dutch collars above their sweaters. He liked their silk stockings and flat shoes. He liked their bobbed hair and the way they walked.

When he was in town their appeal to him was not very strong. He did not like them when he saw them in the Greek's ice cream parlor. He did not want them themselves really. They were too complicated. There was something else. Vaguely he wanted a girl but he did not want to have to work to get her. He would have liked to have a girl but he did not want to have to spend a long time getting her. He did not want to get into the intrigue and the politics. He did not want to have to do any courting. He did not want to tell any more lies. It wasn't worth it.

He did not want any consequences. He did not want any consequences ever again. He wanted to live along without consequences. Besides he did not really need a girl. The army had taught him that. It was all right to pose as though you had to have a girl. Nearly everybody did that. But it wasn't true. You did not need a girl. That was the funny thing. First a fellow boasted how girls mean nothing to him, that he never thought of them, that they could not touch him. Then a fellow boasted that he could not get along without girls, that he had to have them all the time, that he could not go to sleep without them.

That was all a lie. It was all a lie both ways. You did not need a girl unless you thought about them. He learned that in the army. Then sooner or later you always got one. When you were really ripe for a girl you always got one. You did not have to think about it. Sooner or later it would come. He had learned that in the army.

Now he would have liked a girl if she had come to him and not wanted to talk. But here at home it was all too complicated. He knew he could never get through it all again. It was not worth the trouble. That was the thing about French girls and German girls. There was not all this talking. You couldn't talk much and you did not need to talk. It was simple and you were friends. He thought about France and then he began to think about Germany. On the whole he had liked Germany better. He did not want to leave Germany. He did not want to come home. Still, he had come home. He sat on the front porch.

He liked the girls that were walking along the other side of the street. He liked the look of them much better than the French girls or the German girls. But the world they were in was not the world he was in. He would like to have one of them. But it was not worth it. They were such a nice pattern. He liked the pattern. It was exciting. But he would not go through all the talking. He did not want one badly enough. He liked to look at them all, though. It was not worth it. Not now when things were getting good again.

He sat there on the porch reading a book on the war. It was a history and he was reading about all the engagements he had been in. It was the most interesting reading he had ever done. He wished there were more maps. He looked forward with a good feeling to reading all the really good histories when they would come out with good detail maps. Now he was really learning about the war. He had been a good soldier. That made a difference.

One morning after he had been home about a month his mother came into his bedroom and sat on the bed. She smoothed her apron.

"I had a talk with your father last night, Harold," she said, "and he is willing for you to take the car out in the evenings."

"Yeah?" said Krebs, who was not fully awake. "Take the car out? Yeah?"

"Yes. Your father has felt for some time that you should be able to take the car out in the evenings whenever you wished but we only talked it over last night."

"I'll bet you made him," Krebs said.

"No. It was your father's suggestion that we talk the matter over."

"Yeah. I'll bet you made him," Krebs sat up in bed.

"Will you come down to breakfast, Harold?" his mother said.

"As soon as I get my clothes on," Krebs said.

His mother went out of the room and he could hear her frying something downstairs while he washed, shaved, and dressed to go down into the dining room for breakfast. While he was eating breakfast his sister brought in the mail.

"Well, Hare," she said. "You old sleepyhead. What do you ever get up for?"

Krebs looked at her. He liked her. She was his best sister.

"Have you got the paper?" he asked.

She handed him the *Kansas City Star* and he shucked off its brown wrapper and opened it to the sporting page. He folded the *Star* open and propped it against the water pitcher with his cereal dish to steady it, so he could read while he ate.

"Harold," his mother stood in the kitchen doorway, "Harold, please don't muss up the paper. Your father can't read his *Star* if it's been mussed."

"I won't muss it," Krebs said.

His sister sat down at the table and watched him while he read.

"We're playing indoor over at school this afternoon," she said. "I'm going to pitch."

"Good," said Krebs. "How's the old wing?"

"I can pitch better than lots of the boys. I tell them all you taught me. The other girls aren't much good."

"Yeah?" said Krebs.

"I tell them all you're my beau. Aren't you my beau, Hare?"

"You bet."

"Couldn't your brother really be your beau just because he's your brother?"

"I don't know."

"Sure you know. Couldn't you be my beau, Hare, if I was old enough and if you wanted to?"

"Sure. You're my girl now."

"Am I really your girl?"

"Sure."

"Do you love me?"

"Uh, huh."

"Will you love me always?"

"Sure."

"Will you come over and watch me play indoor?"

"Maybe."

"Aw, Hare, you don't love me. If you loved me, you'd want to come over and watch me play indoor."

Krebs's mother came into the dining room from the kitchen. She carried a plate with two fried eggs and some crisp bacon on it and a plate of buckwheat cakes.

"You run along, Helen," she said. "I want to talk to Harold."

She put the eggs and bacon down in front of him and brought in a jug of maple syrup for the buckwheat cakes. Then she sat down across the table from Krebs.

"I wish you'd put down the paper for a minute, Harold," she said.

Krebs took down the paper and folded it.

"Have you decided what you are going to do yet, Harold?" his mother said, taking off her glasses.

"No," said Krebs.

"Don't you think it's about time?" His mother did not say this in a mean way. She seemed worried.

"I hadn't thought about it," Krebs said.

"God has some work for every one to do," his mother said. "There can be no idle hands in His Kingdom."

"I'm not in His Kingdom," Krebs said.

"We are all of us in His Kingdom."

Krebs felt embarrassed and resentful as always.

"I've been worried about you so much, Harold," his mother went on. "I know the temptations you must have been exposed to. I know how weak men are. I know what your own dear grandfather, my own father, told us about the Civil War and I have prayed for you. I pray for you all day long, Harold."

Krebs looked at the bacon fat hardening on his plate.

"Your father is worried, too," his mother went on. "He thinks you have lost your ambition, that you haven't got a definite aim in life. Charley Simmons, who is just your age, has a good job and is going to be married. The boys are all settling down; they're all determined to get somewhere; you can see that boys like Charley Simmons are on their way to being really a credit to the community."

Krebs said nothing.

"Don't look that way, Harold," his mother said. "You know we love you and I want to tell you for your own good how matters stand. Your father does not want to hamper your freedom. He thinks you should be allowed to drive the car. If you want to take some of the nice girls out riding with you, we are only too pleased. We want you to enjoy yourself. But you are going to have to settle down to work, Harold. Your father doesn't care what you start in at. All work is honorable as he says. But you've got to make a start at something. He asked me to speak to you this morning and then you can stop in and see him at his office."

"Is that all?" Krebs said.

"Yes. Don't you love your mother, dear boy?"

"No," Krebs said.

His mother looked at him across the table. Her eyes were shiny. She started crying.

"I don't love anybody," Krebs said.

It wasn't any good. He couldn't tell her, he couldn't make her see it. It was silly to have said it. He had only hurt her. He went over and took hold of her arm. She was crying with her head in her hands.

"I didn't mean it," he said. "I was just angry at something. I didn't mean I didn't love you."

His mother went on crying. Krebs put his arm on her shoulder.

"Can't you believe me, Mother?"

His mother shook her head.

"Please, please, Mother. Please believe me."

"All right," his mother said chokily. She looked up at him. "I believe you, Harold."

Krebs kissed her hair. She put her face up to him.

"I'm your mother," she said. "I held you next to my heart when you were a tiny baby."

Krebs felt sick and vaguely nauseated.

"I know, Mummy," he said. "I'll try and be a good boy for you."

"Would you kneel and pray with me, Harold?" his mother asked.

They knelt down beside the dining room table and Krebs's mother prayed.

"Now, you pray, Harold," she said.

"I can't," Krebs said.

"Try, Harold."

"I can't."

"Do you want me to pray for you?"

"Yes."

So his mother prayed for him and then they stood up and Krebs kissed his mother and went out of the house. He had tried so to keep his life from being complicated. Still, none of it had touched him. He had felt sorry for his mother and she had made him lie. He would go to Kansas City and get a job and she would feel all right about it. There would be one more scene maybe before he got away. He would not go down to his father's office. He would miss that one. He wanted his life to go smoothly. It had just gotten going that way. Well, that was all over now, anyway. He would go over to the schoolyard and watch Helen play indoor baseball.

Questions

1. Why does Krebs have to lie to get people to listen to his war stories?

2. What does Krebs mean in wanting to live his life without "any consequences ever again"? (157)

3. Why does Krebs feel that "it was not worth it" to make the effort to have a girlfriend? (158)

4. What is on Krebs's mind when he tells his mother, "I don't love anybody"? What does he mean when he thinks, "He couldn't tell her, he couldn't make her see it"? (161)

5. Do the things that Krebs's mother, sister, and father do help him to readjust to home life? How could Krebs have communicated to his family what would be most helpful?

6. Why do some civilians get tired of hearing war stories? Why do veterans sometimes get tired of telling these stories?

Ernie Pyle

Ernie Pyle (1900–1945) was one of the most celebrated U.S. journalists of World War II. He studied journalism at Indiana University and became a roving reporter for the Scripps-Howard newspaper chain. He wrote a column that eventually appeared in some 200 newspapers.

Pyle left for Europe at the outbreak of World War II. He was in London during the Blitz and reported on the daily lives of U.S. troops training in England and Ireland. He covered the campaigns in North Africa, Sicily, France, and Italy, winning the Pulitzer Prize. He was in Normandy to cover D-day and accompanied French troops into Paris after its liberation. In 1945 Pyle went to report on the Pacific theater, traveling with U.S. troops. He was on Iwo Jima and then Ie Shima, where he was killed by Japanese machine-gun fire.

Pyle's wartime column ran in the armed forces paper, *Stars and Stripes*. He was beloved by the soldiers, who appreciated his regard for them. Pyle gave voice to the average serviceman overseas, reporting on the bravery of the infantry and telling stories of ordinary men in extraordinary situations. His writing became a link between the men at the front and their families.

Pyle is preeminent in a long line of journalists who have shared the danger and reported the realities of war for the troops and the public at home. He also was one of the first to consider the adjustment from military to civilian life and to assess what is lost as well as gained through military service, for both military personnel and their families.

REPORTING THE WAR IN TUNISIA

THE WAR IN TUNISIA

A forward airdrome in French North Africa—(by wireless)—It is hard for a layman to understand the fine points of aerial combat as practiced at the moment in North Africa. It is hard even for the pilots themselves to keep up, for there are changes in tactics from week to week.

We will have some new idea and surprise Germans with it. Then they'll come across with a surprise maneuver, and we will have to change everything to counteract it.

But basically, at the moment, you can say that everything depends on teamwork. The lone dashing hero in this war is certain to be a dead hero within a week. Sticking with the team and playing it all together is the only guarantee of safety for everybody.

Our fighters go in groups with the bombers, ranging the sky above them, flying back and forth, watching for anything that may appear. But if they see some Germans in the distance nobody goes after them. That would be playing into the Germans' hands. So they stick to their formation above the bombers, making an umbrella.

The German has two choices—to dive down through them, or to wait until somebody is hit by flak and has to drop back. Then they are on him in a flash.

When that happens the fighters attack, but still in formation. Keeping that formation always and forever tight is what the flight leaders constantly drill into the boys' heads. It is a great temptation to dash out and take a shot at some fellow, but by now they've seen too many cases of the tragedy of such action.

The result is that this war doesn't have many individual air heroes. A team may be a composite hero, but not an individual.

One group leader told me: "If everything went according to schedule we'd never shoot down a German plane. We'd cover our bombers and keep ourselves covered and everybody would come home safe."

The fighter pilots seem a little different from the bomber men. Usually they are younger. Many of them were still in school when they joined up. Ordinarily they might be inclined to be more harum-scarum, but their work is so deadly, and the sobering dark cloud of personal tragedy is over them so constantly, that it seems to have humbled them. In fact I think it makes them nicer people than if they were cocky.

They have to get up early. Often I've gone to the room of my special friends at 9:30 in the evening and found them all asleep.

They fly so frequently they can't do much drinking. One night recently when one of the most popular fighter pilots was killed right on the home field, in an accident, some of them assuaged their grief with gin.

"Somehow you feel it more when it happens right here than when a fellow just doesn't come back," they said.

When they first came over here, you'd frequently hear pilots say they didn't hate the Germans, but you don't hear that any more. They have lost too many friends, too many roommates.

Now it is killing that animates them.

The highest spirits I've ever seen in that room were displayed one evening after they came back from a strafing mission. That's what they like to do best, but they get little of it. It's a great holiday from escorting bombers, which they hate. Going out freelancing to shoot up whatever they see, and going in enough force to be pretty sure they'll be superior to the enemy—that's utopia.

That's what they had done that day. And they really had a field day. They ran onto a German truck convoy and blew it to pieces. They'd laugh and get excited as they told about it. The trucks were all full of men, and "they'd fly out like firecrackers." Motorcyclists would get hit and dive 40 feet before they stopped skidding.

Two Messerschmitt 109s made the mistake of coming after our planes. They never had a chance. After firing a couple of wild bursts they went down smoking, and one of them seemed to blow up.

The boys were full of laughter when they told about it as they sat there on their cots in the dimly lighted room. I couldn't help having a funny feeling about them. They were all so young, so genuine, so enthusiastic. And they were so casual about everything—not casual in a hard, knowing way, but they talked about their flights and killing and being killed exactly as they would discuss girls or their school lessons.

Maybe they won't talk at all when they finally get home. If they don't it will be because they know this is a world apart and nobody else could ever understand.

Northern Tunisia—(by wireless)—I was away from the front lines for a while this spring, living with other troops, and considerable fighting took place while I was gone. When I got ready to return to my old friends at the front I wondered if I would sense any change in them.

I did, and definitely.

The most vivid change is the casual and workshop manner in which they now talk about killing. They have made the psychological transition from the normal belief that taking human life is sinful, over to a new professional outlook where killing is a craft. To them now there is nothing morally wrong about killing. In fact it is an admirable thing.

I think I am so impressed by this new attitude because it hasn't been necessary for me to make this change along with them. As a noncombatant, my own life is in danger only by occasional chance or circumstance. Consequently I need not think of killing in personal terms, and killing to me is still murder.

Even after a winter of living with wholesale death and vile destruction, it is only spasmodically that I seem capable of realizing how real and how awful this war is. My emotions seem dead and crusty when presented with the tangibles of war. I find I can look on rows of fresh graves without a lump in my throat. Somehow I can look on mutilated bodies without flinching or feeling deeply.

It is only when I sit alone away from it all, or lie at night in my bedroll re-creating with closed eyes what I have seen, thinking and thinking and thinking, that at last the enormity of all these newly dead strikes like a living nightmare. And there are times when I feel that I can't stand it and will have to leave.

But to the fighting soldier that phase of the war is behind. It was left behind after his first battle. His blood is up. He is fighting for his life, and killing now for him is as much a profession as writing is for me.

He wants to kill individually or in vast numbers. He wants to see the Germans overrun, mangled, butchered in the Tunisian trap. He speaks excitedly of seeing great heaps of dead, of our bombers sinking whole shiploads of fleeing men, of Germans by the thousands dying miserably in a final Tunisian holocaust of his own creation.

In this one respect the front-line soldier differs from all the rest of us. All the rest of us—you and me and even the thousands of soldiers behind the lines in Africa—we want terribly yet only academically for the war to get over. The front-line soldier wants it to be got over by the physical process of his destroying enough Germans to end it. He is truly at war. The rest of us, no matter how hard we work, are not.

THIS IS OUR WAR

The Tunisian campaign was ended. Our air forces moved on farther into Tunisia, to the very edge of the chasm of sea that separated them only so little from Sicily and Sardinia and then from Europe itself. We and the British leaped upon the demolished ports we had captured, cleared out enough wreckage for a foothold for ships, and as the ports grew and grew in usefulness they swarmed with thousands of men, and ships, and trucks. Our combat troops moved back—out of range of enemy strafers— to be cheered and acclaimed momentarily by the cities in the rear, to take a few days of wild and hell-roaring rest, and then to go into an invasion practice that was in every respect, except the one of actually getting shot, as rigorous as a real invasion.

Surely before autumn we of Tunisia would be deep into something new. Most of us realized and admitted to ourselves that horrible days lay ahead. The holocaust that at times seemed so big to us in Tunisia would pale in our memories beside the things we would see and do before another year ran out.

Tunisia for us was not only an end in itself, but without the War of Tunisia we would have been ill-prepared to go on into the bigger wars ahead. Tunisia has been called a warm-up ground. That is a proper word for it, I suppose. We found through actual test which of our weapons and planes and vehicles were good, and which were bad, and which could be made good with a little changing. We seasoned our men in battle, and we found the defects that needed to be found in our communications systems, our supply lines, our methods of organization.

It is hard for you at home to realize what an immense, complicated, sprawling institution a theater of war actually is. As it appears to you in the newspapers, war is a clear-cut matter of landing so many men overseas, moving them from the port to the battlefield, advancing them against the enemy with guns firing, and they win or lose.

To look at war that way is like seeing a trailer of a movie, and saying you've seen the whole picture. I actually don't know what percentage of our troops in Africa were in the battle lines, but I believe it safe to say that only comparatively few ever saw the enemy, ever shot at him, or were shot at by him. All the rest of those hundreds of thousands of men were churning the highways for two thousand miles behind the lines with their endless supply trucks, they were unloading the ships, cooking the meals, pounding the typewriters, fixing the roads, making the maps, repairing the engines, decoding the messages, training the reserves, pondering the plans.

To get all that colossal writhing chaos shaped into something that intermeshed and moved forward with efficiency was a task closely akin to weaving a cloth out of a tubful of spaghetti. It was all right to have wonderful plans ahead of time, but we really learn such things only by doing. Now, after our forces have had more than six months' experience in North Africa, I for one feel that we have washed out the bulk of our miscomprehensions, have abandoned most of our fallacies, and have hardened down into a work-weary and battle-dirtied machine of great effect, capable of assimilating and directing aright those greener men who are to follow by the hundreds of thousands and maybe millions.

What I have seen in North Africa has altered my own feelings in one respect. There were days when I sat in my tent alone and gloomed with the desperate belief that it was actually possible for us to lose this war. I don't feel that way anymore. Despite our strikes and bickering and confusion back home, America is producing and no one can deny that. Even here at the far end of just one line the trickle has grown into an impressive stream. We are producing at home and we are hardening overseas. Apparently it takes a country like America about two years to become wholly at war. We had to go through that transition period of letting loose of life as it was, and then live the new war life so long that it finally became the normal life to us. It was a form of growth, and we couldn't press it. Only time can produce that change. We have survived that long passage of time, and if I am at all correct we have about changed our character and become a war nation. I can't yet see when we shall win, or over what route geographically, or by which of the many means of warfare. But no longer do I have any doubts at all that we shall win.

The men over here have changed too. They are too close to themselves to sense the change, perhaps. And I am too close to them to grasp it fully. But since I am older and a little apart, I have been able to notice it more.

For a year, everywhere I went, soldiers inevitably asked me two questions: "When do you think we'll get to go home?" and "When will the war be over?" The home-going desire was once so dominant that I believe our soldiers over here would have voted—if the question had been put— to go home immediately, even if it meant peace on terms of something less than unconditional surrender by the enemy.

That isn't true now. Sure, they all still want to go home. So do I. But there is something deeper than that, which didn't exist six months ago. I can't quite put it into words—it isn't any theatrical proclamation that the enemy must be destroyed in the name of freedom; it's just a vague but growing individual acceptance of the bitter fact that we must win the war or else, and that it can't be won by running excursion boats back and forth across the Atlantic carrying homesick vacationers.

A year is a long time to be away from home, especially if a person has never been away before, as was true of the bulk of our troops. At first homesickness can almost kill a man. But time takes care of that. It isn't normal to moon in the past forever. Home gradually grows less vivid; the separation from it less agonizing. There finally comes a day—not suddenly but gradually, as a sunset-touched cloud changes its color—when a man is living almost wholly wherever he is. His life has caught up with his body, and his days become full war days, instead of American days simply transplanted to Africa.

That's the stage our soldiers are in now—the ones who have been over since the beginning, I mean. It seems to take about that long. It's only in the last few weeks that I've begun to hear frequent remarks, said enthusiastically and sincerely, about the thrill it will be to see Paris and to march down the streets of Berlin. The immediate goal used to be the Statue of Liberty; more and more it is becoming Unter den Linden. When all of our army has bridged that gap we shall be in the homestretch.

Our men can't make this change from normal civilians into warriors and remain the same people. Even if they were away from you this long under normal circumstances, the mere process of maturing would change them, and they would not come home just as you knew them. Add to that the abnormal world they have been plunged into, the new philosophies they have had to assume or perish inwardly, the horrors and delights and strange wonderful things they have experienced, and they are bound to be different people from those you sent away.

They are rougher than when you knew them. Killing is a rough business. Their basic language has changed from mere profanity to obscenity. More than anything else, they miss women. Their expressed longings, their conversation, their whole conduct show their need for female companionship, and the gentling effect of femininity upon man is conspicuous here where it has been so long absent.

Our men have less regard for property than you raised them to have. Money value means nothing to them, either personally or in the aggregate; they are fundamentally generous, with strangers and with each other. They give or throw away their own money, and it is natural that they are even less thoughtful of bulk property than of their own hard-earned possessions. It is often necessary to abandon equipment they can't take with them; the urgency of war prohibits normal caution in the handling of vehicles and supplies. One of the most striking things to me about war is the appalling waste that is necessary. At the front there just isn't time to be economical. Also, in war areas where things are scarce and red tape still rears its delaying head, a man learns to get what he needs simply by "requisitioning." It isn't stealing, it's the only way to acquire certain things. The stress of war puts old virtues in a changed light. We shall have to relearn a simple fundamental or two when things get back to normal. But what's wrong with a small case of "requisitioning" when murder is a classic goal?

Our men, still thinking of home, are impatient with the strange peoples and customs of the countries they now inhabit. They say that if they ever get home they never want to see another foreign country. But I know how it will be. The day will come when they'll look back and brag about how they learned a little Arabic, and how swell the girls were in England, and how pretty the hills of Germany were. Every day their scope is broadening despite themselves, and once they all get back with their global yarns and their foreign-tinged views, I cannot conceive of our nation ever being isolationist again. The men don't feel very international right now, but the influences are at work and the time will come.

I couldn't say truthfully that they are very much interested in foreign affairs right now, outside of battle affairs. Awhile back a friend of mine in Washington wrote me an enthusiastic letter, telling of the Ball Resolution in the Senate calling for the formation of a United Nations organization to coordinate the prosecution of the war, administer reoccupied countries, feed and economically reestablish liberated nations, and assemble a United Nations military force to suppress any future military aggression.

My friend told of the enthusiasm the bill had created at home, hailed it as the first definite step in winning the peace as well as the war, and asked me almost pleadingly to send back a report on what the men at the front thought of the bill.

I didn't send any report, because the men at the front thought very little about it one way or the other. I doubt that one out of ten of them remembered the thing two days, even though they may have read about it in *Stars and Stripes*. There wasn't anything specific to get their teeth into and argue about. It sounded too much like another Atlantic Charter or committee meeting.

Of course, by digging, a person could find plenty of politically and internationally minded men in our army—all the way from generals to privates—who do spend considerable time thinking of what is to come after the victory, and how we are to handle it. But what I'm trying to get over is that the bulk of our army in Africa, the run-of-the-mine mass of soldiers, didn't think twice about this bill if they heard of it at all. Their thoughts on the peace can be summed up, I believe, in a general statement that after this war is won they want it fixed so it can't happen again and they want a hand in fixing it, but our average guy has not more conception of how it should be done than to say he supposes some kind of world police force is the answer. There is a great deal more talk along the line of, "Those bluenoses back home better not try to put Prohibition over on us while we're away this time," than you hear about bills and resolutions looking toward the post-war world.

Your men have been well cared for in this war. I suppose no soldiers in any other war in history have had such excellent attention as our men overseas. The food is good. Of course we're always yapping about how wonderful a steak would taste on Broadway, but when a soldier is pinned right down he'll admit ungrudgingly that it's Broadway he's thinking about more than the steak, and that he really can't kick on the food. Furthermore, cooking is good in this war. Last time good food was spoiled by lousy cooking, but that is the exception this time. Of course, there were times in battle when the men lived for days on nothing but those deadly cold C rations out of tin cans, and even went without food for a day or two, but those were the crises, the exceptions. On the whole, we figure by the letters from home that we're probably eating better than you are.

A good diet and excellent medical care have made our army a healthy one. Statistics show the men in the mass healthier today than they were in civil life back home.

Our men are well provided with clothing, transportation, mail, and army newspapers. Back of the line they had Post Exchanges where they could buy cigarettes, candy, toilet articles, and all such things. If they were in the combat zone, all those things were issued to them free.

Our fighting equipment was the only thing that didn't stand head and shoulders above everything issued to soldiers of any other country, and that was only because we weren't ready for war at first, and for two years we have been learning what was good and what was bad. Already many of our weapons are unmatched by any other country. Give us another year and surely it can be said that our men are furnished better weapons, along with better food, health, and clothing, than any other army.

Here it is June of 1943 and it seems a long time since we landed at Oran in November of 1942. Of course there were thousands of us even in those first days in Africa, and yet it seemed like a little family then. And specially so when we went on to Tunisia—in those bitter January days we were so small that I knew almost every officer on the staff of every unit, in addition to hundreds of the soldiers. Nothing was very official in our lives then; there was almost no red tape; we correspondents at the front were few and were considered by the army rather like partners in the firm. We made deep friendships that have endured.

During winter I dropped in frequently at corps headquarters, buried deep in a gulch beyond Tebessa. They put up a little tent for me, and I tried to work and sleep in it, but was never very successful at either because of being constantly, paralyzingly cold throughout the twenty-four hours of the day. We ate in a tent with a crushed-stone floor and an iron-bellied stove in the center. It was the only warm place I knew, and so informal was the war in those first days that often I sat around the stove after supper and just gabbed country-storelike with Lieutenant General Lloyd Fredendall, then commander of our armies in Tunisia. I was very fond of General Fredendall, and I admired and respected him. For some unknown reason I always thought of him to myself as "Papa" Fredendall, although I don't think anybody else ever did. I still wear the Armored Corps combat jacket he gave me.

The first pioneering days of anything are always the best days. Everything is new and animating, and acquaintanceships are easy and everyone is knit closely together. In the latter part of the Tunisian War things were just as good for us correspondents—we had better facilities and the fighting army continued to be grand to us—and yet toward the end it became so big that I felt like a spectator instead of a participant. Which is, of course, all that a correspondent is or ever should be. But the old intimacy was gone.

And then finally the Tunisian campaign was over, spectacularly collapsed after the bitterest fighting we had known in our theater. It was only in those last days that I came to know what war really is. I don't know how any of the men who went through the thick of that hill-by-hill butchery could ever be the same again. The end of the Tunisian War brought an exhilaration, then a letdown, and later a restlessness from anticlimax that I can see multiplied a thousand times when the last surrender comes. That transition back to normal days will be as difficult for many as was the change into war, and some will never be able to accomplish it.

Now we are in a lull and many of us are having a short rest period. I tried the city and couldn't stand it. Two days drove me back to the country, where everything seemed cleaner and more decent. I am in my tent, sitting on a newly acquired cot, writing on a German folding table we picked up the day of the big surrender. The days here are so peaceful and perfect they almost give us a sense of infidelity to those we left behind beneath the Tunisian crosses, those whose final awareness was a bedlam of fire and noise and uproar.

Here the Mediterranean surf caresses the sandy beach not a hundred yards away, and it is a lullaby for sleeping. The water is incredibly blue, just as we always heard it was. The sky is a cloudless blue infinity, and the only sounds are the birds singing in the scrub bushes that grow out of the sand and lean precisely away from the sea. Little land terrapins waddle around, and I snared one by the hind leg with a piece of string and tied it in photographer Chuck Corte's tent while he was out, just for a joke. Then I found myself peeking in every few minutes to see how the captive was getting along, and he was straining so hard to get away that I got to feeling sorry for the poor little devil, so I turned him loose and ruined my joke.

An occasional black beetle strolls innocently across the sandy floor. For two hours I've been watching one of them struggling with a cigarette butt on the ground, trying to move it. Yesterday a sand snake crawled by just outside my tent door, and for the first time in my life I looked upon a snake not with a creeping phobia but with a sudden and surprising feeling of compassion. Somehow I pitied him, because he was a snake instead of a man. And I don't know why I felt that way, for I feel pity for all men too, because they are men.

It may be that the war has changed me, along with the rest. It is hard for anyone to analyze himself. I know that I find more and more that I wish to be alone, and yet contradictorily I believe I have a new patience with humanity that I've never had before. When you've lived with the unnatural mass cruelty that mankind is capable of inflicting upon itself, you find yourself dispossessed of the faculty for blaming one poor man for the triviality of his faults. I don't see how any survivor of war can ever be cruel to anything, ever again.

Yes, I want the war to be over, just as keenly as any soldier in North Africa wants it. This little interlude of passive contentment here on the Mediterranean shore is a mean temptation. It is a beckoning into somnolence. This is the kind of day I think I want my life to be composed of, endlessly. But pretty soon we shall strike our tents and traipse again after the clanking tanks, sleep again to the incessant lullaby of the big rolling guns. It has to be that way, and wishing doesn't change it.

It may be I have unconsciously made war seem more awful than it really is. It would be wrong to say that war is all grim; if it were, the human spirit could not survive two and three and four years of it. There is a good deal of gaiety in wartime. Some of us, even over here, are having the time of our lives. Humor and exuberance still exist. As some soldier once said, the army is good for one ridiculous laugh per minute. Our soldiers are still just as roughly good-humored as they always were, and they laugh easily, although there isn't as much to laugh about as there used to be.

And I don't attempt to deny that war is vastly exhilarating. The whole tempo of life steps up, both at home and on the front. There is an intoxication about battle, and ordinary men can sometimes soar clear out of themselves on the wine of danger-emotion. And yet it is false. When we leave here to go on into the next battleground, I know that I for one shall go with the greatest reluctance.

On the day of final peace, the last stroke of what we call the "Big Picture" will be drawn. I haven't written anything about the "Big Picture," because I don't know anything about it. I only know what we see from our worm's-eye view, and our segment of the picture consists only of tired and dirty soldiers who are alive and don't want to die; of long darkened convoys in the middle of the night; of shocked silent men wandering back down the hill from battle; of chow lines and Atabrine tablets and foxholes and burning tanks and Arabs holding up eggs and the rustle of high-flown shells; of jeeps and petrol dumps and smelly bedding rolls and C rations and cactus patches and blown bridges and dead mules and hospital tents and shirt collars greasy-black from months of wearing; and of laughter too, and anger and wine and lovely flowers and constant cussing. All these it is composed of; and of graves and graves and graves.

That is our war, and we will carry it with us as we go on from one battlefield to another until it is all over, leaving some of us behind on every beach, in every field. We are just beginning with the ones who lie back of us here in Tunisia. I don't know whether it was their good fortune or their misfortune to get out of it so early in the game. I guess it doesn't make any difference, once a man has gone. Medals and speeches and victories are nothing to them any more. They died and others lived and nobody knows why it is so. They died and thereby the rest of us can go on and on. When we leave here for the next shore, there is nothing we can do for the ones beneath the wooden crosses, except perhaps to pause and murmur, "Thanks, pal."

Questions

1. What does Pyle mean when he says, "A team may be a composite hero, but not an individual"? (165)

2. When Pyle returns to the front lines, how does he account for the change in the men from "the normal belief that taking human life is sinful, over to a new professional outlook where killing is a craft"? (167)

3. How can veterans make the transition back to a "normal" moral belief that killing is wrong, after having practiced killing as a "craft"? (167)

4. What does Pyle mean when he says that the front-line soldiers are the only ones who are "truly at war"? (168)

5. In explaining the nature of war to those at home, why does Pyle emphasize that of the troops, "only comparatively few ever saw the enemy, ever shot at him, or were shot at by him"? (169)

6. Why does Pyle think that after a while, for warriors in combat, "home gradually grows less vivid; the separation from it less agonizing"? (170–171)

7. Why does Pyle feel compassion for the snake that invades his tent and pity the snake because he is not a man? How is this feeling related to his war experience?

8. As a news correspondent embedded with the troops, is Pyle right to include himself when he speaks of "our war"? (177) Should news reporters on the front line be considered participants in the war effort instead of merely spectators?

Frank O'Connor

Frank O'Connor (1903–1966) was born Michael O'Donovan in the slums of Cork, Ireland. At that time, Irish nationalists had been struggling for years for independence from British rule. In April 1916 the nationalist Easter Rising failed, and fifteen rebel leaders were executed. Outraged by these events, O'Connor, still a teenager, began volunteering for the Irish Republican Army.

In 1922 O'Connor was taken prisoner in the civil strife, but he was able to further his education through the prison's lectures, concerts, and library. He used the pseudonym Frank O'Connor for the first time in 1925. In 1931 he sold his short story "Guests of the Nation" to the *Atlantic Monthly* magazine, and a collection of his stories was published the same year to great acclaim. He would go on to publish more than one hundred fifty stories.

In "Guests of the Nation," O'Connor explores the tragic dissonance between soldiers' personal attitudes toward enemy troops, regarding them as young men just like themselves, and the official obligation to carry out their military duty. The tension between human connection and ideological differences is played out as various characters struggle with their impulses and their orders.

O'Connor's piece raises fundamental issues of compassion and humanity. The fraternal bonds—even between foes—are apparent, and yet concerted efforts are made by the military command to dehumanize the prisoners and alienate one group of men from the other. O'Connor's story prompts questions about the degree of empathy that is possible and advisable between enemies in wartime, who are, after all, fellow human beings.

GUESTS OF THE NATION

1

At dusk the big Englishman Belcher would shift his long legs out of the ashes and ask, "Well, chums, what about it?" and Noble or me would say, "As you please, chum" (for we had picked up some of their curious expressions), and the little Englishman 'Awkins would light the lamp and produce the cards. Sometimes Jeremiah Donovan would come up of an evening and supervise the play, and grow excited over 'Awkins's cards (which he always played badly), and shout at him as if he was one of our own, "Ach, you divil you, why didn't you play the tray?" But, ordinarily, Jeremiah was a sober and contented poor devil like the big Englishman Belcher and was looked up to at all only because he was a fair hand at documents, though slow enough at these, I vow. He wore a small cloth hat and big gaiters over his long pants, and seldom did I perceive his hands outside the pockets of that pants. He reddened when you talked to him, tilting from toe to heel and back and looking down all the while at his big farmer's feet. His uncommon broad accent was a great source of jest to me, I being from the town, as you may recognise.

I couldn't at the time see the point of me and Noble being with Belcher and 'Awkins at all, for it was and is my fixed belief you could have planted that pair in any untended spot from this to Claregalway and they'd have stayed put and flourished like a native weed. I never seen in my short experience two men that took to the country as they did.

They were handed on to us by the Second Battalion to keep when the search for them became too hot, and Noble and myself, being young, took charge with a natural feeling of responsibility. But little 'Awkins made us look like right fools when he displayed he knew the countryside as well as we did and something more. "You're the bloke they calls Bonaparte?" he said to me. "Well, Bonaparte, Mary Brigid Ho'Connell was arskin abaout you and said 'ow you'd a pair of socks belonging to 'er young brother." For it seemed, as they explained it, that the Second used to have little evenings of their own, and some of the girls of the neighbourhood would turn in, and, seeing they were such decent fellows, our lads couldn't well ignore the two Englishmen, but invited them in and were hail-fellow-well-met with them. 'Awkins told me he learned to dance "The Walls of Limerick" and "The Siege of Ennis" and "The Waves of Tory" in a night or two, though naturally he could not return the compliment, because our lads at that time did not dance foreign dances on principle.

So whatever privileges and favours Belcher and 'Awkins had with the Second they duly took with us, and after the first evening we gave up all pretence of keeping a close eye on their behaviour. Not that they could have got far, for they had a notable accent and wore khaki tunics and overcoats with civilian pants and boots. But it's my belief that they never had an idea of escaping and were quite contented with their lot.

Now, it was a treat to see how Belcher got off with the old woman of the house we were staying in. She was a great warrant to scold, and crotchety even with us, but before ever she had a chance of giving our guests, as I may call them, a lick of her tongue, Belcher had made her his friend for life. She was breaking sticks at the time, and Belcher, who hadn't been in the house for more than ten minutes, jumped up out of his seat and went across to her.

"Allow me, madam," he says, smiling his queer little smile; "please allow me," and takes the hatchet from her hand. She was struck too parlatic to speak, and ever after Belcher would be at her heels, carrying a bucket, or basket, or load of turf, as the case might be. As Noble wittily remarked, he got into looking before she leapt, and hot water or any little thing she wanted, Belcher would have it ready before her. For such a huge man (and though I am five foot ten myself I had to look up to him) he had an uncommon shortness—or should I say lack—of speech. It took us some time to get used to him walking in and out like a ghost, without a syllable out of him. Especially because 'Awkins talked enough for a platoon, it was strange to hear big Belcher with his toes in the ashes come out with a solitary "Excuse me, chum," or "That's right, chum." His one and only abiding passion was cards, and I will say for him that he was a good card player. He could have fleeced me and Noble many a time; only if we lost to him, 'Awkins lost to us, and 'Awkins played with the money Belcher gave him.

'Awkins lost to us because he talked too much, and I think now we lost to Belcher for the same reason. 'Awkins and Noble would spit at one another about religion into the early hours of the morning; the little Englishman as you could see worrying the soul out of young Noble (whose brother was a priest) with a string of questions that would puzzle a cardinal. And to make it worse, even in treating of these holy subjects, 'Awkins had a deplorable tongue; I never in all my career struck across a man who could mix such a variety of cursing and bad language into the simplest topic. Oh, a terrible man was little 'Awkins, and a fright to argue! He never did a stroke of work, and when he had no one else to talk to he fixed his claws into the old woman.

I am glad to say that in her he met his match, for one day when he tried to get her to complain profanely of the drought, she gave him a great comedown by blaming the drought upon Jupiter Pluvius (a deity neither 'Awkins nor I had ever heard of, though Noble said among the pagans he was held to have something to do with the rain). And another day the same 'Awkins was swearing at the capitalists for starting the German war, when the old dame laid down her iron, puckered up her little crab's mouth, and said: "Mr. 'Awkins, you can say what you please about the war, thinking to deceive me because I'm an ignorant old woman, but I know well what started the war. It was that Italian count that stole the heathen divinity out of the temple in Japan, for believe me, Mr. 'Awkins, nothing but sorrow and want follows them that disturbs the hidden powers!" Oh, a queer old dame, as you remark!

2

So one evening we had our tea together, and 'Awkins lit the lamp and we all sat in to cards. Jeremiah Donovan came in, too, and sat down and watched us for a while. Though he was a shy man and didn't speak much, it was easy to see he had no great love for the two Englishmen, and I was surprised it hadn't struck me so clearly before. Well, like that in the story, a terrible dispute blew up late in the evening between 'Awkins and Noble, about capitalists and priests and love of your own country.

"The capitalists," says 'Awkins with an angry gulp, "the capitalists pays the priests to tell you abaout the next world, so's you waon't notice what they do in this!"

"Nonsense, man," says Noble, losing his temper. "Before ever a capitalist was thought of people believed in the next world."

'Awkins stood up as if he was preaching a sermon. "Oh, they did, did they?" he says with a sneer. "They believed all the things you believe, that's what you mean? And you believe that God created Hadam, and Hadam created Shem, and Shem created Jehoshophat. You believe all the silly hold fairy tale about Heve and Heden and the happle. Well, listen to me, chum. If you're entitled to 'old to a silly belief like that, I'm entitled to 'old to my own silly belief—which is that the fust thing your God created was a bleedin' capitalist, with mirality and Rolls-Royce complete. Am I right, chum?" he says then to Belcher.

"You're right, chum," says Belcher, with his queer smile, and gets up from the table to stretch his long legs into the fire and stroke his moustache. So, seeing that Jeremiah Donovan was going, and there was no knowing when the conversation about religion would be over, I took my hat and went out with him. We strolled down towards the village together, and then he suddenly stopped, and blushing and mumbling and shifting, as his way was, from toe to heel, he said I ought to be behind keeping guard on the prisoners. And I, having it put to me so suddenly, asked him what the hell he wanted a guard on the prisoners at all for, and said that so far as Noble and me were concerned we had talked it over and would rather be out with a column. "What use is that pair to us?" I asked him.

He looked at me for a spell and said, "I thought you knew we were keeping them as hostages." "Hostages—?" says I, not quite understanding. "The enemy," he says in his heavy way, "have prisoners belong' to us, and now they talk of shooting them. If they shoot our prisoners, we'll shoot theirs, and serve them right." "Shoot them?" said I, the possibility just beginning to dawn on me. "Shoot them, exactly," said he. "Now," said I, "wasn't it very unforeseen of you not to tell me and Noble that?" "How so?" he asks. "Seeing that we were acting as guards upon them, of course." "And hadn't you reason enough to guess that much?" "We had not, Jeremiah Donovan, we had not. How were we to know when the men were on our hands so long?" "And what difference does it make? The enemy have our prisoners as long or longer, haven't they?" "It makes a great difference," said I. "How so?" said he sharply; but I couldn't tell him the difference it made, for I was struck too silly to speak. "And when may we expect to be released from this anyway?" said I. "You may expect it tonight," says he. "Or tomorrow or the next day at latest. So if it's hanging around here that worries you, you'll be free soon enough."

I cannot explain it even now, how sad I felt, but I went back to the cottage a miserable man. When I arrived the discussion was still on, 'Awkins holding forth to all and sundry that there was no next world at all and Noble answering in his best canonical style that there was. But I saw 'Awkins was after having the best of it. "Do you know what, chum?" he was saying, with his saucy smile. "I think you're jest as big a bleedin' hunbeliever as I am. You say you believe in the next world, and you know jest as much abaout the next world as I do, which is sweet damn-all. What's 'eaven? You dunno. Where's 'eaven? You dunno. Who's in 'eaven? You dunno. You know sweet damn-all! I arsk you again, do they wear wings?"

"Very well then," says Noble, "they do; is that enough for you? They do wear wings." "Where do they get them, then? Who makes them? 'Ave they a fact'ry for wings? 'Ave they a sort of store where you 'ands in your chit and tikes your bleedin' wings? Answer me that."

"Oh, you're an impossible man to argue with," says Noble. "Now, listen to me—." And the pair of them went off again.

It was long after midnight when we locked up the Englishmen and went to bed ourselves. As I blew out the candle I told Noble what Jeremiah Donovan had told me. Noble took it very quietly. After we had been in bed about an hour he asked me did I think we ought to tell the Englishmen. I having thought of the same thing myself (among many others) said no, because it was more than likely the English wouldn't shoot our men, and anyhow it wasn't to be supposed the brigade who were always up and down with the Second Battalion and knew the Englishmen well would be likely to want them bumped off. "I think so," says Noble. "It would be sort of cruelty to put the wind up them now." "It was very unforeseen of

Jeremiah Donovan anyhow," says I, and by Noble's silence I realised he took my meaning.

So I lay there half the night, and thought and thought, and picturing myself and young Noble trying to prevent the brigade from shooting 'Awkins and Belcher sent a cold sweat out through me. Because there were men on the brigade you daren't let nor hinder without a gun in your hand, and at any rate, in those days disunion between brothers seemed to me an awful crime. I knew better after.

It was next morning we found it so hard to face Belcher and 'Awkins with a smile. We went about the house all day scarcely saying a word. Belcher didn't mind us much; he was stretched into the ashes as usual with his usual look of waiting in quietness for something unforeseen to happen, but little 'Awkins gave us a bad time with his audacious gibing and questioning. He was disgusted at Noble's not answering him back. "Why can't you tike your beating like a man, chum?" he says. "You with your Hadam and Heve! I'm a communist—or an anarchist. An anarchist, that's what I am." And for hours after he went round the house, mumbling when the fit took him, "Hadam and Heve! Hadam and Heve!"

3

I don't know clearly how we got over that day, but get over it we did, and a great relief it was when the tea things were cleared away and Belcher said in his peaceable manner, "Well, chums, what about it?" So we all sat round the table and 'Awkins produced the cards, and at that moment I heard Jeremiah Donovan's footsteps up the path, and a dark presentiment crossed my mind. I rose quietly from the table and laid my hand on him before he reached the door. "What do you want?" I asked him. "I want those two soldier friends of yours," he says reddening. "Is that the way it is, Jeremiah Donovan?" I ask. "That's the way. There were four of our lads went west this morning, one of them a boy of sixteen." "That's bad, Jeremiah," says I.

At that moment Noble came out, and we walked down the path together talking in whispers. Feeney, the local intelligence officer, was standing by the gate. "What are you going to do about it?" I asked

Jeremiah Donovan. "I want you and Noble to bring them out: you can tell them they're being shifted again; that'll be the quietest way." "Leave me out of that," says Noble suddenly. Jeremiah Donovan looked at him hard for a minute or two. "All right so," he said peaceably. "You and Feeney collect a few tools from the shed and dig a hole by the far end of the bog. Bonaparte and I'll be after you in about twenty minutes. But whatever else you do, don't let anyone see you with the tools. No one must know but the four of ourselves."

We saw Feeney and Noble go round to the houseen, where the tools were kept, and sidle in. Everything, if I can so express myself, was tottering before my eyes, and I left Jeremiah Donovan to do the explaining as best he could, while I took a seat and said nothing. He told them they were to go back to the Second. 'Awkins let a mouthful of curses out of him at that, and it was plain that Belcher, though he said nothing, was duly perturbed. The old woman was for having them stay in spite of us, and she did not shut her mouth until Jeremiah Donovan lost his temper and said some nasty things to her. Within the house by this time it was pitch-dark, but no one thought of lighting the lamp, and in the darkness the two Englishmen fetched their khaki topcoats and said goodbye to the woman of the house. "Just as a man mikes a 'ome of a bleedin' place," mumbles 'Awkins shaking her by the hand, "some bastard at headquarters thinks you're too cushy and shunts you off." Belcher shakes her hand very hearty. "A thousand thanks, madam," he says, "a thousand thanks for everything . . ." as though he'd made it all up.

We go round to the back of the house and down towards the fatal bog. Then Jeremiah Donovan comes out with what is in his mind. "There were four of our lads shot by your fellows this morning, so now you're to be bumped off." "Cut that stuff out," says 'Awkins, flaring up. "It's bad enough to be mucked about such as we are without you plying at soldiers." "It's true," says Jeremiah Donovan. "I'm sorry, 'Awkins, but 'tis true," and comes out with the usual rigmarole about doing our duty and obeying our superiors. "Cut it out," says 'Awkins irritably. "Cut it out!"

Then, when Donovan sees he is not being believed he turns to me. "Ask Bonaparte here," he says. "I don't need to arsk Bonaparte. Me and Bonaparte are chums." "Isn't it true, Bonaparte?" says Jeremiah Donovan solemnly to me. "It is," I say sadly, "it is." 'Awkins stops. "Now, for Christ's sike . . ." "I mean it, chum," I say. "You daon't saound as if you mean it. You knaow well you don't mean it." "Well, if he don't I do," says Jeremiah Donovan. "Why the 'ell sh'd you want to shoot me, Jeremiah Donovan?" "Why the hell should your people take out four prisoners and shoot them in cold blood upon a barrack square?" I perceive Jeremiah Donovan is trying to encourage himself with hot words.

Anyway, he took little 'Awkins by the arm and dragged him on, but it was impossible to make him understand that we were in earnest. From which you will perceive how difficult it was for me, as I kept feeling my Smith and Wesson and thinking what I would do if they happened to put up a fight or run for it, and wishing in my heart they would. I knew if only they ran I would never fire on them. "Was Noble in this?" 'Awkins wanted to know, and we said yes. He laughed. But why should Noble want to shoot him? Why should we want to shoot him? What had he done to us? Weren't we chums (the word lingers painfully in my memory)? Weren't we? Didn't we understand him and didn't he understand us? Did either of us imagine for an instant that he'd shoot us for all the so-and-so brigadiers in the so-and-so British army? By this time I began to perceive in the dusk the desolate edges of the bog that was to be their last earthly bed, and so great a sadness overtook my mind I could not answer him. We walked along the edge of it in the darkness, and every now and then 'Awkins would call a halt and begin again, just as if he was wound up, about us being chums, and I was in despair that nothing but the cold and open grave made ready for his presence would convince him that we meant it all. But all the same, if you can understand, I didn't want him to be bumped off.

4

At last we saw the unsteady glint of a lantern in the distance and made towards it. Noble was carrying it, and Feeney stood somewhere in the darkness behind, and somehow the picture of the two of them so silent in the boglands was like the pain of death in my heart. Belcher, on recognising Noble, said, "'Allo, chum," in his usual peaceable way, but 'Awkins flew at the poor boy immediately, and the dispute began all over again, only that Noble hadn't a word to say for himself and stood there with the swaying lantern between his gaitered legs.

It was Jeremiah Donovan who did the answering. 'Awkins asked for the twentieth time (for it seemed to haunt his mind) if anybody thought he'd shoot Noble. "You would," says Jeremiah Donovan shortly. "I wouldn't, damn you!" "You would if you knew you'd be shot for not doing it." "I wouldn't, not if I was to be shot twenty times over; he's my chum. And Belcher wouldn't—isn't that right, Belcher?" "That's right, chum," says Belcher peaceably. "Damned if I would. Anyway, who says Noble'd be shot if I wasn't bumped off? What d'you think I'd do if I was in Noble's place and we were out in the middle of a blasted bog?" "What would you do?" "I'd go with him wherever he was going. I'd share my last bob with him and stick by 'im through thick and thin."

"We've had enough of this," says Jeremiah Donovan, cocking his revolver. "Is there any message you want to send before I fire?" "No, there isn't, but . . ." "Do you want to say your prayers?" 'Awkins came out with a cold-blooded remark that shocked even me and turned on Noble again. "Listen to me, Noble," he said. "You and me are chums. You won't come over to my side, so I'll come over to your side. Is that fair? Just you give me a rifle and I'll go with you wherever you want."

Nobody answered him.

"Do you understand?" he said. "I'm through with it all. I'm a deserter or anything else you like, but from this on I'm one of you. Does that prove to you that I mean what I say?" Noble raised his head, but as Donovan began to speak he lowered it again without answering. "For the last time, have you any messages to send?" says Donovan in a cold excited voice.

"Ah, shut up, you, Donovan; you don't understand me, but these fellows do. They're my chums; they stand by me and I stand by them. We're not the capitalist tools you seem to think us."

I alone of the crowd saw Donovan raise his Webley to the back of 'Awkins's neck, and as he did so I shut my eyes and tried to say a prayer. 'Awkins had begun to say something else when Donovan let fly, and as I opened my eyes at the bang, I saw him stagger at the knees and lie out flat at Noble's feet, slowly, and as quiet as a child, with the lantern light falling sadly upon his lean legs and bright farmer's boots. We all stood very still for a while watching him settle out in the last agony.

Then Belcher quietly takes out a handkerchief and begins to tie it about his own eyes (for in our excitement we had forgotten to offer the same for 'Awkins), and, seeing it is not big enough, turns and asks for a loan of mine. I give it to him, and as he knots the two together he points with his foot at 'Awkins. "'E's not quite dead," he says. "Better give 'im another." Sure enough 'Awkins's left knee as we see it under the lantern is rising again. I bend down and put my gun to his ear; then, recollecting myself and the company of Belcher, I stand up again with a few hasty words. Belcher understands what is in my mind. "Give 'im 'is first," he says. "I don't mind. Poor bastard, we dunno what's 'appening to 'im now." As by this time I am beyond all feeling, I kneel down again and skilfully give 'Awkins the last shot so as to put him forever out of pain.

Belcher, who is fumbling a bit awkwardly with the handkerchiefs, comes out with a laugh when he hears the shot. It is the first time I have heard him laugh, and it sends a shiver down my spine, coming as it does so inappropriately upon the tragic death of his old friend. "Poor blighter," he says quietly. "And last night he was so curious abaout it all. It's very queer, chums, I always think. Naow, 'e knows as much abaout it as they'll ever let 'im know, and last night 'e was all in the dark."

Donovan helps him to tie the handkerchiefs about his eyes. "Thanks, chum," he says. Donovan asks him if there are any messages he would like to send. "Naow, chum," he says, "none for me. If any of you likes to write to 'Awkins's mother, you'll find a letter from 'er in 'is pocket. But my missus left me eight years ago. Went away with another fellow and took the kid with her. I likes the feelin' of a 'ome, (as you may 'ave noticed), but I couldn't start again after that."

We stand around like fools now that he can no longer see us. Donovan looks at Noble, and Noble shakes his head. Then Donovan raises his Webley again, and just at that moment Belcher laughs his queer nervous laugh again. He must think we are talking of him; anyway, Donovan lowers his gun. "'Scuse me, chums," says Belcher. "I feel I'm talking the 'ell of a lot . . . and so silly . . . abaout me being so 'andy abaout a 'ouse. But this thing come on me so sudden. You'll forgive me, I'm sure." "You don't want to say a prayer?" asks Jeremiah Donovan. "No, chum," he replies, "I don't think that'd 'elp. I'm ready if you want to get it over." "You understand," says Jeremiah Donovan, "it's not so much our doing. It's our duty, so to speak." Belcher's head is raised like a real blind man's, so that you can only see his nose and chin in the lamplight. "I never could make out what duty was myself," he said, "but I think you're all good lads, if that's what you mean. I'm not complaining." Noble, with a look of desperation, signals to Donovan, and in a flash Donovan raises his gun and fires. The big man goes over like a sack of meal, and this time there is no need of a second shot.

I don't remember much about the burying but that it was worse than all the rest, because we had to carry the warm corpses a few yards before we sunk them in the windy bog. It was all mad lonely, with only a bit of lantern between ourselves and the pitch-blackness, and birds hooting and screeching all round, disturbed by the guns. Noble had to search 'Awkins first to get the letter from his mother. Then, having smoothed all signs of the grave away, Noble and I collected our tools, and said goodbye to the others, and went back along the desolate edge of the treacherous bog without a word. We put the tools in the houseen and went into the house. The kitchen was pitch-black and cold, just as we left it, and the old woman was sitting over the hearth telling her beads. We walked past her into the room, and Noble struck a match to light the lamp. Just then she rose quietly and came to the doorway, being not at all so bold or crabbed as usual.

"What did ye do with them?" she says in a sort of whisper, and Noble took such a mortal start the match quenched in his trembling hand. "What's that?" he asks without turning round. "I heard ye," she said. "What did you hear?" asks Noble, but sure he wouldn't deceive a child the way he said it. "I heard ye. Do ye think I wasn't listening to ye putting the things back in the houseen?" Noble struck another match, and this time the lamp lit for him. "Was that what ye did with them?" she said, and Noble said nothing—after all, what could he say?

So then, by God, she fell on her two knees by the door and began telling her beads, and after a minute or two Noble went on his knees by the fireplace, so I pushed my way out past her and stood at the door, watching the stars and listening to the damned shrieking of the birds. It is so strange what you feel at such moments, and not to be written afterwards. Noble says he felt he seen everything ten times as big, perceiving nothing around him but the little patch of black bog with the two Englishmen

Questions

1. Why do Donovan and Bonaparte disagree on whether the length of time the prisoners have been held in custody makes any difference?

2. Given Bonaparte's familiarity with the prisoners and his strong objection to killing them, why doesn't he help them escape?

3. Why does Donovan insist on keeping the execution secret, if it is done in retaliation for the execution of Irish prisoners by the British?

4. Why does Belcher forgive his executioners?

5. Is Donovan making a legitimate distinction when he says that "it's not so much our doing. It's our duty, so to speak"? (190–91)

6. Were Donovan and his Irish compatriots justified in killing Belcher and Hawkins?

J. Saunders Redding

Understanding why their nation engages in a particular war has been a concern for the military and their families in each generation that has been called up to serve in the armed forces. Every conflict is accompanied by questions that force society and individuals to reexamine their deepest values.

In the following essay, J. Saunders Redding (1906–1988) writes from the perspective of an African American during World War II, a time when racial equality both within and outside the United States military was still a distant goal. Redding had a long career as a university professor and prominent African American scholar. His books reflect his belief in the integration of races in American society and include studies of African American literature as well as the psychology of race relations.

In "A Negro Looks at This War," Redding expresses his surprise that he can find reasons to give his support to the Allied cause in World War II. Previously, he had felt that the only war that he could support would be a race war, fighting for equality with whites. He has no belief in heroics, and his family long regarded cynically the public and private reasons for war. After their service in World War I, African American soldiers returned to the United States and found that the sacrifices they had made did not guarantee progress in securing their civil rights on the home front. And though at first Redding can understand their disillusionment, his own reflections on the situation eventually lead him to a different point of view.

Redding's essay raises questions about how both civilians and servicemen and servicewomen can support a nation's common cause in wartime while at the same time having deep-seated doubts about their nation's commitment to providing justice and equality for all its citizens.

A NEGRO LOOKS AT THIS WAR

1

I was listening sleeplessly to an all-night program of music interspersed with war news, bad news. The bad news of the war had not seemed bad news to me. Indeed, on this night, it was again giving me a kind of grim, perverted satisfaction. Some nonwhite men were killing some white men and it might be that the nonwhites would win. This gratified me in a way difficult to explain. Perhaps, in a world conquered and ruled by yellow men, there would be no onus attached to being black and I, a Negro. . . . Then a peculiar thing happened. Something seemed to burst and I knew suddenly that I believed in this war we Americans are fighting. I think I said aloud, with a kind of wonder: "I, a Negro, believe in this war we Americans are fighting." The thought or revelation gave rise to an emotion—keen, purging, astringent.

The thought and the conviction amazed me, for I had thought that I could never believe in war again, or that any war in which I might believe would be truly a race war; and then, naturally, I would believe as I had been taught by innumerable circumstances to believe. I would believe in the side of the darker peoples. But I could envision no such war even in the remote future, for I had been trained in the principles called Christian. I had been trained to believe in the brotherhood of man and that we were approaching that glorious state—slowly, but before complete catastrophe could overtake us.

War had no heroic traditions for me. Wars were white folks'. All wars in historical memory. The last war, and the Spanish-American War before that, and the Civil War. I had been brought up in a way that admitted of no heroics. I think my parents were right. Life for them was a fierce, bitter, soul-searing war of spiritual and economic attrition; they fought it without heroics, but with stubborn heroism. Their heroism was screwed up to a pitch of idealism so intense that it found a safety valve in cynicism about the heroics of white folks' war. This cynicism went back at least as far as my paternal grandmother, whose fierce eyes used to lash the faces of her five grandchildren as she said, "An' he done som'pin big an' brave away down dere to Chickymorgy an' dey made a iron image of him 'cause he got his head blowed off an' his stomick blowed out fightin' to keep his slaves." I cannot convey the scorn and cynicism she put into her picture of that hero-son of her slave-master, but I have never forgotten.

I was nearly ten when we entered the last war in 1917. The European fighting, and the sinking of the *Lusitania*, had seemed as remote, as distantly meaningless to us, as the Battle of Hastings. Then we went in and suddenly the city was flag-draped, slogan-plastered, and as riotously gay as on circus half-holidays. I remembered one fine Sunday we came upon an immense new billboard with a new slogan: GIVE! TO MAKE THE WORLD SAFE FOR DEMOCRACY. My brother, who was the oldest of us, asked what making the world safe for democracy meant. My father frowned, but before he could answer, my mother broke in.

"It's just something to say, like . . ."—and then she was stuck until she hit upon one of the family's old jokes—"like 'Let's make a million dollars.'" We all laughed, but the bitter core of her meaning lay revealed, even for the youngest of us, like the stone in a halved peach.

Even then the war was only as relevant and as close as the powder plant across the river. Explosions at the plant often rattled the windows and shook the crockery in our house. But Negroes were making big money. The river steamers carried three shifts of them a day. They were a reckless and a profane lot, full of swagger and talk on seventy-five dollars a week and double time for overtime. They did not mind having their skins turn nicotine yellow from the powder they were making for white men to kill each other. "They're white, ain't they? Well, let 'em fight. We hates peace!"

For it was thought at first that the war was more exclusively than ever a white folks' war. Long before the first contingent of draftees left the city, there was a mess about drafting. It seems that President Wilson, or someone, did not want colored soldiers. Later, the someone changed his mind and some colored men went away. By this time, trainloads of soldiers were rolling through our station every day. The Red Cross ladies were always at the station, giving away chocolates and cigarettes, doughnuts and coffee. "Nothing's too good for our soldier boys." But we heard that whenever a colored troop train rolled in, the ladies retired to the station-master's office until it was gone again.

But someone really had changed his mind completely and colored boys were not merely staying in the camps to clean up after the white boys. Somebody said the Ninth and Tenth Cavalry units had gone across. Somebody said they would not let Colonel Young go, however. They said that they did not want to make him a brigadier general and that he was somewhere, Cuba or Haiti or down on the Mexican border, dying of a broken heart. Whoever in the world ever heard of a nigger general!

Then somebody said that colored boys were really getting killed. And finally, we learned that in Washington they had called out a Negro detachment to guard government property. We even saw pictures in a colored paper. White soldiers could not always be trusted, the article said. A white soldier might be an Austrian or a German, anything, dressed up in a soldier's suit. But a "nigger" (I remember the word was in quotes) in khaki was Uncle Sam himself. You knew what he was the moment you looked at him. "Yes," I remember my father saying in a weary, strangely bitter voice, "that's the trouble. You take him for granted."

There was an excited, theatrical, patriotic glamour. Every Saturday evening during that summer, under the vast façade of the courthouse and county building, there was a community sing. The city band played. The words were flashed from a magic lantern onto a huge screen and everyone sang his heart out. "Over There"; "Long, Long Trail"; "Keep the Home Fires Burning"; and "Tipperary." By the time we came to the close and the throat-caught singing of the "Star-Spangled Banner," a great many men and women were crying openly, unashamedly. But my Uncle Silas, who was with us in those days, always broke into a ribald parody of the national anthem as we went down the hill toward home.

After she discovered that Negro soldiers really were dying, my mother did Red Cross work in the small segregated unit. Her youngest brother, who won a commission in the segregated officers' training camp in Iowa, was killed. My father worked in the segregated unit to subscribe the Liberty Loans. But both my parents laughed at the little wizened white man who came to our door selling a cheap lithograph. It represented a colored soldier and a colored sailor, one on each side of crossed American flags. Below them was a legend:

You fought and died at San Juan Hill;
Now go and get old Kaiser Bill.

There were several opinions. Negroes were not fighting. They were dying of influenza and dysentery behind the lines, where they served as flunkies. Negroes were fighting. They were holding positions white soldiers could not hold in the most dangerous salients. When they died, they were being dumped into graves without markers of any kind. The positions they were fighting had no medical detachments, no Red Cross units, no hospital facilities. But they died. In any event, quite a few of them died before the war was over.

I remember that first, false, mad armistice. Everyone seemed crazy drunk and everywhere there was a spontaneous and unabashed breakdown of lines. Banker and butcher, coal heaver and clerk, black and white, men and women went worming and screaming joyously through the streets. I also remember the real armistice, and that there was a block party which Negroes could not attend, and that the police would not give them a permit to hold one of their own in the narrow, factory-flanked streets where most of them lived. When the lynchings and the riots started again—in East St. Louis, Chicago, Chester, even in Washington— we knew that, so far as the Negro was concerned, the war had been a failure, and "making the world safe for democracy" a good phrase bandied about by weak or blind or unprincipled men.

And so, since I have reached maturity and thought a man's thoughts and had a man's—a Negro man's—experiences, I have thought that I could never believe in war again. Yet I believe in this one.

2

There are many things about this war that I do not like, just as there are many things about "practical" Christianity that I do not like. But I believe in Christianity, and if I accept the shoddy and unfulfilling in the conduct of this war, I do it as voluntarily and as purposefully as I accept the trash in the workings of "practical" Christianity. I do not like the odor of political pandering that arises from some groups. I do not like these "race incidents" in the camps. I do not like the world's not knowing officially that there were Negro soldiers on Bataan with General Wainwright. I do not like the constant references to the Japs as "yellow bastards," "yellow bellies," and "yellow monkeys," as if color had something to do with treachery, as if color were the issue and the thing we are fighting rather than oppression, slavery, and a way of life hateful and nauseating. These and other things I do not like, yet I believe in the war.

The issue is plain. The issue, simply, is freedom. Freedom is a precious thing. Proof of its preciousness is that so many men wait patiently for its fulfillment, accept defilement and insult in the hope of it, die in the attainment of it. It used to seem shamefully silly to me to hear Negroes talk about freedom. But now I know that we Negroes here in America know a lot about freedom and love it more than a great many people who have long had it. It is because we have so little of it, really, that it used to seem silly to me to hear talk about preserving it. Giving me a penny, my father would remark in a satirical way, "That's not enough money, son, to do you any good. You might as well throw it away." I did not see that there was enough freedom to do me much good. It's a stage most public-schooled Negroes go through.

We go through a stage of blind, willful delusion. Later, we come to see that in the logic of a system based on freedom and the dignity of man we have a chance. We see that now and again there are advances. And this new seeing kindles the hope that Americans are really not proud of their silly prejudices, their thick-skinned discriminations, their expensive segregations. And now, I think, we know that whatever the mad logic of the New Order, there is no hope for us under it. The ethnic theories of the Hitler "master folk" admit of no chance of freedom, but rather glory in its expungement.

This is a war to keep men free. The struggle to broaden and lengthen the road of freedom—our own private and important war to enlarge freedom here in America—will come later. That this private, intra-American war will be carried on and won is the only real reason we Negroes have to fight. We must keep the road open. Did we not believe in a victory in that intra-American war, we could not believe in nor stomach the compulsion of this. If we could not believe in the realization of democratic freedom for ourselves, certainly no one could ask us to die for the preservation of that ideal for others. But to broaden and lengthen the road of freedom is different from preserving it. And our first duty is to keep the road of freedom open. It must be done continuously. It is the duty of the whole people to do this. Our next duty (and this, too, is the whole people's) is to broaden that road so that more people can travel it without snarling traffic. To die in these duties is to die for something.

There are men who do not like the road of freedom, men who would block it, who would destroy it, and that is what the war is about. What we on our side fight for now has nothing to do with color, nor political forms. It has everything to do with the estimation in which we hold ourselves and in which, therefore, others hold us. There are these men, these "master folk," who hold that all other peoples are of less worth than they. It is an article of faith with them: not a thing of intellection, but an emotional thing, and it is hard to be rid of. Where these men find human dignity and aspiration, they set about to degrade and quench it. This is an insult and an injury that has at last to be avenged in blood. Nine-tenths of the world's people have been insulted. And certainly, since this insult is so patently the issue, once we Negroes have fought to avenge it to other men (and ourselves, also) our brothers in blood-revenge will not return that insult to us again, as, I say it softly, they have so long done. Certainly now, over the stink of blood, the Holocaust, they will know that this war for their freedom will be a dead end, unless the road of freedom is made a broad, through highway for all peoples forever.

This, of course, is hope. But you cannot fight wars without hope. This is also belief. And you cannot fight a victorious war without a belief in the thing you fight for. Here in America we believe, however falteringly, in the individual worth and dignity of man. Human dignity counts here.

3

But if the satanic destinies of the New Order fulfill themselves? I, a Negro, would not count. The master folk plainly say I will not count if their will prevails. There are people already who do not count: they are in ghettos and concentration camps. There are Jews and Poles and Chinese who do not count. And we Negroes would be done in purposefully, coldly, "according to plan." None of the precious techniques of survival which we learned in slavery would avail. They are smart and they are zealous, those master folk. They are zealous enough in pursuit of their racial purity to brook no interference, and smart enough to know that the lips and thighs of black women have been found sweet before. None of our skills, none of our will to live would count. We would die; and it would be better to die because we are a menace to what we hate than to live in safety in support of it.

I believe in this war, finally, because I believe in the ultimate vindication of the wisdom of the brotherhood of man. This is not foggy idealism. I think that the growing manifestations of the interdependence of all men is an argument for the wisdom of brotherhood. I think that the shrunk compass of the world is an argument. I think that the talk of united nations and of planned interdependence is an argument. I do not know what social forms these arguments will be molded into to achieve the final vindication of wisdom, but I believe that these arguments are themselves so wise and strong that they will push men up, not to a final victory over baseness and fear and selfishness, but to the height from which they can look wisdom in the eye and know that there is only the choice between brotherhood and anarchy.

More immediately, I believe in this war because I believe in America. I believe in what America professes to stand for. Nor is this, I think, whistling in the dark. There are a great many things wrong here. There are only a few men of good will. I do not lose sight of that. I know the inequalities, the outraged hopes and faith, the inbred hate; and I know that there are people who wish merely to lay these by in the closet of the national mind until the crisis is over. But it would be equally foolish for me to lose sight of the advances that are made, the barriers that are leveled, the privileges that grow. Foolish, too, to remain blind to the distinction that exists between simple race prejudice, already growing moribund under the impact of this war, and theories of racial superiority as a basic tenet of a societal system—theories at bottom are the avowed justification for suppression, defilement, and murder.

Questions

1. Why does Redding's change of attitude concerning the war happen when he is listening to bad news about the war?

2. Why does Redding refer to his new opinion about the war as "keen, purging, astringent"? (195)

3. Does Redding think supporting a war against foreign regimes that oppose freedom will directly influence the "private, intra-American war" for the freedom of all people within the United States? (199)

4. What does Redding mean when he says, "But to broaden and lengthen the road of freedom is different from preserving it"? (200)

5. How much do you think our opinions about the value of war are determined by the influences of our upbringing and our position in society?

6. Do people who have been deprived of freedom value it more than those who have had it for a long time?

James Agee

James Agee (1909–1955) was a film critic, novelist, poet, and screenwriter. In 1936 Agee accepted a commission to spend time with sharecroppers in the American South and to produce, with photographer Walker Evans, a record of the experience for the general public. The two men spent several weeks with families in Alabama and the resulting book, *Let Us Now Praise Famous Men* (1941), was a powerful depiction of the depths of Depression-era suffering. After World War II, Agee moved to Hollywood where he worked as a screenwriter, notably with director John Huston; his screenplay for *The African Queen* (1951) was nominated for an Academy Award.

In "These Terrible Records of War," a review for the *Nation*, Agee compares two newsreels depicting the Battle of Iwo Jima. After noting their strong images and sound effects, he introduces a more controversial perspective. Agee questions whether it is appropriate for audiences to watch news coverage from war zones, asking what effect viewing this violence has on viewers and their attitude toward what occurs in combat.

Agee's concerns are even more relevant today, as armed conflict has become more widely depicted in the media, especially on television and the Internet, and the value of frontline footage has been challenged repeatedly. Today, journalists embedded with combat troops enable audiences to see in minute detail the experiences of soldiers on duty, and questions of censorship, bias, and appropriate content are hotly debated. The motives of the home front audience in wanting to be able to see what is happening may be sincere. But does their viewing experience give them a more accurate or a more distorted and emotionally numbing perception of the distant events of war?

THESE TERRIBLE RECORDS OF WAR

The Paramount newsreel issue about Iwo Jima subjects the tremendous material recorded by Navy and Marine Corps and Coast Guard cameramen to an unusually intelligent job of editing, writing, and soundtracking. I noticed with particular respect a couple of good uses of flat silence; the use of a bit of dialogue on "intercoms," recorded on the spot, in a tank; and the use, at the end, of a still photograph down whose wall the camera moved slowly. Still photographs of motionless objects have a very different quality from motion-picture photographs of motionless objects; as Jean Cocteau observed, time still moves in the latter. The still used here was of dead men, for whom time no longer moved. The device is not a new one; Griffith (or William Bitzer) used it for the same purpose at the end of a battle in *The Birth of a Nation*, and René Clair used stop-shots for a somewhat related purpose in *The Crazy Ray*. But it is a device too basic to poetic resource on the screen to discard as plagiarized, and I am glad to see it put back into use so unpretentiously and well.

The Fox version of the same battle—the only other version I could find—drew on the same stock, and is interesting to compare with the Paramount. In one way it is to its credit that it is much less noisy and much less calculated to excite; it is in other words less rhetorical, and the temptations to rhetoric must be strong in handling such material, and usually result in falseness. But in the Paramount issue it seems to me that rhetoric was well used, to construct as well as might be in ten hours' work and in ten minutes on the screen an image of one of the most terrible battles in history. And that is not to mention plain sense: the coherent shape of violence in the Paramount version, which moves from air to sea to land; its intact, climactic use of the footage exposed through a tank-slit, which in the Fox version is chopped along through the picture; and its use of the recorded dialogue, which Fox didn't even touch. The

Fox version does on the other hand have two shots—a magically sinister slashing of quicksilvery water along the sand, and a heartrending picture of a wounded Marine, crawling toward help with the scuttling motions of a damaged insect—which I am amazed to see omitted from a piece of work so astute as Paramount's.

Very uneasily, I am beginning to believe that, for all that may be said in favor of our seeing these terrible records of war, we have no business seeing this sort of experience except through our presence and participation. I have neither space nor mind, yet, to try to explain why I believe this is so; but since I am reviewing and in ways recommending that others see one of the best and most terrible of war films, I cannot avoid mentioning my perplexity. Perhaps I can briefly suggest what I mean by this rough parallel: whatever other effects it may or may not have, pornography is invariably degrading to anyone who looks at or reads it. If at an incurable distance from participation, hopelessly incapable of reactions adequate to the event, we watch men killing each other, we may be quite as profoundly degrading ourselves and, in the process, betraying and separating ourselves the farther from those we are trying to identify ourselves with; none the less because we tell ourselves sincerely that we sit in comfort and watch carnage in order to nurture our patriotism, our conscience, our understanding, and our sympathies.

Questions

1. Why does Agee think that the "temptations to rhetoric must be strong" for the makers of documentary films of combat? Why does he say that the result is usually "falseness"? (205)

2. What is Agee's "perplexity" about viewing films of actual combat? (206)

3. Why does Agee think that viewing films of actual combat separates us "farther from those we are trying to identify ourselves with"? (206) Do you think this is true?

4. Do you think that a film of actual combat is more or less likely to evoke reactions "adequate to the event" than a written news report? (206)

5. Should there be censorship of films of actual combat? If so, what would be the guidelines and who would determine them?

Robert Sherrod

Robert Sherrod (1909–1994) was a correspondent for *Time* and *Life* magazines and covered combat during World War II. He was embedded with the first drafted Marines in the Pacific theater and felt they represented a generation that had not grown up expecting war. Unprepared for warfare, this new generation of soldiers was learning about it through direct and painful experience.

Sherrod was with the Marines during their successful battle to reclaim Tarawa by amphibious landing in 1943. Although Tarawa was a significant victory and provided a model for subsequent island attacks, leading ultimately to victory over Japan, it was hard-won with many lives lost. When news of the casualties reached the United States, the public was outraged. Sherrod asks why there is such a gap between the reality of the war as communicated to the press directly from the front and the way the news media reported on the war to the public at home.

Sherrod's article raises questions that persist today. Why is civilian life so removed from the military? Can the civilian population ever truly understand the experience of warfare? Without a draft, the military today seems ever more distant from the daily life of many people. Servicemen and servicewomen make up only a small fraction of the population and their experiences often seem to have no relation to those of the civilian population. During World War II, when the majority of people in the country were touched personally by the war, there was still a gap in understanding between the home front and the front line. How much larger is the gap today, when only a small number of the population has direct involvement with the military?

TARAWA: THE STORY OF A BATTLE

(selection)

COULD OUR MEN FIGHT?

I spent a lot of time studying the Marines. They looked like any group of ordinary, healthy young Americans. The range of their background was as broad as America: farmers, truck drivers, college students, runaway kids, rich men's sons, orphans, lawyers, ex-soldiers. One day Lieutenant William B. Sommerville, the battalion supply officer, himself a Baltimore lawyer, was showing me around the ship. On deck we passed a Marine corporal with a bandaged thumb. Sommerville stopped and asked what happened.

"I let my air hose get away from me," grinned the corporal. We walked on. "That guy," said Sommerville, "was a country judge in Texas when he enlisted."

All these Marines were volunteers. Only now, several months after voluntary enlistments had been stopped—to the unconcealed disgust of old-line Marine sergeants who had from time immemorial been able to fall back on the final, scathing word, "Nobody asked you to be a Marine, bub"—were the first Marine draftees being sent overseas as replacements.

The Marines ate the same emergency rations that soldiers ate in battle. They used the same weapons. They came from the same places. They went to the same schools. What, then, had gained the Marines a reputation as fighting men far excelling any attributed to the average young U.S. citizen in a soldier's uniform?

I had been curious about this question for at least a year before the United States went to war. I recalled a White House press conference in June 1940, when President Roosevelt said angrily that a year of military training would be good for the mollycoddled youth of the United States—at least, it would teach them to live with their fellow men. The weeks I spent on maneuvers with the army in the swamps of Louisiana and in the Carolina hills did not serve to ease my fears that perhaps we had grown too soft to fight a war; at that time some low-moraled outfits were threatening to desert, rather than stay in the army. Almost none of them deserted, but the threat was an unhealthy sign, and it could not be blamed entirely on poor leadership.

When I came back to the United States after half a year in Australia, in August 1942, I went around Cassandra-fashion, crying, "We are losing the war—you don't realize it, but we are losing the war!" I talked to several men at the top of the army and navy. I went to the White House and sang my mournful tune to the president. To bear bad tidings is a very rocky road to popularity, but I felt that somebody had to do it.

What worried me was not our productive ability, although it was barely in evidence at the time. I knew we could make the machines of war. But I didn't know whether we had the heart to fight a war. Our men who had to do the fighting didn't want to fight. Their generation had been told in the all-important first ten years, in its teens, and at the voting age that it was not necessary to fight. Sometimes it almost seemed that they had been taught that peace was more important than honor. Our men just wanted to go home.

I could not forget my conversation one chilly August day in a room in Lennon's Hotel in Brisbane. My companion was an army general, a friend of many years. I asked his opinion of the American soldier. He became very depressed. He said, "I'm afraid, Bob. I'm afraid the Americans of this generation are not the same kind of Americans who fought the last war."

In the spring of 1943 I went to the Aleutians. The Battle of Attu in its early stages was not well handled. Our equipment was poor. Nearly fifteen hundred men became casualties from exposure because of their poor equipment, and because their leaders allowed them to be pinned down for days in icy water on the floor of Massacre Valley. But the Battle of Attu did not make me feel any worse. In this primitive, man-against-man fighting enough of our men rose up to win. I thought I learned a lesson on Attu which probably applied to all armies: not all soldiers are heroes—far from it; the army that wins, other things being fairly equal, is the army which has enough men to rise above duty, thus inspiring others to do their duty. There were many such Americans on Attu—men received the fairly commonplace Silver Star for deeds that would have earned a Congressional Medal of Honor earlier in the war. I thought I learned another lesson on Attu: no man who dies in battle dies in vain. There is no time for mourning during a battle, but the aftereffect a soldier's battlefield grave has on his comrades is sometimes overpowering. Five weeks after the Battle of Attu ended, a memorial service was held for the six hundred Americans who died there. No man of the Seventeenth, Thirty-Second, or Fourth Regiments who attended this service is likely ever to forget that hundreds of men scaled Attu's summer-clad brown peaks to pick wild mountain flowers, with which they made wreaths for the graves of their brothers-in-arms. Could the living fail to gain from their own dead an inspiration which would sustain them in future battles? Can one American watch another die in his cause, by his side, without realizing that that cause must be worthwhile, and, therefore, must be pursued to a victorious end, whatever the cost?

This was the hard way of gaining an education, but, since we in America had made such an abominable job of educating a generation, we had no other method during the first two years of war. Therefore, our soldiers showed up poorly in their first battles. The number of "war neuroses" or "shell shock" cases among them simply reflected the fact, in my opinion, that they were not mentally prepared to bridge the vast gap between the comforts of peace and the horrors of war. In other words, they had been brought up to believe that it was only necessary to wish for peace to have peace, and the best way to avoid war was to turn our heads the other way when war was mentioned. I had no words to describe the effect the first bombs and bullets had on many of the men educated in such fashion. Fortunately, most of them recovered their equilibrium after the initial shock. Fortunately, there were signs after two years of war that the oncoming generation of soldiers—those who had been conscious for two years of the nearness of war to them—would go into battle better prepared, better educated.

I thought Attu could be told in the story of the sergeant. On top of one of those snowy, marrow-chilling peaks in May 1943, the platoon leader, a second lieutenant, ordered the sergeant to take a squad and go over there and knock out that Jap machine-gun nest. The sergeant just stared. His mouth was open. He was horrified. He had been in the army two years; now, all of a sudden, he was told to go out and risk his life. He, like most Americans, had never thought of the war in terms of getting killed. In disgust, the second lieutenant said, "All right, sergeant, you just sit here. If any of you bastards," turning to the rest of his men, "have got the guts, follow me. We've got to get that machine gun. A lot of our men are getting killed by that machine gun."

Well, about ten men followed the second lieutenant. They killed the Japs and the machine gun didn't kill any more Americans.

That afternoon the sergeant went to the second lieutenant and said, "Sir, I am ashamed of myself. Give me another chance." By then there was another machine gun to be knocked out. So, the second lieutenant ordered the sergeant to take a squad and knock it out. The sergeant did just that. In fact, he knocked it out personally. The necessity of risking his life had finally been demonstrated to him.

Why didn't the sergeant on Attu do as he was told? Why did he volunteer to do the same thing the second time? I think men fight for two reasons: (1) ideals, (2) esprit de corps. The sergeant's education had not included any firm impression of the things that are worth fighting for, so he didn't see why he should risk his life the first time. But the second time he was willing to risk his life for his fellows, for the lieutenant and the ten men who had risked *their* lives, possibly for him, in the morning. The bonds of their common peril of the moment had gripped him as nothing in the past could.

In talking to the Marines aboard the *Blue Fox* I became convinced that they didn't know what to believe in, either—except the Marine Corps. The Marines fought almost solely on esprit de corps, I was certain. It was inconceivable to most Marines that they should let another Marine down, or that they could be responsible for dimming the bright reputation of their corps. The Marines simply assumed that they were the world's best fighting men. "Are you afraid?" Bill Hipple asked one of them. "Hell, no, mister," he answered, "I'm a Marine."

THE HARD FACTS OF WAR

Just eight days after the first Marines hit the beach at Betio, I was again in Honolulu. Already there were rumblings about Tarawa. People on the

U.S. mainland had gasped when they heard the dread phrase, "heavy casualties." They gasped again when it was announced that 1,026 Marines had been killed, 2,600 wounded. "This must not happen again," thundered an editorial. "Our intelligence must have been faulty," guessed a member of Congress.

This attitude, following the finest victory U.S. troops had won in this war, was amazing. It was the clearest indication that the peacetime United States (i.e., the United States as of December 1943) simply found it impossible to bridge the great chasm that separates the pleasures of peace from the horrors of war. Like the generation they educated, the people had not thought of war in terms of men being killed—war seemed so far away.

Tarawa, it seemed to me, marked the beginning of offensive thrusts in the Pacific. Tarawa appeared to be the opening key to offensive operations throughout the whole Pacific—as important in its way as Guadalcanal was important to the defense of the U.S.-Australian supply line. Tarawa required four days; Guadalcanal, six months. Total casualties among Marines alone, not even including malaria cases, were about twenty percent higher on Guadalcanal.

Tarawa was not perfectly planned or perfectly executed. Few military operations are, particularly when the enemy is alert. Said Julian Smith: "We made mistakes, but you can't know it all the first time. We learned a lot which will benefit us in the future. And we made fewer mistakes than the Japs did." Tarawa was the first frontal assault on a heavily defended atoll. By all the rules concerning amphibious assaults, the Marines should have suffered far heavier casualties than the defenders. Yet, for every Marine who was killed more than four Japs died—four of the best troops the emperor had. Looking at the defenses of Betio, it was no wonder our colonels could say: "With two battalions of Marines I could have held this island until hell froze over."

Tarawa must have given the Japanese General Staff something to think about.

The lessons of Tarawa were many. It is a shame that some very fine Americans had to pay for those lessons with their lives, but they gave their lives that others on other enemy beaches might live. On Tarawa we learned what our best weapons were, what weapons needed improving, what tactics could best be applied to other operations. We learned a great deal about the most effective methods of applying naval gunfire and bombs to atolls. Our capacity to learn, after two years of war, had improved beyond measure. The same blind refusal to learn, which had characterized many of our operations early in the war, had almost disappeared. We were learning, and learning how to learn faster.

The facts were cruel, but inescapable: probably no amount of shelling and bombing could obviate the necessity of sending in foot soldiers to finish the job. The corollary was this: there is no easy way to win the war; there is no panacea which will prevent men from getting killed. To me it seemed that to deprecate the Tarawa victory was almost to defame the memory of the gallant men who lost their lives achieving it.

Why, then, did so many Americans throw up their hands at the heavy losses on Tarawa? Why did they not realize that there would be many other bigger and bloodier Tarawas in the three or four years of Japanese war following the first Tarawa? After two years of observing the Japanese I had become convinced that they had only one strategy: to burrow into the ground as far and as securely as possible, waiting for the Americans to dig them out; then to hope that the Americans would grow sick of their own losses before completing the job. Result: a Japanese victory through negotiated peace. It seemed to me that those Americans who were horrified by Tarawa were playing into Japanese hands. It also seemed that there was no way to defeat the Japanese except by extermination.

Then I reasoned that many Americans had never been led to expect anything but an easy war. Through their own wishful thinking, bolstered by comfort-inspiring yarns from the war theaters, they had really believed that this place or that place could be "bombed out of the war." It seemed to many that machines alone would win the war for us, perhaps with the loss of only a few pilots, and close combat would not be necessary. As a matter of fact, by the end of 1943 our airplanes, after a poor start, had far outdistanced anything the Japanese could put in the air. We really did not worry particularly about Japanese airpower. If we could get close enough we could gain air supremacy wherever we chose. But did that mean we could win the war by getting only a few pilots killed? It did not. Certainly, air supremacy was necessary. But airpower could not win the war alone. Despite airplanes and the best machines we could produce, the road to Tokyo would be lined with the grave of many a foot soldier. This came as a surprise to many people.

Our information services had failed to impress the people with the hard facts of war. Early in the war our communiqués gave the impression that we were bowling over the enemy every time our handful of bombers dropped a few pitiful tons from 30,000 feet. The stories accompanying the communiqués gave the impression that any American could lick any twenty Japs. Later, the communiqués became more matter-of-fact. But the communiqués, which made fairly dry reading, were rewritten by press association reporters who waited for them back at rear head-quarters. The stories almost invariably came out liberally sprinkled with "smash" and "pound" and the other "vivid" verbs. These "vivid" verbs impressed the headline writers back in the home office. They impressed the reading public which saw them in tall type. But they sometimes did not impress the miserable, bloody soldiers in the front lines where the action had taken place. Gloomily observed a sergeant: "The war that is being written in the newspapers must be a different war from the one we see." Sometimes I thought I could see a whole generation losing its faith in the press. One night a censor showed me four different letters saying, in effect: "I wish we could give you the story of this battle without the sugarcoating you see in the newspapers."

Whose fault was this? Surely, there must have been some reason for tens of millions of people getting false impressions about the war. Mostly, it was not the correspondents' fault. The stories which gave false impressions were not usually the front-line stories. But the front-line stories had to be sent back from the front. They were printed somewhat later, usually on an inside page. The stories which the soldiers thought deceived their people back home were the "flashes" of rewritten communiqués, sent by reporters who were nowhere near the battle. These communiqué stories carrying "vivid" verbs were the stories that got the big headlines. And the press association system willy-nilly prevented these reporters from making any evaluation of the news, from saying: "Does this actually mean anything, and if it does, what does it mean in relation to the whole picture?" The speed with which the competing press associations had to send their dispatches did not contribute to the coolness of evaluation. By the time the radio announcers had read an additional lilt into the press association dispatches—it was no wonder that our soldiers spat in disgust.

Said a bomber pilot, after returning from the Pacific: "When I told my mother what the war was really like, and how long it was going to take, she sat down and cried. She didn't know we were just beginning to fight the Japs."

My third trip back to the United States since the war began was a letdown. I had imagined that everybody, after two years, would realize the seriousness of the war and the necessity of working as hard as possible toward ending it. But I found a nation wallowing in unprecedented prosperity. There was a steel strike going on, and a railroad strike was threatened. Men lobbying for special privilege swarmed around a Congress which appeared afraid to tax the people's newfound, inflationary wealth. Justice Byrnes cautioned a group of newsmen that we might expect a half million casualties within a few months—and got an editorial spanking for it. A "high military spokesman" generally identified as General Marshall said bitterly that labor strikes played into the hands of enemy propagandists. Labor leaders got furious at that. The truth was that many Americans were not prepared psychologically to accept the cruel facts of war.

The men on Tarawa would have known what the general and the justice meant. On Tarawa, late in 1943, there was a more realistic approach to the war than there was in the United States.

Questions

1. What does Sherrod mean when he says that "the army that wins, other things being fairly equal, is the army which has enough men to rise above duty, thus inspiring others to do their duty"? (210)

2. Why is Sherrod confident that "the oncoming generation of soldiers" will be better prepared psychologically for the realities of combat than the first troops that went into battle? (211)

3. If Sherrod is correct—that men fight for two reasons: ideals and esprit de corps—is it helpful or detrimental to fight for one without fighting for the other?

4. Why does Sherrod think that "Americans had never been led to expect anything but an easy war" and that it seemed to them that "machines alone would win the war for us"? (214)

5. Do you agree with Sherrod that the "vivid verbs" used in media coverage of combat misrepresent the reality of warfare? (215)

6. During wartime, does the prosperity on the home front that often results from a stimulated economy detract from an awareness of the seriousness of war?

7. How can the civilian population be made aware of the "cruel facts of war" so that they can better help returning soldiers readjust? (216)

Eric Sevareid

In 1939 the noted American journalist Eric Sevareid (1912–1992) was recruited as European correspondent for CBS, and he was with the French military during the opening months of World War II. After the Fall of France in 1940, he reported from China, Burma, India, and Italy, finally traveling with U.S. forces into southern France and across the Rhine to Germany.

When Sevareid wrote "The Price We Pay in Italy" in late 1944, the Allied campaign to retake Italy from the Germans, begun in 1943, was far advanced, although the final outcome was still uncertain. In the fighting up the peninsula to Rome, both sides had suffered an immense number of casualties, amplified by the extremely difficult terrain in which the war was being waged. Even while the campaign was going on, Sevareid had doubts about its strategic value. But out of loyalty to the men engaged in combat, he held back from making his views public during the heaviest fighting.

In our day journalists traveling with soldiers are much more outspoken about their doubts and frustrations, and the questioning of military policy and strategy has become much more prevalent in the media. Military personnel are now more accountable to media questioning, and the 24-hour news cycle has led to more intense and immediate scrutiny of military actions. During World War II, Sevareid waited until the fighting was almost over before publishing his doubts, but in modern wars the questioning and analysis happen almost simultaneously with the action. Sevareid's sharp critique of the strategic decisions behind the Italian campaign raises the issue of the legitimate role of the media in influencing public opinion about military matters.

THE PRICE WE PAY IN ITALY

London, November 7

General Sir Harold L. G. Alexander, Allied commander-in-chief in Italy, has just had his first press conference in some nine months with the war correspondents there. He defended the Italian campaign as a whole and explained that the Eighth and Fifth Armies cannot reasonably be expected to drive the Germans from the Po valley unless the enemy makes some mistake which can be exploited. This most important statement was generally overlooked by the press.

Here in London one senses that the British public has never been much taken with the Italian campaign as a vital contribution to Germany's defeat. Have we, in fact, had a victory in Italy? A clear-cut victory speaks for itself, and the very fact that General Alexander felt compelled to state his claims indicates that public opinion is justified in feeling doubt about the whole thing and wishing to reserve judgment until all the facts are in. I spent five spring and summer months in Italy as war correspondent and while men were dying in their great effort felt constrained from publicly questioning their mission—indeed, the Allied censorship in Italy, actually run by the British, was always quick to blue-pencil even implied criticisms. Members of Alexander's staff even made a habit of telling correspondents not only what they should not write but what they should. Since the commander-in-chief has now spoken about the past, perhaps a reporter may also take the occasion to look back and issue some reminders.

I for one—and many of my colleagues from that front are of like mind—am impressed by the major miscalculations made in high places. There is not the slightest doubt that the original decision to invade Italy proper was based on a belief that the Germans would not give battle in southern Italy, and that if they did they could not possibly maintain more than three or four divisions there because of their very long supply lines and our own mastery of the sky. The Germans surprised us, and the fight was very hard. It was just the first of many surprises. They held us on the Cassino line, where we lost thousands of men, particularly in the tragic winter attempt by the American Thirty-Sixth Division to cross the Rapido River, an attempt which the divisional commander pleaded against with tears. We landed at Anzio in January under the illusion that the Germans, in their alarm, would pull back from the southern front to Rome or beyond. While Churchill was announcing that we would soon have Rome and Alexander was scolding the Anzio reporters for being "alarmists," our cooks and truck drivers were being thrown into the line to stem the German counterattacks which threatened to drive us into the sea. We recovered our safety, but we lost a strategic, mountainous ten percent of the original beachhead and never regained it until the breakout began on May 23. By that date 3,000 Americans lay in the Anzio cemetery; the total of British dead I do not know. We had taken some 4,000 German prisoners, and they had captured "rather more" of our men, as a G-2 colonel put it. After the breakout in May, General Clark's Fifth Army headquarters issued a statement which broadly implied that Anzio was now fully justified—a statement many reporters refused to send to their papers.

We tried to smash the German resistance at Cassino in mid-March with a much-publicized obliteration bombing, followed by an attack by Indians and New Zealanders. It failed completely, and the front went static until the grand offensive opened on May 11 from Cassino to the Tyrrhenian Sea. On that day Alexander issued an order defining his objective as the *destruction of the German armies in Italy.* His troops were told, "You will be supported by overwhelming air forces, and in guns and tanks we are far superior." Nothing was then said about Rome, although of course we expected to take it. Rome was regarded by the generals as purely a political objective, of no military value whatever—actually a liability, since we would have to divert transport and men to feed it. Reporters were told that this offensive was directly connected with the coming invasion of Europe: that we were to oblige the Germans to divert large forces to Italy, that we could accomplish this only by destroying the formations already there, and that if we merely compelled a slow German retreat we would have failed in the primary mission.

Now, in his November 1 statement—I am going by the account in the London *Times*—Alexander says that he aimed to destroy "as much as possible of the enemy forces" and to produce a first-class victory before the second front opened in France, and that "Rome was that victory." He says we inflicted 194,000 casualties on the Germans—though casualty figures for the enemy can never be more than an approximation—at a cost of 116,000 of our own. At the same time he says that only five German divisions were sent into Italy from other fronts after May 11, a reinforcement or replacement of only one-fifth, since twenty-five German divisions were in Italy on that date. Did we, then, give important aid to the second front?

The general, in defending his record, declared further that at no time had he had more than a slight numerical superiority over the Germans. But at various crucial moments of contact we certainly had more than a "slight" superiority. On the southern front, on May 11, we opposed fourteen Allied divisions to the Germans' five. When the battle on the Anzio front opened on May 23, we had seven plus against their five. The Germans, of course, were later reinforced, but it should also be pointed out that the German divisions were nearly always much smaller than ours, running from one-half to two-thirds of our divisional strength. With only a few exceptions, such as the First Parachute and the Hermann Göring Divisions, these were hand-me-down enemy divisions, containing troops too old or too young, interspersed with reluctant Russians and other undependable odd lots. The Germans had far fewer guns and tanks, almost no planes at all, and only a fraction of the Allied transport. In May it was estimated we had on the beachhead alone as many vehicles as they had in the whole of Italy.

After Rome, the Allied objective was to capture the Po valley, which we have not done yet. Today General Alexander says he was left with too little strength, because the invasion of southern France took a number of his divisions. It did take several excellent divisions, including all the French and some American. But his statement makes strange reading to any correspondent who was in Rome in early August. When high officers then described their plans for getting the valley, and, indeed, for driving on into South Germany, they had full knowledge—as did the correspondents—of the total diversion for southern France.

We have been fighting in Italy now for fourteen months. We have killed and captured many Germans and wrecked a great deal of their equipment. We knocked the remaining Italian Fascists out of the war. We got bases in the south from which to do important strategic bombing of France, Austria, Hungary, and Rumania and from which we sent considerable aid to Marshal Tito. And, if you find satisfaction in it, we helped to lay waste and impoverish for many years the major part of Italy.

It was the kind of warfare in which wide, sweeping movements are impossible, in which troops have no alternative to orthodox, steamroller advance, crushing towns and villages in their path, laying waste the countryside. As Churchill said, we have drawn a hot rake up the length of Italy. The consequence is that Italy has become such an economic ruin that the Allies must pour in money and materials for years to come, or be prepared to help millions of Italians to emigrate. I am informed that of the total productive capacity of that part of Italy which has been liberated, approximately one-sixth remains. Destruction of industrial power alone between Rome and Naples is so complete that a year will probably be required to bring it back to 15 percent of its prewar level. One can hardly begin to speak of the erasure of ancient Roman towns and monuments, which belonged not to the Italians but to all civilized peoples.

The Italian campaign is not all debit, by any means. But someday people will want to know whether the returns balance the enormous investment of Allied lives, ships, transport, and planes. They will ask if we could not have achieved almost as much by stopping in southern Italy at the Volturno line, securing our ports and our bases and using the bulk of our forces in more fruitful encounters elsewhere. They will ask, "Did not the Italian ground fighting really become a war of attrition and nothing more?"

To this observer at least, it seems very late for commanders to continue to place blame for failure on weather and insufficient forces. Why should we not be frank about Italy and admit that Kesselring, on a very small budget, has done a masterful job in making a primary Allied force pay bitterly for every dubious mile of a secondary battlefield; that no matter what heroism our superb fighters showed, the monstrously difficult terrain of the peninsula, with its few roads winding through precipitous mountains, made encirclement and destruction of a retreating enemy impossible at any stage; that the terrain was not an unknown quantity when the original plans were made?

The Allied peoples—and history—may well ask whether the bloody Italian campaign has been a "victory," whether, indeed, it has accomplished anything of a decisive nature.

Questions

1. Referring to General Alexander's remark about the difficulty of driving the Germans from the Po valley, why does Sevareid point out, "This most important statement was generally overlooked by the press"? (219)

2. Why does Sevareid make his public statement indicting the Italian campaign before the Allies have defeated the Germans in Italy?

3. In carrying out combat operations, do commanders have a responsibility to safeguard cultural treasures such as the ones that Sevareid says "belonged not to the Italians but to all civilized peoples"? (222)

4. Why does Sevareid ask whether the Allies should be frank in acknowledging that the German commander "has done a masterful job in making a primary Allied force pay bitterly"? (222)

5. Should the military dictate not only what journalists should not write but also what they should write?

6. Should journalists publicly question combat operations while war is still being waged?

Edward W. Wood Jr.

Edward W. Wood Jr. (1924–) was born in Alabama and spent most of his early childhood in the Deep South. His family had a long tradition of military service and he grew up instilled with the belief that being a soldier was part of what it meant to be a man, and that when war broke out, it was a man's duty to volunteer.

Wood joined the U.S. Army in 1943 and began his service in the Army Specialized Training Program (ASTP), which sent servicemen to universities for specialized training before they were commissioned as officers. However, as World War II intensified and casualties mounted, Wood voluntarily left the ASTP to enter front-line combat duty as a replacement soldier. Like many other replacements, Wood was not adequately prepared for combat: he was placed in a unit that had already been engaged in fighting for a considerable amount of time, and the men viewed him as an outsider. Consequently, Wood did not fit in, making him significantly more vulnerable in combat.

After only a short time on the European front in September 1944, Wood was severely wounded by artillery shrapnel. The lasting effects of his wounding, both physical and emotional, profoundly affected Wood's ability to reintegrate himself into the life of his family when he returned home. After decades of distress and feelings of inadequacy, he decided to devote himself to writing as honestly as he could about his wounding and its pervasive significance in his life. The following selection consists of Wood's reflection on his memoir, *On Being Wounded* (1991), along with an excerpt from the memoir itself. Wood explores many of the issues faced by injured veterans as they search for ways to communicate how they feel to their families, friends, and communities in an effort to begin to heal their wounds.

REVISITING MY MEMOIR

Fifteen years ago this September I returned to the place of my wounding in WWII at the first attempted crossing of the Moselle River in eastern France in the fall of 1944. Later that month, in 1984, I settled in Chartres, near the cathedral, where I wrote the first draft of my memoir, *On Being Wounded*.

Now, a decade and a half later, and eight years after the book was published, I have a better sense of what my book is about, its successes, its regrets, the direction it has given my life and my writing.

In retrospect I understand that the most important act I performed in writing *On Being Wounded*, not even realizing it at the time, was *to write, without being pejorative or preachy*, a book both antiwar and anti-violence.

My book deals with the consequences of a serious wound received in combat, how it changed my life in ways I, at the time, neither understood nor expected. In the deepest sense, my wounding destroyed my relation to my parents, never to be made whole again. The wounding, certainly for years, inhibited my sexual life. It brought me under the care of a psychiatrist for as many years. It caused me to break irrevocably with my past, turn to other paths for career, avocations, pleasures. Finally, it led me to "give up the gun," seek gentler ways of living outside the frame of weapons and war in which I, as a Southern boy, had been raised.

My book details in what I hope is my deepest honesty the consequences of a wounding in war—the impacts of war on one individual, impacts seldom seriously considered in America, with its pervasive, shoddy worship of violence in its media and its video games. Yet, on another level, I also understand that my slim book scarcely penetrates the mysterious skein of wars and woundings, scarcely penetrates what war did to me on the deepest levels of my unconscious, and how war hurt those close to me in childhood and youth.

I did not see when writing *On Being Wounded*—was I afraid to look at my darkness?—that in my unconscious coiled the terrible shame of combat. After a lifetime of struggling to understand war, I now am sure that every person in serious combat, under the terrible pressure of that pitiless place, does something for which they are always ashamed. For me, it was the simple act of being wounded after but four days in my division and one day at the front. What kind of man was I not to have lasted any longer? For others "the shame of combat" may involve acts of commission, the simple act of breaking the commandment "Thou Shall Not Kill," the more complex infliction of atrocities, sometimes, more often than we think, the betrayal of a friend. "The shame of combat" includes acts of omission, betrayals of all sorts, refusals to fire, realities seldom discussed in the literature of war.

So, as I say, I was haunted by the question, had I really been a man?—with all that may mean for an American male, particularly one with ancestors participating in every major American war, beginning with the French and Indian War of 1756. It took returning to my place of wounding forty years after the event, struggling to write a book, then years absorbing its most serious meanings to finally face this condition of shame, to recognize that what I had done—entering combat alone, a replacement—had actually been an act of immense courage: doing what I was told under fire without emotional support of any kind. The shame lay in the simple reality of being wounded, my flesh, my soma so badly hurt, not as a consequence of my actions at the front, but simply the result of war. Had I not written my book, I would have never made that discovery, never been as whole as I am today.

Regrets about the book I wrote?

Most of all I did not understand when I finished and published *On Being Wounded* how profoundly I wished I'd talked to my parents about my wounding before their death. And how I wished they had talked to me. My wound became a secret among us, a dark and dirty fact none of us could admit. My father, I have learned from letters written to his brother, always wondered why I was in combat for such a short time, though he never questioned me. My mother's deep and maternal compassion for my wounded flesh was more than I could bear: it threatened me, turned me back into her child, intensified my unconscious shame in unbearable emotion. I fled from her embrace. The healthiest thing I could have done—*we* could have done—was speak of what had happened to me. It would have helped me see my father and mother with greater clarity. My father, a pilot in WWI, had cracked up, lost his front teeth, *but had never been in combat*. Were his Silver Wings the equivalent of my Combat Infantryman's Badge? Both symbols of what we sensed as failure? Did my father wonder about his manhood, having never been in air combat? Could we have shared the same story of human weakness, discovered our courage in adversity together, eschewed our shame? Oh, how much I would that we had!

If my mother and I had talked, could I have absorbed my mother's tears, cared for her in turn, then salved her wounds in those awful days when cancer wracked her flesh and it was too late to share our mutual pain? I most bitterly regret that I did not write my book before my parents' deaths. Had I, we might have talked. Had we talked, we might have loved, recaptured the joy of a family in the distant days of my youth and childhood. And yet, by waiting so long, so many years, to write the book, then absorb its layered meanings, I've finally reached new understandings, richer and more complex than those in my memoir.

I finally begin to grasp how *woundings,* the weapons that cause them, are passed on from generation to generation, in large part because of an inability to talk of inflicted pain, the shame of men killing and being killed. I see that opening one door to such discussions may well be the best contribution I have made. And I understand that by walking through this door myself, I have stepped into a room much wider than I knew existed when I first finished *On Being Wounded.*

—*Denver, Colorado, 1999*

From *On Being Wounded*

My loneliness, my sense of alienation, intensified as the members of the squad took their regular seats on the half-track in which we would roll toward Germany. Their words and laughter poured over me, around me, under me. Until I proved myself in combat, I simply did not exist. I had been told by fellow replacements at the repple-depple* that this was the way I would be treated when I joined the squad. Replacements knew no one as their friends. Sometimes they were even given the tasks of greatest danger as guinea pigs, targets of opportunity, while the rest of the squad crouched in greater security.

Meat for the butcher.

We rolled toward the Moselle that morning, stopping only when great tanks at our side fired their artillery pieces high above barren hills. I marveled at the peasants who came up to the tanks and methodically seized empty shell casings (so they could later sell the brass), seemingly oblivious to German fire.

Twice we dismounted. Once at a rumor of poison gas. Then to penetrate a French village—a high brick wall at our side, five yards between each man, alert for the hand grenade that might come lobbing over the wall. At the edge of the village, we halted in the ditch at the side of the road.

"Put on those fuckin' bayonets!" the sergeant said when he ran back from crouching at the lieutenant's side. "We gonna cross the road and clean those motherfuckers outta that house behind the wall."

My fingers trembled as I fastened my bayonet to the end of my rifle.

We ran in little groups across the road and ducked behind the wall. Nothing happened. The Germans had fled.

My bayonet jammed when I tried to remove it from my rifle. The soldier seated on the ground next to me pulled it free, glaring at me with contempt.

Somewhere later that afternoon, north and west of Metz, the track halted near a road sign to Luxembourg. We lay behind it while shells from a German 88-millimeter artillery piece smashed into a farmhouse across the road. (The explosions lacked all the drama of a shelling in a movie; rather, they looked like dirty backfires from an old car.) We retreated back down the highway as a tank joined us.

At dusk we dismounted from the half-track. We walked at the side of the tank. Once we stopped, and the lieutenant talked fiercely to a

---

* [Military slang for "replacement depot."]

Frenchman who then motioned us down a darkened side road, its trees forming great menacing arches above our heads. We moved warily into a forest where fog slipped through black branches and rain dripped from sodden leaves. As we penetrated deeper into that darkness, gravel suddenly splattered my leggings, stinging me. The pavement in front of me exploded with an orange burst of fire; a blue hole cut into the fog ahead. I scrambled toward the ditch, crawling on my hands and knees like a terrified animal.

The spectacle had just ended, the movie choreographed by Hemingway, starring John and Gary and Humphrey. I was no longer an observer; I was suddenly, instantly, peeingly, playing a part in it: SOMEONE OUT THERE WANTED ME DEAD, little ol' Eddie Wood, his momma's boy, dead!

I buried myself in the ditch, branches snapping above my head.

"WHO THE FUCK IS THAT?" the soldier behind me cried.

My teeth chattered so I could not speak.

"I goddamn near shot ya. Be quiet, for chrissake."

The lieutenant fired over our heads at a blur that suddenly popped up from the ditch ahead of us and ran; the silhouette sprawled back upon the road, its rifle clattering to the black pavement.

The lieutenant hesitated. He waved us ahead. I walked by the dead German, a boy no older than I, his blond hair plastered to his face with rain.

Whenever the lieutenant crossed a culvert, he leaned over and fired bursts from his machine gun into the opening. I shuddered, imagining myself trapped in a tunnel beneath the ground, bullets slamming from the concrete, shredding my unprotected flesh.

At dawn we stopped, mounted the track again. We entered another town, its streets deserted. The signs were in German. Nobody visible. Nobody. As if all human beings had disappeared. Shutters on the buildings slammed in the early morning wind. We parked in the middle of the square. Shells whispered over our heads, tearing through the gray sky. They should have been the ducks I shot with my father as a boy.

We left the village with its closed shutters and doors. The road swung to our left, then our right, a ninety-degree turn. We could not see around the corner.

The lieutenant and the sergeant dismounted. The soldier who had cursed me in the dark the night before jumped from the track. He shouted to the lieutenant, then pointed up at me, glaring ferociously. The lieutenant slowly calmed him, then jerked his arm at our squad. I clambered from the half-track with the other men, my rifle awkward in my arms. As we started around the curve in the road, expecting enemy fire at any moment, my mouth could not form words, my breath seemed louder than any shellfire. I hugged the ditch at the side of the road. When nothing happened, I stepped from the shrubs to the macadam pavement. The air was still. Fog hovered around the trees, masking the mansard roof of a French farmhouse that towered above the poplars to my right. For that moment, that small moment in time, though I did not know it, we were in front of the whole Third Army. The Germans had fallen back across the Moselle River ahead to regroup.

Up the road I could just distinguish the outline of a bridge. I walked toward it. With each faltering step I seemed to penetrate a great vaulted tomb of silence, a silence never known or experienced before—as if all time and motion had ceased and I was the only living being in the universe. This was the silence I had encountered the day I first joined the men of the division—their refusal to help the stranger, the replacement, until he had proven himself under fire. Men did not support each other in comradeship as they did in all those movies I had seen. They entered a place of intense stillness where each lived alone in terror of immediate death. The silence deepened, hovering above me, palpable, almost as if I must soon slip into it and sink into eternity.

I sank to my knees when the lieutenant joined us. I could not speak, my throat constricted with fear.

Just ahead of us, on our side of the river, west of the Moselle, lay a barge canal twenty or thirty yards wide. Before retreating, the Germans had blown a bridge spanning it. Made of steel I-beams, the bridge had broken apart at the explosion and jackknifed into the green water of the canal, forming a V. Gingerly, we clambered down one side, holding the steel trusses with one hand, our rifles with the other. I feared I might be shot and tumble, helpless, into the canal. The gap between the two sets of trusses, just before they penetrated the water, was two or three yards. I tensed my legs. Jumped. One foot swung into the water. I yanked it up, climbed the slippery steel to the other bank. The lieutenant joined us there.

We stood beneath the abutment on the other side of the bridge. A machine gun fired, its bullets whining off the concrete. The lieutenant gentled us as if we were wild animals. He motioned us to the top of the abutment when the machine gun stopped its chattering.

In the distance, several hundred yards to our left, I could see another bridge, much longer, rising out of the mist over the Moselle. Little figures of men ran upon the abutment.

"Fire, goddamnit!" the lieutenant cried. "Fire!"

I threw my rifle to my shoulder, settling on a running silhouette. I led it as I did the quail I had shot as a boy. I started to pull the trigger. The bridge exploded like a concrete geyser: rubble and steel and smoke hid the man at whom I aimed. I fired into the haze.

"Shit!" the lieutenant cursed. "We'll have to cross the fucking river in boats now."

He motioned us back down the slope and across the canal, not knowing we were the forward contingent of the whole Third Army.

The bank of the canal offered us protection from enemy fire. Our tanks were ranged below it. We dropped, exhausted, at the forward lip of the bank. The tanks fired over the rise.

I rolled over on my back and looked down the hill.

A great plain lay behind me. Though it was misty and gray, I could see for miles. The road was lined with tanks and trucks and half-tracks and jeeps and men who stood in little clumps like ants. Airplanes, small artillery spotters, buzzed overhead. Dirty smoke from shellfire drifted over the road and hid it for an instant like dark mist following a heavy rain. Men shouted at each other, gesticulated; I could not hear their words. The air snapped with the shriek of lightning.

One of the men who had crossed the canal with me stood at the bottom of the hill. He yelled commands to a mortar squad firing at a group of apartment buildings, just this side of the Moselle. A dirty puff of smoke suddenly exploded at his side. He spun as if a giant had slammed him in the shoulder, bouncing off the ground as he fell. A medic ran to him where he flopped up and down like a chicken with its head cut off, spurting blood from his arm.

Another puff of smoke dirtied the air. A piece of shrapnel slammed into the earth at my side. The grass around it curled. The lieutenant made hand signals to us to assemble at a stand of trees farther back, near the road that led to the farmhouse. I grabbed a box of .30-caliber machine gun ammunition and ran, understanding, for the first time, how to survive here: live for the moment. Don't think about the near future, not even the next few minutes.

We started to dig foxholes under the trees. I hit a root almost immediately. I struck furiously at it, using the edge of my metal entrenching tool as an ax. The blade was too dull; the root would not snap. At any moment I was sure another artillery shell would split the air above me, send hot shrapnel tearing into my flesh. I frantically slammed at the pulpy mass. My breath was choked. I could not breathe. Sweat poured from my face, though a cold September mist drifted through the grove of trees.

The men at my side had their holes half dug. They had moved farther out from the tree trunk where the roots were smaller. I scrambled over the ground to their side. No one spoke to me.

I started to dig. My blade met no roots. The shovel pierced the deep black earth, the sweet earth in which I would soon hide . . . and then, then, the slam of a sledgehammer lifted me high and I whirled up and up and up through a tunnel of green leaves toward the sky, my hands extended as if to grasp those leaves and the dark brown limbs rushing by me, halting my flight into eternity. My fingers brushed over them. They would not hold.

I flew higher into the sky and seemed to merge with the clouds, mix with their wispy tendrils, not knowing whether to continue this arc toward eternity or fall back to the sweet, sweet earth. With a falling, sliding swoop I tumbled out of the sky. Fell to my knees. I put my fingers up to my face. Blood, thick and red and dark, swiftly pumping, covered them. I reached up and touched my head. My helmet was gone. Blood poured from a hole on the left side of my skull. A hard lump protruded from my torn scalp. A piece of shrapnel was embedded in the bone. I looked behind me. My pants were ripped away, my right buttock was blown open. Beneath the yellow-white fat, I could see the raw, red meat, like the steaks my father had once fed me.

"Hold still, Wood! Hold still!" the medic cried, blood from the tip of his wounded nose spraying my face. "Stop wiggling, goddamnit! I gotta get this morphine in ya." The blood from his own wound sprinkled over me like spittle from a dying sneeze.

As he poked at my arm, I heard the whisper of the shells above me and wondered why their sigh sounded like the wings of the ducks my father and I had once shot in Mississippi bayous. Not yet in pain, I lay there, loose-jointed, until they tumbled me into a stretcher and ran with me toward the ambulance parked on the macadam road near the grove of trees. Once they dropped me, leaving me helpless, as an artillery shell slammed too close. I stared up at them as they hovered in the lee of the ambulance, their place of sanctuary.

When the shelling stopped, they lifted me into the ambulance.

"You didn't like it much up here, did you, Wood?" the lieutenant asked as they slammed the door.

My journey into the land of the wounded began in that ambulance after one day of combat, before I had proven myself, those men in arms still uncertain of my courage and my strength, the lieutenant's words my epitaph.

Being moved by ambulance from Battalion Aid Station into World War I bunkers, I smelled the cloying odor of blood, feeling it drip on me from the stretcher above. Here at the front, before there were forms and bureaucrats to describe and fasten to me some categories of wound and pain, I touched men who, for an instant, cared for me with greater compassion than I had ever experienced at any time or place in my life—men who lit my cigarette and held it in their fingers while I puffed, men who returned to me again and again, seeing if my paralyzed hand would yet move, if my bowels were free, my urine not pink with blood, murmuring to me gently, even crying. I remember one boy my age who had ridden to the front with me, weeping as he cut off my bloody clothes in Battalion Aid Station. I remember the soldier I had watched being wounded visiting me in the field hospital, his arm still bloody in its sling, offering me a package of cigarettes.

Gentleness and compassion, a softness so difficult for the American male to express—always there but held back, contained by some impenetrable shell, breaking open now and warming me after I was wounded, as if love could be given only within the frame of violence and one must be expressed in conjunction with the other. The language of war and peace, violence and love, hate and compassion that I have sought to understand on my journey through the land of the wounded.

Questions

1. According to Wood, why are the effects of war on individuals rarely considered in America?

2. Why do Wood's combat experiences leave him "haunted by the question, had I really been a man?" (228)

3. Does Wood blame the soldiers for not supporting each other in combat, or does he see it as inevitable that they enter "a place of intense stillness where each lived alone in terror of immediate death"? (232)

4. Why does Wood think that the men who care for him in the field are able to show a "gentleness and compassion" that are usually held back in American men? (235)

5. Do you agree with Wood that all those who have been in combat have something they are ashamed of?

6. Has violence in movies, video games, and other media made people less sensitive to the damage inflicted by warfare?

Estela Portillo Trambley

Born in El Paso, Texas, Estela Portillo Trambley (1927–1999) was a pioneering writer, teacher, and broadcaster. With her collection of short stories, *Rain of Scorpions and Other Writings* (1975), she was part of a wave of Chicana authors and performers who began to achieve success in the 1970s.

Although Portillo Trambley was neither in the military nor ever close to combat, in "Village" she demonstrates an artist's capacity for accurately imagining what it is like. Portillo's protagonist, Rico, is fighting in the U.S. Army in Vietnam, but he sees many similarities between the conditions for villagers in rural Vietnam and his own upbringing in a poor barrio in the United States. He struggles to think of Vietnamese villagers as the enemy, instead seeing parallels between their lives and his. "Village" portrays several dilemmas faced by soldiers during war when they are forced to confront questions of personal dignity and freedom. Tasked with a military order he finds repellent, Rico must decide how to act. His moral intuition and his compassion toward the villagers tell him one thing, his commanding officer another.

Military obedience and personal beliefs have clashed throughout the history of war. "Village" raises questions about the extent to which the military must suppress dissent within its ranks and impose strict obedience on its members in order to operate effectively. And by highlighting important issues of individual responsibility and freedom, it raises the related question of where to draw the line between discipline and individual conscience.

VILLAGE

Rico stood on top of a bluff overlooking Mai Cao. The whole of the wide horizon was immersed in a rosy haze. His platoon was returning from an all-night patrol. They had scoured the area in a radius of thirty-two miles, following the length of the canal system along the delta, furtively on the lookout for an enemy attack. On their way back, they had stopped to rest, smoke, and drink warm beer after parking the carryalls along the edge of the climb leading to the top of the bluff. The hill was good cover, seemingly safe.

Harry was behind him on the rocky slope. Then, there was the sound of thunder overhead. It wasn't thunder, but a squadron of their own helicopters on the usual run. Rico and Harry sat down to watch the 'copters go by. After that, a stillness, a special kind of silence. Rico knew it well; it was the same kind of stillness that was a part of him back home, the kind of stillness that makes a man part of his world—river, clearing, sun, wind. The stillness of a village early in the morning—barrio stillness, the first stirrings of life that come with dawn.

Harry was looking down at the village of Mai Cao. "Makes me homesick." He lit a cigarette.

Rico was surprised. He thought Harry was a city dude. From Chicago, no less. "I don't see no freeway or neon lights," he joked.

"I'm just sick of doing nothing in this goddamned war."

No action yet. But who wanted action? Rico had been transformed into a soldier, but he knew he was no soldier. He had been trained to kill the enemy in Vietnam. He watched the first curl of smoke coming out of one of the chimneys. They were the enemy down there. Rico didn't believe it. He would never believe it. Perhaps because there had been no confrontation with Vietcong soldiers or village people. Harry flicked away his cigarette and started down the slope. He turned, waiting for Rico to follow him. "Coming?"

"I'll be down after a while."

"Suit yourself." Harry walked swiftly down the bluff, his feet carrying with them the yielding dirt in a flurry of small pebbles and loose earth. Rico was relieved. He needed some time by himself, to think things out. But Harry was right. To come across an ocean just to do routine checks, to patrol ground where there was no real danger . . . it could get pretty shitty. The enemy was hundreds of miles away.

The enemy! He remembered the combat creed—kill or be killed. Down a man—the lethal kick: a strangling is neater and quieter than the slitting of a throat; grind your heel against a face to mash the brains. Stomp the rib cage to carve the heart with bone splinters. Kill . . .

Hey, who was kidding who? They almost made him believe it back at boot camp in the States. In fact only a short while ago, only that morning, he had crouched down in the growth following a mangrove swamp, fearing an unseen enemy, ready to kill. Only that morning. But now, as he looked down at the peaceful village with its small rice field, its scattered huts, something had struck deep, something beyond the logic of war and enemy, something deep in his guts.

He had been cautioned: the rows of thatched huts were not really peoples' homes, but "hootches," makeshift stays built by the makeshift enemy. But then they were real enemies. There were enough dead Americans to prove it. The hootches didn't matter. The people didn't matter. These people knew how to pick up their sticks and go. Go where? How many of these villages had been bulldozed? Flattened by gunfire? Good pyres for napalm, these Vietnamese villages. A new kind of battleground.

Rico looked down and saw huts that were homes clustered in an intimacy that he knew well. The village of Mai Cao was no different than Valverde, the barrio where he had grown up. A woman came out of a hut, walking tall and with a certain grace, a child on her shoulder. She was walking toward a stream east of the slope. She stopped along the path and looked up to say something to the child. It struck him again, the feeling—a bond—that people were all the same everywhere.

The same scent from the earth, the same warmth from the sun, a woman walking with a child—his mother, Trini. His little mother who had left Tarahumara country and crossed the Barranca del Cobre, taking with her seeds from the hills of Batopilas, withstanding suffering, danger—for what? For a dream, a piece of ground in the land of plenty, the United States of America. She had waded across the Rio Grande from Juárez, Mexico, to El Paso, Texas, when she felt the birth pangs of his coming. He had been born a U.S. citizen because his mother had had a dream. She had made the dream come true—an acre of river land in Valverde, the edge of the border. His mother, like the earth and sun, mattered. The woman with the child on her shoulder mattered. Every human life in the village mattered. He knew this not only with the mind but with the heart.

Rico remembered a warning from combat training, from the weary, wounded soldiers who had fought and killed and survived, soldiers sent to Saigon, waiting to go home. His company had been flown to Saigon before being sent to the front. And this was the front, villages like Mai Cao. He felt relieved knowing that the fighting was hundreds of miles away from the people of Mai Cao—but the warning was still there: Watch out for pregnant women with machine guns. Toothless old women are experts with the knife between the shoulders. Begging children with hidden grenades, the unseen VC hiding in the hootches. Village people were not people, they were the enemy. The woman who knew the child on her shoulder, who knew the path to her door, who knew the coming of the sun—she was the enemy.

It was a discord not to be believed by instinct or intuition. And Rico was an Indian, the son of a Tarahumara chieftain. Theirs was a world of instinct and intuitive decisions. Suddenly he heard the sounds of motors. He looked to the other side of the slope, down to the road where the carryalls had started queuing their way back to the post. Rico ran down the hill to join his company.

In Rico's dream, Sergeant Keever was shouting in code, "Heller, heller!" Rico woke with a start. It wasn't a dream. The men around him were scrambling out of the pup tent. Outside, most of the men were lining up in uneven formation. Rico saw a communiqué in the sergeant's hand. Next to Keever was a lieutenant from communications headquarters. Keever was reading the communiqué:

"Special mission 72 for Company C, Platoon 2, assigned at 2200 hours. Move into the village of Mai Cao, field manual description—hill 72. Destroy the village."

No! It was crazy. Why? Just words on a piece of paper. Keever had to tell him why. There had to be a reason. Had the enemy come this far? It was impossible. Only that morning he had stood on the slope. He caught up with Keever, blurting out, "Why? I mean—why must we destroy it?"

Sergeant Keever stopped in his tracks and turned steel blue eyes at Rico. "What you say?"

"Why, I said."

"You just follow orders, savvy?"

"Are the Vietcong . . ."

"Did you hear me? You want trouble, Private?"

"There's people . . ."

"I don't believe you, soldier! But okay. Tell you as much as I know. We gotta erase the village in case the Vietcong come this way. So they won't use it as a stronghold. Now move your ass!"

Keever walked away from him, his lips tight in some kind of disgust. Rico did not follow this time. He went to get his gear and join the men in one of the carryalls. Three carryalls for the assault; three carryalls moving up the same road. Rico felt the weight and hardness of his carbine. Now it had a strange, hideous meaning. The machine guns were some kind of nightmare. The mission was to kill and burn and erase all memories. Rico swallowed a guilt that rose from the marrow and with it, all kinds of fear. He had to do something, something to stop it, but he didn't know what. And despite all those feelings there was a certain reluctance to do anything but follow orders. In the darkness, his lips formed words from the anthem: "My country 'tis of thee . . ."

They came to the point where the tree line straggled between two hills that rose darkly against the moon. Rico wondered if all the men were of one mind—one mind to kill. Was he a coward? No! It was not killing the enemy that his whole being was rejecting, but firing machine guns into a village of sleeping people . . . people. Rico remembered when only the week before, returning from their usual patrol, the men from the company had stopped at the stream, mingling with the children, old men, and women of the village. There had been an innocence about the whole thing. His voice broke the silence in the carryall, a voice harsh and feverish. "We can get the people out of there. Help them evacuate . . ."

"Shut up." Harry's voice was tight, impatient.

The carryalls traveled through the tall, undulant grass following the dirt road that led to the edge of the bluff. It was not all tall grass. Once in a while trees appeared again, clumped around scrub bushes. Ten miles out the carryalls stopped. It was still a mile's walk to the bluff in the darkness, but they had to avoid detection. Sergeant Keever was leading the party. Rico, almost at the rear, knew he had to catch up to him. He had to stop him. Harry was ahead of him, a silent black bundle walking stealthily through rutted ground to discharge his duty. For a second, Rico hesitated. That was the easy thing to do: carry out his duty, die a hero, do his duty blindly and survive—hell, why not? He knew what happened to men who backed down in battle. But he wasn't backing down. Hell, what else was it? How often had he heard it among the gringos in his company?

"You Mexican? Hey, you Mexicans are real fighters. I mean, everybody knows Mexicans have guts."

A myth perhaps. But no. He thought of the old guys who had fought in World War II. Many of them were on welfare back in the barrio. But, man, did they have medals! He had never seen so many purple hearts. He remembered old Toque, the wino, who had tried to pawn his medals to buy a bottle. No way, man. They weren't worth a nickel.

He quickly edged past Harry, pushing by the men ahead of him to reach the sergeant. He was running, tall grass brushing his shoulder, tall grass that had swayed peacefully like wheat. The figure of Sergeant Keever was in front of him now. He had a sudden impulse to reach out and hold Keever back. But the sergeant had stopped. Rico did not touch him, but whispered hoarsely, desperately, in the dark. "Let's get the people out—evacuate . . ."

"What the hell . . ." Keever's voice was ice. He recognized Rico and hissed, "Get back to your position, soldier, or I'll shoot you myself."

Rico did as he was told, almost unaware of the men around him. But in the distance he heard something splashing in the water of the canal, in his nostrils the sweet smell of burnt wood. He looked toward the clearing and saw the cluster of huts bathed in moonlight. In the same moonlight he saw Keever giving signals. In the gloom he saw the figures of the men carrying machine guns. They looked like dancing grasshoppers as they ran ahead to position themselves on the bluff. He felt like yelling, "For Christ's sake! Where is the enemy?"

The taste of blood was in his mouth, and he suddenly realized he had bitten his quivering lower lip. As soon as Sergeant Keever gave the signal, all sixteen men would open fire on the huts—machine guns, carbines would erase everything. No more Mai Cao—the execution of duty without question, without alternative. They were positioned on the south slope. Sergeant Keever up ahead, squatting on his heels, looking at his watch. He stood, after a quick glance at the men. As Sergeant Keever raised his hand to give the signal for attack, Rico felt the cold, metallic deadness of his rifle. His hands began to tremble as he released the safety catch. Sergeant Keever was on the rise just above him. Rico stared at the sergeant's arm, raised, ready to fall—the signal to fire. The crossfire was inside Rico, a heavy-dosed tumult—destroy the village, erase all memory. There was ash in his mouth. Once the arm came down, there was no turning back.

In a split second Rico turned his rifle at a forty-degree angle and fired at the sergeant's arm. Keever half-turned with the impact of the bullet, then fell to his knees. In a whooping whisper the old-time soldier blew out the words, "That fucking bastard—get him." He got up and signaled the platoon back to the carryalls as two men grabbed Rico, one hitting him on the side of the head with the butt of his rifle. Rico felt the sting of the blow as they pinned his arms back and forced him to walk the path back to the carryall. He did not resist. There was a lump in his throat, and he blinked back tears, tears of relief. The memory of the village would not be erased. Someone shouted in the dark, "They're on to us! There's an old man with a lantern and others coming out of the hootches."

"People—just people . . ." Rico whispered, wanting to shout it, wanting to tell them that he had done the right thing. But the heaviness that filled his senses was the weight of another truth. He was a traitor, a maniac. He had shot his superior in a battle crisis. He was being carried almost bodily back to the truck. He glanced at the thick brush along the road, thinking that somewhere beyond it was a rice field, and beyond that a mangrove swamp. There was a madman inside his soul that made him think of rice fields and mangrove swamps instead of what he had done. Not once did he look up. Everyone around him was strangely quiet and remote. Only the sound of trudging feet.

In the carryall, the faces of the men sitting around Rico were indiscernible in the dark, but he imagined their eyes, wide and confused, peering through the dark at him with a wakefulness that questioned what he had done. Did they know his reason? Did they care? The truck suddenly lurched. Deep in his gut, Rico felt a growing fear. He choked back a hysteria rising from his diaphragm. The incessant bumping of the carryalls as they moved unevenly on the dirt road accused him too. He looked up into the night sky and watched the moon eerily weave in and out of tree branches. The darkness was like his fear. It had no solutions. Back at the post, Sergeant Keever and a medic passed by Rico, already handcuffed, without any sign of recognition. Sergeant Keever had already erased him from existence. The wheels of justice would take their course. Rico had been placed under arrest and temporarily shackled to a cot in one of the tents. Three days later he was moved to a makeshift bamboo hut, with a guard in front of the hut at all times. His buddies brought in food like strangers, awkward in their silence, anxious to leave him alone. He felt like some kind of poisonous bug. Only Harry came by to see him, after a week.

"You dumb ass, were you on loco weed?" Harry asked in disgust.

"I didn't want people killed, that's all."

"Hell, that's no reason, those Chinks aren't even—even . . ."

"Even what?" Rico demanded. He almost screamed it a second time. "Even what?"

"Take it easy, will you? You better go for a Section 8."* Harry was putting him aside like everyone else. "They're sending you back to the States next week. You'll have to face Keever sometime this afternoon. I thought I'd better let you know."

"Thanks." Rico knew the hopelessness of it all. But there was still that nagging question he had to ask. "Listen, nobody tells me anything. Did you all go back to Mai Cao? I mean, is it still there?"

---

* [A discharge from the U.S. Army for military inaptitude or undesirable habits.]

"Still there. Orders from headquarters to forget it. The enemy were spotted taking an opposite direction. But nobody's going to call you a hero, you understand? What you did was crud. You're no soldier. You'll never be a soldier." Rico said nothing to defend himself. He began to scratch the area around the steel rings on his ankles. Harry was scowling at him. He said it again, almost shouting, "I said, you'll never be a soldier."

"So?" There was soft disdain in Rico's voice.

"You blew it, man. You'll be locked up for a long, long time."

"Maybe." Rico's voice was without concern.

"Don't you care?"

"I'm free inside, Harry." Rico laughed in relief. "Free . . ."

Harry shrugged, peering at Rico unbelievingly, then turned and walked out of the hut.

Questions

1. What does Rico's "instinct or intuition" tell him about the village? (241) Does he act on these instincts?

2. Before shooting Sergeant Keever, why does Rico think more about whether he is a coward than about the consequences of his actions?

3. At the end of the story, when Harry says Rico will be "locked up for a long time," why does Rico say, "I'm free inside" and laugh in relief? (246)

4. Does the outcome of Rico's actions justify his decision?

5. Is it justifiable to ask why when given an order in the military? Does asking why make for a better soldier or a poorer one?

6. In war, is refusing orders to save lives ever justifiable?

Margaret Atwood

Canadian writer Margaret Atwood (1939–) is a prolific poet and novelist. Her most famous novels include *The Handmaid's Tale* (1985) and the Booker Prize–winning *The Blind Assassin* (2000).

Atwood's poem "It Is Dangerous to Read Newspapers" appears in the collection *The Animals in That Country*, which was published in 1968, in the midst of the Vietnam War. Escalating U.S. military involvement in Vietnam prompted widespread antiwar protests around the world. Thousands of young Americans fled to Canada rather than submit to the draft, but at the same time many Canadians volunteered to fight in the war.

By the age of twenty-nine, Atwood's life had already spanned World War II, the Korean War, the Cold War, and the Vietnam War. In this poem, she traces her growth from childhood to young adulthood through the lens of world events. She juxtaposes childish and personal moments with images of destructive violence, and helpless innocence with seeming complicity in global atrocities.

Atwood's poem highlights the dissemination and assimilation of disturbing news imagery. While she refers to reading newspapers, the ways in which acts of war are made visible and communicated to those far from the front line has changed enormously over time. With media coverage now feeding images to a global audience twenty-four hours a day, war has become an even more visual presence in our homes. Atwood asks whether, once people are made aware of the violence of war through media coverage, they become in some way implicated in that violence.

IT IS DANGEROUS TO READ NEWSPAPERS

While I was building neat
castles in the sandbox,
the hasty pits were
filling with bulldozed corpses

and as I walked to the school
washed and combed, my feet
stepping on the cracks in the cement
detonated red bombs.

Now I am grownup
and literate, and I sit in my chair
as quietly as a fuse
and the jungles are flaming, the under-
brush is charged with soldiers,
the names on the difficult
maps go up in smoke.

I am the cause, I am a stockpile of chemical
toys, my body
is a deadly gadget,
I reach out in love, my hands are guns,
my good intentions are completely lethal.

Even my
passive eyes transmute
everything I look at to the pocked
black and white of a war photo,
how
can I stop myself

It is dangerous to read newspapers.

Each time I hit a key
on my electric typewriter,
speaking of peaceful trees

another village explodes.

Questions

1. Why does the poet juxtapose her actions as a child with the violence that was happening simultaneously in the larger world?

2. Why does the poet describe the maps whose names go up in smoke as "difficult"? (249)

3. Why does the poet say that she is the cause of the horrors she describes?

4. Why does the poet describe her body as a "deadly gadget" and her hands as "guns"? (249)

5. What does the poet mean when she says, "It is dangerous to read newspapers"? For whom is it dangerous? (250)

6. Does news of terrible events outside our immediate experience that we receive through the media confer on us any responsibility to do something about these events?

Philip Caputo

Philip Caputo (1941–) served in the U.S. Marine Corps from 1964 to 1967, reached the rank of lieutenant, and was a platoon leader in the Vietnam War. In 1968 Caputo joined the *Chicago Tribune* as a journalist and was part of a team that won the Pulitzer Prize for its work uncovering election fraud. He later worked as a foreign correspondent covering the Middle East, the Soviet Union, and Vietnam. Since 1977 he has written several novels, essays, and screenplays. Caputo's writing often revisits his experience in Vietnam.

Caputo was in Vietnam from 1965 to 1966. Even during those early years of the war, U.S. involvement was hampered by oversights, errors, and inadequacies that worsened the situation on the ground. The U.S. military and the public had been assured that the war in Vietnam would be quick and clean, but that assessment proved wrong. The Vietcong fighters used guerrilla tactics that were unfamiliar to American strategists and for which combat troops were neither trained nor equipped. Casualties mounted, the goals of the war remained poorly defined, and signs of success were elusive.

Caputo notes distressing behavior, in himself and in his men, that prompts him eventually to question every aspect of the Vietnam War, from the mindset of individual soldiers to the rationale of the American military command. The stress of combat led him and others to commit acts that went far beyond conventional rules of engagement and codes of morality. This selection, the last chapter from Caputo's memoir *A Rumor of War* (1977), recounts Caputo's final months as a Marine in Vietnam and the ordeal he faced as the result of his involvement in one of these acts.

A RUMOR OF WAR

(selection)

Merry it was to laugh there—
Where death becomes absurd and life absurder.
For power was on us as we slashed bones bare
Not to feel sickness or remorse of murder.

WILFRED OWEN, "Apologia Pro Poemate Meo"

iling up the trail that weaved through the stunted scrub jungle surrounding the outpost, the six men in the patrol walked on their bruised and rotted feet as if they were walking barefoot over broken glass. The patrol was waved in, and the Marines climbed over the rusty perimeter wire one by one. The foothills where they had been all morning stretched behind them, toward the moss-green mountains wavering in the heat-shimmer.

The heat was suffocating, as it always was between monsoon storms. The air seemed about to explode. Sun-dazed, half the platoon were dozing beneath their hooches. Others cleaned their rifles, which would start to corrode in a few hours and have to be cleaned again. A few men squatted in a circle around a tin of cheese which had been brought to Charley Hill with the twice-weekly ration resupply. The cheese was a special treat: a change from the dreary diet of C rations, and it eased the diarrhea that gripped us. Squatting around the tin, the men ate with their fingers, grunting their approval.

"Hey, we got some cheese," one of them said to Crowe's patrol. "Good cheese. You guys want some cheese?"

Too tired to eat, the men in the patrol shook their heads and hobbled toward their foxholes. Their skin was pallid except for their faces and necks, their hands, and a V-shaped spot on their chests, which were tanned. One rifleman's bicep bore a tattoo: a skull and crossbones underscored by the words "USMC—*Death before Dishonor.*" I laughed to myself. With the way things had been going since Operation Long Lance, I was confident that the Marine would not have to worry about facing the choice. Page and Navarro, killed a few days before, had faced no choice. The booby-trapped artillery shell had not given them any time to choose, or to take cover, or to do anything but die instantly. Both had had only four days left of their Vietnam tours, thus confirming the truth in the proverb "You're never a short-timer until you're home."

I was sitting on the roof of the outpost's command bunker, sunning my legs. The corpsmen said that sun and air would help dry the running sores on feet and lower legs. The disease had been diagnosed as tropical impetigo. I had probably contracted it on our last patrol—three days in a monsoon rain that would have impressed Noah; three days of slogging through the slime of drowned swamps. The corpsmen had given me penicillin shots, but even antibiotics were not effective in that climate. Pus continued to ooze from the ulcers, so that whenever I took off my boots to change socks I had to hold my breath against the stench of my own rotting flesh. Well, I could have caught something a lot worse than a skin disease.

Holding a map in one hand, Crowe walked up to me to make his report. Crowe, called Pappy by the teenage platoon because he had reached the advanced age of twenty-three—growing older than twenty-one was an achievement for most combat riflemen—had a face that made his nickname seem appropriate. The months of wincing at snipers' bullets, the sleepless nights, and the constant strain of looking for trip wires had aged him. Behind his glasses, Crowe's eyes were as dull as an old man's.

He said his patrol had picked up some intelligence information. Spreading the map over the bunker's sandbagged roof, he pointed to a village called "Giao-Tri (2)."

"You remember those three VCs we found in this ville two weeks ago, sir?"

I said that I did. He was referring to an earlier patrol and the three young men we had brought in for questioning. Since Giao-Tri was a village usually controlled by the Vietcong, it was unusual to find young men there. The three youths, moreover, had been carrying papers that were obvious forgeries, and their ages had been falsified. McCloy, who by this time spoke fluent Vietnamese, and an ARVN militia sergeant gave them a perfunctory interrogation. They were released when the sergeant determined that their papers had been forged and their ages falsified so they could stay in school and out of the army. They were draft-dodgers, not Vietcong.

"Well, sir," Crowe went on, "it looks like two of 'em are Charlies after all, the two older ones."

"How'd you find that out?"

"The younger one told me, Le Dung I think his name is. We found him in the ville again and I started to question him. You know, a little English, a little Vietnamese, a little sign language. He said the other two was VC, sappers who was makin' mines and booby traps. I think he's tellin' the truth because one of the other two walked by when we was talkin' and the kid shut up. He looked scared as hell and shut up. So, when the other dude's out of sight, I ask the kid, 'VC? Him VC?' And the kid nods his head and says 'VC.' The third guy is standin' over by a house, buildin' a gate or somethin'. I pointed at the guy and said, 'VC there?' The kid nods again and says that both the Charlies live in that house. Then I broke out my map and the kid said there were five Cong in Binh Thai, sappers too, and armed with automatic rifles. He drew me a picture of the weapons. Here." Crowe handed me a piece of paper with a crude drawing of a top-loading automatic rifle that resembled a British Bren. "Then he says there's a platoon—fifteen VC—in Hoi-Vuc and they've got a mortar and a machine gun."

Angry, I swung off the bunker. "Crowe, why in the hell didn't you capture those two and bring 'em in?"

"Well, I don't know, sir. I mean, Mister McCloy cleared 'em. He said they was okay before."

"Goddamnit, we didn't know this before. Crowe, this company's lost thirty-five men in the last month. All of them to mines and booby traps, and you get a guy who shows you two sappers and you leave them there."

"Sorry, sir. It's just that they were cleared. Hell, we never know who's the guerrilla and who ain't around here."

"No shit. Listen, the info's good. You did all right. Shove off and take a break."

"Yes, sir."

I went down into the bunker, where Jones was cleaning his rifle. It was stifling inside, the air stale with the smells of sweat, rifle oil, and the canvas haversacks hanging from pegs driven into the mud walls. Cranking the handle of the field phone, I called company HQ with Crowe's report, dreading the lecture I would get from Captain Neal. *Why didn't he capture them? What's the matter with that platoon of yours, lieutenant? Aren't your people thinking?*

Having lost about thirty percent of his command in the past month alone, Neal had become almost intolerable. I assumed battalion was putting a great deal of pressure on him; since Operation Long Lance ended, the company had killed only three guerrillas and captured two more, while suffering six times as many casualties itself. C Company's kill ratio was below standard. Bodies. Bodies. Bodies. Battalion wanted bodies. Neal wanted bodies. He lectured his officers on the importance of aggressiveness and made implied threats when he thought we lacked that attribute. "Your people aren't being aggressive enough," he told me when one of my squads failed to pursue two VC who had fired on them one night. I argued that the squad leader had done the sensible thing: with only eight men, at night, and a mile from friendly lines, he had no idea if those two guerrillas were alone or the point men for a whole battalion. Had he pursued, his squad might have fallen into a trap. "Mister Caputo, when we make contact with the enemy, we maintain it, not break it," said Neal. "You had best get those people of yours in shape." Meekly, so meekly that I despised myself as much as I despised him, I said, "Yes, sir. I'll get them in shape." A few days later, Neal told me and the other officers that he was adopting a new policy: from now on, any Marine in the company who killed a confirmed Vietcong would be given an extra beer ration and the time to drink it. Because our men were so exhausted, we knew the promise of time off would be as great an inducement as the extra ration of beer. So we went along with the captain's policy, without reflecting on the moral implications. That is the level to which we had sunk from the lofty idealism of a year before. We were going to kill people for a few cans of beer and the time to drink them.

McCloy answered the phone. Neal was busy elsewhere, so I was spared another chewing out. I read Crowe's report to McCloy, who of course asked, "Why didn't they bring them in?" I explained. Murph said he would pass the information on to battalion S-2. Yes, I thought, putting the receiver back in its canvas-covered case, and they'll pass it on to regimental S-2, who'll pass it on to division G-2, who'll bury it in a file cabinet, and the sappers will go on blowing up Charley Company. An immense weariness came over me. I was fed up with it, with the futile patrols and the inconclusive operations, with the mines and the mud and the diseases. Only a month remained to my Vietnam tour, and my one hope was to leave on my own feet and not on a stretcher or in a box. Only a month. What was a month? In Vietnam, a month was an eternity. Page and Navarro had had only four days left. I was much haunted by their deaths.

Jones, leaning against a wall of the bunker, was still cleaning his rifle. There was a sheen of sweat on his face. His cleaning rod, drawn back and forth through the rifle bore, made a monotonous, scraping sound. I lay down on the poncho that was spread across the floor. Sleep. I had to get some sleep. Taking one of the haversacks off its peg, I propped it against my helmet to make a pillow and rolled onto my side, grimacing when my trousers, which had been glued to the pussy sores, pulled loose and tore away bits of flesh. To sleep, to sleep, perchance not to dream. I had again begun to have some very bad dreams.

The month that followed the attack in the Vu Gia valley had itself been a bad dream. I can recall only snatches of that time; fragmentary scenes flicker on my mental screen like excerpts from a film: There is a shot of the company marching near a tree line that was napalmed during the assault. Through my field glasses, I see pigs rooting around forms which resemble black logs, but which are charred corpses. *Click.* The next scene. A crazy, running firefight on the last day of the operation, the Vietcong dashing down one side of a wide river, firing as they run, my platoon running down a dike on the other side, firing back. Bullets dance in the rice paddy between the river and the dike, then spurt toward Jones and me. As the rounds strike at our feet the two of us dive over backward into a heap of buffalo dung from which we leap up laughing insanely, the offal dripping from our faces. Then the company's mortar crew is dropping sixties on the enemy and my platoon pours rifle fire into the pall of shell smoke. An artillery observer, flying over in a spotter plane, calls on the radio to say that he sees seven enemy bodies lying on a trail near the river bank.

Click. The next scenes take place at the company's operation area near Danang. They are all of a piece, shots of patrols coming back diminished by two or three or half a dozen men. The soundtrack is monotonous: the thud of exploding mines, the quick rattle of small-arms fire, the thrashing of marines pursuing enemy ambush parties, almost never finding them, men crying "Corpsman!" and the *wap-wap-wap* noise of the medevac helicopters. *Click.* There is one piece of time-lapse footage, but instead of showing flowers blooming, it shows our company slowly dissolving. With each frame, the ranks get shorter and shorter, and the faces of the men are the faces of men who feel doomed, who are just waiting their turn to be blown up by a mine. *Click.* A shot of my platoon on a night patrol, slogging through a blackness so deep that each man must hold onto the handle of the entrenching tool on the back of the man in front of him. A driving rain whips us as we stumble blindly through the dark. Holding onto an E-tool handle with one hand, I am holding a compass in the other. I cannot see the Marine who is an arm's length in front of me, only the pale, luminous dial of the compass. *Click.* There is a scene of PFC Arnett, who has been hit by a mine. He is lying on his back in the rain, wrapped in scarlet ribbons of his own blood. He looks up at me with the dreamy, far-off expression of a saint in a Renaissance painting and says, "This is my third Purple Heart and they ain't gettin' no more chances. I'm goin' home."

Other episodes reflect what the war has done to us. A corporal is chasing a wounded Vietcong after a firefight. He follows the man's blood trail until he finds him crawling toward the entrance to a tunnel. The enemy soldier turns his face toward his pursuer, perhaps to surrender, perhaps to beg for mercy. The corporal walks up to him and casually shoots him in the head. *Click.* Sergeant Horne is standing in front of me with a nervous smile on his face. He says, "Sir, Mister McKenna's gone crazy." I ask how he has arrived at this diagnosis. "We were set in in a daylight ambush near Hoi-Vuc," Horne says. "An old woman came by and spotted us, so we held her so she wouldn't warn the VC that we were around. She was chewing betel nut and just by accident spit some of it in Mister McKenna's face. The next thing I knew, he took out his pistol and shot her in the chest. Then he told one of the corpsmen to patch her up, like he didn't realize that he'd killed her." There is a quick-cut to the officer's tent that night. In the soft light of a kerosene lamp, McKenna and I are talking about the murder. He says, "Phil, the gun just went off by itself. You know, it really bothers me." I reply that it should. "No, that isn't what I mean," McKenna says. "I mean the thing that bothers me about killing her is that it doesn't bother me."

I slept briefly and fitfully in the bunker and woke up agitated. Psychologically, I had never felt worse. I had been awake for no more than a few seconds when I was seized by the same feeling that had gripped me after my nightmare about the mutilated men in my old platoon: a feeling of being afraid when there was no reason to be. And this unreasoning fear quickly produced the sensation I had often had in action: of watching myself in a movie. Although I have had a decade to think about it, I am still unable to explain why I woke up in that condition. I had not dreamed. It was a quiet day, one of those days when it was difficult to believe a war was on. Yet, my sensations were those of a man actually under fire. Perhaps I was suffering a delayed reaction to some previous experience. Perhaps it was simply battle fatigue. I had been in Vietnam for nearly a year, and was probably more worn out than I realized at the time. Months of accumulated pressures might have chosen just that moment to burst, suddenly and for no apparent reason. Whatever the cause, I was outwardly normal, if a little edgier than usual; but inside, I was full of turbulent emotions and disordered thoughts, and I could not shake that weird sensation of being split in two.

Thinking fresh air might help, I climbed out of the musty bunker. I only felt worse, irritated by the pain that came each time my trousers tore loose from the ulcers. The sores itched unbearably, but I couldn't scratch them because scratching would spread the disease. The late-afternoon air was oppressive. Heat came up from the baked earth and pressed down from the sky. Clouds were beginning to build in gray towers over the mountains, threatening more rain. Rain. Rain. Rain. When would it stop raining? From the heads rose the stench of feces, the soupy deposits of our diseased bowels. My need for physical activity overcame my discomfort and I set out to walk the perimeter. Around and around I walked, sometimes chatting with the men, sometimes sitting and staring into the distance. A few yards outside the perimeter, the walls of a half-ruined building shone bright white in the sun's glare. It made me squint to look at them, but I did anyway. I looked at them for a long time. I don't know why. I just remember staring at them, feeling the heat grow more oppressive as the clouds piled up and advanced across the sky. The building had been a temple of some kind, but it was now little more than a pile of stones. Vines were growing over the stones and over the jagged, bullet-scarred walls, which turned from white to hot pink as the sun dropped into the clouds. Behind the building lay the scrub jungle that covered the slopes of the hill. It smelled of decaying wood and leaves, and the low trees encircled the outpost like the disorderly ranks of a besieging army. Staring at the jungle and at the ruined temple, hatred welled up in me; a hatred for this green, moldy, alien world in which we fought and died.

My thoughts and feelings over the next few hours are irretrievably jumbled now, but at some point in the early evening, I was seized by an irresistible compulsion to do something. "Something's got to be done" was about the clearest thought that passed through my brain. I was fixated on the company's intolerable predicament. We could now muster only half of our original strength, and half of our effectives had been wounded at least once. If we suffered as many casualties in the next month as we had in the one past, we would be down to fifty or sixty men, little more than a reinforced platoon. It was madness for us to go on walking down those trails and tripping booby traps without any chance to retaliate. *Retaliate.* The word rang in my head. *I will retaliate.* It was then that my chaotic thoughts began to focus on the two men whom Le Dung, Crowe's informant, had identified as Vietcong. My mind did more than focus on them; it fixed on them like a heat-seeking missile fixing on the tailpipe of a jet. They became an obsession. I would get them. I would get them before they got any more of us; before they got me. I'm going to get those bastards, I said to myself, suddenly feeling giddy.

"I'm going to get those bastards," I said aloud, rushing down into the bunker. Jones looked at me quizzically. "The VC, Jones, I'm going to get them." I was laughing. From my map case, I took out an overlay of the patrol route which second squad was to follow that night. It took them to a trail junction just outside the village of Giao-Tri. It was perfect. If the two VC walked out of the village, they would fall into the ambush. I almost laughed out loud at the idea of their deaths. If the VC did not leave the village, then the squad would infiltrate into it, Crowe guiding them to the house Le Dung had pointed out, and capture them—"snatch," in the argot. Yes, that's what I would do. A snatch patrol. The squad would capture the two VC and bring them to the outpost. I would interrogate them, beat the hell out of them if I had to, learn the locations of other enemy cells and units, then kill or capture those. I would get all of them. But suppose the two guerrillas resisted? The patrol would kill them, then. Kill VC. That's what we were supposed to do. Bodies. Neal wanted bodies. Well, I would give him bodies, and then my platoon would be rewarded instead of reproved. I did not have the authority to send the squad into the village. The patrol order called only for an ambush at the trail junction. But who was the real authority out on that isolated out-post? *I* was. I would take matters into my own hands. Out there, I could do what I damned well pleased. And I would. The idea of taking independent action made me giddier still. I went out to brief the patrol.

In the twilight, Allen, Crowe, Lonehill, and two other riflemen huddled around me. Wearing bush hats, their hands and faces blackened with shoe polish, they looked appropriately ferocious. I told them what they were to do, but, in my addled state of mind, I was almost incoherent at times. I laughed frequently and made several bloodthirsty jokes that probably left them with the impression I wouldn't mind if they summarily executed both Vietcong. All the time, I had that feeling of watching myself in a film. I could hear myself laughing, but it did not sound like my laugh.

"Okay, you know what to do," I said to Allen, the patrol leader. "You set in ambush for a while. If nobody comes by, you go into the ville and you get them. *You get those goddamned VC.* Snatch 'em up and bring 'em back here, but if they give you any problems, kill 'em."

"Sir, since we ain't supposed to be in the ville, what do we say if we have to kill 'em?"

"We'll just say they walked into your ambush. Don't sweat that. All the higher-ups want is bodies."

"Yes, sir," Allen said, and I saw the look in his eyes. It was a look of distilled hatred and anger, and when he grinned his skull-like grin, I knew he was going to kill those men on the slightest pretext. And, knowing that, I still did not repeat my order that the VC were to be captured if at all possible. It was my secret and savage desire that the two men die. In my heart, I hoped Allen would find some excuse for killing them, and Allen had read my heart. He smiled and I smiled back, and we both knew in that moment what was going to happen. There was a silent communication between us, an unspoken understanding: blood was to be shed. There is no mystery about such unspoken communication. Two men who have shared the hardships and dangers of war come to know each other as intimately as two natural brothers who have lived together for years; one can read the other's heart without a word being said.

The patrol left, creeping off the outpost into the swallowing darkness. Not long afterward, I began to be teased by doubts. It was the other half of my double self, the calm and lucid half, warning that something awful was going to happen. The thought of recalling the patrol crossed my mind, but I could not bring myself to do it. I felt driven, in the grip of an inexorable power. Something had to be done.

And something was done. Allen called on the radio and said they had killed one of the Vietcong and captured the other. They were coming in with the prisoner. Letting out a whoop, I called Neal on the field phone. He said he had monitored Allen's radio transmission. He congratulated us:

"That's good work your men did out there."

I was elated. Climbing out of the bunker, I excitedly told Coffell, "They got both of 'em! Both of 'em! Yeeeah-hoo!" The night was hot and stiff. Off to the west, heat lightning flashed like shellfire in the clouds that obscured the sky above the mountains. It was clear directly overhead, and I could see the fixed and lofty stars.

Waiting by the perimeter for the patrol to return, I heard a burst of rifle fire and the distinctive roar of Crowe's shotgun. Allen called on the radio again: the prisoner had whipped a branch into Crowe's face and tried to escape. They had killed him.

"All right, bring the body in. I want to search it," I said.

They came in shortly. The five men were winded from their swift withdrawal and a little more excited than such veterans should have been. Allen was particularly overwrought. He started laughing as soon as he was inside the perimeter wire. Perhaps it was the release from tension that made him laugh like that, tinny, mirthlessly. When he calmed down, he told me what had happened:

"We sneaked into the ville, like you told us, sir. Crowe guided us to the house where he'd talked to the informant. It was empty, so we went to the hooch where the VC lived. Me, Crowe, and Lonehill went inside. The other two stayed on the trail to guard our rear. It was dark in the house, so Crowe turned on his flashlight and there's the two Cong, sleepin' in their beds. Lonehill goes into the other room and this girl in there starts screamin'. 'Shut her up,' I said and Lonehill cracks her with his rifle barrel." Allen started to laugh again. So did Crowe and a few of the men who were listening. I was laughing, too. How funny. Old Lonehill hit her with his rifle. "So about then, one of the Cong jumps up in his bed and the broad starts screamin' again. Crowe went in and slapped her and told her to keep her damned mouth shut. Then he comes back into the room and pops the Cong sittin' up with his forty-five. The dude jumps up and runs—he was hit in the shoulder—and Crowe runs after him. He was runnin' around outside yellin' 'Troi Oi! Troi Oi!'" (Oh God) "and then Crowe greased him and he didn't do no more yellin'. The other dude made a break for the door, but Lonehill grabbed him. 'Okay, let's take him back,' I said, and we moved the hell out. We was right at the base of the hill when the gook whipped the branch in Crowe's face. Somebody said, 'He's makin' a break, grease the motherfucker,' and Lonehill greased him and Crowe blasted him with the shotgun. I mean, that dude was *dead*." Madly and hysterically, we all laughed again.

"Okay," I said, "where's the body?"

"Right outside the wire, sir."

The dead man was lying on his belly. The back of his head was blown out, and, in the beam of my flashlight, his brains were a shiny gray mass. Someone kicked the body over onto its back and said, "Oh, excuse me, Mr. Charles, I hope that didn't hurt," and we all doubled over with laughter. I beamed the flashlight on the corpse's face. His eyes were wide and glowing, like the eyes in a stuffed head. While Coffell held the flashlight, I searched the body. There was something about the dead man that troubled me. It was not the mutilation—I was used to that. It was his face. It was such a young face, and, while I searched him, I kept thinking, He's just a boy, just a boy. I could not understand why his youth bothered me; the VC's soldiers, like our own, were all young men.

Tearing off his bloodstained shirt, shredded, like his chest, by shotgun pellets, I looked for his papers. Someone quipped, "Hey, lieutenant, he'll catch cold." Everyone laughed again. I joined in, but I was not laughing as hard as before.

There were no documents in the boy's pockets, no cartridge belt around his waist. There was nothing that would have proved him to be a Vietcong. That troubled me further. I stood up and, taking the flashlight from Coffell, held it on the boy's dead face.

"Did you find anything on the other one?" I asked Allen.

"No, sir."

"No documents or weapons?"

"No, sir. Nothing."

"How about the house? Did you find anything that looked like booby-trap gear in the house?"

"No, sir."

"And no forged papers or anything like that?"

"No, sir. We didn't find nothing."

The laughter had stopped. I turned to Crowe.

"Are you *sure* this one was one of the two that kid pointed out?"

"Yes, sir," Crowe said, but he looked away from me.

"Tell me again why you shot him."

"Whipped a branch in my face, like Allen said." Crowe would not look at me. He looked at the ground. "He whipped a branch in my face and tried to make a break, so we wasted him."

The air seemed charged with guilt. I kept looking at the corpse, and a wave of horror rolled through me as I recognized the face. The sensation was like snapping out of a hypnotic trance. It was as jarring as suddenly awakening from a nightmare, except that I had awakened from one nightmare into another.

"Allen, is that how it happened?" I asked. "The prisoner tried to escape, right?"

"As far as I know, yes sir. Crowe shot him."

He was already covering himself. "Okay, if anyone asks you about this, you just say both these guys walked into your ambush. That's what you'll say, and you stick to that, all of you. They walked into your ambush and you killed one and captured the other. Then the prisoner tried to escape, so you killed him, too. Got that? You don't tell anybody that you snatched him out of the village."

"Yes, sir," Allen said.

"Shove off and pass that on to the others. You too, Crowe."

"Yes, sir," Crowe said, hanging his head like a naughty child.

They walked off. I stayed for a while, looking at the corpse. The wide, glowing, glassy eyes stared at me in accusation. The dead boy's open mouth screamed silently his innocence and our guilt. In the darkness and confusion, out of fear, exhaustion, and the brutal instincts acquired in the war, the Marines had made a mistake. An awful mistake. They had killed the wrong man. No, not they; *we*. We had killed the wrong man. That boy's innocent blood was on my hands as much as it was on theirs. I had sent them out there. My God, what have we done? I thought. I could think of nothing else. My God, what have we done. Please God, forgive us. What have we done?

Clicking off the flashlight, I told Coffell to get a burial party together. I did not know what else to do with the body of Crowe's informant, the boy named Le Dung.

The typewriters in the quonset hut began to click promptly at eight o'clock, when the legal clerks came in to begin another routine day of typing up routine reports. The red light on the electric coffee pot glowed and the electric fans on the clerks' desks stirred the warm, dense air. Having slept undisturbed for eight hours, as they did every night, and breakfasted on bacon and eggs, as they did every morning except when the division HQ mess served pancakes, the clerks were happy, healthy-looking boys. They appeared slightly bored by their dull work, but were content in the knowledge that their rear-echelon jobs gave them what their contemporaries in the line companies lacked: a future.

Sitting in one corner of the hut with my defense counsel, Lieutenant Jim Rader, I looked at the clerks and wished I were one of them. How pleasant it would be to have a future again. A crowd of witnesses milled around outside: Marines and Vietnamese villagers, the latter looking utterly bewildered by the courtroom drama in which they would soon play their assigned roles. One of the clerks muttered a curse as a fan blew some papers off his desk. The artificial gust blew against the wall behind them, rustling the pages of his short-timer's calendar. The calendar was graced by a pornographic drawing, beneath which the word "June" was flanked by the number "1966." All the dates had been crossed off except today's, the 30th, the day on which Lance Corporal Crowe was to be tried on two counts of premeditated murder.

I was to appear as a witness for the prosecution. There was an absurdity in that, as I was to be tried on the same charges by the same prosecutor the following morning. But then, the fact that we had been charged in the first place was absurd. They had taught us to kill and had told us to kill, and now they were going to court-martial us for killing.

A bound sheaf of papers as thick as a small-town telephone book and entitled "Investigating Officer's Report" sat on Rader's desk. It was the product of five months' labor on the part of various military lawyers, and the two top forms—DD457 and DD458—contained the charges against me: ". . . in that First Lieutenant Philip J. Caputo . . . did murder with premeditation Le Dung, a citizen of the Republic of Vietnam. In that First Lieutenant Philip J. Caputo . . . did murder with premeditation Le Du . . ." There was a third charge, resulting from my panicked attempt to deny that I had tried to cover up the killings: "In that First Lieutenant Philip J. Caputo . . . did subscribe under lawful oath a false statement in substance as follows: 'I did not tell them to stick by their statements,' which statements he did not then believe to be true."

There was a lot of other stuff—statements by witnesses, inquiry reports, and so forth—but one square on form DD457 was conspicuously blank. It was the square labeled EXPLANATORY OR EXTENUATING CIRCUMSTANCES ARE SUBMITTED HEREWITH. Early in the investigation, I wondered why the investigating officer had not submitted any explanatory or extenuating circumstances. Later, after I had time to think things over, I drew my own conclusion: the explanatory or extenuating circumstance was the war. The killings had occurred in war. They had occurred, moreover, in a war whose sole aim was to kill Vietcong, a war in which those ordered to do the killing often could not distinguish the Vietcong from civilians, a war in which civilians in "free-fire zones" were killed every day by weapons far more horrible than pistols or shotguns. The deaths of Le Dung and Le Du could not be divorced from the nature and conduct of the war. They were an inevitable product of the war. As I had come to see it, America could not intervene in a people's war without killing some of the people. But to raise those points in explanation or extenuation would be to raise a host of ambiguous moral questions. It could even raise the question of the morality of American intervention in Vietnam; or, as one officer told me, "It would open a real can of worms." Therefore, the five men in the patrol and I were to be tried as common criminals, much as if we had murdered two people in the course of a bank robbery during peacetime. If we were found guilty, the Marine Corps's institutional conscience would be clear. Six criminals, who, of course, did not represent the majority of America's fine fighting sons, had been brought to justice. Case closed. If we were found innocent, the Marine Corps would say, "Justice has taken its course, and in a court-martial conducted according to the facts and the rules of evidence, no crime was found to have been committed." Case closed again. Either way, the military won.

"I was talking to your old skipper outside," Rader said. "He told me you seemed nervous."

"Well, how the hell do you expect me to feel? By tomorrow night, I could be on my way to Portsmouth for life." Portsmouth, the U.S. naval prison, is a penal institution that was said to combine the worst aspects of Marine boot camp and a medieval dungeon. Nevertheless, a life sentence there was better than the alternative—execution by firing squad. That possibility had been hanging over our heads until only a few weeks before, when it was ruled that our case would be tried as noncapital. We were not to be shot if found guilty. A boon!

"Look, I don't want you thinking that way," Rader said. "I'm confident about what the outcome'll be. Even if you're convicted, we'll appeal. All the way up to the president if we have to."

"Terrific. Meanwhile I'll have brig guards playing the drums on my head with billy clubs. Christ, you've heard what it's like in that place. Can you imagine what they'll do to a busted officer?"

"I don't want you getting bitter. I want you to do well on that stand today. I can tell you that I admire you for the way you've borne up under all this. Don't mess it up now. Really, I would've cracked long ago."

"Well, I don't break, Jim. That's one thing I'm not going to do. I broke once and I'm never going to break again."

"Hell, when did you ever break?"

"That night. The night I sent those guys out there. I just cracked. I couldn't take it anymore. I was frustrated as hell and scared. If I hadn't broken, I would've never sent those guys out."

"Oh, that. We've been over this a dozen times. No drama, okay? This is the real world. We've been over that, over and over. You told them to capture those Vietnamese and to kill them if they had to. You didn't order an assassination. That's what you'll say on the stand and you'll say it because it's the truth."

Rader and I had argued the point before. We had argued it from the day that he was appointed my defense counsel. That had been in February, after several villagers from Giao-Tri lodged a complaint with their village chief, who went to the district chief, a Vietnamese army colonel, who took the matter to the American military authorities in Danang. Two young men from Giao-Tri, both civilians, had been assassinated by a Marine patrol. The investigation got under way. The battalion was meanwhile establishing new permanent positions forward of the old front line. The Vietcong protested the intrusion into their territory with land mines, infiltrators, mortars, and snipers. My platoon lost several more men, including Jones, who was seriously wounded in a booby trap. The other two platoons suffered about sixteen casualties between them, and C Company became so short-handed that Neal had to make riflemen out of the mortar crews attached to the company, leaving no one to man the eighty-ones.

It was in this depressing atmosphere of steady losses that the five Marines and I were called to battalion HQ to be questioned about what came to be known as "the incident at Giao-Tri."

Most of the particulars of that long and complicated inquiry have faded from memory. What remains most vividly is the mind-paralyzing terror that came over me when the investigating officer told me I was under suspicion of murder. *Murder.* The word exploded in my ears like a mortar shell. *Murder.* But they were Vietcong, I told the IO, a hearty lawyer-colonel from the division legal section. At least one of them was. No, he said, they did not appear to be VC. That had been confirmed by the village police chief and the village chief. *Murder.* I knew we had done something wrong, but the idea of homicide had never occurred to me. Bewildered and frightened, I answered the colonel's questions as best as I could, but when he asked, "Did you tell your men to stick to their statements?" I blurted out "No!"

Accompanied by his reporter, a lance corporal who had tapped out my answers on a transcript machine, the colonel left a few minutes later with his papers, case books, and machine, all the paraphernalia from the tidy world of division HQ, the world of laws, which are so easy to obey when you eat well, sleep well, and do not have to face the daily menace of death.

I was badly shaken afterward, so badly I thought I was going to break in two. It was not only the specter of a murder charge that tormented me; it was my own sense of guilt. Lying in a tent at HQ, I saw that boy's eyes again, and the accusation in their lifeless stare. Perhaps we had committed homicide without realizing it, in much the same way McKenna had. Perhaps the war had awakened something evil in us, some dark, malicious power that allowed us to kill without feeling. Well, I could drop the "perhaps" in my own case. Something evil had been in me that night. It was true that I had ordered the patrol to capture the two men if at all possible, but it was also true that I had wanted them dead. There was murder in my heart, and, in some way, through tone of voice, a gesture, or a stress on *kill* rather than *capture*, I had transmitted my inner violence to the men. They saw in my overly aggressive manner a sanction to vent their own brutal impulses. I lay there remembering the euphoria we had felt afterward, the way we had laughed, and then the sudden awakening to guilt. And yet, I could not conceive of the act as one of premeditated murder. It had not been committed in a vacuum. It was a direct result of the war. The thing we had done was a result of what the war had done to us.

At some point in this self-examination, I realized I had lied to the investigating officer. Walking over to the adjutant's tent, I called the colonel and said I wanted to amend my statement and to exercise my right to counsel. He returned to battalion HQ with Rader, a tall redhead in his late twenties.

"Sir," I said, "that part in my statement where I said that I didn't tell the men to stick by their statements? Well, that isn't true. I wasn't thinking straight. I'd like it deleted and replaced with the truth."

Sorry, he said, that statement had been made under oath. It could not be deleted. That was the law. If I wished to say something else, fine, but the original statement would remain in the record. The colonel smiled, quite pleased with himself and the inexorable logic of his precious law. He had me on another charge. I made another statement.

Afterward, Rader and I had the first of our many long interviews. He asked me to describe everything that had happened that night.

"All right," I said, "but before I do, I want you to read this. I wrote it while I was waiting for you and the colonel to get here."

I handed him a turgid essay on front line conditions. In a guerrilla war, it read, the line between legitimate and illegitimate killing is blurred. The policies of free-fire zones, in which a soldier is permitted to shoot at any human target, armed or unarmed, and body counts further confuse the fighting man's moral senses. My patrol had gone out thinking they were going after enemy soldiers. As for me, I had indeed been in an agitated state of mind and my ability to make clear judgments had been faulty, but I had been in Vietnam for eleven months. . . .

Rader crumpled up my literary ramblings and said, "This is all irrelevant, Phil."

"Why? It seems relevant to me."

"It won't to a court-martial."

"But *why*? We didn't kill those guys in Los Angeles, for Christ's sake."

Rader replied with a lecture on the facts of life. I cannot remember exactly what he said, but it was from him that I got the first indication that the war could not be used to explain the killings, because it raised too many embarrassing questions. We were indeed going to be charged as if we had killed both men on the streets of Los Angeles. The case was to be tried strictly on the facts: who said what to whom; what was done and who did it. A detective story. The facts, Rader said, are what he wanted. He did not want philosophy.

"Did you order your men to assassinate the two Vietnamese?" he asked.

"No."

"Did you say they were to capture them, or to shoot first and ask questions later?"

"No. They were supposed to capture them, kill them if they had to. But the thing is, I must have given them the impression that I wouldn't mind if they just killed them. Jim, I wasn't right in the head that night . . ."

"Don't try temporary insanity. There's a legal definition for that, and unless you were bouncing off walls, you won't fit it."

"I'm not saying I was crazy. What I'm saying is that I was worn out as hell. And scared. Goddamnit, I admit it. I was scared that one of those damned mines was going to get me if I didn't do something. You've got to realize what it's like out there, never knowing from one minute to the next if you're going to get blown sky-high."

"Look, a court-martial isn't going to care what it's like out there. You've got to realize that. This isn't a novel, so drop the dramatics. Nothing would've happened if those villagers hadn't complained. But they did and that started an investigation. Now the machine's in gear and it won't stop until it's run its course. Now, did anyone else hear you brief the patrol?"

"Yeah, Sergeant Coffell and the platoon sergeant were there."

"So, in other words, you gave orders to capture if possible, kill if necessary, or words to that effect. That's what you said, and there are two witnesses who'll corroborate you. Right?"

"That's what I said. I'm not sure if I completely meant it. I had this feeling that night . . . a sort of violent feeling . . ."

"Feelings aren't admissible evidence. I'm not worried about your psyche. The important thing is whether or not you ordered your men to commit an assassination."

"Damnit, Jim. It keeps coming back to the war. I wouldn't have sent those guys out there and they would never have done what they did if it hadn't been for this war. It's a stinking war and some of the stink rubs off on you after a while."

"Will you please drop that. If you ordered an assassination, tell me now. You can plead guilty and I'll try to get you a light sentence—say, ten to twenty in Portsmouth."

"I'll tell you this. I'll have a helluva time living with myself if those guys get convicted and I get off."

"Do you want to plead guilty to murder?"

"No."

"Why?"

"Because it wasn't murder. Whatever it was, it wasn't murder. And if it was murder, then half the Vietnamese killed in this war have been murdered."

"No. You don't want to plead guilty because you're innocent as charged. You did not order an assassination."

"All right. I'm innocent."

"So, what we have is this: you gave orders to a patrol to capture two Vietcong suspects who were to be killed only if necessary. That's lawful order under combat. And there are two NCOs who'll support you on that, right?"

"You're the boss. Whatever you say. Just get me out of this mess."

"Don't give me the 'you're the boss' routine. Are those the facts or aren't they?"

"Yes, those are the facts."

And so I learned about the wide gulf that divides the facts from the truth. Rader and I had a dozen similar conferences over the next five months. "Preparing testimony," it was called. With each session, my admiration for Rader's legal skills increased. He prepared my case with the hard-minded pragmatism of a battalion commander preparing an attack on an enemy-held hill. In time, he almost had me convinced that on the night of the killings, First Lieutenant Philip Caputo, in a lucid state of mind, issued a clear, legitimate order that was flagrantly disobeyed by the men under his command. I was fascinated by the testimony that was produced by our Socratic dialogues. Rader had it all written on yellow legal tablets, and I observed that not one word of it was perjured. There were qualifying phrases here and there—"to the best of my recollection," "if I recall correctly," "words to that effect"—but there wasn't a single lie in it. And yet it wasn't the truth. Conversely, the attorneys for the enlisted men had them convinced that they were all good, God-fearing soldiers who had been obeying orders, as all good soldiers must, orders issued by a vicious killer-officer. And that was neither a lie nor the truth. The prosecution had meanwhile marshaled facts to support its argument that five criminal Marines, following the unlawful orders of their criminal platoon leader, had cold-bloodedly murdered two civilians whom they then tried to claim as confirmed Vietcong to collect the reward their captain had offered for enemy dead, a reprehensible policy not at all in keeping with the traditions of the U.S. Marine Corps. And that was neither a lie nor the truth. None of this testimony, none of these "facts" amounted to the truth. The truth was a synthesis of all three points of view: the war in general and U.S. military policies in particular were ultimately to blame for the deaths of Le Du and Le Dung. That was the truth and it was that truth which the whole proceeding was designed to conceal.

Still, I was not without hope for an acquittal. Throughout the investigation, a number of officers told me: "What's happened to you could've happened to anybody in this war." In their eyes, I was a victim of circumstances, a good officer unjustly charged. I had an above-average service record, and was normal to outward appearances. Those other officers saw in me a mirror image of themselves. I was one of them.

And the enlisted men were all good soldiers. There wasn't a mark on their records, not even for AWOL. Four of the five had been honorably wounded in combat. Two—Allen and Crowe—were family men. And yet, paradoxically, they had been accused of homicide. If the charges were proved, it would prove no one was guaranteed immunity against the moral bacteria spawned by the war. If such cruelty existed in ordinary men like us, then it logically existed in the others, and they would have to face the truth that they, too, harbored a capacity for evil. But no one wanted to make that recognition. No one wanted to confront his devil.

A verdict of innocence would solve the dilemma. It would prove no crime had been committed. It would prove what the others wanted to believe: that we were virtuous American youths, incapable of the act of which we had been accused. And if we were incapable of it, then they were too, which is what they wanted to believe themselves.

It was nine o'clock. Witnesses began to file into the neighboring hut, where the court-martial was being held. In our hut, the clerks continued to peck at their typewriters. Radar and I again went over my testimony. He told me how to behave on the stand: use a firm, but not strident, tone of voice; look at the six officers who were to be my judges when I answered questions; appear earnest and forthcoming.

I was called sometime in the late afternoon. Crowe, sitting at the defendant's table, looked very small. I confess I don't remember a word of what I said on the stand. I only recall sitting there for a long time under direct and cross-examination, looking at the six-man court as I had been instructed to do and parroting the testimony I had rehearsed a hundred times. I must have sounded like Jack Armstrong, all-American boy. Later, during a recess, I heard the prosecutor congratulating Rader. "Your client did very well on the stand today, Mister Rader." I felt pleased with myself. I was good for something. I was a good witness.

The trial dragged on to its conclusion. In my tent awaiting the verdict, I felt in limbo, neither a free man nor a prisoner. I could not help thinking about the consequences of a guilty verdict in my own case. I would go to jail for the rest of my life. Everything good I had done in my life would be rendered meaningless. It would count for nothing.

I already regarded myself as a casualty of the war, a moral casualty, and like all serious casualties, I felt detached from everything. I felt very much like a man who has lost a leg or an arm, and, knowing he will never have to fight again, loses all interest in the war that has wounded him. As his physical energies are spent on overcoming his pain and on repairing his bodily injuries, so were all of my emotional energies spent on maintaining my mental balance. I had not broken during the five-month ordeal. I would not break. No matter what they did to me, they could not make me break. All my inner reserves had been committed to that battle for emotional and mental survival. I had nothing left for other struggles. The war simply wasn't my show any longer. I had declared a truce between me and the Vietcong, signed a personal armistice, and all I asked for now was a chance to live for myself on my terms. I had no argument with the Vietcong. It wasn't the VC who were threatening to rob me of my liberty, but the United States government, in whose service I had enlisted. Well, I was through with that. I was finished with governments and their abstract causes, and I would never again allow myself to fall under the charms and spells of political witch doctors like John F. Kennedy. The important thing was to get through this insane predicament with some degree of dignity. I would not break. I would endure and accept whatever happened with grace. For enduring seemed to me an act of penance, an inadequate one to be sure, but I felt the need to atone in some way for the deaths I had caused.

Lying there, I remembered the South Vietnamese insurrection that had begun three months before and ended only in May. That insurrection, as much as my own situation, had awakened me to the senselessness of the war. The tragifarce began when General Thi, the commander of I Corps, was placed under arrest by the head of the Saigon government, Nguyen Cao Ky. Ky suspected him of plotting a coup. Thi's ARVN divisions in I Corps rallied to his support. There were demonstrations and riots in Danang, where Thi's headquarters were located. This prompted Ky to declare that Danang was in the hands of Communist rebels and to send his divisions to the city to "liberate it from the Vietcong." Soon, South Vietnamese soldiers were fighting street battles with other South Vietnamese soldiers as the two mandarin warlords contended for power.

And while the South Vietnamese fought their intramural feud, we were left to fight the Vietcong. In April, with the insurrection in full swing, One-Three suffered heavy casualties in an operation in the Vu Gai Valley. Because of the investigation, I had been transferred from the battalion to regimental HQ, where I was assigned as an assistant operations officer. There, I saw the incompetent staff work that had turned the operation into a minor disaster. Part of the battalion was needlessly sent into a trap, and one company alone lost over one hundred of its one hundred and eighty men. Vietnamese civilians suffered too. I recalled seeing the smoke rising from a dozen bombed villages while our artillery pounded enemy positions in the hills and our planes darted through the smoke to drop more bombs. And I recalled seeing our own casualties at the division hospital. Captain Greer, the intelligence officer, and I were sent there from the field to interview the survivors and find out what had gone wrong. We knew what had gone wrong—the staff had fouled up—but we went along with the charade anyway. I can still see that charnel house, crammed with wounded, groaning men, their dressings encrusted in filth, the cots pushed one up against the other to make room for the new wounded coming in, the smell of blood, the stunned faces, one young platoon leader wrapped up like a mummy with plastic tubes inserted in his kidneys, and an eighteen-year-old private, blinded by shellfire, a bandage wrapped around his eyes as he groped down the aisle between the cots. "I can't find my rack," he called. "Can somebody help me find my rack?"

Meanwhile, the armies of Thi and Ky continued to spar in Danang. One morning in May, after I had been sent to division HQ, I led a convoy of Marine riflemen into the city. They were part of a security detachment that was to guard American installations—not against the VC, but against the rebelling South Vietnamese troops. I returned to HQ in the afternoon. Division's command post was on Hill 327, which gave us a ringside seat. Looking to the west, we could see Marines fighting the VC; to the east, the South Vietnamese Army fighting itself. Early that evening, I saw tracers flying over the city, heard the sound of machine-gun fire, and then, in utter disbelief, watched an ARVN fighter plane strafing an ARVN truck convoy. It was incredible, a tableau of the madness of the war. One of the plane's rockets fell wide of the mark, exploding near an American position and wounding three Marines. The prop-driven Skyraider roared down again, firing its rockets and cannon once more into the convoy, packed with South Vietnamese soldiers. And I knew then that we could never win. With a government and an army like that in South Vietnam, we could never hope to win the war. To go on with the war would be folly—worse than folly: it would be a crime, murder on a mass scale.

The insurrection ended on May 25. General Walt sent a message to all Marine units in I Corps. In it, he said that the "rebellion" had been crushed and that we could "look forward to an era of good relations with our South Vietnamese comrades-in-arms."

The message shocked me. Even Lew Walt, my old hero, was blind to the truth. The war was to go on, senselessly on.

A few days later, my antiwar sentiments took an active form. The division HqCo commander ordered me to take part in a parade in honor of some visiting dignitary. I refused. He said I could not refuse to obey an order. I replied, yes, I could and would. I thought the whole thing was a mess, a folly and a crime, and I was not going to participate in some flag-waving sham. I was in no position to make such statements, he said. Oh yes I was. I was already up for the most serious crime in the book—one more charge made no difference to me. He could get somebody else to strut around to Sousa marches. Much to my surprise, I won.

It was then that I tried to do a bit of proselytizing among the clerks in the HqCo office. The war, I said, was unwinnable. It was being fought for a bunch of corrupt politicians in Saigon. Every American life lost was a life wasted. The United States should withdraw now, before more men died. The clerks, their patriotism unwavering, having never heard a shot fired in anger, looked at me in disbelief. I wasn't surprised. This was 1966 and talk such as mine was regarded as borderline treason.

"Sir," said a lance corporal, "if we pull out now, then all our efforts up to now would have been in vain."

"In other words, because we've already wasted thousands of lives, we should waste a few thousand more," I said. "Well, if you really believe that 'not in vain' crap, you should volunteer for a rifle company and go get yourself killed, because you deserve it."

Rader walked into the tent in the early evening. "Phil," he said, "they've come in with a verdict on Crowe. Not guilty on all counts."

I sat up and lit a cigarette, not sure what to think. "Well, I'm happy for him. He's got a wife and kids. But how does that make it look for us?"

"Well, I think it looks good. Just hang loose until tomorrow. You go up at oh-nine-hundred."

Curiously, I slept very well that night. Maybe it was my sense of fatalism. Worrying could do no good. Whatever was going to happen, I could do nothing about it. The next morning, I ate an enormous breakfast and managed a few quips about the condemned man's last meal. Then, long before I was due, I walked to the quonset hut, feeling much as I had before going into action: determined and resigned at the same time. I waited in the hut for about an hour, watching the same desk clerks sitting at the same desks typing the same reports. The red light on the coffee pot glowed and the fans whirred, rustling the pages of the calendar, which was now turned to July. The same crowd of witnesses milled around outside. Captain Neal was there. He looked worn and old. I went out and offered him a cigar. Smoking it, his eyes fixed on the ground, he shook his head and said, "We lost half the company. I hope they realize that. We'd lost half the company then."

At a quarter to nine, Rader called me back inside.

"Here's the situation. The general is thinking of dropping all charges against the rest of you because Crowe was acquitted. In your own case, you'd have to plead guilty to the third charge and accept a letter of reprimand from the general. What do you want to do?"

"You mean if I plead guilty to charge three, there's no court martial?"

"Unless you want one."

"Of course I don't want one. Okay, I'm guilty."

"All right," Rader said ebulliently, "wait here. I'll let them know and get back to you."

I paced nervously for fifteen or twenty minutes. It looked as if my instincts had been right: the higher-ups wanted this case off their backs as much as I wanted it off mine. Wild thoughts filled my head. I would atone in some way to the families of Le Du and Le Dung. When the war was over, I would go back to Giao-Tri and . . . and what? I didn't know.

Rader returned grinning. "Congratulations," he said, pumping my hand. "The charges have been dropped. The general's going to put a letter of reprimand in your jacket, but hell, all that'll do is hurt your chances for promotion to captain. You're a free man. I also heard that the adjutant's cutting orders for you. You'll be going home in a week, ten days at most. It's all over."

We stood waiting in the sun at the edge of the runway. There were about a hundred and fifty of us, and we watched as a replacement draft filed off the big transport plane. They fell into formation and tried to ignore the dusty, tanned, ragged-looking men who jeered them. The replacements looked strangely young, far younger than we, and awkward and bewildered by this scorched land to which an indifferent government had sent them. I did not join in the mockery. I felt sorry for those children, knowing that they would all grow old in this land of endless dying. I pitied them, knowing that out of every ten, one would die, two more would be maimed for life, another two would be less seriously wounded and sent out to fight again, and all the rest would be wounded in other, more hidden ways.

The replacements were marched off toward the convoy that waited to carry them to their assigned units and their assigned fates. None of them looked at us. They marched away. Shouldering our sea-bags, we climbed up the ramp into the plane, the plane we had all dreamed about, the grand, mythological Freedom Bird. A joyous shout went up as the transport lurched off the runway and climbed into the placid sky. Below lay the rice paddies and the green, folded hills where we had lost our friends and our youth.

The plane banked and headed out over the China Sea, toward Okinawa, toward freedom from death's embrace. None of us was a hero. We would not return to cheering crowds, parades, and the pealing of great cathedral bells. We had done nothing more than endure. We had survived, and that was our only victory.

Questions

1. Given the company's "intolerable predicament," is Caputo's wish to kill the two suspected men excusable? (260)

2. After the investigating officer leaves a blank on the DD457 form, why does Caputo conclude that "the explanatory or extenuating circumstance was the war"? (266)

3. Is Caputo right to blame his "overly aggressive manner" for providing his patrol with a "sanction to vent their own brutal impulses"? (269)

4. Do you agree with Caputo that "the whole proceeding" of the trial was designed to conceal the truth? (273)

5. At the end of the selection, what does Caputo mean in calling survival a victory?

6. In combat, is it possible to distinguish murder from waging war? If so, what standards separate the former from the latter?

Karl Marlantes

Karl Marlantes (1945–) was born in Oregon and earned his under-graduate degree from Yale while in the Marine Corps Reserve. In 1968 he chose to postpone his graduate education at Oxford and fight in the Vietnam War. During his time as a Marine lieutenant, he was awarded the Navy Cross, two Navy Commendation Medals for Valor, two Purple Hearts, and ten Air Medals.

In the late 1990s, Marlantes called the Veterans Health Administration for help with symptoms of posttraumatic stress disorder. He regards his subsequent published works as part of his healing process: in 2009, he published a fictionalized Vietnam War novel, *Matterhorn*, which he had been revising and seeking to pub-lish since 1977; and in 2011, he published his nonfiction memoir, *What It Is Like to Go to War*, from which the following selection is taken.

This selection focuses on a characteristic aspect of the Vietnam War—veteran alienation. As the controversial war dragged on, some U.S. protesters expressed their strong opposition by abusing return-ing veterans. Young men who had both witnessed and carried out violent acts in the course of waging war, enduring uncertainty and danger, returned to mistreatment, anger, and rejection from their fellow Americans.

In recent years, antiwar Americans have generally separated their feelings about policy decisions from veterans themselves. But veterans from any era will recognize Marlantes's post-combat feelings of alienation, guilt, and confusion, particularly when the switch from the combat zone to civilian life is so abrupt. The issue of how returning servicemen and servicewomen can reintegrate into their communities is a difficult one. Comprising a relatively small proportion of the population, returning veterans are often surrounded by those with no exposure to war or to the experiences of those who were there.

WHAT IT IS LIKE TO GO TO WAR

(selection)

My first day back home my mother and father were at the airport, and so was, to my surprise, Maree Ann, a girl I'd dated when I was in high school. With Maree Ann were her four-year-old daughter, Lizzy, and Maree Ann's aunt, a friend of my mother's. My small hometown is only a hundred miles from the city and my close relatives still live in the area. Many had followed jobs to the city itself. My mother had called all of them to tell them I was coming home and when I'd arrive. Could they please come to the airport to welcome me back? There was only this little anxious group: Mom, trying unsuccessfully to hold back tears; Dad, more successful than she but still close to losing it; Maree Ann; little Lizzy; and Maree Ann's aunt.

It would have been nice if some of my extended family had come to the airport. But I told Mom I didn't much mind. I'm not a public person. We'd see them later.

There was nothing later. To me, and to my parents, I'd been gone an eternity; to everyone else, a flash. This is no one's fault. Life is busy and full.

Still, I wish it were otherwise. Maybe if there had been some sort of hokey family potluck dinner. A toast by Uncle George, who was wounded in Italy (funny how we say wounded in Italy instead of wounded in the leg); or my dad, who hauled gasoline to Patton's tanks in France and was at the Battle of the Bulge; or Uncle Kim, who fought the Japanese in the Pacific. Maybe some teary speech by one of my aunts saying how glad she was that I'd come back safe, or even my old communist grandmother could have gotten up and said how it was all because of those Wall Street millionaires but now that her lumpen proletariat grandson was back home she was happy again. And maybe, well, was it too much to at least expect a thank-you from the people who voted to send us over there?

This was mistake number one—lack of extended family involvement. The psychology of the young warrior is, I think, almost entirely related to hearth and kin. You can subvert that into patriotism and nationalism if you're clever and work at it long enough, but I'd been detoxified. A homecoming of yellow ribbons and throwing out the first ball at the local game would have made me feel like puking.

So we stood around, nervous, happy, after stiff public hugs, waiting for my seabag to come through the baggage hole. I hadn't seen Maree Ann since I left high school, but one day on a blasted hilltop in Vietnam a package arrived from her and her aunt. The first of many. In the diary I kept throughout my tour I copied a scrawled "L" and some indistinguishable following marks from where Lizzy had carefully written her name on Maree Ann's Christmas package.

Maree Ann was a fourteen-year-old freshman when I last knew her, the age when girls spell their name with two e's instead of y and dot their i's with little round circles. She was smart and funny, a great rider and rodeo princess who loved animals and belonged to 4-H. I was the big senior class president and probable valedictorian and an all-league football player. She asked me to the Sadie Hawkins Day dance. Well, I was surprised. I went.

Back then I was always looking to get out of town, looking to the future, and not seeing her in it. She, just starting high school, was bound in the present, too smart with a too finely tuned mind and sense of humor to be content with remaining where fate had landed her, a high school girl from an alcoholic and broken home in a cultural vacuum.

Shortly after I was graduated she got pregnant by some guy from out of town. He left her, or she left him, or each had left the other. How it is, outsiders never know. I think her aunt in the city took her in while she had Lizzy. She somehow managed to finish high school there.

I told them about my flight all the way across the Pacific Ocean, about seeing my older brother at Stanford, what it was like in California. They told me about old friends of mine and the garden. Then my seabag came out on the baggage conveyor. I shouldered it and we started for the door. Then Maree Ann asked me if I wanted to come home with her.

Well, I was surprised.

I could see that some things about Maree Ann hadn't changed. I looked at my mother and father. I looked at Maree Ann. Maree Ann is a good-looking woman. I went home with Maree Ann. This was mistake number two and entirely my own. I started feeling bad about leaving my folks, and a few other things, just after I reached Maree Ann's single room and kitchenette, which she rented in an old house in one of the city's poorer, but still respectable, neighborhoods.

The homecoming soldier may want to make love to any woman who moves, but any young man who hasn't seen a woman for even a few days wants to do the same. I was no exception, but I now know this was a part of me that needed some help and guidance. Other things having to do with returning warriors, not lonely young men with sex on their minds, needed to be put in place first. They weren't. No one knew any better. This was mistake number three, which had already been committed two weeks earlier on Okinawa.

We talked, we drank some tea, and I watched and listened while Maree Ann put Lizzy to bed, reading her a story. It felt so warm and comfortable there, the old lighting soft on the fir tongue-and-groove walls with their patina of years. I was so grateful she'd come to the airport to see me. We talked some more. We were tender with each other in many ways. But when she put on her nightgown and got into bed I couldn't go through with it.

I'd contracted NSU from one of the prostitutes who lined Gate Number Two Street outside Kadena Air Base on Okinawa. This was the result of a lot of alcohol to satisfy the shy one and a seventy-two-hour nonstop answer to the needs of that other part of me I just mentioned. This piece of information I never passed on to my parents to explain why my arrival home was delayed ten days. I claimed military inefficiency. The fact was that the navy doctor wouldn't endorse my orders until the NSU had cleared up.

Although I wasn't dripping anymore, I still wasn't completely sure the penicillin had totally wiped out the problem. I couldn't imagine transmitting NSU to Maree Ann. But there was more to it than just that.

The fact was I felt unclean, insecure, strange, and awkward. I didn't feel right—with anyone. This feeling of being "wrong" somehow had dogged me since the minute I boarded the chartered 707 for California. The NSU was my own doing, or at least my own bad luck and my lack of someone to take me aside and say, "Look, what you think you need isn't what you need. All that's egging you on is the misplaced idea that being masturbated by a paid pair of labia is somehow manlier or more satisfying than doing it to yourself. They're exploiting your loneliness. You're exploiting their poverty. You're both just using each other and it is going to make everyone feel bad. And, oh, by the way, you can catch a venereal disease."

Perhaps the awkward wrong feeling started with the stewardesses on the airplane treating us as if we were tourists. The thing no one recognized, including the stewardesses and even most of us, was that just two or three days earlier many of us had been in combat, scared to death we were going to die and watching the deaths of others just like us. Now we were being served peanuts and Cokes by stewardesses, most of them unaware except on a vague subconscious level of what was happening to us. It was the same jolting juxtaposition of the infinite and the mundane that hit me on my R&R to Australia. It wasn't the stewardesses' fault. They were just doing their job, handing out smiles and Cokes. We loved it. But we should have come home by sea. We should have had time to talk with our buddies about what we all had shared. We joined our units alone, and we came home alone, and this was a key difference between us and veterans of other wars, including today's.

Perhaps the awkward wrong feeling started when my brother mumbled something to try to make me feel better as we drove past the war protesters at Travis Air Force Base just outside San Francisco, where he picked me up. They were pounding his car with their signs and snarling at us through the closed car window. Or maybe it got started when he showed me around the Stanford campus—being looked at by girls in long clean hair and boys in long not-so-clean hair, all dressed somewhere between Newport Beach and Haight-Ashbury, me in no hair, with jungle-rot scars on my face and hands, dressed in clothes that smelled like mothballs and looked like something handed down from the Kingston Trio.

No one shouted obscenities, or even said anything, maybe out of deference to my brother. No one needed to. You know the feeling, as if you've made a mistake coming to the party but no one is going to tell you to your face.

At one point I waited at the Stanford bookstore for my brother to get out of class. I had to squeeze by a girl in one of the aisles. I said excuse me, politely. She looked at me with contempt and wouldn't move aside. I tried to slip past her and accidentally knocked a book down from the shelf. I hated my clumsiness and flushed face as she watched me stoop to pick it up. I remember wishing she knew I'd won a Navy Cross and was trying to reach the poetry section. She was joined by two long-haired boys who further barred the aisle. Trembling with anger and humiliation, this Marine chose to advance in the other direction.

No matter where I went, I felt something was not right about me. I still felt it at Maree Ann's. I knew that to make love to her would be wrong for me and, if wrong for me, then wrong for her. I was again bound away, this time with orders to Headquarters Marine Corps in Washington, D.C. I simply wasn't interested in a relationship with a woman with a four-year-old daughter, no matter how good-looking or how tender the woman was. She must have known that, and it added a terrible poignancy. I think I told her about the NSU but don't know for sure. I'm quite sure I was incapable in those days of explaining how I felt to anyone.

I didn't want to reject her—far from it. But I didn't want to mislead. There was too much past between us, too much linkage, and perhaps yearning and loneliness. To be sixteen with a baby and no husband, on your own, then seventeen, and then eighteen, must be one of the loneliest situations life can hand us. And here comes the hero back from the war and he doesn't want to make love and maybe tells her he's got NSU, even though he's also afraid of telling her that he's afraid of the emotional consequences. My God, how we waste our lives hurting each other.

Maree Ann didn't know what to do any more than I did, but she showed up. She was the only other person, besides my parents, who'd kept the linkage with my past, with my little town, my tribe, as it were.

It was clear that the others of the tribe, "my fellow Americans," as the politicians say, had worse than abandoned me. Imagine the damage to young Aborigine boys returning from their frightening and mind-altering initiation only to have the villagers pelt them with garbage.

I needed desperately to be accepted back in. I think I ended up assuming unconsciously that I must have done something wrong to have received all this rejection. To be sure, I had been engaged in dirty business. Somebody, usually the man, empties the garbage and turns the compost. But when he's done, he comes back in the house, he washes his hands, and someone says thank you. War is society's dirty work, usually done by kids cleaning up failures perpetrated by adults. What I needed upon returning, but didn't know it, was a bath.

What I needed was for Maree Ann to sit down with me in a tub of water and run her hands over my body and squeeze out the wrong feelings and confusion, soothe the pain, inside and out, and rub the skin back to life. I needed her to Dutch-rub my skull with soap until the tears came, and I needed her to dry the tears, and laugh with me, and cry with me, and bring my body back from the dead.

That body had suffered. It was covered with scars from jungle rot. It had had dysentery, diarrhea, and possibly a mild case of malaria. It had gone without fresh food for months at a time. It had lived on the knife edge of fear, constantly jerked from an aching need for sleep with all the cruel refinement of the best secret police torturer. It had pumped adrenaline until it had become addicted to it. There were scars where hot metal had gone in, searing and surprising in its pain, and scars where a corpsman had dug most of it out. There were bits of metal still in it, some pushing against the skin, itching to get out. The eyeballs were scarred where tiny bits of hand grenade had embedded themselves. The inner ears rang with a constant high-pitched whine that ceased only in sleep, when the nightmares started.

That body was shut down against pain as far as I could get it shut. Shut down to where it would not feel a thing, while my mind was still seven thousand miles away, unattached, floating, watching.

I needed a woman to get me back on the earth, get me down in the water, get me down *under* the water, get my body to feel again, to slough off old skin, old scars, old scabs, to come again into her world, the world that I'd left, and which sometimes I think I've never returned to. But I kissed her and went home.

When my mother shook me awake late the next morning, she tells me I reached out and tried to choke her. I don't remember this. At least I didn't try and choke Maree Ann.

I do remember the careful way my bedroom had been restored with my old letter jacket, pictures, trophies. This care I remember and this a mother can do to welcome someone home—make it feel like a home, not just a house.

We left the next day for Cortes Island, which lies between Vancouver Island and the British Columbia mainland, a favorite place of mine. On the Victoria–Port Angeles ferry I fell asleep. A woman tripped over my feet, startling me. Again I reared up, reaching out to choke her. There was great embarrassment all around, my mother trying to explain to this middle-aged Canadian who was trying to explain how she hadn't meant to step on me and me explaining how I hadn't meant to . . . and how she understood and . . . In any case, this kid was not ready to go on a public ferryboat ride. This kid was still in the jungle. . . .

There is a correct way to welcome your warriors back. Returning veterans don't need ticker-tape parades or yellow ribbons stretching clear across Texas. Cheering is inappropriate and immature. Combat veterans, more than anyone else, know how much pain and evil have been wrought. To cheer them for what they've just done would be like cheering the surgeon when he amputates a leg to save someone's life. It's childish, and it's demeaning to those who have fallen on both sides. A quiet grateful handshake is what you give the surgeon, while you mourn the lost leg. There should be parades, but they should be solemn processionals, rifles upside down, symbol of the sword sheathed once again. They should be conducted with all the dignity of a military funeral, mourning for those lost on both sides, giving thanks for those returned. Afterward, at home or in small groups, let the champagne flow and celebrate life and even victory if you were so lucky—afterward.

Veterans just need to be received back into their community, reintegrated with those they love, and thanked by the people who sent them. I wanted to be hugged by every girl I ever knew. Our more sane ancestors had ceremonies like sweat rituals to physically bring the bodies back into civilian mode. Mongolian warriors were taken into heated yurts and had every muscle that could be reached pressed and rolled with smooth staves, squeezing out toxins, signaling the psyche and the body that it was time to stop pumping adrenaline.

There is also a deeper side to coming home. The returning warrior needs to heal more than his mind and body. He needs to heal his soul.

Questions

1. Why does Marlantes say, "A homecoming of yellow ribbons and throwing out the first ball at the local game would have made me feel like puking"? (284)

2. Why does Marlantes think going home with Maree Ann was a mistake?

3. What does Marlantes believe would have been different about the experience of returning from war if he and those he served with had come home by sea, like veterans of earlier wars?

4. Why does Marlantes believe that quiet handshakes and solemn parades are the "correct" way to welcome warriors back? (289)

5. What is the best way to welcome veterans home?

6. If you have ever been confronted by people who disapproved of your serving in the military, how did you respond to them?

Tobias Wolff

Tobias Wolff (1945–) was born in Alabama and joined the army as a teenager in 1964, hoping to escape his chaotic home life with an abusive stepfather, to gather experiences as a writer, and to satisfy his patriotic aspirations. He served in the U.S. Army Special Forces (Green Berets) and was stationed as an advisor to South Vietnamese troops in the Mekong Delta. Following his military service, Wolff has gone on to a highly successful writing career. He is especially known for his skillfully crafted short stories and his memoir, *This Boy's Life* (1989).

In Pharaoh's Army: Memories of a Lost War (1994), from which "White Man" and "The Rough Humor of Soldiers" are taken, recounts Wolff's time in Vietnam. These excerpts do not depict typical scenes of combat but rather convey the mundane alienation and brutality of daily life for soldiers in the field. Wolff's spare descriptions of everyday events emphasize the boredom and the callousness that could permeate day-to-day experience. Yet these two selections also lay bare soldiers' desperate search for tenderness of some kind—any kind—no matter how fleeting, illusory, or ill-advised.

Wolff's writing depicts the unpredictability of life in Vietnam, where every patrol, meal, and encounter leaves him vulnerable to attack. The interaction among the men brings to the fore the uncomfortable attitudes the American and the South Vietnamese soldiers held toward each other. Life for these allies is filled with undercurrents of tension. Beneath the rough humor and casual teasing, questions of power and superiority, across a range of encounters, sour the cooperation between the two armies. Perceived authority is challenged and even overthrown. Wolff's deceptively simple storytelling uncovers multiple layers of understanding and interaction and poses difficult questions about the place of military legitimacy, cultural control, and the struggle for self-respect, in an environment where normal standards have been dismantled.

IN PHARAOH'S ARMY

(selection)

WHITE MAN

Aweek or so after Sergeant Benet and I made our Thanksgiving raid on Dong Tam, the division was ordered into the field. The plan called for our howitzers and men to be carried by helicopter to a position in the countryside. I was sent ahead with the security force responsible for preparing the ground and making sure it was safe to land. My job was to call in American gunships and medevacs if any were needed. I could even get F-14 Phantom jets if we ran into serious trouble, or trouble that I might consider serious, which would be any kind of trouble at all.

The designated position turned out to be a mud field. We were ordered to secure another site some four or five kilometers away. Our march took us through a couple of deserted villages along a canal. This was a free-fire zone. The people who'd lived around here had been moved to a detention camp, and their home ground declared open to random shelling and bombing. Harassment and interdiction, it was called, H and I. The earth was churned up by artillery and pocked with huge, water-filled craters from B-52 strikes. Pieces of shrapnel, iridescent with heat scars, glittered underfoot. The dikes had been breached. The paddies were full of brackish water covered by green, undulant slime, broken here and there by clumps of sawgrass. The silence was unnatural, expectant. It magnified the sound of our voices, the clank of mess kits and weapons, the rushing static of the radio. Our progress was not stealthy.

The villas were empty, the hooches in shreds, but you could see that people had been in the area. We kept coming across their garbage and cooking fires. Cooking fires—just like a Western. In the second village we found a white puppy. Someone had left him a heap of vegetable slops with some meat and bones mixed in. It looked rotten, but he seemed to be doing okay, the little chub. One of the soldiers tied a rope around his neck and brought him along.

Because the paddies were flooded and most of the dikes broken or collapsed, we had only a few possible routes of march, unless we moved off the trail; but mucking through the paddies was a drag, and our boys wouldn't dream of it. Though I knew better I didn't blame them. Instead we kept to what little remained of dry land, which meant a good chance of booby traps and maybe a sniper. There were several troops ahead of me in the column and I figured they'd either discover or get blown up by anything left on the trail, but the idea of a sniper had me on edge. I was the tallest man out here by at least a head, and I had to stay right next to the radio operator, who had this big squawking box on his back and a long antenna whipping back and forth over his helmet. And of course I was white. A perfect target. And that was how I saw myself, as a target, a long white face quartered by crosshairs.

I was dead sure somebody had me in his sights. I kept scanning the tree lines for his position, feeling him track me. I adopted an erratic walk, slowing down and speeding up, ducking my head, weaving from side to side. We were in pretty loose order anyway so nobody seemed to notice except the radio operator, who watched me curiously at first and then went back to his own thoughts. I prepared a face for the sniper to judge, not a brave or confident face but not a fearful one either. What I tried to do was look well-meaning and slightly apologetic, like a very nice person who has been swept up by forces beyond his control and set down in a place where he knows he doesn't belong and that he intends to vacate the first chance he gets.

But at the same time I knew the sniper wouldn't notice any of that, would notice nothing but my size and my whiteness. I didn't fit here. I was out of proportion not only to the men around me but to everything else—the huts, the villages, even the fields. All was shaped and scaled to the people whose place this was. Time had made it so. I was oafish here, just as the Vietnamese seemed oddly dainty on the wide Frenchified boulevards of Saigon.

And man, was I white! I could feel my whiteness shooting out like sparks. This wasn't just paranoia, it was what the Vietnamese saw when they looked at me, as I had cause to know. One instance: I was coming out of a bar in My Tho some months back, about to head home for the night, when I found myself surrounded by a crowd of Vietnamese soldiers from another battalion. They pressed up close, yelling and pushing me back and forth. Some of them had bamboo sticks. They were mad about something but I couldn't figure out what, they were shouting too fast and all at once. *Tai sao?* I kept asking—Why? Why? I saw that the question infuriated them, as if I were denying some outrage that everyone there had personally seen me commit. I understood that this was a ridiculous misunderstanding, that they had me confused with another man, another American.

"I'm the wrong man," I said. "The wrong man!"

They became apoplectic. I couldn't get anywhere with them, and I soon wearied of trying. As I pushed my way toward the jeep one of them slashed me across the face with his stick and then the rest of them started swinging too, shoving for position, everyone trying to get his licks in. I fought back but couldn't hold them off. Because of my height I took most of the punishment on my shoulders and neck, but they managed to hit me a few more times in the face, not heavy blows but sharp and burning, as from a whip. Blood started running into my eyes. They were swinging and screaming, totally berserk, and then they stopped. There was no sound but the feral rasp and pant of our breathing. Everyone was looking at the bar, where an American lieutenant named Polk stood in the doorway. He was the one they were after, that was clear from his expression and from theirs.

With an unhurried movement Polk unsnapped his holster and took out his .45 and cocked it. He slowly aimed the pistol just above their heads, and in the same dream time they stepped back into the street and walked silently away.

Polk lowered the pistol. He asked if I was all right.

"I guess," I said. "What was that all about, anyway?"

He didn't tell me.

I was halfway home before it occurred to me that I could have saved myself a lot of trouble by pulling my own pistol. I'd forgotten I had it on.

Sergeant Benet cleaned my wounds—a few shallow cuts on my forehead. He had a touch as gentle as a woman's, and feeling him take me so tenderly in hand, dabbing and clucking, wincing at my pain as if it were his own, I started to feel sorry for myself. "I don't get it," I said. "Polk doesn't look anything like me. He's almost as big as you are. He doesn't have a moustache. He's got these piggy little eyes and this big moon face. We don't look *anything* alike!"

"Why, you poor nigger," Sergeant Benet said. "You poor, poor nigger."

Which is all by way of saying that even as I composed my face for the sniper, making it shine forth my youth and good nature and hope for years to come, I had no illusion that he would see anything but its color.

We found the second position to be satisfactory and set up camp for the night. Though the troops weren't supposed to build fires, they did, as always. They dropped their weapons any old place and took off their boots and readied their pans for the fish they'd collected earlier that day by tossing hand grenades into the local ponds. While they cooked they called back and forth to each other and sang along with sad nasal ballads on their radios. The perimeter guards wouldn't stay in position; they kept drifting in to visit friends and check on the progress of the food.

Nights in the field were always bad for me. I had a case of the runs. My skin felt crawly. My right eye twitched, and I kept flinching uncontrollably. I plotted our coordinates and called them in to the firebase and the air support people, along with the coordinates of the surrounding tree lines and all possible avenues of attack. If we got hit I intended to call down destruction on everything around me—the whole world, if necessary. The puppy ran past, squealing like a pig, as two soldiers chased after him. He tumbled over himself and one of the troops jumped for him and caught him by a hind leg. He lifted him that way and gave him a nasty shake, the way you'd snap a towel, then walked off swinging the puppy's nose just above the ground. After I finished my calls I followed them over to one of the fires. They had tied the puppy to a tree. He was all curled in on himself, watching them with one wild eye. His sides were heaving.

I greeted the two soldiers and hunkered down at their fire. They were sitting face-to-face with their legs dovetailed, massaging each other's feet. The arrangement looked timeless and profoundly corporeal, like two horses standing back to front, whisking flies from one another's eyes. Seeing them this way, whipped and sore, mired in their bodies, emptied me of anger. I shared my cigarettes. We agreed that Marlboros were number one.

I motioned toward the dog. "What are you going to call him?"

They looked at me without understanding.

"The dog," I said. "What name are you going to give him?"

The younger of the two gave a snort. The other, a sergeant with gray hair, stared at the puppy and said, "Canh Cho. His name is Canh Cho."

Dog Stew.

The one who had snorted lay back and shrieked like a girl being tickled, banging his knees together. Some other soldiers wandered over to see what was happening.

I addressed myself to the sergeant. He had a thin, scholarly face and a grave manner. When he spoke to me he lowered his head and looked up from under his eyebrows. I said, "Are you really going to eat him?"

"Oh yes." He smacked his lips and made greedy spooning gestures. Then he turned to the newcomers and repeated our conversation. They laughed. Gold teeth flashed in the firelight.

"When are you going to eat him?"

"Oh, tonight."

"Tonight? He's pretty small, isn't he? Don't you want to wait until he's bigger?"

"No," the sergeant said. "Now is the best time. The meat is best now." He made the spooning motions again. He said, "Let's eat!" and stood and untied the puppy, then picked him up by the tail and carried him to the fire. Looking at his friends and dancing a clownish jig, he dangled the yelping little wretch over the flames.

"Don't do that," I said, and everything changed, or became clear. I saw it in the sergeant's face, felt it in the hardening silence of the others. Up to now we'd been a couple of soldiers messing around in a soldierly way. But I had drawn a line, or at least called attention to the line already between us. I had spoken in absolute confidence of my mastery here. Now he had no choice but to show me—I could feel it coming—his own version of the situation.

The sergeant pulled the pup away from the fire and studied me. Then he hung it over the fire again. It gagged in the smoke and raked the air with its paws.

"Stop it!" I said, and got up.

He moved the puppy back long enough to let it catch its breath, then swung it like a censer back and forth through the flames. All this time his eyes were on me. I knew I should keep my mouth shut, but when the pup started choking I couldn't help myself. I ordered him to stop. Again he pulled the pup back, again he held it to the fire, again I told him to stop. And again. He wasn't playing with the dog, he was playing with me, with my whiteness, my Americanness, my delicate sentiments—everything that gave me my sense of superior elevation. And I knew it. But knowing did not free me from these conditions, it only made me feel how hopelessly subject I was to them.

Please, what was I doing here? If I'd been forced to say what I was doing out here in this alien swamp, forced to watch an ignorant man oppress a dog, could I, with a straight face, have said, "I am an advisor"?

I couldn't win. My only choice was to quit. I turned and walked away, until I heard a howl of such despair that I had to stop. It seemed I didn't have a choice after all. Nor did the sergeant, grimly waiting for me with the singed and gasping pup. He was locked in the game too, as much as I was. He had to take it to the end.

I could think of only one way out. I said, as if this had been the question all along, "All right. How much?"

The sergeant was no dope; he saw his opening. He looked at the puppy. "A thousand piastres," he said.

"A thousand piastres? Too much. Five hundred."

"A thousand."

I made an aggrieved face but got out my wallet and paid him. It didn't kill me—five dollars and change. He took the money and gave me the smoking dog. The other soldiers had been stern and watchful, holding him to his task, but now they were joking around again. They were satisfied. Profit was victory.

"Goodbye, Cahn Cho," one of them called.

I took the puppy back to my tent. His fur was scorched and greasy with soot, his eyes bloodshot, his nose blistered. He smelled like rancid bacon. I cleaned him up as well as I could and tried to calm him. He trembled convulsively. Every time I touched him he yipped in fright and shrank away. I spoke to him in low, gentle tones and when he continued to cringe I began to dislike him. I disliked him for being so unlucky. I disliked him for involving me in his bad luck, and making a fool of me. I disliked him for not seeing any difference between me and the man who'd hurt him.

But I held him and petted him and finally he fell asleep in my lap, his nose tucked between my knees. While he slept I went on stroking him, and my hands grew slow and gentle with the memory of all the other dogs they'd known, Sheppy and Tyke, Ringer, Banana, Champion, and without warning tenderness overcame me. It spread through me like a blush, like the sudden heat of unexpected praise—an exotic sensation, almost embarrassing in its intensity. I hardly recognized it. I hadn't felt anything like it in months.

The radio operator brought me a plate of rice and fish. He looked at the pup and made the same eating gesture the sergeant had made. He rubbed his stomach and laughed, and walked away laughing.

From that day on it became the custom of our troops to greet me with spooning motions and signs of ravenous appetite, especially when I took Canh Cho out for a walk. He seemed to understand their meaning. He was a sad little pooch. I tried to teach him a few tricks, bring out some personality, make a proper mascot of him so he'd have a place in the battalion after I was gone. Nothing doing. He wouldn't even chase a ball unless I smeared hamburger on it. All he wanted to do was lie under the big wicker chair with his head sticking out and snap at flies. This engaged his interest, and he was certainly good at it, but it seemed a raw, unfriendly sort of pleasure.

Shortly after Christmas Vera wrote to tell me she'd been seeing someone else, "seriously." She thought it was best to suspend our engagement until things were clearer. I read the letter many times over, not sure how to respond. Though I managed to strike a note of offended trust and virtue in my letter back to Vera, I didn't really feel it, and knew I had no right to it. The truth was, I'd been unfaithful to her ever since I got to My Tho. I made resolutions, and renewed them now and then, but they never survived any temptation worth the name. Nor had I given Vera much to hang on to. My letters home were by turns casual and melodramatic, and had little to say of love. If, as she'd asked me to do, I had written truthfully about my inner life, I would have written about boredom, dread, occasional outright fear, and the sexual hunger that fear left boiling in its wake.

Still, Vera's letter gave me a knock. It caused me to compare myself to the other fellow, Leland. We had never met, but I'd heard Vera speak of him as an old friend. Though only a year my senior, Leland was a college graduate with a good job. She had once said that he was brilliant. The word went down hard even then, as if I'd sensed how it would come back to judge me later.

Using Leland's blazing sun to take my bearings, I looked around and found myself exactly nowhere. No marketable education, no money, no prospects. My writing, my "work" as I'd begun to call it, was supposed to take care of all that. Mindful of the feckless dropout Scott Fitzgerald leaving the army with a finished draft of *This Side of Paradise* in his duffel bag, about to feed lifelong dust to his classmates, I had promised myself that I would use my nights to finish the novel I'd begun in Washington; but it soon came to seem romantic and untrue, and I conceived an implacable hatred for it.

Probably it was romantic. Most first novels are. As to whether it was untrue, that's another question. I believed in it when I first started writing it, believed in its story and the view of things that held it together. The truth of a novel proceeds from just that kind of conviction, carried to extremes. I had it, then I didn't. The ground shifted under my feet; the old view vanished and of the one still taking shape I could make neither poetry nor sense. I put the novel out of sight. Eventually, ceremonially, I burned it.

I was unable to write anything else. Instead I tried to read the books Geoffrey took such pains to choose and send me, but over the past several months my passion for them had gone flat as well. It became a duty to read each sentence, and the books themselves felt awkward and foreign in my hands. Before long I'd catch myself staring off. This was my signal to join Sergeant Benet for *Bonanza* or *The Gong Show*, or brave the road for a run into town. The best thing I had to say for myself was that I was still alive. Not impressively, though. Not brilliantly.

Strange, how the memory of that one word—she didn't use it in the letter—could give me so stark a picture of my condition. Even more than the letter itself, even more than losing Vera, whose loss, to tell the truth, did not seem impossible to bear, that word cast me down. I called Canh Cho over, thinking it would be agreeable to have him lay his head on my knee and look up at me while I stroked him and pondered my state. But he didn't move.

"Come here, damn you."

He pulled his head back under the chair.

I stood and lifted the chair to show him he couldn't hide from me, anywhere. He looked up and understood, then lowered his head in the woe of his knowledge. I put the chair back down. I was sorry, but what a sad dog. I had to conclude that he probably would have been happier with the Vietcong, unless, of course, they ate him.

THE ROUGH HUMOR OF SOLDIERS

My last night in My Tho. The battalion officers were giving me a farewell party. We began the evening at a bar in town, then moved on to Major Chau's house for dinner. Madame Chau was nowhere in evidence, nor were any of their children. When we'd all assembled and settled our-selves in a circle on the floor Major Chau rang a bell and a young woman entered the room. She was made up heavily, even ceremonially, her face whitened, her cheeks rouged, her lips painted red. Her perfume was thick and sweet. Major Chau introduced the young woman as his niece, Miss Bep. She bowed, then took a tray filled with brandy glasses from the sideboard and moved around the circle of men, bending before each of us with downcast eyes. Captain Kale took his glass and thanked her and she moved on to me without a word, but in passing looked back at him and gave him what might have been a smile; it was gone too soon to say. The face she presented to me was impeccably bland.

Then she came around with a large bottle of Martell and filled our glasses. Again she looked at Captain Kale, and again, unmistakably this time, smiled.

"What's your secret?" I asked him.

"Knock it off," he said.

Captain Kale had a wife to whom he intended to be true.

Miss Bep returned the bottle to the sideboard and took the empty place to Major Chau's right. This was the first time in my experience that a woman had joined a circle of officers rather than serving and leaving. Captain Kale was watching her with a rude, unconscious fixity. No one took any notice. The room was blue with smoke, loud with boasts and insults. Pots banged in the kitchen.

We emptied our glasses and Miss Bep went around again with the Martell. She gave more to Captain Kale than to anyone else. When she resumed her place beside Major Chau she turned and whispered in his ear.

Major Chau leaned forward. "My niece says the American captain is very handsome."

Captain Kale shifted, shifted again. The lotus position was torture to those pumped-up haunches. There were wet patches on the back of his shirt, widening rings under his arms. His pink face shone. "Please convey my compliments to Miss Bep on her extremely nice looks," he said, and nodded at her. "Miss Bep is very beautiful."

The other officers whistled and slapped their knees when Major Chau translated this. Miss Bep spoke into his ear again.

"My niece says the American captain looks like the great Fred Astaire."

Miss Bep said something else to Major Chau.

"My niece asks, Has the great Astaire found his Ginger Rogers here in My Tho?"

"No," Captain Kale said in Vietnamese.

Major Chau got up and went over to the stereo Sergeant Benet and I had bought him at the PX. He put on Brenda Lee's "I'm Sorry" and motioned for Captain Kale to rise. "My niece would be honored to dance with the great Astaire," he said.

"I'm not that great," he said, but he stood and walked over to Miss Bep. He held out his hand. She took it and rose lightly and without hesitation moved into his arms. They danced in the center of our circle, swaying to the music, hardly moving their feet at all. At first she looked up at him, then slowly let her head fall forward against his chest. Her eyes were closed. I could see the play of her fingers on the back of his neck.

Then Captain Kale closed his eyes too, and his face became gentle and calm. He was transfigured. The Vietnamese officers were watching him with peculiar concentration. Major Chau rolled his shoulders to the music, mouthing words as he stacked more 45s on the turntable:

> *They tell me*
> *Mistakes*
> *Are part of bein' young*
> *But that don't right*
> *The wrong that's been done . . .*

After the song ended, Captain Kale and Miss Bep went on swaying together to their own music, then roused themselves and stepped grog-gily apart, her hand still in his. The officers called out encouragement. I joined in, though I was nearly deranged with envy and incomprehension. A record fell, the needle hissed, Connie Francis began to sing.

> *Evening shadows make me blue*
> *When each weary day is through*

"You need more room," Major Chau said. "In here is too many peoples. Come." He beckoned to Captain Kale and gestured toward the doorway leading to the back of the house. "Come!" Captain Kale looked at him, looked at Miss Bep. They were still holding hands. She gave him that ghostly smile, then led him out of the circle and through the doorway behind Major Chau. The major returned, took his place, and rang the bell again. A pair of old women carried in trays from the kitchen.

While we filled our plates Major Chau raised his glass and began reciting a toast to me. He praised my implacable enmity toward the communist insurgents, my skill as a leader of men, my reckless courage under fire. He said that my presence here had dealt the Vietcong a blow they'd never recover from. Through all this Major Chau maintained an air of utmost gravity, and so did the other officers. When he was done the adjutant proposed a toast even more elevated. They were all stuffing themselves now, except the adjutant and, of course, me. That was part of the prank. As long as I was being toasted I had to sit there and listen with an expression of humility and gratitude. Lieutenant Nanh spoke next. Then another officer stepped in.

I was hungry. Somewhere in the back of the house Captain Kale was slow-dancing with Miss Bep. The toasts went on.

I'd expected something like this, but I didn't know what a nuisance it would be to sit through. Behind the understanding that all this was a joke, we had another understanding that it was not a joke at all, that in my time here I had succeeded only in staying alive. Their satiric praise created by implication a picture of me that was also a picture of what I feared I had become, a man in hiding.

At last they stopped and let me eat. Spring rolls, clear soup, fish and rice, noodles stirred up with shoots and greens and cubes of tender meat. "Where's This Place Called Lonely Street?" was on the record player. I'd just about finished my first helping when I heard a yell from the back of the house. The officers sat up, searched one another out with swift glances. Silence. Then another yell—a roar, really—and the sound of Captain Kale coming our way. He stomped into the room and stood there, staring at me, his face bleached white. His mouth was smeared with lipstick. He held his hands clenched in front of him like a runner frozen in midstride. I looked at him, he looked at me. Then Lieutenant Nanh made a sobbing sound and buried his face in his hands and fell sideways onto the floor. He kicked his foot out like a ham playing a dying man and knocked over a bowl of rice. Major Chau let off a series of shrill hoots—*whoo whoo whoo*—and then they all doubled over. They were wailing and shrieking and pounding the floor. Captain Kale gave no sign that he heard them.

"Did you know she was a guy?" he said.

I was too surprised to speak. I shook my head.

He gave me his full attention. Then he said, "I'd kill you if you did."

I understood that he meant it. Another close call.

Captain Kale looked at the others as if they'd just materialized in the room. He walked around them and out the door. After I heard the jeep start up and drive away I couldn't keep from treating myself to a few laughs while I ate my dinner. The officers kept trying to pull themselves together, but every time they looked at me they blew a gasket. At first I played along like a sport, thinking they'd lose interest, but they'd entered a state where anything I did—spearing my food, lifting my fork, chewing—set them off again. Finally Lieutenant Nanh managed to sit up and catch his breath. He watched me fill my plate yet again with noodles and diced meat. "*Bon appetit*," he said.

"This is good," I said. "What is it?"

He pitched over onto his back and let out a howl. He lay there, drumming his feet and panting soundlessly. I looked down at my plate. "Oh no," I said. "You didn't do that."

But of course that was exactly what they'd done. What else could I expect? What else could *he* expect, with a name like Dog Stew? That pooch was up against some very strong karma, far beyond the power of my stopgap, sentimental intercessions. In moments of clarity I'd known he would come to this. He knew it himself in his doggy way, and the knowledge had given him a morose, dull, hopeless cast of mind. He bore his life like a weight, yet trembled to lose it. I'd been fretting about his prospects. Now my worries were over. So were his. At least there was some largesse in this conclusion, some reciprocity. I had fed him, now he fed me, and fed me, I have to say, right tastily.

There was only one way left to do him justice. I bent to my plate and polished him off.

Questions

1. When Wolff complains that he looks nothing like Polk, why does Sergeant Benet, and African American, respond by repeating, "You poor, poor nigger"? (296)

2. Why does Wolff call himself "hopelessly subject" to the conditions of "my whiteness, my Americanness, my delicate sentiments"? (298)

3. Why does Wolff question whether he could have said, "I am an advisor" with a straight face if asked what he was doing "in this alien swamp"? (298)

4. Why does Wolff conclude that the dog "probably would have been happier with the Vietcong"? (301)

5. Are the battalion officers mocking Wolff when they testify to his leadership?

6. What does Wolff mean when he says he feared he had become "a man in hiding"? (304)

7. Why do the officers give Wolff his dog to eat? Why does he finish his plate, even though he knows the origin of the meat?

8. In combat, when does humor cross the line from being helpful in alleviating stress to insolence and insubordination?

Tim O'Brien

Tim O'Brien (1946–) was an antiwar activist when he was drafted in 1968. Despite his opposition to the war, he served a year-long tour of duty in some of the most dangerous regions of Vietnam. Following his discharge he turned to writing, working for several years as a reporter for the *Washington Post* and then devoting himself to fiction full-time.

Since that time, O'Brien has written numerous short stories and novels, many based on his service in Vietnam. The following passages are from *The Things They Carried* (1990), a collection of interconnected stories that are considered fiction although the settings and events echo the author's own wartime experiences. Much of O'Brien's writing has an autobiographical aspect and deals with issues of memory, trauma, and forgiveness, as well as the difficulty of depicting combat for those who have not experienced it. Because he was so opposed to the war in which he fought, O'Brien's ambivalent feelings are particularly troubling to him. His grappling with painful memories reflects the experience of many combat veterans.

In "In the Field," O'Brien explores the feelings of guilt and grief experienced by a group of soldiers as they search for a fallen comrade. Though his death is irreversible, his companions cannot abandon him to an unidentified resting place. In "Field Trip," the narrator returns to the site of his friend's death many years later, this time accompanied by his young daughter. In this pair of stories, O'Brien explores the ways in which combat veterans seek closure, both by revisiting battlegrounds and by trying to communicate their experience to their families.

THE THINGS THEY CARRIED

(selection)

IN THE FIELD

At daybreak the platoon of eighteen soldiers formed into a loose rank and began wading side by side through the deep muck of the shit field. They moved slowly in the rain. Leaning forward, heads down, they used the butts of their weapons as probes, wading across the field to the river and then turning and wading back again. They were tired and miserable; all they wanted now was to get it finished. Kiowa was gone. He was under the mud and water, folded in with the war, and their only thought was to find him and dig him out and then move on to someplace dry and warm. It had been a hard night. Maybe the worst ever. The rains had fallen without stop, and the Song Tra Bong had overflowed its banks, and the muck had now risen thigh-deep in the field along the river. A low, gray mist hovered over the land. Off to the west there was thunder, soft little moaning sounds, and the monsoons seemed to be a lasting element of the war. The eighteen soldiers moved in silence. First Lieutenant Jimmy Cross went first, now and then straightening out the rank, closing up the gaps. His uniform was dark with mud; his arms and face were filthy. Early in the morning he had radioed in the MIA report, giving the name and circumstances, but he was now determined to find his man, no matter what, even if it meant flying in slabs of concrete and damming up the river and draining the entire field. He would not lose a member of his command like this. It wasn't right. Kiowa had been a fine soldier and a fine human being, a devout Baptist, and there was no way Lieutenant Cross would allow such a good man to be lost under the slime of a shit field.

Briefly, he stopped and watched the clouds. Except for some occasional thunder it was a deeply quiet morning, just the rain and the steady sloshing sounds of eighteen men wading through the thick waters. Lieutenant Cross wished the rain would let up. Even for an hour, it would make things easier.

But then he shrugged. The rain was the war and you had to fight it.

Turning, he looked out across the field and yelled at one of his men to close up the rank. Not a man, really—a boy. The young soldier stood off by himself at the center of the field in knee-deep water, reaching down with both hands as if chasing some object just beneath the surface. The boy's shoulders were shaking. Jimmy Cross yelled again but the young soldier did not turn or look up. In his hooded poncho, everything caked with mud, the boy's face was impossible to make out. The filth seemed to erase identities, transforming the men into identical copies of a single soldier, which was exactly how Jimmy Cross had been trained to treat them, as interchangeable units of command. It was difficult sometimes, but he tried to avoid that sort of thinking. He had no military ambitions. He preferred to view his men not as units but as human beings. And Kiowa had been a splendid human being, the very best, intelligent and gentle and quiet-spoken. Very brave, too. And decent. The kid's father taught Sunday school in Oklahoma City, where Kiowa had been raised to believe in the promise of salvation under Jesus Christ, and this conviction had always been present in the boy's smile, in his posture toward the world, in the way he never went anywhere without an illustrated New Testament that his father had mailed to him as a birthday present back in January.

A crime, Jimmy Cross thought.

Looking out toward the river, he knew for a fact that he had made a mistake setting up here. The order had come from higher, true, but still he should've exercised some field discretion. He should've moved to higher ground for the night, should've radioed in false coordinates. There was nothing he could do now, but still it was a mistake and a hideous waste. He felt sick about it. Standing in the deep waters of the field, First Lieutenant Jimmy Cross began composing a letter in his head to the kid's father, not mentioning the shit field, just saying what a fine soldier Kiowa had been, what a fine human being, and how he was the kind of son that any father could be proud of forever.

The search went slowly. For a time the morning seemed to brighten, the sky going to a lighter shade of silver, but then the rains came back hard and steady. There was the feel of permanent twilight.

At the far left of the line, Azar and Norman Bowker and Mitchell Sanders waded along the edge of the field closest to the river. They were tall men, but at times the muck came to mid-thigh, other times to the crotch.

Azar kept shaking his head. He coughed and shook his head and said, "Man, talk about irony. I bet if Kiowa was here, I bet he'd just laugh. Eating shit—it's your classic irony."

"Fine," said Norman Bowker. "Now pipe down."

Azar sighed. "Wasted in the waste," he said. "A shit field. You got to admit, it's pure world-class irony."

The three men moved with slow, heavy steps. It was hard to keep balance. Their boots sank into the ooze, which produced a powerful downward suction, and with each step they would have to pull up hard to break the hold. The rain made quick dents in the water, like tiny mouths, and the stink was everywhere.

When they reached the river, they shifted a few meters to the north and began wading back up the field. Occasionally they used their weapons to test the bottom, but mostly they just searched with their feet.

"A classic case," Azar was saying. "Biting the dirt, so to speak, that tells the story."

"Enough," Bowker said.

"Like those old cowboy movies. One more redskin bites the dirt."

"I'm serious, man. Zip it shut."

Azar smiled and said, "Classic."

The morning was cold and wet. They had not slept during the night, not even for a few moments, and all three of them were feeling the tension as they moved across the field toward the river. There was nothing they could do for Kiowa. Just find him and slide him aboard a chopper. Whenever a man died it was always the same, a desire to get it over with quickly, no fuss or ceremony, and what they wanted now was to head for a ville and get under a roof and forget what had happened during the night.

Halfway across the field Mitchell Sanders stopped. He stood for a moment with his eyes shut, feeling along the bottom with a foot, then he passed his weapon over to Norman Bowker and reached down into the muck. After a second he hauled up a filthy green rucksack.

The three men did not speak for a time. The pack was heavy with mud and water, dead looking. Inside were a pair of moccasins and an illustrated New Testament.

"Well," Mitchell Sanders finally said, "the guy's around here somewhere."

"Better tell the LT."

"Screw him."

"Yeah, but—"

"Some lieutenant," Sanders said. "Camps us in a toilet. Man don't *know* shit."

"Nobody knew," Bowker said.

"Maybe so, maybe not. Ten billion places we could've set up last night, the man picks a latrine."

Norman Bowker stared down at the rucksack. It was made of dark green nylon with an aluminum frame, but now it had the curious look of flesh.

"It wasn't the LT's fault," Bowker said quietly.

"Whose then?"

"Nobody's. Nobody knew till afterward."

Mitchell Sanders made a sound in his throat. He hoisted up the rucksack, slipped into the harness, and pulled the straps tight. "All right, but this much for sure. The man knew it was raining. He knew about the river. One plus one. Add it up, you get exactly what happened."

Sanders glared at the river.

"Move it," he said. "Kiowa's waiting on us."

Slowly then, bending against the rain, Azar and Norman Bowker and Mitchell Sanders began wading again through the deep waters, their eyes down, circling out from where they had found the rucksack.

First Lieutenant Jimmy Cross stood fifty meters away. He had finished writing the letter in his head, explaining things to Kiowa's father, and now he folded his arms and watched his platoon crisscrossing the wide field. In a funny way, it reminded him of the municipal golf course in his hometown in New Jersey. A lost ball, he thought. Tired players searching through the rough, sweeping back and forth in long systematic patterns. He wished he were there right now. On the sixth hole. Looking out across the water hazard that fronted the small flat green, a seven iron in his hand, calculating wind and distance, wondering if he should reach instead for an eight. A tough decision, but all you could ever lose was a ball. You did not lose a player. And you never had to wade out into the hazard and spend the day searching through the slime.

Jimmy Cross did not want the responsibility of leading these men. He had never wanted it. In his sophomore year at Mount Sebastian College he had signed up for the Reserve Officer Training Corps without much thought. An automatic thing: because his friends had joined, and because it was worth a few credits, and because it seemed preferable to letting the draft take him. He was unprepared. Twenty-four years old and his heart wasn't in it. Military matters meant nothing to him. He did not care one way or the other about the war, and he had no desire to command, and even after all these months in the bush, all the days and nights, even then he did not know enough to keep his men out of a shit field.

What he should've done, he told himself, was follow his first impulse. In the late afternoon yesterday, when they reached the night coordinates, he should've taken one look and headed for higher ground. He should've known. No excuses. At one edge of the field was a small ville, and right away a couple of old mama-sans had trotted out to warn him. Number ten, they'd said. Evil ground. Not a good spot for good GIs. But it was a war, and he had his orders, so they'd set up a perimeter and crawled under their ponchos and tried to settle in for the night. The rain never stopped. By midnight the Song Tra Bong had overflowed its banks. The field turned to slop, everything soft and mushy. He remembered how the water kept rising, how a terrible stink began to bubble up out of the earth. It was a dead-fish smell, partly, but something else, too, and then later in the night Mitchell Sanders had crawled through the rain and grabbed him hard by the arm and asked what he was doing setting up in a shit field. The village toilet, Sanders said. He remembered the look on Sanders's face. The guy stared for a moment and then wiped his mouth and whispered, "Shit," and then crawled away into the dark.

A stupid mistake. That's all it was, a mistake, but it had killed Kiowa.

Lieutenant Jimmy Cross felt something tighten inside him. In the letter to Kiowa's father he would apologize point-blank. Just admit to the blunders.

He would place the blame where it belonged. Tactically, he'd say, it was indefensible ground from the start. Low and flat. No natural cover. And so late in the night, when they took mortar fire from across the river, all they could do was snake down under the slop and lie there and wait. The field just exploded. Rain and slop and shrapnel, it all mixed together, and the field seemed to boil. He would explain this to Kiowa's father. Carefully, not covering up his own guilt, he would tell how the mortar rounds made craters in the slush, spraying up great showers of filth, and how the craters then collapsed on themselves and filled up with mud and water, sucking things down, swallowing things, weapons and entrenching tools and belts of ammunition, and how in this way his son Kiowa had been combined with the waste and the war.

My own fault, he would say.

Straightening up, First Lieutenant Jimmy Cross rubbed his eyes and tried to get his thoughts together. The rain fell in a cold, sad drizzle.

Off toward the river he again noticed the young soldier standing alone at the center of the field. The boy's shoulders were shaking. Maybe it was something in the posture of the soldier, or the way he seemed to be reaching for some invisible object beneath the surface, but for several moments Jimmy Cross stood very still, afraid to move, yet knowing he had to, and then he murmured to himself, "My fault," and he nodded and waded out across the field toward the boy.

The young soldier was trying hard not to cry.

He, too, blamed himself. Bent forward at the waist, groping with both hands, he seemed to be chasing some creature just beyond reach, something elusive, a fish or a frog. His lips were moving. Like Jimmy Cross, the boy was explaining things to an absent judge. It wasn't to defend himself. The boy recognized his own guilt and wanted only to lay out the full causes.

Wading sideways a few steps, he leaned down and felt along the soft bottom of the field.

He pictured Kiowa's face. They'd been close buddies, the tightest, and he remembered how last night they had huddled together under their ponchos, the rain cold and steady, the water rising to their knees, but how Kiowa had just laughed it off and said they should concentrate on better things. And so for a long while they'd talked about their families and hometowns. At one point, the boy remembered, he'd been showing Kiowa a picture of his girlfriend. He remembered switching on his flashlight. A stupid thing to do, but he did it anyway, and he remembered Kiowa leaning in for a look at the picture—"Hey, she's *cute*," he'd said—and then the field exploded all around them.

Like murder, the boy thought. The flashlight made it happen. Dumb and dangerous. And as a result his friend Kiowa was dead.

That simple, he thought.

He wished there were some other way to look at it, but there wasn't. Very simple and very final. He remembered two mortar rounds hitting close by. Then a third, even closer, and off to his left he'd heard somebody scream. The voice was ragged and clotted up, but he knew instantly that it was Kiowa.

He remembered trying to crawl toward the screaming. No sense of direction, though, and the field seemed to suck him under, and everything was black and wet and swirling, and he couldn't get his bearings, and then another round hit nearby, and for a few moments all he could do was hold his breath and duck down beneath the water.

Later, when he came up again, there were no more screams. There was an arm and a wristwatch and part of a boot. There were bubbles where Kiowa's head should've been.

He remembered grabbing the boot. He remembered pulling hard, but how the field seemed to pull back, like a tug-of-war he couldn't win, and how finally he had to whisper his friend's name and let go and watch the boot slide away. Then for a long time there were things he could not remember. Various sounds, various smells. Later he'd found himself lying on a little rise, face-up, tasting the field in his mouth, listening to the rain and explosions and bubbling sounds. He was alone. He'd lost everything. He'd lost Kiowa and his weapon and his flashlight and his girlfriend's picture. He remembered this. He remembered wondering if he could lose himself.

Now, in the dull morning rain, the boy seemed frantic. He waded quickly from spot to spot, leaning down and plunging his hands into the water. He did not look up when Lieutenant Jimmy Cross approached.

"Right here," the boy was saying. "Got to be right here."

Jimmy Cross remembered the kid's face but not the name. That happened sometimes. He tried to treat his men as individuals but sometimes the names just escaped him.

He watched the young soldier shove his hands into the water, "Right *here*," he kept saying. His movements seemed random and jerky.

Jimmy Cross waited a moment, then stepped closer. "Listen," he said quietly, "the guy could be anywhere."

The boy glanced up. "Who could?"

"Kiowa. You can't expect—"

"Kiowa's *dead*."

"Well, yes."

The young soldier nodded. "So what about Billie?"

"Who?"

"My girl. What about her? This picture, it was the only one I had. Right here, I lost it."

Jimmy Cross shook his head. It bothered him that he could not come up with a name.

"Slow down," he said, "I don't—"

"Billie's *picture*. I had it all wrapped up, I had it in plastic, so it'll be okay if I can . . . Last night we were looking at it, me and Kiowa. Right here. I know for sure it's right here somewhere."

Jimmy Cross smiled at the boy. "You can ask her for another one. A better one."

"She won't *send* another one. She's not even my *girl* anymore, she won't . . . Man, I got to find it."

The boy yanked his arm free.

He shuffled sideways and stooped down again and dipped into the muck with both hands. His shoulders were shaking. Briefly, Lieutenant Cross wondered where the kid's weapon was, and his helmet, but it seemed better not to ask.

He felt some pity come on him. For a moment the day seemed to soften. So much hurt, he thought. He watched the young soldier wading through the water, bending down and then standing and then bending down again, as if something might finally be salvaged from all the waste.

Jimmy Cross silently wished the boy luck.

Then he closed his eyes and went back to working on the letter to Kiowa's father.

Across the field Azar and Norman Bowker and Mitchell Sanders were wading alongside a narrow dike at the edge of the field. It was near noon now.

Norman Bowker found Kiowa. He was under two feet of water. Nothing showed except the heel of a boot.

"That's him?" Azar said.

"Who else?"

"I don't know." Azar shook his head. "I don't know."

Norman Bowker touched the boot, covered his eyes for a moment, then stood up and looked at Azar.

"So where's the joke?" he said.

"No joke."

"Eating shit. Let's hear that one."

"Forget it."

Mitchell Sanders told them to knock it off. The three soldiers moved to the dike, put down their packs and weapons, then waded back to where the boot was showing. The body lay partly wedged under a layer of mud beneath the water. It was hard to get traction; with each movement the muck would grip their feet and hold tight. The rain had come back harder now. Mitchell Sanders reached down and found Kiowa's other boot, and they waited a moment, then Sanders sighed and said, "Okay," and they took hold of the two boots and pulled up hard. There was only a slight give. They tried again, but this time the body did not move at all. After the third try they stopped and looked down for a while. "One more time," Norman Bowker said. He counted to three and they leaned back and pulled.

"Stuck," said Mitchell Sanders.

"I see that. Christ."

They tried again, then called over Henry Dobbins and Rat Kiley, and all five of them put their arms and backs into it, but the body was jammed in tight.

Azar moved to the dike and sat holding his stomach. His face was pale.

The others stood in a circle, watching the water, then after a time somebody said, "We can't just *leave* him there," and the men nodded and got out their entrenching tools and began digging. It was hard, sloppy work. The mud seemed to flow back faster than they could dig, but Kiowa was their friend and they kept at it anyway.

Slowly, in little groups, the rest of the platoon drifted over to watch. Only Lieutenant Jimmy Cross and the young soldier were still searching the field.

"What we should do, I guess," Norman Bowker said, "is tell the LT."

Mitchell Sanders shook his head. "Just mess things up. Besides, the man looks happy out there, real content. Let him be."

After ten minutes they uncovered most of Kiowa's lower body. The corpse was angled steeply into the muck, upside down, like a diver who had plunged headfirst off a high tower. The men stood quietly for a few seconds. There was a feeling of awe. Mitchell Sanders finally nodded and said, "Let's get it done," and they took hold of the legs and pulled up hard, then pulled again, and after a moment Kiowa came sliding to the surface. A piece of his shoulder was missing; the arms and chest and face were cut up with shrapnel. He was covered with bluish green mud. "Well," Henry Dobbins said, "it could be worse," and Dave Jensen said, "How, man? Tell me *how*." Carefully, trying not to look at the body, they carried Kiowa over to the dike and laid him down. They used towels to clean off the scum. Rat Kiley went through the kid's pockets, placed his personal effects in a plastic bag, taped the bag to Kiowa's wrist, then used the radio to call in a dustoff.

Moving away, the men found things to do with themselves, some smoking, some opening up cans of C rations, a few just standing in the rain.

For all of them it was a relief to have it finished. There was the promise now of finding a hootch somewhere, or an abandoned pagoda, where they could strip down and wring out their fatigues and maybe start a hot fire. They felt bad for Kiowa. But they also felt a kind of giddiness, a secret joy, because they were alive, and because even the rain was preferable to being sucked under a shit field, and because it was all a matter of luck and happenstance.

Azar sat down on the dike next to Norman Bowker.

"Listen," he said. "Those dumb jokes—I didn't mean anything."

"We all say things."

"Yeah, but when I saw the guy, it made me feel—I don't know—like he was listening."

"He wasn't."

"I guess not. But I felt sort of guilty almost, like if I'd kept my mouth shut none of it would've ever happened. Like it was my fault."

Norman Bowker looked out across the wet field.

"Nobody's fault," he said. "Everybody's."

Near the center of the field First Lieutenant Jimmy Cross squatted in the muck, almost entirely submerged. In his head he was revising the letter to Kiowa's father. Impersonal this time. An officer expressing an officer's condolences. No apologies were necessary, because in fact it was one of those freak things, and the war was full of freaks, and nothing could ever change it anyway. Which was the truth, he thought. The exact truth.

Lieutenant Cross went deeper into the muck, the dark water at his throat, and tried to tell himself it was the truth.

Beside him, a few steps off to the left, the young soldier was still searching for his girlfriend's picture. Still remembering how he had killed Kiowa.

The boy wanted to confess. He wanted to tell the lieutenant how in the middle of the night he had pulled out Billie's picture and passed it over to Kiowa and then switched on the flashlight, and how Kiowa had whispered, "Hey, she's *cute*," and how for a second the flashlight had made Billie's face sparkle, and how right then the field had exploded all around them. The flashlight had done it. Like a target shining in the dark.

The boy looked up at the sky, then at Jimmy Cross.

"Sir?" he said.

The rain and mist moved across the field in broad, sweeping sheets of gray. Close by, there was thunder.

"Sir," the boy said, "I got to explain something."

But Lieutenant Jimmy Cross wasn't listening. Eyes closed, he let himself go deeper into the waste, just letting the field take him. He lay back and floated.

When a man died, there had to be blame. Jimmy Cross understood this. You could blame the war. You could blame the idiots who made the war. You could blame Kiowa for going to it. You could blame the rain. You could blame the river. You could blame the field, the mud, the climate. You could blame the enemy. You could blame the mortar rounds. You could blame people who were too lazy to read a newspaper, who were bored by the daily body counts, who switched channels at the mention of politics. You could blame whole nations. You could blame God. You could blame the munitions makers or Karl Marx or a trick of fate or an old man in Omaha who forgot to vote.

In the field, though, the causes were immediate. A moment of carelessness or bad judgment or plain stupidity carried consequences that lasted forever.

For a long while Jimmy Cross lay floating. In the clouds to the east there was the sound of a helicopter, but he did not take notice. With his eyes still closed, bobbing in the field, he let himself slip away. He was back home in New Jersey. A golden afternoon on the golf course, the fairways lush and green, and he was teeing it up on the first hole. It was a world without responsibility. When the war was over, he thought, maybe then he would write a letter to Kiowa's father. Or maybe not. Maybe he would just take a couple of practice swings and knock the ball down the middle and pick up his clubs and walk off into the afternoon.

FIELD TRIP

A few months after completing "In the Field," I returned with my daughter to Vietnam, where we visited the site of Kiowa's death, and where I looked for signs of forgiveness or personal grace or whatever else the land might offer. The field was still there, though not as I remembered it. Much smaller, I thought, and not nearly so menacing, and in the bright sunlight it was hard to picture what had happened on this ground some twenty years ago. Except for a few marshy spots along the river, everything was bone dry. No ghosts—just a flat, grassy field. The place was at peace. There were yellow butterflies. There was a breeze and a wide blue sky. Along the river two old farmers stood in ankle-deep water, repairing the same narrow dike where we had laid out Kiowa's body after pulling him from the muck. Things were quiet. At one point, I remember, one of the farmers looked up and shaded his eyes, staring across the field at us, then after a time he wiped his forehead and went back to work.

I stood with my arms folded, feeling the grip of sentiment and time. Amazing, I thought. Twenty years.

Behind me, in the jeep, my daughter Kathleen sat waiting with a government interpreter, and now and then I could hear the two of them talking in soft voices. They were already fast friends. Neither of them, I think, understood what all this was about, why I'd insisted that we search out this spot. It had been a hard two-hour ride from Quang Ngai City, bumpy dirt roads and a hot August sun, ending up at an empty field on the edge of nowhere.

I took out my camera, snapped a couple of pictures, then stood gazing out at the field. After a time Kathleen got out of the jeep and stood beside me.

"You know what I think?" she said. "I think this place stinks. It smells like . . . God, I don't even *know* what. It smells rotten."

"It sure does. I know that."

"So when can we go?"

"Pretty soon," I said.

She started to say something but then hesitated. Frowning, she squinted out at the field for a second, then shrugged and walked back to the jeep.

Kathleen had just turned ten, and this trip was a kind of birthday present, showing her the world, offering a small piece of her father's history. For the most part she'd held up well—far better than I—and over the first two weeks she'd trooped along without complaint as we hit the obligatory tourist stops. Ho Chi Minh's mausoleum in Hanoi. A model farm outside Saigon. The tunnels at Cu Chi. The monuments and government offices and orphanages. Through most of this, Kathleen had seemed to enjoy the foreignness of it all, the exotic food and animals, and even during those periods of boredom and discomfort she'd kept up a good-natured tolerance. At the same time, however, she'd seemed a bit puzzled. The war was as remote to her as cavemen and dinosaurs.

One morning in Saigon she'd asked what it was all about. "This whole war," she said, "why was everybody so mad at everybody else?"

I shook my head. "They weren't mad, exactly. Some people wanted one thing, other people wanted another thing."

"What did *you* want?"

"Nothing," I said. "To stay alive."

"That's all?"

"Yes."

Kathleen sighed. "Well, I don't get it. I mean, how come you were even here in the first place?"

"I don't know," I said. "Because I had to be."

"But *why*?"

I tried to find something to tell her, but finally I shrugged and said, "It's a mystery, I guess. I don't know."

For the rest of the day she was very quiet. That night, though, just before bedtime, Kathleen put her hand on my shoulder and said, "You know something? Sometimes you're pretty weird, aren't you?"

"Well, no," I said.

"You are *too*." She pulled her hand away and frowned at me. "Like coming over here. Some dumb thing happens a long time ago and you can't ever forget it."

"And that's bad?"

"No," she said quietly. "That's weird."

In the second week of August, near the end of our stay, I'd arranged for the side trip up to Quang Ngai. The tourist stuff was fine, but from the start I'd wanted to take my daughter to the places I'd seen as a soldier. I wanted to show her the Vietnam that kept me awake at night—a shady trail outside the village of My Khe, a filthy old pigsty on the Batangan Pensinsula. Our time was short, however, and choices had to be made, and in the end I decided to take her to this piece of ground where my friend Kiowa had died. It seemed appropriate. And, besides, I had business here.

Now, looking out at the field, I wondered if it was all a mistake. Everything was too ordinary. A quiet sunny day, and the field was not the field I remembered. I pictured Kiowa's face, the way he used to smile, but all I felt was the awkwardness of remembering.

Behind me, Kathleen let out a little giggle. The interpreter was showing her magic tricks.

There were birds and butterflies, the soft rustlings of rural anywhere. Below, in the earth, the relics of our presence were no doubt still there, the canteens and bandoliers and mess kits. This little field, I thought, had swallowed so much. My best friend. My pride. My belief in myself as a man of some small dignity and courage. Still, it was hard to find any real emotion. It simply wasn't there. After that long night in the rain, I'd seemed to grow cold inside, all the illusions gone, all the old ambitions and hopes for myself sucked away into the mud. Over the years, that coldness had never entirely disappeared. There were times in my life when I couldn't feel much, not sadness or pity or passion, and somehow I blamed this place for what I had become, and I blamed it for taking away the person I had once been. For twenty years this field had embodied all the waste that was Vietnam, all the vulgarity and horror.

Now it was just what it was. Flat and dreary and unremarkable. I walked up toward the river, trying to pick out specific landmarks, but all I recognized was a small rise where Jimmy Cross had set up his command post that night. Nothing else. For a while I watched the two old farmers working under the hot sun. I took a few more photographs, waved at the farmers, then turned and moved back to the jeep.

Kathleen gave me a little nod.

"Well," she said, "I hope you're having fun."

"Sure."

"Can we go now?"

"In a minute," I said. "Just relax."

At the back of the jeep I found the small cloth bundle I'd carried over from the States.

Kathleen's eyes narrowed. "What's *that*?"

"Stuff," I told her.

She glanced at the bundle again, then hopped out of the jeep and followed me back to the field. We walked past Jimmy Cross's command post, past the spot where Kiowa had gone under, down to where the field dipped into the marshland along the river. I took off my shoes and socks.

"Okay," Kathleen said, "what's going on?"

"A quick swim."

"Where?"

"Right here," I said. "Stay put."

She watched me unwrap the cloth bundle. Inside were Kiowa's old moccasins.

I stripped down to my underwear, took off my wristwatch, and waded in. The water was warm against my feet. Instantly, I recognized the soft, fat feel of the bottom. The water here was eight inches deep.

Kathleen seemed nervous. She squinted at me, her hands fluttering. "Listen, this is stupid," she said, "you can't even hardly get *wet*. How can you *swim* out there?"

"I'll manage."

"But it's not . . . I mean, God, it's not even *water*, it's like mush or something."

She pinched her nose and watched me wade out to where the water reached my knees. Roughly here, I decided, was where Mitchell Sanders had found Kiowa's rucksack. I eased myself down, squatting at first, then sitting. There was again that sense of recognition. The water rose to mid-chest, a deep greenish-brown, almost hot. Small water bugs skipped along the surface. Right here, I thought. Leaning forward, I reached in with the moccasins and wedged them into the soft bottom, letting them slide away. Tiny bubbles broke along the surface. I tried to think of something decent to say, something meaningful and right, but nothing came to me.

I looked down into the field.

"Well," I finally managed. "There it is."

My voice surprised me. It had a rough, chalky sound, full of things I did not know were there. I wanted to tell Kiowa that he'd been a great friend, the very best, but all I could do was slap hands with the water.

The sun made me squint. Twenty years. A lot like yesterday, a lot like never. In a way, maybe, I'd gone under with Kiowa, and now after two decades I'd finally worked my way out. A hot afternoon, a bright August sun, and the war was over. For a few moments I could not bring myself to move. Like waking from a summer nap, feeling lazy and sluggish, the world collecting itself around me. Fifty meters up the field one of the old farmers stood watching from along the dike. The man's face was dark and solemn. As we stared at each other, neither of us moving, I felt something go shut in my heart while something else swung open. Briefly, I wondered if the old man might walk over to exchange a few war stories, but instead he picked up a shovel and raised it over his head and held it there for a time, grimly, like a flag, then he brought the shovel down and said something to his friend and began digging into the hard, dry ground.

I stood up and waded out of the water.

"What a mess," Kathleen said. "All that gunk on your skin, you look like ... Wait'll I tell Mommy, she'll probably make you sleep in the garage."

"You're right," I said. "Don't tell her."

I pulled on my shoes, took my daughter's hand, and led her across the field toward the jeep. Soft heat waves shimmied up out of the earth.

When we reached the jeep, Kathleen turned and glanced out at the field.

"That old man," she said, "is he mad at you or something?"

"I hope not."

"He *looks* mad."

"No," I said. "All that's finished."

Questions

1. What does Jimmy Cross mean when he says Kiowa's death is a crime?

2. Why does the unnamed young soldier in "In the Field" look for the picture of his ex-girlfriend instead of the body of his friend?

3. Is it true, as Jimmy Cross says, that "When a man died, there had to be blame"? (319)

4. Is placing blame for a soldier's death something a commander should encourage or discourage?

5. Why does O'Brien think that in visiting the site of Kiowa's death he might find "forgiveness or personal grace or whatever else the land might offer"? (320)

6. Why does O'Brien want to share with his daughter the Vietnam that keeps him awake at night?

7. After Kathleen says the old man looks mad, what does O'Brien mean when he says, "All that's finished"? (325)

8. Why do people sometimes think that returning to the site of a traumatic event, often from long ago, can have a beneficial effect?

Yusef Komunyakaa

Yusef Komunyakaa (1947–) served in the Vietnam War as an information specialist and as a correspondent and editor for a military newspaper, earning a Bronze Star for his service. Since the 1970s he has authored numerous collections of poetry, including *Neon Vernacular: New and Selected Poems* (1994), which won the Pulitzer Prize and the prestigious Kingsley Tufts Poetry Award.

Komunyakaa's work primarily concerns two formative early experiences: growing up amid the violent segregation of the Jim Crow South, and serving as a young man in the Vietnam War. In his poetry, these two dangerous scenarios are often linked to themes of race and gender conflict and to the shifting nature of human connections. Komunyakaa writes of the temporary nature of interactions between people; the consequences, both oppressive and joyful, recur throughout his poetry.

"Facing It" describes a visit to the Vietnam Veterans Memorial, located on the National Mall in Washington, D.C. Built in 1982, the Vietnam Veterans Memorial consists of highly reflective black granite walls, angled to form a wide V-shape. Etched on the walls are the names of more than 58,000 American servicemen and servicewomen who died or were classified as missing in action during the Vietnam War.

"Facing It" illustrates how the Vietnam Veterans Memorial has become a place of pilgrimage for many, especially for veterans, their families, and their friends. In the poem, the reflective granite surface lends a literal note of reflection to the speaker's thoughtful moment as present reality is overlaid with memories of names from the past. In doing so, the poem prompts us to consider the complex interaction of memories and present realities in our acts of memorializing.

FACING IT

My black face fades,
hiding inside the black granite.
I said I wouldn't
dammit: No tears.
I'm stone. I'm flesh.
My clouded reflection eyes me
like a bird of prey, the profile of night
slanted against morning. I turn
this way—the stone lets me go.
I turn that way—I'm inside
the Vietnam Veterans Memorial
again, depending on the light
to make a difference.
I go down the 58,022 names,
half-expecting to find
my own in letters like smoke.
I touch the name Andrew Johnson;
I see the booby trap's white flash.
Names shimmer on a woman's blouse
but when she walks away
the names stay on the wall.
Brushstrokes flash, a red bird's
wings cutting across my stare.
The sky. A plane in the sky.
A white vet's image floats
closer to me, then his pale eyes
look through mine. I'm a window.
He's lost his right arm
inside the stone. In the black mirror
a woman's trying to erase names:
No, she's brushing a boy's hair.

Questions

1. Why is Komunyakaa initially determined not to cry? Why does he say, "I'm stone. I'm flesh"?

2. Why is Komunyakaa "half-expecting" to find his own name etched on the Vietnam Veterans Memorial?

3. Why does Komunyakaa describe what he sees reflected in the wall, as well as what he sees on the wall itself?

4. Why does Komunyakaa say he is "a window" when he sees the veteran who has lost an arm reflected in the wall?

5. Why does the poem end with Komunyakaa thinking a woman is trying to erase names on the wall and then realizing that she is "brushing a boy's hair"?

6. What purposes can a memorial or monument serve for those who already have their own memories of the event because they participated in it?

Anne Simon Auger *as told to Keith Walker*

During the Vietnam War approximately 265,000 women served in the U.S. armed forces. Over 11,000 of them, mostly nurses, were stationed in Vietnam. Women also served as clerical workers, administrators, flight instructors, and mechanics. Though these roles frequently thrust women into dangerous combat regions, women were not officially allowed in combat roles until well after the Vietnam War.

Anne Simon Auger enlisted in the Army Nurse Corps in 1969, shortly after graduating from nursing school. She served for one year in the 91st Evacuation Hospital in Chu Lai, South Vietnam, treating the wounded of both sides. In the following selection, Auger recounts her experiences as an army nurse and as a veteran in the years since she returned. Her story was recorded by Keith Walker, a Korean War veteran who became interested in the involvement of women in the Vietnam War and published his interviews with twenty-six of them in the book *A Piece of My Heart* (1986).

Auger lays bare her transition in Vietnam from naive, warm-hearted altruism to feelings of frozen numbness and then vengeful anger. She continues to struggle with distress and shame at these changes within herself in her life back home. Since women in the military were not officially exposed to life-threatening situations, they received little psychiatric support or official acknowledgment of the traumatic situations they endured and were often left to cope with their distress alone.

Auger's account highlights the importance of connecting with other veterans and sharing common experiences as a crucial step to reentering civilian life. She also asks us to consider the deeply disturbing consequences for those who are unable or unwilling to do so.

A PIECE OF MY HEART

(selection)

I remember driving down to Fort Sam Houston with two of the girls who had signed up with me. I can still see us flying down those freeways heading south toward Texas. We felt like we were invincible. We owned the world; we were free, independent. It was really neat.

I remember trying on our combat boots and ponchos and our uniforms; we'd never worn anything so ridiculous in our lives. And we would parade 'round and play games in them and think we were really cool. We learned how to march. We thought that was so funny. I remember we had field training. We were given compasses and had to go out and find our way back; we never had so much fun. We got lost twelve times to Tuesday—it didn't matter. We had a little bit of medical training in the field where they would wrap some volunteer up in bandages, put a tag on him saying what was wrong with him, and we had to take care of him. It was totally unrealistic. It was another game. We knew what to do and how to do it from the lesson, but we didn't have any idea of what we were getting ourselves into. We were given weapons training in that they showed us how to fire an M-16, but they wouldn't let us do it. Of course I didn't want to anyway—they were too noisy. They took us through a mock Vietnam village. That was a little scary when they had the punji stick trap come up, but again it was no big deal. And I don't see how the army could have done any different. I hated them for years for not training me better for Vietnam, but I don't think it could possibly be done. I don't think you can train anybody or teach anybody to experience something that horrible without having them simply live it. . . . Anyway. We got through Fort Sam. It was a lark.

I went to Fort Devons in Massachusetts for six months. I was assigned to the orthopedic ward, and one hundred percent of my patients were Vietnam casualties. They were long-term; they had been in Japan before they came to us. I didn't even relate them to Vietnam, and it bothers me now, because they could have been suffering some of the distress that I have, and I didn't recognize it. I know some of them acted really wild and crazy, but I figured it was just because they were kids. While I was there I was dating a psychologist. He was a captain. I'll never forget when I got my orders he was the first one I showed them to, and I was excited. "I'm going to Vietnam!" I told him. He was upset because he was staying there and I was leaving; he thought the man should go. It hadn't dawned on me before that I should be anything but excited. I didn't think to question anything that was going on or to wonder what I was getting myself into. I was just out for experiences at the time, I guess.

So, I remember flying over from Travis. I was the only woman on the plane. There must have been two hundred men on the plane. But everybody was polite and friendly until we got within sight of Vietnam, and then it all just quieted down. Nobody talked; nobody said anything. Everybody had their noses glued to the window. We saw puffs of smoke. The plane took a sudden turn up, and we heard we were being fired on. That was the first time it dawned on me that my life may be in peril. Then I started thinking, "Why would they want to shoot me? I haven't done anything to them." Anyway, we took this steep, real fast dive into Long Binh, and we landed in Vietnam. I remember talking to the nurse in charge of assigning people, and she actually gave me a choice of where I wanted to go. The other nurses with me knew just about where they wanted to go. They all had choices, and I had no idea of one place from another. So I told her to send me wherever she wanted, and she still wouldn't do that. She said, "North or south?" I said, "I don't know." I finally just decided, "Oh hell, send me north. If I'm going to be here I might as well get as close to the North Vietnamese as I can," which is really irrational now, but at the time I didn't know what I was doing. So she assigned me to the 91st Evac.

I was assigned to intensive care and recovery, which is like jumping straight into the fire. I had no preparation for it. I was six months out of nursing school and had worked in a newborn nursery until I joined the army. It was hectic. It was fast paced. It was depressing. I spent six months there. Two of the incidents that really stand out from those six months: One was when I was working recovery. I had been there a few months, long enough to get numb and build a few walls. This eighteen-year-old

GI came into my recovery ward. He had been through surgery. He'd been in an APC that ran over a mine, and I think he was the only survivor. He was just a young kid; I don't even think he had hair on his face yet. And he came out of the anesthesia crying for his mother. I felt so helpless. I was barely older than he was, and he's crying, "Mommy! Mommy! Mommy!" I didn't know what to do. . . . I just held him, and I think that's all I did. It worked, but it was a real experience for me because I certainly wasn't maternal at the time and hadn't thought that that would ever come up. It got me to realize how young and how innocent and how naive these poor kids were. And their choices had been taken away from them.

Then the other incident. We had a sergeant, must have been in his midforties; he was a drinker, an alcoholic. And he wasn't even involved first line in the war—he was a supply sergeant or something. He came into our intensive care unit with a bleeding ulcer. I remember spending two hours pumping ice water into his stomach, pulling it out, and pumping it back in. We were also pumping blood into him. He died, and he had a family back home, and I thought, "My God, it's bad enough to die over here legitimately"—the gunshot wound—but to die that way seemed like such an awful waste.

The patient that chased me off the ward . . . was a lieutenant named . . . I don't remember his last name—his first name was John. He was twenty-one. He'd gotten married just before he came to Vietnam. And he was shot in his face. He absolutely lost his entire face from ear to ear. He had no nose. He was blind. It didn't matter, I guess, because he was absolutely a vegetable. He was alive and breathing; tubes and machines were keeping him alive. . . . I just . . . I couldn't handle it. To think of how one instant had affected his life. . . . His wife's life was completely changed, his parents, his friends, me—it affected me too. And all because of one split second. I got to realizing how vulnerable everybody was. And how vulnerable I was. I took care of him for a week. They finally shipped him to Japan, and I never heard from him again. I don't know if he's dead or alive. I don't know how his wife or his family are doing. I don't know how he's doing. It seems like every patient on that ward, when they left, took a piece of me with them. They came in, we would treat them for a few hours or a few days, and then we'd send them off and never hear a word. I had this real need to see one GI who'd survived the war after an injury, because I never saw them—never heard from them again. There was one time in Vietnam when I came so close to writing to my mother and asking her to check around and see if she could find one whole eighteen-year-old. I didn't believe we could have any left. After John left I just couldn't handle it any more. We had too many bodies lying in those beds minus arms and legs, genitals, and faces, and things like that can't be put back together again.

I found I'd built up walls real effectively. I was patient and tender with the GIs. I didn't talk to them a lot because I was afraid to—afraid of losing my cool. I was very professional, but I was distant. I worry sometimes about the way I treated those GIs in intensive care (this was an insight I only got a year ago). . . . I was afraid, because I didn't feel I had done my best with them. Because of the walls I'd put up I didn't listen to them, didn't hear what they might be trying to tell me even just in gestures or whatever. I wasn't open to them because I was so closed to myself.

I got out of ICU. I couldn't handle any more. I asked to be transferred to the Vietnamese ward. Everybody had to do that—spend a rotation in the ward. This is where I found out that war doesn't just hit soldiers, that nobody is safe from war. I can still see this little boy—he was about nine months old. He had both of his legs in a cast and one arm in a cast and his entire abdomen bandaged, because he'd gotten in the way. I delivered a baby for a POW, a stillborn baby. It amazed me that life still went on even in a war. Because it seemed like everything should just stop. We had lots of medical problems too when we weren't too busy with war injuries. I had an eight-year-old girl who died of malnutrition. That's something that we only read about in our textbooks. Her mother brought her in, reluctantly, and she said we had twenty-four hours to cure her. She didn't trust us. If we couldn't cure the kid in twenty-four hours, she was taking her away. She did take her away, and the kid died the day after. To come from a background like I did, where everybody has plenty to eat, a lot of security, and to witness what these kids went through. They were older at the age of four than I was at eighteen. And I'll never forget that look on their faces, that old-man look on those young kids' faces, because they'd lived through so much. That still haunts me today.

The POWs. I took a lot of my frustrations out on them—in innocuous ways. I made one POW chew his aspirin when he wanted something for pain because I didn't think he had any right to complain while there were so many GIs injured . . . just on the next ward. One of the POWs attacked me once—tried to choke me—and I hit back at him. But I think before I even made contact with him, the two MPs were all over him. I never saw him again. We had one twelve-year-old NVA who had killed five GIs. Twelve years old! And he would brag about it to me. He would spit at me. I have never seen such hate. To see the loathing that he had in his eyes was frightening. But at almost the same time, we had a kid on the other side of the ward who was about the same age. He was a scout for the GIs, so he was on "our side." And the GIs just babied him. They thought he was the coolest kid, and he was so tough he scared me.

One of my most traumatic and long-lasting experiences happened to me while working the POW ward. An NVA was admitted with gunshot wounds he got during an ambush on a platoon of GIs. This POW was personally responsible for the deaths of six of those GIs. When he was wheeled onto my ward, something snapped. I was overwhelmed with uncontrollable feelings of hate and rage. I couldn't go near this guy because I knew, without any doubt, that if I touched him I would kill him. I was shaking from trying to keep my hands off his neck. This scared me to death, and for twelve years after I was scared of experiencing it again. I discovered I was capable of killing and of violently hating another human being. I had been raised to be a loving and giving person. As a nurse, I had vowed to help *all* who need it. As a human being I should love my brother, whoever he was. I was forced to confront a side of myself I never dreamed existed before.

After four months on the Vietnamese ward, I asked to be transferred again. So I was put on the GI medical ward. That was more depressing than the first two wards I'd been on. Mostly because the people that I had labeled as cop-outs were on that ward. The drug abusers, the alcoholics, the guys in there with malaria—because rather than go out in the field they would not take their malaria pills so they could come down with malaria. I was really very unsympathetic to them. I didn't try to understand them. After so many months of taking care of "legitimate" injuries, I couldn't handle that. I just figured, "Hell, even I can take this.

Why can't you? You're supposed to be braver and stronger than I am, and somehow I'm managing."

We were shelled monthly, at least monthly. The closest call we had was when I was on the medical ward. I remember mortars were falling all around us. I had just gotten my sixty patients under their mattresses, and I dove under a bed myself, finally, and then this GI next to me says, "Hey, you forgot . . ." whatever his name was, and sure enough—he was one of our drug ODs—he was lying on top of his bed singing. I had to get out, crawl over to him, pull him out of bed, and put the mattress over him. I remember screaming at him. I was so mad at him for making me take any more chances. This happened the same day that my sister got married. In fact it was almost the same hour, and I thought, "My God, they're partying, and here I am." We had a sapper attack too when I was on that ward. That's when somebody infiltrates our perimeter. There's a certain siren that goes off. At the time, my corpsman on the ward was a conscientious objector, so he wouldn't handle any firearms. I remember I had to grab the M-16 and stand guard after I had locked the doors. I didn't even know how to fire the damn thing! I finally had to haul one of my patients—he was a lieutenant, I remember—out of bed and had him stand with me in case the gun needed to be fired. Once again, I had the preconception that women were supposed to be taken care of, and it seemed like I was doing all the taking care of.

A lot more happened; I just don't like pulling it out. . . . It's behind me now, and I think what became of me is more important anyway.

I remember on the plane home I held my breath until we were probably a thousand miles from Vietnam, because I was so afraid that something would happen and we'd have to go back. We landed at Sea-Tac. I remember getting a hotel room and calling my parents, because they wanted to come out from Michigan to meet me. I ended up going back to the airport to meet them on *my* way home from Vietnam. They wanted to stay for two days in Seattle and sightsee. I can vividly see me sitting in this tour bus, looking out the window at nothing. Feeling up in the air, lost, disoriented. I was still back there. I didn't smile much. They thought I was angry. Well, they didn't know. They were trying to act like things were just the same as always—that a year hadn't gone by and that I hadn't gone anywhere. They were doing that to relax me. . . . I'm sure they were hurting too. I jumped at any noise. I looked at people walking the streets, and there wasn't even fear in their eyes. All I could think was, "If you only knew . . . you wouldn't be so damned complacent." I didn't even feel like going home. I wish I could have gone somewhere for a while—just to be by myself. I was pushed right back into everyday living, when I was still so far away from it and so disjointed that I couldn't possibly fit in. Everybody tried to ignore where I'd been. I guess some people did ask me about Vietnam, and I would say things like "It was okay." Or "Actually it was the pits." That's all I said for ten years.

I got married about six months after I got home. Rick and I had met in Japan. It was my second R&R, and I remember it was a month before I was DEROSing. All I was going to do was have a good time. I felt like I hadn't laughed in months. And I remember getting to the hotel in Osaka and people could just say "Good morning" and I'd start giggling. Everything was funny. I just laughed because I was releasing tension, I know that. But at the time I just couldn't stop laughing. I had no thoughts of commitments. And I met Rick. It was a good thing he was persistent. He's the best thing that's ever happened to me.

After we got married, we lived in Utah for four years. I put him through college. I worked in the local hospital there. I started out working newborn nursery simply because I wanted a happy job. So I worked for six months in the nursery and found I was bored. I was promoted to nursing supervisor after that, which worked out well, because I was in charge of the emergency room. I was coordinating emergency surgeries, assisting with deliveries, running the pharmacy. It was a nice challenge. But still, nobody knew I was a veteran. I had a desire to meet another veteran, but I wasn't broadcasting. I was having periods of real depression at the time—very happily married, a good job, wonderful husband, a beautiful baby—and I would consider suicide. I didn't understand why I was so depressed. I had nightmares, but I didn't attribute them to the war. It took me many, many years to even interpret those nightmares. All of a sudden one day I realized that a lot of them were centered around gooks; I couldn't see a slant-eye without getting upset. And a lot of it was centered on being misinterpreted, being misunderstood, but I didn't realize it at the time. As soon as I woke up, I tried real hard to forget them.

I've pretty much grown out of nursing. My last nursing job was at an ER in a run-down section of Richmond, California. Something happened there that was literally the straw that broke my back. It was six years after Vietnam, and one evening this fifteen-year-old black boy comes in to our ER with a two-inch laceration above his right eye from a street fight. It needed stitching, and soon. At first, he had refused to even come to ER, and after an hour of pleading, his mother finally got him in. But he absolutely, flat out didn't trust any white person touching him. I begged, pleaded, reasoned, and even threatened him, but he wouldn't let me touch him. He ended up walking out with his eye swollen shut, a gaping wound, and full of mistrust and hostility—and he was only fifteen! He took me back to Vietnam. To the hostility I felt from the POWs. To the mistrust I felt for any slant-eye—we could never be sure *who* the enemy was. I saw those young kids again, with their so-old faces. And I couldn't handle it. I had one of my worst episodes of depression—it lasted for days. I still can't go back to nursing because I'm afraid of this happening again.

About nine years after I got out of Vietnam, I read an article in the paper about this guy in Oregon who'd gone berserk and shot somebody. At his trial they named his condition delayed stress syndrome. I had never heard of it before. But the article described some of the symptoms. And I kept saying, "That's me, that's me! This is exactly it. I can't believe this!" So that evening I brought the article to Rick and said, "Don't laugh, but . . ." Rick and I are very open about everything, talk about absolutely everything, but I never talked to him about my nightmares or my depressions. I didn't want to burden him, I guess, or I didn't want to talk about it. I'm not sure which. I asked, "Did you ever notice things like that about me and just not say anything?" And he said, "Yeah, exactly. I figured when you were ready to talk about it, you'd talk." He was in Vietnam too, of course, but where he was at was relatively quiet, and he never saw combat. So anyway, I spent six months reading up on delayed stress. And it was a relief just to find out what it was that was making me do this stuff. But I still had the nightmares; I still had the depression. I'd go through periods of relative calm and serenity, and then I'd turn around and start screaming at the kids, or at Rick, or the dog. I'd ventilate that way for a while, and then we'd go back to serenity again.

I was reading the Sunday paper, and by God there was this article on women Vietnam veterans in it. First one I'd ever seen. I read that article like it was saving my life. It mentioned Lynda Van Devanter and some of the things she'd gone through. It mentioned several psychologists who were interviewed, and they talked about delayed stress in women veterans. It was like a lifeline. I thought, "I've got to talk to Lynda." So I called our local VA. They'd never heard of her, and they'd never heard of women's Vietnam veteran groups. They gave me another number to call—and I got a runaround for three or four different phone calls. So I read the article again. When I read it I knew I wanted help and that something had to be done, but God, I was scared to reach out. But I did it. I made a long-distance call to the vet center in Los Angeles somewhere, asked for the psychologist that was mentioned in the article. I told her I was trying to get ahold of someone I could talk to who was a veteran. And I made it very clear that I wanted to talk to another woman veteran. She didn't know how to help me. She said the only thing she could figure out was that I should call Vietnam Veterans of America in Washington, D.C., and see if they could locate Lynda Van Devanter. I remember sitting down before I lost all my nerve and writing a seven- or eight-page letter. I wrote down all those things that I'd been bottling up and wanting to talk about and not being able to. I didn't have to preface anything with explanations or details or justifications. I just wrote it down straight from my heart. She wrote me a real nice, supportive letter back. She sent me a whole bunch of material on other women veterans who had been interviewed, and I remember pouring over those and underlining everything that I could identify closely with. I felt literally like she was the lifeline, that I had been sinking in a sea unable to swim and she was holding the rope.

A few months later a friend of mine in Anchorage, Alaska, whose daughter was also a friend of mine down here, had read an article where Jan Ott from the Seattle vet center was interviewed. She cut it out and sent it to my friend to give to me because she thought I'd be interested. And it mentioned that there was a support group being formed. I thought, "There's nothing wrong with me. I'm functioning fine." I called Jan anyway to say I thought what she was doing was a good job. She convinced me that it was just a talk group, there was no therapy, nothing else, it didn't mean there was anything wrong with us. So I said, "Yeah, okay." I figured they needed numbers to make the group go. I sat there with my legs crossed and my arms folded, and I wasn't going to talk; I was going to listen. But they were saying the same things I was thinking. It was hard to sit there because in my head I was going, "Oh yeah. Oh yeah!" And it started coming out. It took me a long time. Some of the ladies there—maybe they'd had more practice, I don't know; maybe they're more open with themselves—but they shared really well. I would share but more superficially. Not because I didn't want to share deeper. I don't think I could have at that time. It was a slow evolving through about twelve weeks of the group. I had something more to think about every week. They'd brought out new things that I hadn't ever thought about before.

I think the turning point in the group came when I watched a certain movie on TV. *Friendly Fire*. I remember being just overwhelmed because the guy who played the part of the GI in that film looked exactly like the guy in my nightmares. He was blond; he was young; he was so innocent and so naive. He went over to Vietnam just like most of us did, thinking he was doing what he should be doing . . . and you could just see him evolve. He went from being naive and innocent through being scared and confused into being hard-nosed and cynical. Exactly the way I had gone through it. The movie was done with such perception; they really had a handle on it. I remember sitting down with my notebook and writing as I was going through this movie—thank God for commercials. I had started out describing him as I just did, and how I could relate so well to that. And then something snapped. At the end of the movie, when he was killed and brought home, another useless death, I didn't even realize what I was doing. My letters were all of a sudden three times as large. I was tearing the paper with my pen! I was writing about how angry and bitter I was. It was because those people, whoever they were, who sent us over there made us do all these terrible things, wasted so many lives, so much time and money, and so many resources, are not accountable and will never be really accountable. They've hidden behind so many other people that they will never be brought to justice. I felt really frustrated and impotent knowing that they would not be reckoned with. And I remember saying that I hope that their day of reckoning would come.

I got through the movie, and it just opened up so many things that I hadn't thought about. I realized finally where my anger and my hostility were directed. I realized how sad I was and that it would never go away. For twelve years I've wanted it to go away, to get on with life, and not have that thing hanging around my neck. I realized how badly I felt about the way I saw myself treat some of those GI patients in intensive care. How I wasn't perfect with them like I probably should have been, and how much that affected me. I realized how much each of those GIs had taken of me with them. And how much I wanted it back. Everything came all at once. I had written all this down, and I was going to share it with the group.

I remember reading what I had written because I don't think I could have said it straight out. My one hand bled from my nails biting into my palm because I was still so angry. I think that's where most of the tension and frustration and stress went that evening. I really got it out. Then, a week or two later, we had the male GIs come to our group. That was very powerful. It was really great for me to see the whole GIs. But even more important I remember Dan, this great big hunk of a guy. He was big but he was gentle, kind, caring. He started talking about how he tried to injure himself in Vietnam so he wouldn't have to go out on another firefight. And my first reaction was to tense up and say, "Oh, Goddamn you! You had to be one of those, didn't you." But Dan sat there and went through the buildup to how it got so bad he would get almost physically sick at thinking of having to go out there. To wonder where the next shot was coming from, if it was coming for him, was he going to live or die, was he going to have to kill somebody. He said he got to the point where he just couldn't take it anymore. He honestly thought that he may even have gone a little crazy for a while. He had a friend of his take the butt of his rifle and try to break his collar bone so he couldn't carry a gun. His friend did it as hard as he could, and he ended up just bruising Dan. And he said, "That guy probably saved my life, because I don't think I could have lived with myself if it had worked. I still humped and it hurt with every step, but it was almost like it was my punishment." And this big, gentle man is sitting there crying, talking about how traumatic that experience was for him. It gave me such an insight into what I had labeled as a cop-out. I saw that we all had our own ways of coping. Where I built my walls and hid behind them, that was my form of copping out. I could not judge anybody else for whatever form they took.

Since that time, when I really got everything together and spit it out to the group, things have really been okay. The nightmares are absolutely gone. The depressions are just about gone. But Lynda Van Devanter said it better than I could ever say it again: "The war does not control me anymore. I control it." I know the depressions will still come, but I can handle them because I know why they're there and that they'll go away. I know that I can't forget those experiences, but I understand why I have them and that they're a part of my life. I also know that I'm a better person, actually, for having lived them.

Probably my two biggest goals now are, I'll do my damnedest to keep something like that from ever happening again, and if I can help even one other woman veteran to work it through as I have, then it's all worth it. I'm not normally an outgoing person, but I'll spill everything if I have to, if that will help just one other person. Because nobody needs to live through this. . . .

Questions

1. Why does Auger end up feeling the army couldn't have done any better at preparing her for Vietnam, after she "hated them for years for not training me better"? (333)

2. What does Auger mean when she says she was distant from the GIs she treated "because I was so closed to myself"? (336) Why isn't she able to realize this at the time, but only years later?

3. During her time in Vietnam, why does Auger consider soldiers who abused drugs or alcohol "cop-outs"? (337) Why does Auger revise her ideas about copping out after confronting her own coping mechanisms?

4. When she returns to the United States, why can't Auger talk about her experiences with family or friends? Why does it take her almost ten years to do so?

5. Do you agree with Auger that it is impossible to be fully prepared for combat?

6. What are some ways to respond to someone who is silent about his or her combat experiences?

Myrna E. Bein

For every serviceman or servicewoman killed in Iraq, it is estimated that seven times as many were wounded. Many of these troops returned home paralyzed or with missing limbs, terrible burns, major head trauma, loss of vision, or other catastrophic injuries, facing enormous physical and psychological hardships. They rely heavily on their families to help with their rehabilitation and the process can be excruciating for their loved ones as well.

At about 7:00 a.m. on the morning of May 2, 2004, Myrna E. Bein (1950–) learned that her twenty-six-year-old son, Charles, a U.S. Army infantryman, had barely survived an ambush in Iraq a few hours earlier. Charles had been riding in a five-truck convoy in Kirkuk when insurgents detonated a roadside bomb and unleashed a barrage of gunfire on the American soldiers scrambling out of their crippled, flaming vehicles. One soldier was shot in the head and ten others were injured. Metal fragments from the initial blast shredded the lower half of Charles's right leg and he was ultimately flown to Walter Reed Army Medical Center for long-term care. Charles's mother and his stepfather, Tom, visited him regularly in the hospital. The first time that Bein saw Charles was Sunday, May 9, 2004—Mother's Day. From the morning she heard the news about her son, Bein began e-mailing friends and family with updates on Charles's progress as well as her own state of mind. The following selection consists of some of Bein's e-mails.

In January 2005, a review board of army physicians recommended that Charles be medically discharged because of his disability. Charles successfully appealed the decision, receiving a waiver so that he could stay in the army. He remained in the army for almost four years after being wounded but following complications with his recovery, he was medically discharged in 2008 with the rank of sergeant.

A JOURNEY TAKEN WITH MY SON

May 10

Yesterday afternoon I was finally able to see, touch, hug, kiss, and comfort my precious son. He arrived at Walter Reed Army Medical Center in Washington, D.C., on Saturday evening, May 8, at around 11 p.m. I got a call from the Red Cross informing me he was there within thirty minutes of his arrival. Charles called me around 6 a.m. on Sunday, May 9, to tell me he was scheduled for yet another surgical procedure that day and for Tom and I to delay our initial visit until afternoon. . . .

When I first saw my son, I did not recognize him. His face was very thin and drawn and he had about a week's growth of beard. There was a lot of pain in his eyes. He grabbed my hand and would not let it go. . . . I'm a registered nurse and I've seen a lot of people with amputations, so I know what to expect. But seeing my son's less than half a leg for the first time, wrapped up in that big, bulky, surgical bandage, was an experience of indescribable grief. Seeing him maneuver so awkwardly in bed, and seeing the pain that he was experiencing, just to do the simplest activity, was something I had tried to prepare myself for, but now I don't think I could have ever been prepared.

Once he was settled and medicated with morphine again, the pain began to ease to what he described as a constant 4 out of 10. He never really complained about anything. He just gritted his teeth and did what he had to do. "Mom, don't try to help me unless I ask you," he said, "I need to learn to manage everything for myself." His left leg is also very painful as he has numerous smaller shrapnel wounds, which are sutured and the leg bandaged from toes to hip. Charles said he's had many larger shrapnel pieces removed, but some of the smaller pieces will just be left.

Charles held my hand and talked extensively to Tom and me. Much of what he said, including thoughts and impressions, he did not want repeated to anyone. He has begun to express that he would like to stay in the army, if possible, after he is fitted with his prosthesis and finishes his rehabilitation. According to Charles, his orthopedic surgeons have told him they believe he could do that, with a different MOS other than infantry.

After several hours Charles asked to be taken to the Medical Intensive Care Unit to try to see Spc. J. H. We called to the MICU and got permission to bring Charles down. It took Charles approximately thirty minutes of pain and maneuvering to get himself dressed in shorts and a T-shirt, put a sock and shoe on his left foot, and manage his transfer from his bed to his wheelchair. His determination and courage astound me. After another dose of morphine, Charles held onto his IV pole and pump in front of him, while Tom and I got his wheelchair down the hall, into the elevator, and down another set of hallways to the MICU.

I tried to prepare Charles, and myself, for what we could expect to find with Spc. J. H. Again, I've spent a lot of hours in ICUs in my time and seen a lot of heartbreaking situations, but nothing can compare to what I experienced yesterday. Spc. J. H. remains very ill and highly sedated. Charles asked me to get him as close to Spc. J. H.'s bed as possible where he was able to touch his hands, arms, and face. He talked to him for about thirty minutes. Charles was deeply affected by Spc. J. H.'s condition. Spc. J. H. and Charles were side by side when the IED exploded under their HMMWV. Listening to Charles speaking to Spc. J. H., I know that if he survives this, there will be a bond between Charles and him that will never be broken.

May 15

I thought I'd take the time to send another missive regarding Charles's condition. Unfortunately, he has had some very rough days since Friday. He went to surgery that day for what he thought would be his last procedure on his right leg, to create the best stump possible for his prosthesis. However, Charles has had an infection set in, caused by an organism common in soldiers returning with wounds from Iraq. The organism is *Acinetobacter baumannii*. It's a very nasty creature and resistant to almost all antibiotic therapy. The orthopedic surgery team working with Charles was only able to do part of the procedure they had planned, since the infection in the wound has caused too much inflammation in the soft tissues to proceed further at this point. The infection, coupled with the trauma of all the surgeries, is also causing Charles to feel very sick and to have very severe, unrelenting pain. . . .

I know Charles is having moments of despair and I can now, two weeks after the event, see the inevitable depression creeping in around his edges. The Walter Reed staff tell me that they've now seen enough amputees come through there from Afghanistan and Iraq to know that the depression, and its resolution, will generally follow a pattern. Apparently, Charles is on schedule. All of the wounded are followed by psychiatry and receive appropriate medication and counseling throughout the course of their care to deal with this life-changing event and the fear, anxiety, and grief that inevitably follow this type of injury. Thank God for that. I know the army has learned a lot about taking care of the whole soldier since the days of Vietnam. Charles told me tonight, "I know this will get better." Tom and I are trying our best to support him through this horrible ordeal. Most of the time we feel pretty helpless, but we do what we can both in prayer and in practical matters to assist him where he needs it.

In spite of what I can see he's going through, I've never once heard Charles whine or complain. When the nurses and physicians ask, he rates the pain on a scale of 0-10, but he basically just grits his teeth and waits for it to eventually subside. He doses himself with morphine from his patient-controlled IV pump and gets in his wheelchair and goes down to check on Spc. J. H. every day, because he's his buddy and they are in this together. He's pushing himself in physical therapy to do as much as he can, as soon as he can. My admiration for his courage and determination is so profound. . . .

There's great news about Spc. J. H. My husband, Tom, and I saw him on May 15, along with Charles. We rolled Charles and all his associated intravenous pumps and tubes downstairs to visit Spc. J. H. and his family. Spc. J. H.'s mother and brother were both with him. He had been transferred to an intermediate care unit, from the Medical Intensive Care Unit, and was being prepared for further transfer to a regular care unit as we were there. He was awake and for the first time he absolutely recognized Charles. As Charles rolled through the door of his room, you should have seen the look on Spc. J. H.'s face! He lit up like a Christmas tree. He was able to motion for Charles to come in. Spc. J. H. still cannot speak, but I believe that will come in a bit more time. The nurse in charge of the unit, a major, said he was extremely encouraged by the progress Spc. J. H. had made over the past 48 hours. Spc. J. H. nodded his head in response to questions, gave a thumbs-up sign, grasped Charles's hand very strongly and wouldn't let go, and made excellent eye contact. He was sitting up in a chair. He still has one nasogastric tube in place and many tubes for intravenous fluids, but when I touched him he did not feel as if he had a fever. He still has the evidence of many abrasions, etc., from the blast on his face and upper body. He was moving about in the chair to make himself more comfortable.

At times he would get a sort of panicked look in his eyes, which his brother attributed to "flashbacks." When that would happen, his brother and mother would speak very soothingly to him and he would return to normal. His brother said that Spc. J. H. has only just begun to realize that he is back in the U.S. and in a hospital. Charles emphasized to Spc. J. H. that they are both out of Iraq and "we made it." Charles updated Spc. J. H. on Spc. J. S. and Pfc. C. F. Charles also told Spc. J. H. that he had lived for a short time in Washington, D.C., and, "I know this town, man." I think that means he knows where the "chicks" are, but some things a mother is probably better off not inquiring about in too much detail ☺.

Last night, Charles wanted to try to go outside into the fresh air, so Tom and I got permission from his nurse to take him out onto the hospital grounds in his wheelchair. It was the first time since the incident that he's been outside of buildings, aircrafts, or vehicles. I thought it was very telling that Charles said that it felt "totally weird" to be outside without a weapon in his hand. He said he would have to get used to not feeling as if he had to be constantly alert to watching his back and the backs of others around him. He said he, too, is having flashbacks and that noises similar to the sound of the explosion are very upsetting. He knows all of this is a normal progression of his recovery from this event and injury. I think that talking about it is probably the best thing for him.

[To First Sergeant R. J., in Kirkuk, Iraq]   *May 25*

The expected depression and anxiety have now very obviously kicked in with Charles. His whole world has been totally turned inside out and he's having a lot of uncertainty about what he's going to be able to do in the army, or out of the army if he has to take a medical discharge. He fears that he is not far enough advanced in rank and that the army doesn't have "enough invested in me yet" to really want to keep him. Charles has never been one to gravitate toward jobs that don't have a certain amount of adrenaline rush, so he fears the loss of his leg will very much limit him in doing what he would like to do in the army. I've tried to remind him that he is an exceptionally intelligent young man and the army must value that. I don't know if you may have any eventual influence over what happens with Charles's army career, but if so, he could certainly use all the help he can get. I hope that once Charles actually gets up on a prosthesis and is walking again, he will have a brighter outlook. I also know that his depression is normal and a part of the process he has to work through to deal with this loss of his leg and change in his body image and lifestyle.

Donald Rumsfeld visited Charles a few days ago when he came to Walter Reed. Usually Charles opts out of the visits by the football players, congressmen and congresswomen, and others who pay frequent visits to Walter Reed. He has had limited energy and also has said he really doesn't care to be part of their "photo ops." However, he said that Rumsfeld came without press, just with his security personnel, and he did see him. He said his impression was that Rumsfeld was much older and smaller in physical stature than he had expected. He said that the visit to the injured troops at Walter Reed seemed to be a sort of "decompression" for Rumsfeld; a time without reporters, photographers, and probing, hostile questioning. It encourages me that Rumsfeld was taking the time to go and see for himself the ravages of this war. I know he must lose sleep at night over the cost of it. I hope he does anyway.

[To First Sergeant R. J., in Kirkuk, Iraq]   *May 27*

Dear First Sgt. J., I have wonderful news regarding Spc. J. H. I saw him last night, along with his mother and brother, when James and I visited Charles at Walter Reed. Spc. J. H. looked fabulous! He is talking up a storm now and appears totally normal, neurologically. Just before we saw Spc. J. H., the psychiatrist who's following both Charles and Spc. J. H. stopped by Charles's room to tell him that Spc. J. H. had begun speaking again that day. He thanked Charles for his support, regular visits, and continued communications with Spc. J. H. while he was so critically ill and coming out of his mental fog after the incident. . . .

Spc. J. H. continued to have a lot of questions and conversation with Charles regarding the specifics of the May 2 incident. Basically, Spc. J. H. remembers nothing except that he heard the explosion of the IED, and then found himself lying on top of Charles feeling pain in his abdominal area. Then he said he looked at his abdomen and saw "my guts hanging out." He could remember that he began firing his weapon. He has no memory of anything after that until he woke up at Walter Reed. He said he did realize that it was Charles coming to see him in the intensive care unit, even though he seemed only semi-responsive. . . . As far as I'm concerned, a true miracle has occurred with Spc. J. H. There have certainly been many, many people all over the world praying for his recovery. When I first saw him in the intensive care unit at Walter Reed, I had real doubt that he would survive; or, if he did survive, that he would ever be able to live a normal life. After seeing him last night, I now believe he will make a full recovery.

June 1

It's strange and ironic how my perceptions of what is "good" have changed since May 2. I don't have the awful feeling of personal dread watching the news on television or reading the newspaper now, because my son is not over there anymore in that hell hole. He's no longer trying to survive the politics or the fanaticism or the insanity that is Iraq and Afghanistan. Now, when I go to Walter Reed, I think how fortunate he is to have "only" lost his leg. As I've gone to visit him at Walter Reed, I've walked many times by the neurotrauma unit and said a prayer of thanks that he's not in there with a brain or spinal cord injury. Over the past three weeks on the orthopedic surgery ward, I've seen so many beautiful young men with such horribly mutilating injuries from this war: the Marine across the hall, with both arms gone up to his elbows plus a leg gone below the knee from a rocket-propelled grenade; the young man in the patient computer room, typing out his e-mail with the one hand he has left. The almost ghostly apparition of a twenty-something soldier I met on the sidewalk in front of the hospital one dusky evening, with a prosthesis on his left arm almost up to his shoulder, and his other arm absent at the same level, so affected me I had to stop and compose myself before I went in to Charles.

I'm not a sage, or a politician, or anyone with answers to all the hard questions. I'm just a mother. I know what I'm feeling down in my soul is what countless other mothers have felt over the centuries. I know the mothers in Iraq and Afghanistan feel the same thing. It's a timeless and universal grief. I see it in the eyes of the other women I meet at Walter Reed; that semi-shocked, "I'm trying to be brave and hold it all together" look. We recognize each other.

I know I'm going through a "normal" emotional process, but it feels pretty awful at times. It's not always like this; I know I'm tired and I had a bad night. I do feel God's love all around me, even in the midst of the suffering. I know that things will get better and that there will be blessings that spring from this experience for Charles, for me, and for others. There are already blessings and I am so thankful for each and every one of them. Most of all, I'm thankful to still have my son.

June 10

A sock did me in a few nights ago, a plain white sock. I'm doing so much better with the grief, but sometimes I just get blindsided again in a totally unexpected way. Some memory or sharp realization will prick at the places healing in my heart, and I feel the grief wash over me in a massive wave. Sometimes I almost feel I could double over with the pain of it. That's what happened with the sock.

I had brought Charles's soiled clothes home from Walter Reed to wash. Everything had gone through the wash and dry cycles and I had dumped the freshly laundered clothes onto the bed to fold them. It was late and I was quite weary, so I wanted to finish and get to bed to try for a better night's sleep than I've been having lately. I found one sock . . . just one. I folded all the rest of the clothes and still, just one sock. Without even thinking, I walked back to the laundry room and searched the dryer for the mate. Nothing was there. I looked between the washer and dryer and all around the floor, in case I'd dropped the other sock somewhere during the loading and unloading processes. Still, my tired and preoccupied brain didn't get it. As I walked back to the bedroom with the one sock in hand, it hit me like a punch to the gut. There was no other sock. There was also no other foot, or lower leg, or knee. I stood there in my bedroom and clutched that one clean sock to my breast and an involuntary moan came from my throat; but it originated in my heart.

I guess, as a nurse, I know too much. I know all the details of the physical difficulties and long-term complications of life for an amputee that most others have no reason to comprehend. I know about the everyday activities of daily living that the rest of us take for granted, and for which we never give a moment's consideration, that Charles will now always have to struggle to accomplish. I do know he will eventually win the struggle; he is made of very strong stuff. I'm in awe and so proud of his strength and determination. But my "mother's heart" still feels very tender and sore. The wounds there are fresh and bleed easily when disturbed. God's peace to you all. Myrna.

August 20

It's now been sixteen weeks since Charles was wounded in Iraq. Life goes on and things settle down. Charles is very stable physically now. His right leg is totally healed and the stump continues to atrophy and decrease in size. The scars on both of his legs from the surgeries and the shrapnel remain red and very noticeable, but are beginning to fade a bit. He has put on a bit more weight and looks much healthier. Now he's in the midst of the long hard slog of learning to live with the chronic remaining pain, adapting to a prosthetic leg, and learning to achieve an active life again. On August 1, he was in New York City with about twenty other soldiers from Walter Reed who were invited there by the Achilles Track Club to participate in a 5K race. Charles participated in the race on a hand cycle, as he's not yet able to attempt running. He finished the course and enjoyed the trip very much.

Charles's attitude remains generally very positive and he considers himself to be one of the "lucky ones." I know that's true as I travel back and forth to Walter Reed and see more and more wounded there. There are so many of them with terrible burns, often multiple amputations, deep and ragged scars, and mutilations. I still find myself especially shocked when I see the young female soldiers who are so severely wounded. This war has no front line and everywhere is a combat zone. There is no "safer place."

As more and more wounded come into Walter Reed, especially with so many traumatic amputations from improvised explosive devices and rocket-propelled grenades, the prosthetics department is fairly over-whelmed. The sheer number of amputees from all the explosive injuries, all needing artificial limbs made and adjusted frequently, means that there are long waits of days to weeks for Charles, back on his crutches and in his wheelchair when his "leg is in the shop." When this happens, his rehabilitation progress more or less comes to a standstill until his prosthesis is ready again and returned to him. I see his spirits sag when he is forced back into this mode and is unable to continue moving for-ward toward his goals.

At times I have to stop and compose myself before I go into Mologne House to meet Charles. Last week I had one of those times when I met a young father out with his two little sons. He had all of a leg missing and was pushing himself along in a wheelchair. His younger son, about three, was sitting on the young father's lap, while his brother, about five, skipped along beside the moving wheelchair. There are many other heart-rending sights and many shocking mutilations, but I will spare you the details. It's a humbling experience to move about the Walter Reed complex. The gritty determination of these wounded and the support they offer to each other puts a lot of the other details of daily life in clearer perspective. Regardless of your politics or how you may feel about this war, these wounded, and the dead, are an inescapable reality. I pray to God that we as a nation don't forget the sacrifices that are being made on our behalf. From now on, Veteran's Day will be a great deal more meaningful to me than just a day to take off from work and to fly the flag, if I remember.

I keep thinking a time will come when it doesn't hurt so much to watch Charles struggling to recover. Watching what is left of his right leg withering up and growing ever smaller is something I know is normal, but in my dreams at night I see him at about seventeen, running so smoothly and beautifully, and when I awake to reality I know how cruel this new "normal" is. Sometimes, still, when I see him I find my heart clutching and I have to take a deep breath and swallow hard to keep the tears at bay. My tears won't help him; hopefully my support and encouragement will.

God's peace to you all,
Myrna

Questions

1. In what way are Bein's experiences with her wounded son a "journey"? Where does this journey take them?

2. Why is visiting Spc. J. H. so important to Charles? Why do they continue to have conversations about the attack in which they were wounded?

3. In caring for the wounded, what does it mean to take care of the "whole soldier"? (349)

4. Compared to the changes in Bein's perceptions of what is "good," how has the war altered your perceptions of what is "good"? (352)

5. In speaking of the wounded servicemen and servicewomen in the hospital, what does Bein mean when she says, "This war has no front line and everywhere is a combat zone. There is no 'safer place'"? (355)

6. Why does Bein call the new normal "cruel"? Is adapting to the "new normal" a helpful goal in the recovery of the severely wounded? (356)

John Berens

A veteran of the 1991 Gulf War, Lieutenant Colonel John Berens (1955–) was called out of the U.S. Marine Reserve in January 2003 to serve in Iraq with Task Force Tarawa, Second Marine Expeditionary Force. Growing up, Berens had never aspired to join the military; he wanted to be a chef. But in November 1979, when he was twenty-four years old and studying at the Culinary Institute of America, Berens heard that Americans had been taken hostage in Iran. He immediately enlisted in the Marine Corps to, in his words, "make a difference in the world." In late April 2003, as he and his fellow Marines—along with a contingent of British and other coalition troops—worked to secure Iraq in the early days of the war, Berens assumed that he would be employing his more than twenty years of infantry skills to assist with combat operations. Instead, he was assigned a task in the town of Al Kut that initially seemed to be of little value to the overall mission. Berens wrote the following narrative about the assignment shortly before his unit left Iraq in June 2003.

After leaving Iraq, Berens completed his military career by deploying twice to Africa for training missions, including riverine operations training for the one-boat Gambian Navy. He retired in 2006 and settled in South Carolina where he spends his time writing, woodworking, tending his three dogs, and working part-time at a local store.

RECLAMATION

Brigadier General F. A. Houghton, in the gloom of his dirty tent, sat down to eat. It was early April and the temperatures often surpassed one hundred degrees. Heat, disease, starvation, and enemy assaults were devastating his men, and Houghton was trying his best to present a brave demeanor. He had witnessed men die following his orders, and it was weighing heavily on him. Food was also running dangerously low and today another rider had been forced to sacrifice his horse to provide as many men as possible a small taste of meat.

The siege of Al Kut had gone on much longer than he had expected, but Houghton was still hopeful that reinforcements would come north from Basrah and get his brigade out of this horrific stalemate. The general ate a bite of *saq*, called "spinach" by the troops, but it tasted particularly bitter. He asked one of the men who had prepared the meal if he was certain that he had picked *saq* and not the poisonous look-alike. The soldier assured him that the correct weed had been picked. Houghton slowly finished eating.

The soldier was wrong, and within a few hours the general was dead from accidental poisoning.

Eighty-eight years later in the one-hundred-degree heat of April 2003, Brigadier General Rich Natonski, the brigade commander for the U.S. Marines Task Force Tarawa, stood looking at General Houghton's gravestone in the ruins of a World War I British cemetery in Al Kut. General Natonski had just led his brigade through combat at An Nasiriyah, where, against fierce resistance, the task force had seized and held two vital bridges. It was the most brutal combat Marines had seen since Vietnam, and it cost the lives of nineteen of his men. The deaths of those nineteen Marines would remain with General Natonski for the rest of his life—a commander's burden shared with General Charles Townshend,

359

who, almost ninety years ago in Al Kut, led the men of his British Sixth Indian Division against the Turks. Townshend lost men in the thousands, including one of his brigade commanders, General Houghton.

General Natonski turned to me and asked, "I wonder how this general died?" He stood there and studied the grave of a fellow brigade commander and officer like himself, who had died doing his duty at this very place.

All who have ever gone to war carry with them the same burdens, regardless of when or where they have served. So when Task Force Tarawa fought on the same ground, under the same harsh conditions, with the same timeless burdens as British soldiers of World War I, the connection to those long-dead soldiers was close and visceral.

General Natonski assigned me to clean this cemetery, which was little more than a sunken acre of rotting garbage and donkey carcasses hidden under twelve-foot reed grass and dead, skeletal trees. Below the surface lay the remains of four hundred and twenty men.

On the face of it, the job was a nasty task that seemed to have no direct benefit to the Iraqi people. My personal misgivings, that we could be addressing more urgent needs, were irrelevant. My duty was to execute the mission I was given.

Al Kut is an ancient, crumbling place that would have died long ago, except that it sits on the banks of the Tigris River. Commerce still flows the eighty miles downriver from Baghdad. The site has made Al Kut a critical stopping point not only for supplies of grain and salt, but also for military units seeking a staging ground close to Baghdad. In 2003, Task Force Tarawa stopped its northern push at an abandoned Iraqi airfield just south of Al Kut. In 1915, the British Sixth Indian Division stopped here as well and became trapped by Turkish forces. That siege resulted in thousands of deaths, including the bodies hidden here beneath garbage and grass.

"It is no problem for you to put up a cross here. We respect all religions." I turned to face a dark-skinned Iraqi, probably early thirties, very thin and smiling. He introduced himself as Hussein Zamboor, and he spoke with a clear British accent. "There are Christians who live in this neighborhood, and the only reason the cross was taken in the first place was so the metal could be used as reinforcement in cement—because of sanctions." We were looking at a truncated cement obelisk that was the base of a missing cross in the center of the devastated cemetery.

His English was very good. When I complimented him, there was something poignant about the way he looked down modestly and said, "Thank you." Hussein had learned his English by listening to the BBC. He became my translator but refused to be paid, saying that he wanted only to learn to speak better English.

Hussein and I were not alone in the cemetery. When we first arrived, there was a great buzz of excitement and barefoot children came from everywhere. Men moved about in large groups, some wearing traditional gowns, called *jellabas*, though most were in Western trousers and polyester shirts with colorful geometric designs. They were talking excitedly, with a fierce energy. They began to walk slowly around the site as if they too were evaluating the sanity of cleaning up this place.

After inspecting the cemetery, I was reeling from the magnitude of the project. I was about to return to the airfield to figure out a plan, when a large group of men pulled Hussein aside. With animated gestures they all seemed to be talking at once. Hussein then turned to me. When he spoke, all the men became quiet. "They want to know what you are going to do about the protestors," he said.

Driving through the town to the cemetery that morning, I had encountered about a hundred men in front of the town hall holding black banners and chanting over loudspeakers, "NO CHALABI! NO CHALABI!" They were protesting the possible insertion by the United States of Ahmed Chalabi, an Iraqi expatriate with a suspicious background, into power in Baghdad. There was no violence, but the chant was clearly directed toward us.

In Iraq, men guard their words like gems that might be stolen. They whisper their true thoughts only to those whom they know they can trust. The old regime had killed men for merely uttering words against it. Political protest had been a crime just weeks before. I answered that we would do nothing about the protest. "Those men are being peaceful. They're doing nothing wrong."

They asked: "Will anyone stop them?"

I said no. "Saddam is gone, and you are free to say anything you want to say. You can speak freely without fear."

The animated chattering stopped, and the faces of the men immediately changed. They looked hopeful, like a code they had been trying to decipher was beginning to make sense. These modest, hardworking men looked at me in wonder. They shook my hand, smiled big, mostly toothless, head-shaking grins.

The next day, we rolled in with every type of heavy equipment imaginable. Marine combat engineers and Seabees went to work with backhoes, bulldozers, and an assortment of smoke-belching, earth-moving machinery. We never made it past the front gate; the equipment sank in the soft soil, and the rest of the day was spent recovering the useless machines.

At the same time, the Seabees began to measure the obelisk so a new cross could be constructed. Another crew of Marines struggled to excavate an ornate gate, which was buried, half open, in a mound of dirt and garbage at the front of the cemetery.

Hussein came up and asked me, again with a group of men crowded around him, "Why are you doing this cleaning? Our most dire need is electricity. What are you doing for that problem? We do not understand why so much work is going on here when we cannot use the lights in our houses." Electricity had been off for many months.

"It is our biggest effort right now," I tried to console them. "We have helicopters flying from Al Kut to An Nasiriyah and to Baghdad to assess how many poles and electrical lines are down and to document any other problems."

They told me how Saddam used to punish the town by shutting off the electricity. Each day I kept hoping I would see lights come on in the houses. Still I offered no explanation as to why we were doing the cleanup.

General Natonski confided to me that he, too, was taking flak for spending the man-hours and resources for the reclamation, and he had thought hard about the justifications for the task. A student of history, a man of deep moral convictions, and a warrior-philosopher, he decided simply, "It's the right thing to do."

I inspected the grounds of the cemetery once again. Trash was everywhere, piled up against the perimeter wall, between the headstones, even stuck in the branches of the dead trees. I found a torn-out bit of notebook paper with an Iraqi child's English homework on it that, in shaky block letters, said, WHERE ARE YOU FROM?

This filth had been building up since 1991, when Saddam, angered by the Brits after the first Gulf War, ordered this place destroyed. Instead, the villagers just dumped their garbage here. When I poked around the putrid mounds of refuse, I realized that I would not be able to accomplish this mission without enlisting the help of the residents of Al Kut. That night I sought—and was given permission to hire—local Iraqis to help us with the garbage.

The next day Hussein introduced me to Methag Jabar Abdulla, a quiet, well-groomed man who owned a glass installation shop across the street from the cemetery. Methag said he could get the men to remove all the garbage. We needed to discuss terms of a contract, so he gestured to his shop and soon we were sitting in the damp coolness of the cement building. Methag drew water from a plastic cooler and offered the tin cup to me. Ignoring the sanitation risk, I drank the water, savoring my first cold drink in three months. The negotiations could now begin. I wrote on a piece of notebook paper exactly what needed to be done: In six days, remove all the garbage down to ground level and haul it away. Hussein wrote the words in Arabic under my writing.

Methag consulted his brother and the other men in the room. He insisted that he must hire five trucks and at least fifty men. I said that this would be fine and asked him how much he expected to be paid. He said, "As you wish." It surprised me. As I wish . . . I wished I could pay him more, I wished I could bring in dentists, doctors, electricity . . . I wished this dignified man were not having to bargain to clean up garbage. We settled on $1,700, and he agreed to start the following day.

When I arrived in the morning, the Iraqis were already working. I was in awe of the simplicity of their approach. I counted only two tools. There was an old man standing on the highest pile of garbage with a shovel, the blade of which was broken in half along its length. Beside him was a younger man with a pickax that had a shaved tree branch for a handle. The younger man would plunge the pickax into the pile and loosen a small amount of the garbage that the older man could shovel. The rest of the crew carried sturdy vinyl bags as they climbed the mound and then leaned down to receive one shovelful of filth. One sack, one man, one shovelful, one trip to the sidewalk and back, over and over.

They began work at seven in the morning. In the course of the day, the heat rose to over one hundred degrees, but work never stopped. By seven that night, one small bagful at a time, the biggest garbage pile in the cemetery had been displaced to the sidewalk. In the process, the Iraqis uncovered four headstones.

As work progressed, we learned more about the soldiers buried under our feet. The British had dug in with only two months' worth of food, and the Turks kept British reinforcements from breaching the siege. Hanny Tahir, a fifty-year-old general contractor who had come by seeking work, said that his grandfather once told him that many of the people of Al Kut had died along with the British. In fact, the reason the Brits' food did not last was that they fed the six thousand people of Al Kut during the fighting. He cursed the Turks.

The British soldiers were no longer anonymous. As their names and their struggles were slowly revealed, our work became more personal. The dates on the headstones related individual stories: Private J. H. Mitchell, of the First Battalion Durham Light Infantry, died along with fourteen other men buried here on December 10, the day the Turks launched multiple attacks on the Sixth Division's first trench line. Two hundred and two men died that day.

The Iraqis continued their methodical work. One day I pulled aside a boy of about twelve who was carrying his sack to the sidewalk and, through Hussein, I asked him if he had yet been paid. He grinned widely and showed me a handful of dinars from all his work. I asked him how much he was being paid, and he said an amount that was equal to two dollars a day, twice the going rate. When I asked him what he was going to do with the money, he became serious.

"I will buy food for my family," he responded.

I asked him how many were in his family.

"My mother and my two sisters and me. I am the only man and I must work to feed them." He appeared to me then not like a boy, but like a very young man, full of decency and purpose. I asked Hussein what had happened to the boy's father, and he told me that Saddam's men had carried him away in 1998 and he had never been seen again.

The next day Methag shook my hand in the warm Arab greeting (clasp hands, then place your hand to your heart) and thanked me for asking the boy whether he had been paid. I told him he need not thank me, as I was just making sure that the contract was being adhered to. In fact, I was checking up on him. But for Methag, it was a new experience to have the people in charge give a damn about where the money was going. Under the last regime, no one cared where it went so long as certain officials got their share of it.

Most of the men hauling the garbage showed up each morning wearing the same shirts they had worn the day before. We did, too. But the striking difference was that while their clothes were always immaculate, ours were not. No matter how hard they worked and how dirty their clothes became, they washed them each night because they wanted to appear neat and clean the next day.

I looked at the men toting the sacks. There was a dignity about them, an innate bearing of nobility that, at least for today, they could hold their heads up because they were working. This was the first work they had been offered in nearly a year, and they were eager to earn the money. But it was more than money itself they were looking for; it was a sense of worth. Cleaning this cemetery was beginning to affect me. Amid a war, it was bolstering my faith in mankind.

Hussein and I were sitting in the shade one day when he felt comfortable enough to ask me about my family. Just a wife, I said, and I showed him her picture. He lowered his head and with a shy, charming grin said, "She is very beautiful."

I thanked him and asked him if he were married.

He said, wistfully, "No . . . no . . . I am not married. I am not wealthy enough to be married."

I asked him if there was a woman he liked.

He brightened. "Oh yes." He told me her name, and I asked, "Does she know you like her?"

"Oh, no. I think she does not."

Then I asked him why. He looked at me directly and said, "I am a professor of mathematics. I make a small salary. In our culture I must have enough money so that I can take care of the woman I love. She does not know because I cannot tell her now."

Here was a noble man, an honest man with a tenderness and depth of spirit rarely encountered. He had been caught in the grinding poverty brought on by a mindless regime and the punishing effects of sanctions. It was not just love unrequited; it was human ambition beaten to the ground and dreams extinguished. In conversation with one of the other translators, I learned that Hussein made only enough money each week to buy one carton of eggs.

Hussein introduced me to a man who looked to be about forty and was very handsome, but his hands were malformed. He explained, using Hussein to translate, that two years ago he had been taken from his home and tortured. The men responsible wanted him to incriminate his friends even though they had done nothing wrong. This man needed to tell his story, and he wanted an American to hear it. To torture him, the man continued, they tied him from a rafter by his thumbs and shocked him with electrical wires all over his body. He said he withstood their punishment, and when they finally believed he had no useful information, they released him by swinging a machete right through his thumbs, leaving them dangling in the air above his head.

The closer one comes to death, the more urgent it becomes to live genuinely. Military men know this simple openness. Men at war speak plainly, make peace with their possible fate, and in moments of reflection they tell one another what to do with their belongings if they die. There is no individual more honest than one who sees clearly the end of his life. The people of Iraq have lived close to the edge of death since Saddam came to power, and it has endowed most of them with an open, raw authenticity that strikes me as honest and admirable.

Six days passed and, as promised, the garbage was removed. Methag said that he was prepared for me to evaluate the quality of his work. I walked slowly over each area where the piles of garbage had been, and the grounds were spotless. A small group of Iraqis quietly followed as I made my inspection.

I told them the work was excellent.

Methag asked me when he would get paid, and I told him, "Now."

He was in shock. He seemed to be expecting some unforeseen complication, some official reason why he could not be paid. I had already gone to the disburser and withdrawn the money we had agreed on, and, with Hussein helping me count, I placed the money in Methag's hand. His grin and barely suppressed laugh told me that he was surprised to find it so easy and honest. I was proud to be the one giving the cash, knowing that this man would make sure it helped his community. I also believed, in the deepest recesses of my heart, that we had made a difference here. Despite my skepticism, the best thing we brought with our big machines, our loud talk, and our American money . . . was hope. I think now they believed we were truly here to help, and they were then free to hope for better lives for themselves.

While the work on the grounds was ongoing and the stones were being reset, the restoration work on the cross in the center of the cemetery began. Ali Jabar Abdulla, Methag's brother, had a 1982 picture of the cemetery in pristine condition. It clearly shows the cross. The intent was to make one that resembled, as closely as possible, the original. The Seabees constructed a three-hundred-pound cement cross and a flat, black metal cross that would be affixed to it, but offset by a couple of inches to create a shadow effect. It was creative metalwork on an industrial scale.

While I was busy supervising the reclamation, Brigadier General Natonski asked me to coordinate a ceremony to honor the British dead in Iraq, past and present. At this point in Operation Iraqi Freedom, British casualties almost equaled our own. Our goal was to hand off the cemetery in whatever improved condition we could achieve by May 8, 2003, with the hope that the British would undertake its continued improvement.

The Seabees were busy installing the cross on May 7. It was a beautifully rendered bit of ironwork, and I was admiring it when Hussein came to my side. We greeted each other as friends, "*As Salaam alaikum*," "*Alaikum salaam.*" We shook hands and then put our hands to our hearts. We had been friends for only three weeks, but under such pressurized circumstances the bond seemed unusually strong. We had spoken honestly about our lives. We trusted and respected each other, and when I told him that day I would be leaving after the ceremony, I saw sadness in his eyes. I too felt acute sorrow because I loved this uncomplicated man, and I felt as if I were abandoning him.

When I got back to the airfield that night, I filled a small gift box with things I thought Hussein could use, along with one hundred dollars of my own money and a heartfelt note. I gave him the box after the ceremony but never got to see him open it.

His gift to me was a poem that I treasure:

> *You are a good human.*
> *USA have honor that you belong to.*
> *Your faithful face will not be forgotten.*
> *Everything will pass away, gold, kingdoms,*
> *But goodness will stay alive, engraved in hearts.*
> *Here you are in front of a member of Saddam's victims,*
> *An easy example for his misery,*
> *But the perfume of freedom has opened silently the doors.*
> *You and I were looking for life among the tombs.*

The cemetery was as improved as we could make it. The reed grass was gone, the dead trees were removed, and the garbage had been hauled away. It certainly smelled better, and you could see every gravestone although some were still leaning and cracked.

The ceremony was meant to tie the past with the present, the dead to the living, Iraq to Britain, and to America. But it became a reflection on loss, a somber moment to honor both the men who had died recently and those who were buried in the cemetery. And, by extension, it became a gentle, dignified way of reflecting on the war, our grief, and the cost of this grim profession. It was the funeral we never got to attend for our nineteen Task Force Tarawa Marines. It provided a quiet moment to help the generals make peace with the fact that those deaths would be a part of them for the rest of their lives. I can only imagine the guilt, uncertainty, regret, and sorrow that plague the mind of someone whose decisions have cost the lives of his men, and this ceremony was a salve for those deeply personal wounds. It also tied our American grief at losing our young men to the honor paid to the British for their losses. Major General Brims, the commanding general of the First UK Armored Division, had lost thirty men. He was our guest of honor.

When the ceremony got under way, I staked out a little privacy for myself and stood alone behind the chairs. My mission was almost complete, and this was the first time I could begin to relax. Behind me stood most of the men of the neighborhood. Hussein, in a very subdued voice, translated throughout the ceremony for his countrymen.

At 3:00 p.m. Iraq time on May 8, the dignitaries arrived. Two bag-pipes played "Amazing Grace" as everyone took their seats. General Natonski said this:

> As the fighting men of Task Force Tarawa labored in the sun
> to clear the cemetery, to help restore its dignity and solemnity,
> they did it as brothers to those who lie herein. Just to the right
> of where I am standing, Private J. J. Jennings's headstone reads,
> "Second Queens Own, Royal West Kent Regiment, Died March
> 22 1916. Age 21."
>
> To the young Marine who sweated and strained to clear the
> site around his grave, Private Jennings is not a lost member of
> another generation, not just a soldier from the ranks of our clos-
> est ally, he is another twenty-one-year-old fighting man, a peer;
> his death is linked to the lives of those we lost. We mourn the
> passing of our young men with timeless, universal grief. Our
> bond to Private Jennings and to all the soldiers buried here is
> deep and spiritual. It transcends nationality and is rooted in
> the understanding that when we as soldiers and Marines go to
> foreign shores, our deepest hope is to see our homes and loved
> ones again.

As I thought about the work, the words, the men we had lost, and the men I had befriended, I was surprised by the deep emotion that sur-faced. My biggest contribution to the war was, in the end, healing, not killing. But now I had to leave. I had been allowed to see into the lives of everyday Iraqis, and I knew there was so much more to be done. I would not be here to see the men make plans to marry, have children, regain their lives, or simply be able to flip on a light switch. I had, in three weeks, become close to these men. They, not the cemetery, had become my mission.

As General Natonski came to the heart of his speech, his voice fal-tered—and I began to cry. I just stood there and let my tears fall without moving and without shame. But I was not the only old warrior who had put his head down and let the wave of sorrow and relief wash over him.

Questions

1. Why does Berens title his narrative "Reclamation"?

2. Do you agree with General Natonski that cleaning up the cemetery is "the right thing to do"? (362)

3. Why is Berens so surprised that the Iraqi villagers always make sure their clothing is immaculate at the start of each workday?

4. When Hussein writes the poem to Berens, do you think that Hussein still questions the value of cleaning up the cemetery? Why does he write, "You and I were looking for life among the tombs"? (368)

5. Why does Berens feel both "sorrow and relief" as he cries during General Natonki's speech? (369)

6. How does knowing the history of the place where you are fighting affect your feelings about serving there?

David Finkel

David Finkel (1955–) is a Pulitzer Prize–winning reporter and editor for the *Washington Post*. In 2007 Finkel spent eight months in Iraq embedded with the 2-16 army unit (Second Battalion, Sixteenth Infantry Regiment of the Fourth Infantry Brigade Combat Team, First Infantry Division). The unit was sent to Rustamiyah in Baghdad as part of "the surge"—a fifteen-month, 21,000-troop push to quell insurgent violence across the country. *The Good Soldiers* (2009), from which the following excerpt is taken, is Finkel's award-winning chronicle of his experiences alongside the men of 2-16.

Daily life for the soldiers, their families, and the Iraqis working on base becomes increasingly fragmented and distant from loved ones. During deployments, but also during return trips home, rifts develop between husbands and wives, parents and children. The two distinct worlds seem incompatible and the relatively swift movement between the two is unsettling and alienating.

This selection details many of the journeys made by soldiers between combat and home and back again. Every arrival and every departure carries practical and emotional risks, with often surprising consequences. Through small moments in daily life, Finkel presents a portrait of damaged lives as compelling as any battlefield account. For the soldiers he shadowed, the damage continues long after the front line. Finkel also asks us to consider how well equipped the families of these men are to deal with the physical and mental changes resulting from their loved ones' combat experience.

THE GOOD SOLDIERS

(selection)

Home: it was less a place than an act of imagination now, a realm fundamentally disconnected from what life had become. The time difference was part of it—dawn in America was dusk in Iraq— but after nine months it was more than that. Soldiers had a hard time explaining Iraq to one another; how could they explain it to someone whose life had nothing to do with the pucker factor of climbing yet again into a Humvee? Or being caught in a flimsy-walled shitter during a rocket attack? Or busting into a building at 3:00 a.m. and finding a little torture room with blood-spattered walls and a bloodstained mattress and a rubber hose and scratchings on a wall of a crazed face and a partly eaten piece of bread? Or touching the bread with a boot and realizing with additional horror that it was still fresh? Or developing the absolute need, as Brent Cummings had developed, of never, never, *ever* standing in his room with half of his foot on the floor and half of it on the cheap rug he'd bought to make his room feel homier, because the one time he stood that way was the day of a KIA?

If Cummings told his wife that, was there any way she would understand?

If he told a soldier that, was there any way he wouldn't?

Nine months along, where *was* home now? Was it back there, where Kauzlarich's wife, Stephanie, recorded a video for him of their three children on his birthday, or was it here, where he interrupted the rhythms of a day in order to watch it?

"Happy birthday, cha-cha-cha," they sang.

"My little buddies," he said. He played it again. And again, amazed at how much taller they had become.

Was home the place where children grew so steadily it was invisible, or here, where their father noticed it in increments, like a distant relative?

Jumpy videos, slapdash e-mails, occasional phone calls, Internet messaging—these were the tether lines from here to there, and there to here, that were becoming ever more frayed by distance and time.

"The weather this weekend has been glorious!" Kauzlarich's mother wrote in October. "The leaves are all turning color, no wind, and temperatures in the upper 60s, low 70s! Are there any other signs of fall in Iraq except the more reasonable temperatures? Your lovin' Mom and Dad."

"Dear Mom and Dad," Kauzlarich wrote back. "It's still 100 degrees here. The leaves are not turning color. Love, Ralph."

"Hi Love! I Love you! Well, today I've spent in vacation research craziness . . ." Stephanie began an e-mail in early December, and she went on from there to describe different scenarios for Kauzlarich's upcoming leave and their plans to go to Florida. She had found flights, ticket packages, hotels, and resorts, and she laid out the prices of each. Would he prefer this hotel or that hotel? Standard room or suite? A hotel or a condo? With meals or without meals? Disney or Universal? And what about Sea World? "SOOOO THOUGHTS???????"

"Stephanie Corie," he wrote back. "As long as I get to spend all the time with you and the kids we can do it in a bungalow upside down for all I care. Money ain't an issue. Do need a heated pool. Your choice on all . . . Hugs, Ralph Lester."

"OK!!" she wrote back, and before he could fully absorb that she hadn't started with the word "love," he was reading: "I stayed up 2 extra hours last night to get all the details straight for you so that you could be a part of making the decision on our trip. I know you're making lots of decisions over there & I shouldn't bother you with this. I've been making all the decisions here for 10 months by myself . . ."

Meanwhile, Brent Cummings called home and didn't know whether to laugh or cry as his wife, Laura, told him she had just come back from taking their two daughters to the sports bar the family would go to every Friday afternoon when he was there. It was a tradition of theirs, and it moved him that she had done this, but then Laura was saying that their four-year-old daughter, who has Down syndrome, began vomiting all over herself at the table, and their eight-year-old daughter kept saying, "Gross gross gross," and the waitress was horrified, and Laura couldn't find enough napkins, and as the vomit kept coming, people all over the sports bar were averting their eyes and covering their mouths and noses as they realized it wasn't the aroma of french fries drifting their way . . .

Meanwhile, a soldier who was one of the snipers was storming around in a rage because he had telephoned his wife at one o'clock in the morning her time and no one had answered and *where the hell was his wife at one o'clock in the morning?* So he called her again at two o'clock in the morning and she didn't answer *and where the hell was she at two in the morning?*

"For a lot of soldiers, home is a place of disaster right now," a mental health specialist named James Tczap, who worked in Combat Stress and was a captain, said one day. "It's a broken relationship, a fractured relationship, a suspicious relationship. Even the functional relationships are challenged by the disconnect." Worse, even, he said, was the belief soldiers held that when they went home on their mid-deployment leave, everything would be better than it ever was. "There's an anger in guys when they go back. They want to go home and be normal, and they're not quite normal," he said, and added, "Coming back from leave is the worst part of the deployment."

On their leaves, they got eighteen days at home to not wear camouflage, not wear armor, not wear gloves, not wear eye protection, and not drive around wondering what was in that pile of trash they were passing, although most of them did wonder, because eighteen days is not enough time to shake such a thing. It was a point of honor with Kauzlarich that he would be among the last to go, and so he stayed put month after month as his soldiers disappeared on helicopters and returned three weeks later with all manner of stories to tell.

A specialist named Brian Emerson ended up in Las Vegas at the Sweethearts Wedding Chapel with his girlfriend of two years, getting married as her mother listened in on a cell phone. He spent $5,000, he said when he got back, ring not included, much of it at the Bellagio. "The penthouse suite," he said proudly. "It was like five-hundred-and-something dollars a night. We stayed for two." And then it was time to go. "Worse than leaving the first time," he said.

Sergeant Jay Howell ended up in Branson, Missouri, at a place called the Dixie Stampede. "It's like a rodeo while you're eating, but the theme is the Civil War," he said. "You go in, you pick a side, North or South, they do some singing and dancing, then they do some horse races; they got weapons, they have pigs even; then they pull out kids from the audience and the kids chase chickens. The North versus the South. We've been there a few times, and it always ends in a tie. The kids love it." And then it was time to come back.

Sergeant Major Randy Waddell simply went home, and as glad as he was to be there, his heart sank when he saw that his seventeen-year-old son, Joey, was driving around in a truck that had 160,000 miles on it, was leaking oil and transmission fluid, and had a plastic bag taped over a broken-out window.

"So we go looking for a truck," Waddell, back now, told Brent Cummings of what he had done on leave, "and golly, these cars are so expensive." The one they liked the most was at a Toyota place, he said, a used gray Dodge with 25,000 miles on it, but the price was $17,000. *Only $17,000*, the salesman, a little ball of energy, had said, but there was no *only* about it.

Cummings shook his head in sympathy.

"And one night I was sitting out on the porch by myself and I was thinking about it," Waddell continued. "I was thinking, 'You know, Randy, if you don't make it back, for whatever reason, if you don't come back, what will Joey have to drive if you don't get him something before you leave?'" Alone on the porch, he went back and forth, he told Cummings. Fix the old truck? That he could afford. "Or I could go buy him something and be done with it, and at least when I go back to Iraq I'll have a clear conscience that I did the right thing when I was home.

"So I bought him a seventeen-thousand-dollar truck."

"Wow," Cummings said.

"And let me tell how I did this," Waddell said. "This is great. This is how I surprised him. We find this truck and we drive it and then we go away for a couple of days, and I do all the paperwork while he's at school. So the day that we're ready to sign all the paperwork—because I did it over the phone—I said, 'Joey,' I said, 'Let's drive back up to the Toyota place and see if that truck's still there.' He said, 'There ain't no need in going up there, Dad. We can't afford it. We've already talked about it. It costs too much.' I said, 'Well, let's go talk to him. Let's see if we can get him down to fifteen instead of seventeen.' So we pull up there, and the truck's moved, because they're getting it ready for me to pick up. So we walk up to one of the salesmen, and that guy didn't know me. I said, 'So, what's going on with that gray Dodge?' 'Oh, somebody came by this morning and bought it.' Aww, you shoulda *seen* Joey's face. 'I told you, Dad! I told you somebody already bought it! I told you!' I said, 'Well let's go in and talk to the guy and see.' So we go inside, and the little guy comes running up to me, 'Hey, Mr. Waddell, how you doing? Blah blah blah.' And I said, 'So, I hear you sold that truck out there today.' He said, 'Yeah. We did. We sold it to *you*!' And Joey turned around and looked at me, and I said, 'Oh yeah, you own that truck outside.'

"And that's how we got the truck."

"That's awesome!" Cummings said.

"It turned out well," Waddell said.

"I spent seven grand," said Jay March, who was just back from leave and once again beneath the tree from which hung the sack of poison filled with dead flies.

"You're shittin' me," a sergeant he was sitting with said.

"Nope," March said, and then went on to describe what he had done after he turned twenty-one, left James Harrelson's memorial service, and went home to Ohio in search of new slides for the continuing show in his head.

"The first thing I did was take fifteen hundred dollars and take my two brothers to the mall," he began, and then backtracked to say that the very first thing he did was strip off his uniform in the airport parking lot, put on shorts and a T-shirt that his brothers had brought him, and then go to the mall. For three hours, they bought whatever they wanted, sale or no sale, as if they weren't poor, and what he bought were new pants, a new shirt, and new athletic shoes, all in white, pure white, because he wanted to feel clean.

From the mall, he went home to see the rest of his family, where the questions began. "So what do you do?" they asked. "Well, we go out," he said, and unsure of how to describe it, he showed them photographs instead. There was Harrelson's Humvee, on fire. There was Craig's Humvee just after Craig died. There were some kids in Kamaliyah. "And my grandma started crying," March said. "She knew about the deaths, but this was seeing how people lived. The shit trenches and stuff. I showed her a picture of a Humvee stuck in a shit trench, and she asked if that was mud, and I tried to explain it was shit, and that those lakes on the sides were shit and piss, and she didn't want to see anymore. She got up and went in the other room and she got busy ordering me my favorite dinner, which is chicken Parmesan."

And his first day went from there, he said. He ate some marvelous chicken Parmesan, he bought his first legal six-pack of beer, and then he went with his brother and some friends to a place called the Yankee Bar and Grill for the Friday night wet T-shirt contest.

He danced. He drank a beer. He drank tequila. He drank Crown Royal. He drank another beer. He drank a Flaming Dr Pepper. He drank something else: "I don't even know what the fuck it was, but they put something on fire and dropped it in the beer."

He danced with a girl and mentioned he was home from Iraq, and danced with another girl and mentioned it again. He was wearing his new white shirt and white pants and white shoes and was feeling pretty good about things, and yes, he was drunk, totally drunk, but not so drunk that he didn't hear them calling out his name and telling him to come up on the stage.

So he and his brother went up onstage and sat back-to-back in two chairs with a stripper's pole in between, and as six women in T-shirts came onstage and began dancing in a circle around them, he yelled to his brother, "Dude, there's no fucking way." Here came the water hoses now, and soon the women were soaked head to toe and dancing through puddles while pulling off their shirts, and was that the moment he had a new slide for the show inside his head, or was it from what came next? Because now one of the women was stepping onto his new white shoes and leaning toward him and pushing her chest toward his face, and now she was climbing onto his lap and standing on his thighs with her wet dirty feet to get to the stripper's pole, and now she was trying to step onto his shoulders, and now, drunk as he was, all he could think about was:

My new white shoes!
My new white pants!
My new white shirt!
Once again, he was filthy.

"But I remembered it didn't matter," he said. "I had more money. I could buy new clothes tomorrow." So he began laughing, and then cheering as someone yelled into the microphone, "Welcome back from Iraq," and then a woman was saying, "I'll give you a ride home tonight," and then they were in front of his house kissing, and then she was removing her shirt, and then "I passed out on her chest. Drunk. Done. She woke me up. 'Maybe we should do this another night.' 'Yeah.'"

So he went inside, passed out again, and dreamed of an explosion.

"Dude, what's wrong?" his brother said as he sat up wide-eyed.

He passed out again and then the phone began ringing.

"They're trying to call me! They're trying to call me!" he began screaming, and then he had a cigarette, and then he passed out again, and then it was morning and his grandmother was the one leaning toward him, saying, "Here's some orange juice," and he was thinking:

Seventeen days to go.

In the first hours of his leave, Nate Showman walked through the Atlanta airport and couldn't look anyone in the eye. The businessmen on cell phones, the families on vacation—all of it was too strange. The normal abnormal, Cummings called Iraq, but this was exactly the opposite: the abnormal normal. Eyes down so he wouldn't betray any emotion, Showman made his way to a connecting flight home and a girlfriend he wasn't sure he knew how to talk to anymore.

In the final hours of his leave, he ended up getting married, the last thing he had gone home intending to do.

Showman was the twenty-four-year-old lieutenant whose earnestness and optimism about the war had made people think of him as a young version of Kauzlarich. But by the time he headed home, that optimism had been tempered. After being in charge of Kauzlarich's personal security detail for the first few months of the deployment, he was promoted to a platoon leader in Alpha Company, directly responsible for the lives of two dozen men who in horrible June, and horrible July, and horrible August, and horrible September, would roll their eyes at Kauzlarich's "It's all good" pronouncements. Over time, he began to see their point. "I think it's difficult for them, and difficult for me, to hear about these strides we're making, these improvements we're making, when we know—

when *I* know—for a fact, that this place hasn't changed a damn bit since we set foot here in February," he said one day.

Mid-August was the worst of it, when two of his soldiers were severely wounded in an EFP attack. Two days later, the rest of his soldiers decided they'd had enough. They were tired of waiting to be blown up, they were tired of being mortared every day at the COP, they were tired of being told they were winning when they knew they weren't. Among themselves, they decided that the following morning they weren't going to go out of the wire. Maybe they would sabotage their Humvees. Or maybe they would just refuse orders to go, even if it meant charges of insubordination. Either way, when Showman heard whispers of it, he realized he had a potential mutiny on his young hands, and he went to Kauzlarich for advice.

"Fix it," Kauzlarich suggested.

He did in the end, by hatching a plan with two of his platoon sergeants to wake up the soldiers in the middle of the night, when they would be at their groggiest, and get in their faces until they were on their way. It would not go down in military history as the most sophisticated plan of all time, but to Showman's relief, it worked. One sleepy soldier headed toward a Humvee, another followed, then another. Problem solved. But of course it was not.

By the time Showman flew to the United States at the end of September, an effusive young man who would write earnest letters home—"We are holding a snake by the tail here . . . Keep the faith . . . Let us finish the fight"—had become largely silent. He and his girlfriend headed to a cabin deep in the woods, but even there, safe and sealed off, he was reluctant to talk. One day he did, though, and when he found himself unable to stop, as if he had become one more war wound in need of a tourniquet, he came up with another plan, this one more elaborate.

It involved a limousine to a restaurant and a bouquet of roses waiting on a chair. Out came a bottle of wine and two glasses, one etched with the words "Will you marry me?" And the other with "Say yes."

"Yes," she said. "Yes."

"What if we did it now?" he said.

"What if we did it now?" she repeated, and so it was that on day seventeen of his leave, in the backyard of her house, as their families and a few friends watched, Nate Showman's optimism returned.

They spent one night together, and then they were at the airport saying goodbye. It would be six months before he would see her again, and he wanted to find the right words that would last that long, or if it were to come to that, longer.

"My wife," he finally said, saying those words for the first time.

She laughed.

"My husband," she said.

And then he came back.

Adam Schumann was going home, too. But unlike the others, he was not coming back. Five months after carrying Sergeant Emory down the stairs in Kamaliyah, his bad-news vessel, as David Petraeus might describe it, was no longer able to drain.

This was Schumann's third deployment to Iraq. He'd been here thirty-four months by his own count, just over a thousand days, and it didn't matter anymore that he was one of the 2-16's very best soldiers. His war had become unbearable. He was seeing over and over his first kill disappearing into a mud puddle, looking at him as he sank. He was seeing a house that had just been obliterated by gunfire, a gate slowly opening, and a wide-eyed little girl about the age of his daughter peering out. He was seeing another gate, another child, and this time a dead-aim soldier firing. He was seeing another soldier, also firing, who afterward vomited as he described watching head spray after head spray through his magnifying scope. He was seeing himself watching the vomiting soldier while casually eating a chicken-and-salsa MRE.

He was still tasting the MRE.

He was still tasting Sergeant Emory's blood.

He needed to go home. That was what Combat Stress had said after he finally gave in and admitted that his thoughts had turned suicidal. The traveling psychiatrist who spent a few days a week on the FOB diagnosed him as depressed and suffering from posttraumatic stress disorder, a diagnosis that was becoming the most common of the war. There had been internal studies suggesting that 20 percent of soldiers deployed to Iraq were experiencing symptoms of PTSD ranging from nightmares, to insomnia, to rapid breathing, to racing hearts, to depression, to obsessive thoughts about suicide. They also suggested that those symptoms

381

increased significantly with multiple deployments and that the cost of treating the hundreds of thousands of soldiers suffering from them could eventually cost more than the war itself.

Every study that had been done indicated the seriousness of this, and yet in the culture of the army, where mental illness has long been equated with weakness, there remained a lingering suspicion of any diagnosis for which there wasn't visible evidence. A soldier who lost a leg, for instance, was a soldier who lost a leg. Losing a leg couldn't be faked. Same with being shot, or pierced by shrapnel from a lob bomb, or incinerated by an EFP. Those were legitimate injuries. But to lose a mind? Early in the deployment, a soldier had one day climbed onto the roof of an Iraqi police station, stripped off everything he was wearing, then ascended a ladder to the top of a guard tower, and in full view of a busy section of New Baghdad began hollering at the top of his lungs and masturbating. Was it an act of mental instability, as some thought, or was it the calculated act of someone trying to get home, which was Kauzlarich's growing suspicion? Trying to figure it out, Kauzlarich kept returning to the fact that the soldier had paused in the midst of his supposed meltdown to remove sixty pounds of clothing and gear before climbing the ladder, which suggested a deliberateness to his thinking. Perhaps he hadn't been so out of control after all. Perhaps he was just a lousy, disloyal soldier. And so, in the end, he was sent home not with a recommendation for treatment, but for a court martial and incarceration.

Kauzlarich himself was another example of the army's conflicted attitude about all this. On one hand, he endorsed the idea of his soldiers being debriefed by the FOB's Combat Stress team after witnessing something especially traumatic. But when Kauzlarich was the one in need of debriefing after he saw the remains of three of his soldiers scattered along the road on September 4, he made it clear that he needed no help whatsoever. "I don't need that bullshit," he told Cummings, and so Cummings, who knew better, discreetly arranged for a Combat Stress specialist to casually drop by Kauzlarich's office. An hour later, he was still leaning in Kauzlarich's doorway, tossing out questions, and afterward Kauzlarich mentioned to Cummings that he was feeling a lot better. He understood what had just happened and was glad for it, and yet even with that he had no intention of ever being seen walking

into the aid station and disappearing through the doorway marked
COMBAT STRESS. And as reports of soldiers supposedly having problems continued to reach him, he continued to reduce some of those
reports to the infantry's historically preferred diagnosis: "He's just a
pussy."

With Schumann, though, there was no such pronouncement, because
it was obvious to everyone what had happened, that a great soldier had
reached his limit. "He is a true casualty of battle," Ron Brock, the battalion's physician assistant, said one day as Schumann was preparing to
leave Rustamiyah for good. "There's not a physical scar, but look at the
man's heart, and his head, and there are scars galore."

You could see it in his nervous eyes. You could see it in his shaking
hands. You could see it in the three prescription bottles in his room: one
to steady his galloping heart rate, one to reduce his anxiety, one to mini-
mize his nightmares. You could see it in the screensaver on his laptop—a
nuclear fireball and the words FUCK IRAQ—and in the private journal he
had been keeping since he arrived.

His first entry, on February 22:

> Not much going on today. I turned my laundry in, and we're
> getting our TAT boxes. We got mortared last night at 2:30 a.m.,
> none close. We're at FOB Rustamiyah, Iraq. It's pretty nice, got
> a good chow hall and facilities. Still got a bunch of dumb shit to
> do though. Well, that's about it for today.

His last entry, on October 18:

> I've lost all hope. I feel the end is near for me, very, very near.
> Day by day my misery grows like a storm, ready to swal-
> low me whole and take me to the unknown. Yet all I can fear
> is the unknown. Why can't I just let go and let it consume me.
> Why do I fight so hard, just to be punished again and again, for
> things I can't recall? What have I done? I just can't go on any-
> more with this evil game.
> Darkness is all I see anymore.

So he was finished. Down to his final hours, he was packed, weapon-
less, under escort, and waiting for the helicopter that would take him

away to a wife who had just told him on the phone: "I'm scared of what you might do."

"You know I'd never hurt you," he'd said, and he'd hung up, wandered around the FOB, gotten a haircut, and come back to his room, where he now said, "But what if she's right? What if I snap someday?"

It was a thought that made him feel sick. Just as every thought now made him feel sick. "You spend a thousand days, it gets to the point where it's *Groundhog Day*. Every day is over and over. The heat. The smell. The language. There's nothing sweet about it. It's all sour," he said. He remembered the initial invasion, when it wasn't that way. "I mean it was a front seat to the greatest movie I've ever seen in my life." He remembered the firefights of his second deployment. "I loved it. Anytime I get shot at in a firefight, it's the sexiest feeling there is." He remembered how this deployment began to feel bad early on. "I'd get in the Humvee and be driving down the road and I would feel my heart pulsing up in my throat." That was the start of it, he said, and then Emory happened, and then Crow happened, and then he was in a succession of explosions, and then a bullet was skimming across his thighs, and then Doster happened, and then he was waking up thinking, "Holy shit, I'm still here, it's misery, it's hell," which became, "Are they going to kill me today?" which became, "I'll take care of it myself," which became, "Why do that? I'll go out killing as many of them as I can, until they kill me.

"I didn't give a fuck," he said. "I wanted it to happen. Bottom line—I wanted it over as soon as possible, whether they did it or I did it."

The amazing thing was that no one knew. Here was all this stuff going on, pounding heart, panicked breathing, sweating palms, electric eyes, and no one regarded him as anything but the great soldier he'd always been, the one who never complained, who hoisted bleeding soldiers onto his back, who'd suddenly begun insisting on being in the right front seat of the lead Humvee on every mission, not because he wanted to be dead but because that's what selfless leaders would do.

He was the great Sergeant Schumann, who one day walked to the aid station and went through the door marked COMBAT STRESS and asked for help from James Tczap and now was on his way home.

Now he was remembering what Tczap had told him: "With your stature, maybe you've opened the door for a lot of guys to come in."

"That made me feel really good," he said. And yet he had felt so awful the previous day when he told one of his team leaders to round up everyone in his squad.

"What'd we do now?"

"You didn't do anything," he said. "Just get them together."

They came into his room, and he shut the door and told them he was leaving the following day. He said the hard part: that it was a mental health evacuation. He said to them, "I don't even know what I'm going through. I know that I don't feel right."

"Well, how long?" one of his soldiers asked, breaking the silence.

"I don't know," he said. "There's a possibility I won't be coming back."

They had rallied around him then, shaking his hand, grabbing his arm, patting his back, and saying whatever nineteen- and twenty-year-olds could think of to say.

"Take care of yourself," one of them said.

"Drink a beer for me," another said.

He had never felt so guilt-ridden in his life.

Early this morning, they had driven away on a mission, leaving him behind, and after they'd disappeared, he had no idea what to do. He stood there alone for a while. Eventually he walked back to his room. He turned up his air conditioner to high. When he got cold enough to shiver, he put on warmer clothes and stayed under the vents. He started watching *Apocalypse Now* on his computer and paused when Martin Sheen said, "When I was here, I wanted to be there; when I was there, all I could think of was getting back into the jungle." He backed it up and played it again. He packed his medication. He stacked some packages of beef jerky and mac-n-cheese and smoked oysters, which he wouldn't be able to take with him, for the soldiers he was leaving behind and wrote a note that said, "Enjoy."

Finally it was time to go to the helicopter, and he began walking down the hall. Word had spread through the entire company by now, and when one of the soldiers saw him, he came over. "Well, I'll walk you as far as the shitters, because I have to go to the bathroom," the soldier said, and as last words, those would have to do, because those were the last words he heard from any of the soldiers of the 2-16 as his deployment came to an end.

His stomach hurt as he made his way across the FOB. He felt himself becoming nauseated. At the landing area, other soldiers from other battalions were lined up, and when the helicopter landed, everyone was allowed to board except him. He didn't understand.

"Next one's yours," he was told, and when it came in a few minutes later, he realized why he'd had to wait. It had a big red cross on the side. It was the helicopter for the injured and the dead.

That was him, Adam Schumann.

He was injured. He was dead. He was done.

"You okay?"

Laura Cummings asked this.

"Yeah. Just watching the storm," Cummings said. He was home, too, now, sitting on his front porch since waking up in the dark to the sound of explosions. Just thunder, he'd realized, so he'd gone outside to see his first rainstorm in months. He'd watched the lightning flashes come closer. He'd felt the air turn moist. The rain, when it came down on the roof, and fell through the downspouts, and washed across his lawn, and flowed along his street, sounded musical to him, and he listened to it, wondering what time it was in Iraq. Was it two in the afternoon? Three in the afternoon? Had anything happened? Unlikely. Anything bad? Anything good?

"We're going to have to get the umbrellas out for the girls," Laura said now, and he wondered whether the umbrellas were still kept in the same place as when he had left.

At Radina's, the coffee shop he liked to go to, one of the regulars clapped him on the back and motioned to a friend. "Come on over and meet Brent Cummings," he said. "He's just back from Iraq. He's a hero."

Before the Kansas State University football game, as he stood in the stadium parking lot, dressed in school colors, just like always, and wondering if he would ever again think of a football game as life and death, people had questions.

"How are things in Iraq?"

"It's been difficult—but we're doing good," he said.

"Is the war worth it?"

"Yeah, I think it's worth it," he said.

"You can ask him," he overheard a man saying to a woman, who then asked, "Is Bush a good man?"

Sometimes he would look at his daughters and think about the day that a little Iraqi girl waved at him and a man standing next to the girl saw this and slapped her hard across the face, and he grabbed the man and called him a coward and said if he ever did that again he would be arrested or killed. "It felt good to say it," he had said that day, right afterward. "It felt good to snatch him off the street in front of people. It felt good to see the fear in his eyes. That felt good."

He would sit on the porch and listen to the automatic lawn sprinklers that Laura had mentioned in an e-mail that she was having installed.

He would sit in the living room and listen to his daughters play the piano that Laura had mentioned she was thinking of buying.

Back at Radina's, someone said, "We saw a few soldiers in the paper," and he knew what they meant and wished they would talk about something else. And soon they did. The conversations were once again about football or vacations or the weather or, for the thousandth time, how good the coffee was, and he was grateful.

One day he said to Laura, "How much do you want to know?"

They were in the bedroom, just back from a memorial service at the Fort Riley chapel, where he had delivered a eulogy for Doster, who had died a few hours after Cummings had flown out of Rustamiyah to begin his leave. "Whatever you do, when you get up to speak, don't look at the family," the chaplain had said beforehand, advising Cummings on how not to lose his composure, and he hadn't looked, but he had heard them, as had everyone in the chapel, including a few of the 2-16 soldiers who had been injured and sent back to Kansas. The soldier who had been shot in the chest at the gas station and dragged to safety by Rachel the interpreter was there. A soldier who had been shot in the throat and appeared to Cummings as if he were in the midst of a perpetual flashback was there. A soldier who had been in Cajimat's Humvee way back when and now spent his days watching one of his arms wither away was there. There were five in all, and Cummings had made plans after the service to see them again, maybe for lunch, and then he and Laura had gone home to the one place in the world where he didn't worry about whether his foot was halfway on the carpet and halfway on the floor. "How'd I sound?" he'd asked as he hung up his uniform. "You were good," Laura had answered, sitting on the edge of the bed, looking at him, and suddenly he was crying and saying, "It's so stupid, Laura, it's so stupid, it's so stupid," and feeling as if the rainstorm he had watched the first night was now moving through him.

He felt better after that. He went for bike rides. He got his daughters ready for school. He drank the best beer he had ever tasted. He went to the gym with Laura. He sat on his porch with his dogs. He went to Radina's and saw the man with the big beard who always sat in the corner reading a novel, there as ever, as if there weren't a concern in the world.

"Oh man, it was so good, just to be home," he said, back in Baghdad now, about to take an Ambien, hoping he would be able to sleep. "It was the best time of my life."

He had not seen the injured soldiers again, even though he'd intended to.

He'd also intended to go to the Fort Riley cemetery and visit the grave of the lone 2-16 soldier who had been buried there. Back in the war again, he wondered why he hadn't.

But he hadn't.

The grave was that of Joel Murray, one of the three soldiers who died on September 4 and whose home now was an old cemetery filled to its edges with dead soldiers from half a dozen wars. On December 11, his grave and that cemetery were covered in ice from a massive storm that was blowing through Kansas on its way from the Great Plains into the Midwest. Seventeen people so far were dead. Hundreds of thousands were without electricity. Trees were crashing down everywhere. Down came a huge limb in the cemetery, collapsing onto a line of headstones and just missing Murray's. Down came more limbs all over Fort Riley, including in the front yard of a house near the cemetery, where a sign out front read, LT COL KAUZLARICH and where the morning newspaper with a story about the two most recent battle deaths in Iraq was buried under a layer of ice.

Stephanie Kauzlarich would get to the paper eventually, but at the moment she had too much to do.

"Next time I'll buy the Jungle Pancakes," she was saying to Allie, who was eight years old now and bored with her Eggos.

"You want more syrup?" she was saying to Jacob, who was six now.

"You gonna eat breakfast?" she was saying to Garrett, who was four now and racing around the house in a T-shirt and underpants while screaming, *I can't stop running!*

Last night's pizza slices were still in the sink. Flash cards were on the counter. Lego pieces were everywhere. Stephanie opened the refrigerator and the orange juice came tumbling out, which somehow caused the Eggos to fall out of their box and go skidding across the floor. "It's snowing waffles!" Jacob hollered as Stephanie, who had turned forty since the deployment began, ran after them.

Here was home in its truest form, when the soldier who lived there was not on the front porch watching the thunderstorm, or proposing, or passing out on the couch, or buying a truck, but was still in Iraq. It was what home was like not on the eighteen days that Kauzlarich would be there, but on the four hundred days he would not.

It was boxes of Christmas decorations that Stephanie had hauled down from the attic and needed to put up. It was thickening ice on the sidewalk and steps, and where in the world was the big bag of ice melter they bought last year? It was the lights flickering in the storm, and where were the AA batteries for the flashlight, in case the electricity went out? Here were the C batteries. Here were the AAAs. But where were the AAs? The framed photograph of Ralph on top of the refrigerator also needed batteries to power the motion sensor that triggered the memory chip on which he had recorded a message so the kids wouldn't forget his voice. "Hey. Whatcha doin' over there? I seeeee you," he had recorded, trying to be funny, after Stephanie had said that his original message, about how much he missed them, might be too sad. And it worked. He got on a plane to go to Iraq, and the kids came home and walked into the kitchen and heard him saying, "I seeeee you." They went out and came back in. "I seeeee you." They woke up the next morning and came into the kitchen for breakfast. "I seeeee you." Every morning, there he was, even before Stephanie had coffee. "I seeeee you." She went upstairs to get dressed and came back. "I seeeee you." She went to get the mail and came back. "I seeeee you." She began ducking when she came into the kitchen. "I seeeee you." What could she do, though? She couldn't turn the photo upside down. She couldn't take the batteries out, or cover the sensor, or do anything that would seem disrespectful of the circumstances that had led to the buying of the frame and the recording of the message. "I seeeee you." "I seeeee you." "I seeeee you." "I seeeee you." And then, one day, the batteries ran out, and she meant to replace them, but now it was months later, and anyway they were probably AAs, and if she could find any AAs she'd better put them in the flashlight, because the storm was getting worse. Down came a branch. "I wonder if I should move the car," she said. But it was miserable out there. Down came more branches. "I should move the car," she said.

His war, her war. They were vastly different and largely unshared with each other.

In April, when he wrote to tell her that Jay Cajimat died, he didn't go into detail about what an EFP could do, and when she wrote back she didn't go into detail about painting Easter eggs with the kids.

In July, when the 2-16 was being attacked several times a day, she didn't dwell on her own drama: that she and the kids were driving home from out of state, and the car died and had to be jump-started, and they went to a Wendy's, and the kids had to go to the bathroom, and she couldn't turn off the car because she was afraid it would die again, and she couldn't let them go in by themselves . . .

In September, she didn't tell him much about the colonel's wife who'd approached her and asked, "How are you doing?" "I'm doing okay." "Are you sure?" "Yes." "Are you *sure*?" "Yes, I'm doing okay." "No, you're *not*. You're *not* doing okay." It would have been an uncomfortable conversation anytime, but making it worse was the setting: the memorial service for the three dead soldiers. "And what am I supposed to say?" she said now, sitting in her kitchen. "I'm sick of being a single parent? I'm sick of not having sex? Is that what I say? That life sucks?"

Instead, she kept anything like that to herself. She wasn't going to tell a colonel's wife that, and she wasn't going to tell Ralph, who she was sure needed her to be nothing other than upbeat.

"Happy birthday, cha-cha-cha," the kids sang, and there was no way she was going to tell him how much work those videos were: that the boys preferred to be watching TV or playing with friends, that no one would say anything and she'd have to prompt them with whispered commands.

"Hi Love! Well, guess who loves you! Me & A, J, & G!!!!! I hope that you enjoyed the pictures I sent earlier . . . quite a remarkable storm!" was how she began her e-mail to him the night of the storm, after getting the kids into bed.

She didn't tell him about the branch that just missed the car, or the way she attacked the ice on the sidewalk, with a hammer and knife, because she couldn't find the melter, or that when she sent the pictures, she was sure he would notice that she hadn't brought in the garden hose for the winter.

She didn't tell him that before she could find a moment to write to him, the night had been a parade of footsteps and flushing toilets and coughs and a tired mother trying to soothe some anxious little boys by saying, "Good night, my handsome men."

She came back downstairs. She looked at the silent photograph on top of the refrigerator. He was in a white shirt. They had all worn white shirts that day and gone to Sears to be photographed. It was right before he left. Almost eleven months later, of course she missed him, but it was more than that. "I think it's hurt. Deep down personal hurt. Resentment. That it's fifteen months. That I'm parenting alone. That I'm just doing life alone," she said.

"I hate the war and what it has done to my life."

She didn't tell him that, either. Instead, giving no indication of her exhaustion, except for the time stamp on the e-mail that said it was sent at 12:44 a.m., she wrote, "Schools are closed again tomorrow. Some more precipitation fell, and well I think that perhaps we may be able to hit the slopes and go for some ice sledding. WOW! That would be fast & fun. Yes a perfect way to introduce the kids to Extreme Sports!!! I've been waiting for this opportunity to live on the edge!! ha-ha! Yea I know without you it won't be quite as fun, but about living on the edge—I bet we can accommodate that feat in January!!!"

January was when he would be home. He was due to leave Baghdad in sixteen days.

"I'm worried about January," she said. "Who will he be?"

"I'm proud of you!" she wrote to him. "Your wife, Stephanie."

Questions

1. Why does Cummings not "know whether to laugh or cry" when his wife tells him about taking their daughters to the sports bar? (374)

2. Why does James Tczap say, "Coming back from leave is the worst part of the deployment"? (375)

3. During his leave, why doesn't Cummings get together with the injured soldiers he saw at the memorial service, even though he had intended to do so?

4. Why doesn't Stephanie Kauzlarich tell her husband about "her war" at home without him? (390)

5. Why are soldiers suffering acutely from combat stress often unwilling to admit they need help?

6. Is it possible for those who remain at home to understand what a warrior in combat has experienced?

Abraham Rodriguez Jr.

Abraham Rodriguez Jr. (1961–) was born in New York and grew up in the South Bronx. He began writing at age ten but later dropped out of high school at sixteen. After earning his high school equivalency, Rodriguez attended the City College of New York for four years. Rodriguez published *The Boy Without a Flag: Tales of the South Bronx* in 1992, and the *New York Times* named it a Notable Book in 1993. Since then, Rodriguez has become well-known as a talented chronicler of the Nuyorican experience—that of Puerto Ricans living in New York.

In "The Boy Without a Flag," the precocious young narrator tries to reconcile his own developing worldview with those of his teachers and his father in the context of the political and social unrest of the 1960s and 1970s. Throughout the story, the characters define themselves in relation to controversial historic events: the long imprisonment of Puerto Rican nationalist Pedro Albizu Campos in the 1930s; the U.S.-backed neutralization of Juan Bosch, elected president of the Dominican Republic in the 1960s; the 1970 Kent State University killing of four student war protesters by national guardsmen; and the 1973 death of Chilean President Salvador Allende during a coup led by U.S.-backed dictator Augusto Pinochet.

In Rodriguez's story, the young narrator and the adults around him grapple with questions of identity, belonging, and nationhood. Both the American and Puerto Rican flags become dense symbols, and the various, changing attitudes toward each flag help define each character's search for identity. Questions of patriotism, respect, and loyalty circle throughout the story as each character attempts to define his own feelings towards the nation and its flag.

THE BOY WITHOUT A FLAG

To Ms. Linda Falcón, wherever she is

Swirls of dust danced in the beams of sunlight that came through the tall windows, the buzz of voices resounding in the stuffy auditorium. Mr. Rios stood by our Miss Colon, hovering as if waiting to catch her if she fell. His pale mouse features looked solemnly dutiful. He was a versatile man, doubling as English teacher and gym coach. He was only there because of Miss Colon's legs. She was wearing her neon pink nylons. Our favorite.

We tossed suspicious looks at the two of them. Miss Colon would smirk at Edwin and me, saying, "Hey, face front," but Mr. Rios would glare. I think he knew that we knew what he was after. We knew, because on Fridays, during our free period when we'd get to play records and eat stale pretzel sticks, we would see her way in the back by the tall windows, sitting up on a radiator like a schoolgirl. There would be a strange pinkness on her high cheekbones, and there was Mr. Rios, sitting beside her, playing with her hand. Her face, so thin and girlish, would blush. From then on, her eyes, very close together like a cartoon rendition of a beaver's, would avoid us.

Miss Colon was hardly discreet about her affairs. Edwin had first tipped me off about her love life after one of his lunchtime jaunts through the empty hallways. He would chase girls and toss wet bathroom napkins into classrooms where kids in the lower grades sat, trapped. He claimed to have seen Miss Colon slip into a steward's closet with Mr. Rios and to have heard all manner of sounds through the thick wooden door, which was locked (he tried it). He had told half the class before the day was out, the boys sniggering behind grimy hands, the girls shocked because Miss Colon was married, so married that she even brought the

395

poor unfortunate in one morning as a kind of show-and-tell guest. He was an untidy dark-skinned Puerto Rican type in a colorful dashiki. He carried a paper bag that smelled like glue. His eyes seemed sleepy, his Afro an uncombed Brillo pad. He talked about protest marches, the sixties, the importance of an education. Then he embarrassed Miss Colon greatly by disappearing into the coat closet and falling asleep there. The girls, remembering him, softened their attitude toward her indiscretions, defending her violently. "Face it," one of them blurted out when Edwin began a new series of Miss Colon tales, "she married a bum and needs to find true love."

"She's a slut, and I'm gonna draw a comic book about her," Edwin said, hushing when she walked in through the door. That afternoon, he showed me the first sketches of what would later become a very popular comic book entitled *Slut at the Head of the Class*. Edwin could draw really well, but his stories were terrible, so I volunteered to do the writing. In no time at all, we had three issues circulating under desks and hidden in notebooks all over the school. Edwin secretly ran off close to a hundred copies on a copy machine in the main office after school. It always amazed me how copies of our comic kept popping up in all the unlikeliest places. I saw them on radiators in the auditorium, on benches in the gym, tacked up on bulletin boards. There were even some in the teachers' lounge, which I spotted one day while running an errand for Miss Colon. Seeing it, however, in the hands of Miss Marti, the pig-faced assistant principal, nearly made me puke up my lunch. Good thing our names weren't on it.

It was a miracle no one snitched on us during the ensuing investigation, since only a blind fool couldn't see our involvement in the thing. No bloody purge followed, but there was enough fear in both of us to kill the desire to continue our publishing venture. Miss Marti, a woman with a battlefield face and constant odor of Chiclets, made a forceful threat about finding the culprits while holding up the second issue, the one with the hand-colored cover. No one moved. The auditorium grew silent. We meditated on the sound of a small plane flying by, its engines rattling the windows. I think we wished we were on it.

It was in the auditorium that the trouble first began. We had all settled into our seats, fidgeting like tiny burrowing animals, when there was a general call for quiet. Miss Marti, up on stage, had a stare that could make any squirming fool sweat. She was a gruff, nasty woman who never smiled without seeming sadistic.

Mr. Rios was at his spot beside Miss Colon, his hands clasped behind his back as if he needed to restrain them. He seemed to whisper to her. Soft, mushy things. Edwin would watch them from his seat beside me, giving me the details, his shiny face looking worried. He always seemed sweaty, his fingers kind of damp.

"I toldju, I saw um holdin hands," he said. "An now lookit him, he's whispering sweet shits inta huh ear."

He quieted down when he noticed Miss Marti's evil eye sweeping over us like a prison-camp searchlight. There was silence. In her best military bark, Miss Marti ordered everyone to stand. Two lone, pathetic kids, dragooned by some unseen force, slowly came down the center aisle, each bearing a huge flag on a thick wooden pole. All I could make out was that great star-spangled, unfurling, twitching thing that looked like it would fall as it approached over all those bored young heads. The Puerto Rican flag walked beside it, looking smaller and less confident. It clung to its pole.

"The Pledge," Miss Marti roared, putting her hand over the spot where her heart was rumored to be.

That's when I heard my father talking.

He was sitting on his bed, yelling about Chile, about what the CIA had done there. I was standing opposite him in my dingy Pro-Keds. I knew about politics. I was eleven when I read William Shirer's book on Hitler. I was ready.

"All this country does is abuse Hispanic nations," my father said, turning a page of his *Post*, "tie them down, make them dependent. It says democracy with one hand while it protects and feeds fascist dictatorships with the other." His eyes blazed with a strange fire. I sat on the bed, on part of his *Post*, transfixed by his oratorical mastery. He had mentioned political things before, but not like this, not with such fiery conviction. I thought maybe it had to do with my reading Shirer. Maybe he had seen me reading that fat book and figured I was ready for real politics.

Using the knowledge I gained from the book, I defended the Americans. What fascism was he talking about, anyway? I knew we had stopped Hitler. That was a big deal, something to be proud of.

"Come out of fairy-tale land," he said scornfully. "Do you know what imperialism is?"

I didn't really, no.

"Well, why don't you read about that? Why don't you read about Juan Bosch and Allende, men who died fighting imperialism? They stood up against American big business. You should read about that instead of this crap about Hitler."

"But I like reading about Hitler," I said, feeling a little spurned. I didn't even mention that my fascination with Adolf led to my writing a biography of him, a book report one hundred and fifty pages long. It got an A-plus. Miss Colon stapled it to the bulletin board right outside the classroom, where it was promptly stolen.

"So, what makes you want to be a writer?" Miss Colon asked me quietly one day, when Edwin and I, always the helpful ones, volunteered to assist her in getting the classroom spiffed up for a Halloween party.

"I don't know. I guess my father," I replied, fiddling with plastic pumpkins self-consciously while images of my father began parading through my mind.

When I think back to my earliest image of my father, it is one of him sitting behind a huge rented typewriter, his fingers clacking away. He was a frustrated poet, radio announcer, and even stage actor. He had sent for diplomas from fly-by-night companies. He took acting lessons, went into broadcasting, even ended up on the ground floor of what is now Spanish radio, but his family talked him out of all of it. "You should find yourself real work, something substantial," they said, so he did. He dropped all those dreams that were never encouraged by anyone else and got a job at a Nedick's on Third Avenue. My pop the counterman.

Despite that, he kept writing. He recited his poetry into a huge reel-to-reel tape deck that he had, then he'd play it back and sit like a critic, brow furrowed, fingers stroking his lips. He would record strange sounds and play them back to me at outrageous speeds, until I believed that there were tiny people living inside the machine. I used to stand by him and watch him type, his black pompadour spilling over his forehead. There was energy pulsating all around him, and I wanted a part of it.

I was five years old when I first sat in his chair at the kitchen table and began pushing down keys, watching the letters appear magically on the page. I was entranced. My fascination with the typewriter began at that point. By the time I was ten, I was writing war stories, tales of pain and pathos culled from the piles of comic books I devoured. I wrote unreadable novels. With illustrations. My father wasn't impressed. I guess he was hard to impress. My terrific grades did not faze him, nor the fact that I was reading books as fat as milk crates. My unreadable novels piled up. I brought them to him at night to see if he would read them, but after a week of waiting I found them thrown into the bedroom closet, unread. I felt hurt and rejected, despite my mother's kind words. "He's just too busy to read them," she said to me one night when I mentioned it to her. He never brought them up, even when I quietly took them out of the closet one day or when he'd see me furiously hammering on one of his rented machines. I would tell him I wanted to be a writer, and he would smile sadly and pat my head, without a word.

"You have to find something serious to do with your life," he told me one night, after I had shown him my first play, eighty pages long. What was it I had read that got me into writing a play? Was it Arthur Miller? Oscar Wilde? I don't remember, but I recall my determination to write a truly marvelous play about combat because there didn't seem to be any around.

"This is fun as a hobby," my father said, "but you can't get serious about this." His demeanor spoke volumes, but I couldn't stop writing. Novels, I called them, starting a new one every three days. The world was a blank page waiting for my words to re-create it, while the real world remained cold and lonely. My schoolmates didn't understand any of it, and because of the fat books I carried around, I was held in some fear. After all, what kid in his right mind would read a book if it wasn't assigned? I was sick of kids coming up to me and saying, "Gaw, lookit tha fat book. Ya teacha make ya read tha?" (No, I'm just reading it.) The kids would look at me as if I had just crawled out of a sewer. "Ya crazy, man." My father seemed to share that opinion. Only my teachers understood and encouraged my reading, but my father seemed to want something else from me.

Now, he treated me like an idiot for not knowing what imperialism was. He berated my books and one night handed me a copy of a book about Albizu Campos, the Puerto Rican revolutionary. I read it through in two sittings.

"Some of it seems true," I said.

"Some if it?" my father asked incredulously. "After what they did to him, you can sit there and act like a Yankee flag-waver?"

I watched that Yankee flag making its way up to the stage over indifferent heads, my father's scowling face haunting me, his words resounding in my head.

"Let me tell you something," my father sneered. "In school, all they do is talk about George Washington, right? The first president? The father of democracy? Well, he had slaves. We had our own Washington, and ours had real teeth."

As Old Glory reached the stage, a general clatter ensued.

"We had our own revolution," my father said, "and the United States crushed it with the flick of a pinkie."

Miss Marti barked her royal command. Everyone rose up to salute the flag.

Except me. I didn't get up. I sat in my creaking seat, hands on my knees. A girl behind me tapped me on the back. "Come on, stupid, get up." There was a trace of concern in her voice. I didn't move.

Miss Colon appeared. She leaned over, shaking me gently. "Are you sick? Are you okay?" Her soft hair fell over my neck like a blanket.

"No," I replied.

"What's wrong?" she asked, her face growing stern. I was beginning to feel claustrophobic, what with everyone standing all around me, bodies like walls. My friend Edwin, hand on his heart, watched from the corner of his eye. He almost looked envious, as if he wished he had thought of it. Murmuring voices around me began reciting the Pledge while Mr. Rios appeared, commandingly grabbing me by the shoulder and pulling me out of my seat into the aisle. Miss Colon was beside him, looking a little apprehensive.

"What is wrong with you?" he asked angrily. "You know you're supposed to stand up for the Pledge! Are you religious?"

"No," I said.

"Then what?"

"I'm not saluting that flag," I said.

"What?"

"I said, I'm not saluting that flag."

"Why the . . . ?" He calmed himself; a look of concern flashed over Miss Colon's face. "Why not?"

"Because I'm Puerto Rican. I ain't no American. And I'm not no Yankee flag-waver."

"You're supposed to salute the flag," he said angrily, shoving one of his fat fingers in my face. "You're not supposed to make up your own mind about it. You're supposed to do as you are told."

"I thought I was free," I said, looking at him and at Miss Colon.

"You are," Miss Colon said feebly. "That's why you should salute the flag."

"But shouldn't I do what I feel is right?"

"You should do what you are told!" Mr. Rios yelled into my face. "I'm not playing no games with you, mister. You hear that music? That's the anthem. Now you go stand over there and put your hand over your heart." He made as if to grab my hand, but I pulled away.

"No!" I said sharply. "I'm not saluting that crummy flag! And you can't make me, either. There's nothing you can do about it."

"Oh yeah?" Mr. Rios roared. "We'll see about that!"

"Have you gone crazy?" Miss Colon asked as he led me away by the arm, down the hallway, where I could still hear the strains of the anthem. He walked me briskly into the principal's office and stuck me in a corner.

"You stand there for the rest of the day and see how you feel about it," he said viciously. "Don't you even think of moving from that spot!"

I stood there for close to two hours or so. The principal came and went, not even saying hi or hey or anything, as if finding kids in the corners of his office was a common occurrence. I could hear him talking on the phone, scribbling on pads, talking to his secretary. At one point I heard Mr. Rios outside in the main office.

"Some smart-ass. I stuck him in the corner. Thinks he can pull that shit. The kid's got no respect, man. I should get the chance to teach him some."

"Children today have no respect," I heard Miss Marti's reptile voice say as she approached, heels clacking like gunshots. "It has to be forced upon them."

She was in the room. She didn't say a word to the principal, who was on the phone. She walked right over to me. I could hear my heart beating in my ears as her shadow fell over me. Godzilla over Tokyo.

"Well, have you learned your lesson yet?" she asked, turning me from the wall with a finger on my shoulder. I stared at her without replying. My face burned, red hot. I hated it.

"You think you're pretty important, don't you? Well, let me tell you, you're nothing. You're not worth a damn. You're just a snotty-nosed little kid with a lot of stupid ideas." Her eyes bored holes through me, searing my flesh. I felt as if I were going to cry. I fought the urge. Tears rolled down my face anyway. They made her smile, her chapped lips twisting upward like the mouth of a lizard.

"See? You're a little baby. You don't know anything, but you'd better learn your place." She pointed a finger in my face. "You do as you're told if you don't want big trouble. Now go back to class."

Her eyes continued to stab at me. I looked past her and saw Edwin waiting by the office door for me. I walked past her, wiping at my face. I could feel her eyes on me still, even as we walked up the stairs to the classroom. It was close to three already, and the skies outside the grated windows were cloudy.

"Man," Edwin said to me as we reached our floor, "I think you're crazy."

The classroom was abuzz with activity when I got there. Kids were chattering, getting their windbreakers from the closet, slamming their chairs up on their desks, filled with the euphoria of soon-home. I walked quietly over to my desk and took out my books. The other kids looked at me as if I were a ghost.

I went through the motions like a robot. When we got downstairs to the door, Miss Colon, dismissing the class, pulled me aside, her face compassionate and warm. She squeezed my hand.

"Are you okay?"

I nodded.

"That was a really crazy stunt there. Where did you get such an idea?"

I stared at her black flats. She was wearing tan panty hose and a black miniskirt. I saw Mr. Rios approaching with his class.

"I have to go," I said, and split, running into the frigid breezes and the silver sunshine.

At home, I lay on the floor of our living room, tapping my open note-book with the tip of my pen while the Beatles blared from my father's stereo. I felt humiliated and alone. Miss Marti's reptile face kept appear-ing in my notebook, her voice intoning, "Let me tell you, you're nothing." Yeah, right. Just what horrible hole did she crawl out of? Were those people really Puerto Ricans? Why should a Puerto Rican salute an American flag?

I put the question to my father, strolling into his bedroom, a tiny M-1 rifle that belonged to my GI Joe strapped to my thumb.

"Why?" he asked, loosening the reading glasses that were perched on his nose, his newspaper sprawled open on the bed before him, his cig-arette streaming blue smoke. "Because we are owned, like cattle. And because nobody has any pride in their culture to stand up for it."

I pondered those words, feeling as if I were being encouraged, but I didn't dare tell him. I wanted to believe what I had done was a brave and noble thing, but somehow I feared his reaction. I never could impress him with my grades, or my writing. This flag thing would probably upset him. Maybe he, too, would think I was crazy, disrespectful, a "smart-ass" who didn't know his place. I feared that, feared my father saying to me, in a reptile voice, "Let me tell you, you're nothing."

I suited up my GI Joe for combat, slipping on his helmet, strapping on his field pack. I fixed the bayonet to his rifle, sticking it in his clutching hands so he seemed ready to fire. "A man's gotta do what a man's gotta do." Was that John Wayne? I don't know who it was, but I did what I had to do, still not telling my father. The following week, in the auditorium, I did it again. This time, everyone noticed. The whole place fell into a weird hush as Mr. Rios screamed at me.

I ended up in my corner again, this time getting a prolonged, pen-sive stare from the principal before I was made to stare at the wall for two more hours. My mind zoomed past my surroundings. In one strange vision, I saw my crony Edwin climbing up Miss Colon's curvy legs, giv-ing me every detail of what he saw.

"Why?" Miss Colon asked frantically. "This time you don't leave until you tell me why." She was holding me by the arm, masses of kids flying by, happy blurs that faded into the sunlight outside the door.

"Because I'm Puerto Rican, not American," I blurted out in a weary torrent. "That makes sense, don't it?"

"So am I," she said, "but we're in America!" She smiled. "Don't you think you could make some kind of compromise?" She tilted her head to one side and said, "Aw, c'mon," in a little-girl whisper.

"What about standing up for what you believe in? Doesn't that matter? You used to talk to us about Kent State and protesting. You said those kids died because they believed in freedom, right? Well, I feel like them now. I wanna make a stand."

She sighed with evident aggravation. She caressed my hair. For a moment, I thought she was going to kiss me. She was going to say something, but just as her pretty lips parted, I caught Mr. Rios approaching.

"I don't wanna see him," I said, pulling away.

"No, wait," she said gently.

"He's gonna deck me," I said to her.

"No, he's not," Miss Colon said, as if challenging him, her eyes taking him in as he stood beside her.

"No, I'm not," he said. "Listen here. Miss Colon was talking to me about you, and I agree with her." He looked like a nervous little boy in front of the class, making his report. "You have a lot of guts. Still, there are rules here. I'm willing to make a deal with you. You go home and think about this. Tomorrow I'll come see you." I looked at him skeptically, and he added, "To talk."

"I'm not changing my mind," I said. Miss Colon exhaled painfully.

"If you don't, it's out of my hands." He frowned and looked at her. She shook her head, as if she were upset with him.

I reread the book about Albizu. I didn't sleep a wink that night. I didn't tell my father a word, even though I almost burst from the effort. At night, alone in my bed, images attacked me. I saw Miss Marti and Mr. Rios debating Albizu Campos. I saw him in a wheelchair with a flag draped over his body like a holy robe. They would not do that to me. They were bound to break me the way Albizu was broken, not by young smiling American troops bearing chocolate bars, but by conniving, double-dealing, self-serving Puerto Rican landowners and their ilk, who dared say they were the future. They spoke of dignity and democracy while teaching Puerto Ricans how to cling to the great coat of that powerful northern neighbor. Puerto Rico, the shining star, the great lap dog of the Caribbean. I saw my father, the nationalist hero, screaming from his podium, his great oration stirring everyone around him to acts of bravery. There was a shining arrogance in his eyes as he stared out over the sea of faces mouthing his name, a sparkling audacity that invited and incited. There didn't seem to be fear anywhere in him, only the urge to rush to the attack, with his armband and revolutionary tunic. I stared up at him, transfixed. I stood by the podium, his personal adjutant, while his voice rang through the stadium. "We are not, nor will we ever be, Yankee flag-wavers!" The roar that followed drowned out the whole world.

The following day, I sat in my seat, ignoring Miss Colon as she neatly drew triangles on the board with the help of plastic stencils. She was using colored chalk, her favorite. Edwin, sitting beside me, was beaning girls with spitballs that he fired through his hollowed-out Bic pen. They didn't cry out. They simply enlisted the help of a girl named Gloria who sat a few desks behind him. She very skillfully nailed him with a thick wad of gum. It stayed in his hair until Edwin went running to Miss Colon. She used her huge teacher's scissors. I couldn't stand it. They all seemed trapped in a world of trivial things, while I swam in a mire of oppression. I walked through lunch as if in a trance, a prisoner on death row waiting for the heavy steps of his executioners. I watched Edwin lick at his regulation cafeteria ice cream, sandwiched between two sheets of paper. I was once like him, laughing and joking, lining up for a stickball game in the yard without a care. Now it all seemed lost to me, as if my youth had been burned out of me by a book.

Shortly after lunch, Mr. Rios appeared. He talked to Miss Colon for a while by the door as the room filled with a bubbling murmur. Then, he motioned for me. I walked through the sudden silence as if in slow motion.

"Well," he said to me as I stood in the cool hallway, "have you thought about this?"

"Yeah," I said, once again seeing my father on the podium, his voice thundering.

"And?"

"I'm not saluting that flag."

Miss Colon fell against the doorjamb as if exhausted. Exasperation passed over Mr. Rios's rodent features.

"I thought you said you'd think about it," he thundered.

"I did. I decided I was right."

"*You* were right?" Mr. Rios was losing his patience. I stood calmly by the wall.

"I told you," Miss Colon whispered to him.

"Listen," he said, ignoring her, "have you heard of the story of the man who had no country?"

I stared at him.

"Well? Have you?"

"No," I answered sharply; his mouse eyes almost crossed with anger at my insolence. "Some stupid fairy tale ain't gonna change my mind anyway. You're treating me like I'm stupid, and I'm not."

"Stop acting like you're some mature adult! You're not. You're just a puny kid."

"Well, this puny kid still ain't gonna salute that flag."

"You were born here," Miss Colon interjected patiently, trying to calm us both down. "Don't you think you at least owe this country some respect? At least?"

"I had no choice where I was born. And I was born poor."

"So what?" Mr. Rios screamed. "There are plenty of poor people who respect the flag. Look around you, dammit! You see any rich people here? I'm not rich either!" He tugged on my arm. "This country takes care of Puerto Rico, don't you see that? Don't you know anything about politics?"

"Don't you know what imperialism is?"

The two of them stared at each other.

"I don't believe you," Mr. Rios murmured.

"Puerto Rico is a colony," I said, a direct quote of Albizu's. "Why I gotta respect that?"

Miss Colon stared at me with her black saucer eyes, a slight trace of a grin on her features. It encouraged me. In that one moment, I felt strong, suddenly aware of my territory and my knowledge of it. I no longer felt like a boy but some kind of soldier, my bayonet stained with the blood of my enemy. There was no doubt about it. Mr. Rios was the enemy, and I was beating him. The more he tried to treat me like a child, the more defiant I became, his arguments falling like twisted armor. He shut his eyes and pressed the bridge of his nose.

"You're out of my hands," he said.

Miss Colon gave me a sympathetic look before she vanished into the classroom again. Mr. Rios led me downstairs without another word. His face was completely red. I expected to be put in my corner again, but this time Mr. Rios sat me down in the leather chair facing the principal's desk. He stepped outside, and I could hear the familiar clack-clack that could only belong to Miss Marti's reptile legs. They were talking in whispers. I expected her to come in at any moment, but the principal walked in instead. He came in quietly, holding a folder in his hand. His soft brown eyes and beard made him look compassionate, rounded cheeks making him seem friendly. His desk plate solemnly stated: Mr. Sepulveda, PRINCIPAL. He fell into his seat rather unceremoniously, opened the folder, and crossed his hands over it.

"Well, well, well," he said softly, with a tight-lipped grin. "You've created quite a stir, young man." It sounded to me like movie dialogue.

"First of all, let me say I know about you. I have your record right here, and everything in it is impressive. Good grades, good attitude, your teachers all have adored you. But I wonder if maybe this hasn't gone to your head? Because everything is going for you here, and you're throwing it all away."

He leaned back in his chair, "We have rules, all of us. There are rules even I must live by. People who don't obey them get disciplined. This will all go on your record, and a pretty good one you've had so far. Why ruin it? This'll follow you for life. You don't want to end up losing a good job opportunity in government or in the armed forces because as a child you indulged your imagination and refused to salute the flag? I know you can't see how childish it all is now, but you must see it, and because you're smarter than most, I'll put it to you in terms you can understand.

"To me, this is a simple case of rules and regulations. Someday, when you're older," he paused here, obviously amused by the sound of his own voice, "you can go to rallies and protest marches and express your rebellious tendencies. But right now, you are a minor, under this school's jurisdiction. That means you follow the rules, no matter what you think of them. You can join the Young Lords later."

I stared at him, overwhelmed by his huge desk, his pompous mannerisms and status. I would agree with everything, I felt, and then, the following week, I would refuse once again. I would fight him then, even though he hadn't tried to humiliate me or insult my intelligence. I would continue to fight, until I . . .

"I spoke with your father," he said.

I started. "My father?" Vague images and hopes flared through my mind briefly.

"Yes. I talked to him at length. He agrees with me that you've gotten a little out of hand."

My blood reversed direction in my veins. I felt as if I were going to collapse. I gripped the armrests of my chair. There was no way this could be true, no way at all! My father was supposed to ride in like the cavalry, not abandon me to the enemy! I pressed my wet eyes with my fingers. It must be a lie.

"He blames himself for your behavior," the principal said. "He's already here," Mr. Rios said from the door, motioning my father inside. Seeing him wearing his black weather-beaten trench coat almost asphyxiated me. His eyes, red with concern, pulled at me painfully. He came over to me first while the principal rose slightly, as if greeting a head of state. There was a look of dread on my father's face as he looked at me. He seemed utterly lost.

"Mr. Sepulveda," he said, "I never thought a thing like this could happen. My wife and I try to bring him up right. We encourage him to read and write and everything. But you know, this is a shock."

"It's not that terrible, Mr. Rodriguez. You've done very well with him, he's an intelligent boy. He just needs to learn how important obedience is."

"Yes," my father said, turning to me, "yes, you have to obey the rules. You can't do this. It's wrong." He looked at me grimly, as if working on a math problem. One of his hands caressed my head.

There were more words, in Spanish now, but I didn't hear them. I felt like I was falling down a hole. My father, my creator, renouncing his creation, repentant. Not an ounce of him seemed prepared to stand up for me, to shield me from attack. My tears made all the faces around me melt.

"So you see," the principal said to me as I rose, my father clutching me to him, "if you ever do this again, you will be hurting your father as well as yourself."

I hated myself. I wiped at my face desperately, trying not to make a spectacle of myself. I was just a kid, a tiny kid. Who in the hell did I think I was? I'd have to wait until I was older, like my father, in order to have "convictions."

"I don't want to see you in here again, okay?" the principal said sternly. I nodded dumbly, my father's arm around me as he escorted me through the front office to the door that led to the hallway, where a multitude of children's voices echoed up and down its length like tolling bells.

"Are you crazy?" my father half-whispered to me in Spanish as we stood there. "Do you know how embarrassing this all is? I didn't think you were this stupid. Don't you know anything about dignity, about respect? How could you make a spectacle of yourself? Now you make us all look stupid."

He quieted down as Mr. Rios came over to take me back to class. My father gave me a squeeze and told me he'd see me at home. Then, I walked with a somber Mr. Rios, who oddly wrapped an arm around me all the way back to the classroom.

"Here you go," he said softly as I entered the classroom, and everything fell quiet. I stepped in and walked to my seat without looking at anyone. My cheeks were still damp, my eyes red. I looked like I had been tortured. Edwin stared at me, then he pressed my hand under the table.

"I thought you were dead," he whispered.

Miss Colon threw me worried glances all through the remainder of the class. I wasn't paying attention. I took out my notebook, but my strength ebbed away. I just put my head on the desk and shut my eyes, reliving my father's betrayal. If what I did was so bad, why did I feel more ashamed of him than I did of myself? His words, once so rich and vibrant, now fell to the floor, leaves from a dead tree.

At the end of the class, Miss Colon ordered me to stay after school. She got Mr. Rios to take the class down along with his, and she stayed with me in the darkened room. She shut the door on all the exuberant hallway noise and sat down on Edwin's desk, beside me, her black pumps on his seat.

"Are you okay?" she asked softly, grasping my arm. I told her everything, especially about my father's betrayal. I thought he would be the cavalry, but he was just a coward.

"Tss. Don't be so hard on your father," she said. "He's only trying to do what's best for you."

"And how's this the best for me?" I asked, my voice growing hoarse with hurt.

"I know it's hard for you to understand, but he really was trying to take care of you."

I stared at the blackboard.

"He doesn't understand me," I said, wiping my eyes.

"You'll forget," she whispered.

"No, I won't. I'll remember every time I see that flag. I'll see it and think, 'My father doesn't understand me.'"

Miss Colon sighed deeply. Her fingers were warm on my head, stroking my hair. She gave me a kiss on the cheek. She walked me downstairs, pausing by the doorway. Scores of screaming, laughing kids brushed past us.

"If it's any consolation, I'm on your side," she said, squeezing my arm. I smiled at her, warmth spreading through me. "Go home and listen to the Beatles," she added with a grin.

I stepped out into the sunshine, came down the white stone steps, and stood on the sidewalk. I stared at the towering school building, white and perfect in the sun, indomitable. Across the street, the dingy row of tattered uneven tenements where I lived. I thought of my father. Her words made me feel sorry for him, but I felt sorrier for myself. I couldn't understand back then about a father's love and what a father might give to ensure his son safe transit. He had already navigated treacherous waters and now couldn't have me rock the boat. I still had to learn that he had made peace with the Enemy, that the Enemy was already in us. Like the flag I must salute, we were inseparable, yet his compromise made me feel ashamed and defeated. Then I knew I had to find my own peace, away from the bondage of obedience. I had to accept that flag, and my father, someone I would love forever, even if at times to my young, feeble mind he seemed a little imperfect.

Questions

1. Why does the boy in the story stop saluting the flag? Why does he agree to start saluting it again?

2. What reasons for saluting or not saluting the flag do the adults in the story give the boy? What other reasons besides those offered would you give the boy?

3. Why does the father behave as he does, first at home and later when he is called to the school?

4. What does Miss Colon mean when she tells the boy, "I'm on your side"? (410)

5. At the end of the story, why does the boy link his father to the flag and say he must accept both?

6. What does the story say about how children develop a civic identity and a sense of belonging to a larger community?

Brian Turner

Brian Turner (1967–) served in the military from 1999 to 2005, first in Bosnia-Herzegovina and then in Iraq, where he was a team leader in the Third Stryker Brigade Combat Team. Turner's brigade was the first in an Iraqi combat zone to use the new Stryker combat vehicle.

Turner, who holds an MFA in poetry from the University of Oregon, wrote poetry and kept a journal during his service in Iraq. His first collection of poems, *Here, Bullet*, was published in 2005, soon after his discharge. One of the poems in this collection, "The Hurt Locker," provided the title for Kathryn Bigelow's Oscar-winning film. Turner's second collection, *Phantom Noise* (2010), addresses the enduring torments that veterans face once they return to civilian life, as well as the further alienation of having returned from a war that has been largely ignored on the home front. Although the last U.S. troops were not sent home until 2011, the American public remained largely disengaged from the nation's involvement in the region, leaving active-duty military and veterans feeling that their combat experiences had become mere background noise. As Turner put it, "America has several wars going on right now, but I found back home that you wouldn't know it. . . . I realized I had to find images that created doorways between the two realities."

"Perimeter Watch" is taken from *Phantom Noise*. In it, he captures the intensity of remembered images and their disorienting tendency to feel more real than the present. How to respond to these experiences in civilian life is a question for many veterans who are still profoundly affected by their combat experience.

PERIMETER WATCH

I lock the doors tonight, check the bolts twice
just to make sure. Turn off all the lights.
Only the fan blades rotate above, slow as helicopters
winding down their oily gears.
                                        Water buffalo
chew the front lawn, snorting. When the sprinklers
switch on, white cowbirds lift up from the grass
with heavy wing-beats, a column of feathers
rising over my rooftop, their wing-tips
backlit by the moon.
                        Through Venetian blinds
I see the Iraqi prisoners in that dank cell at Firebase Eagle
staring back at me. They say nothing, just as they did
in the winter of 2004, shivering in the piss-cold dark,
on scraps of cardboard, staring.
                                        Snipers traverse the skyline
from the neighbor's rooftop. Helicopters on station,
fifteen minutes out. And it's difficult to tell the living
from the dead, walking the dim elephant grass, papyrus thickets
lining the asphalt streets. I see Bosch, my old rifleman,
sleepwalking—on fire and unaware of it.
                                        I see the Stryker,
Ghost 3, parked at the curb. I know the guys inside
watch Iraqi women in the white-hot lens
of the gun-mount camera, eager for the smolder
of their sex. A minivan idles with passengers dying inside
while down the street, an explosion sets off
the neighbor's car alarm.
                        Then, quiet.

The wounded wait with great patience for Doc High,
who treats them by the pool in the backyard,
where I can see the Turkish cook with shrapnel
in the back of his head, his mouth still foaming.
Beside him, the dead infant from that cold blue morning
in the orange groves of Balad, while in the pool
a battalion scout floats face down
in the current.
                    Where is my M-4? My smoke grenades?
My flak vest and plates of body armor? I wander the house
searching for them, hear the twelve-year-old voice just outside
the front door—*Where is my father? Let free my father.*
My father no bad man. Let go my father.
                           When I dial 911,
the operator tells me to use proper radio procedure,
reminding me that my call sign is *Ghost 1-3 Alpha*,
and that it's time, long past time, to unlock the door
and let these people in.

Questions

1. Why does the poet keep seeing images from the war in Iraq as he walks around his house?

2. Why does the poet hear a child's voice outside the front door saying, *"Where is my father? Let free my father"*?

3. Why does the poet dial 911?

4. At the end of the poem, why does the poet hear the operator telling him "it's time, long past time, to unlock the door / and let these people in"? Whom would he be letting in?

5. What is the extent of the perimeter the poet is watching? How does he know where it lies?

6. Does the poem end on a positive or negative note for the poet?

Benjamin Busch

Benjamin Busch (1968–) joined the United States Marine Corps in 1992 after graduating from Vassar College with a major in studio art. He resigned from active duty in 1996 and became a member of the Marine Corps Reserve, later deploying twice to Iraq as an infantry and light armored reconnaissance officer. During his second tour, the battalion in which Busch served suffered high casualty rates, and he was wounded during an IED attack, for which he was awarded a Purple Heart. In addition, he received the Bronze Star for his service in Operation Iraqi Freedom.

In 1997 Busch began a career in acting, and in 2004, between deployments, he began playing Officer Anthony Colicchio on the HBO series *The Wire*. Busch later played Major Todd Eckloff in the HBO miniseries *Generation Kill*. While in Iraq, Busch photographed daily events and interactions between the U.S. forces and the Iraqi people, later exhibiting the images as *The Art in War*.

In 2012 Busch published a memoir, *Dust to Dust*. In it, he writes of his childhood in New York State, his father—the writer Frederick Busch—and his affinity with nature, all woven together by reflections on his lifelong fascination with combat and his experiences in Iraq.

In the following selection from *Dust to Dust*, Busch writes about the aftermath of one of his injuries and about his attitude toward being in perpetual danger. He reflects on his parents' fears for his safety and on the bewilderment of his young daughter when he finally returns. In doing so, Busch raises the issue of how returning veterans can communicate their feelings about their combat experience to their families, their friends, and, ultimately, their society.

DUST TO DUST

(selection)

The soldier arrives home to discover that the war he has returned from has already been forgotten, and because he has survived as a witness to it, neither he nor his country are innocent. Both try to dream again, the soldier by remembering himself before the war, and the country by forgetting the soldier it sent away. The legionnaire returns to find Rome in ruins, its roads still straight, leading out the way he had once marched. It is, perhaps, better that his home is deserted. It can never be what it was before, and the people who can forgive us cannot know what we have done. But the arch at the entrance to Rome still stands, its carved letters clear in the marble. It recounts only victory. The paved roads are also there, leading to conquered lands where free people dig for the buried empire, its value being in that it is now lost.

A calm doctor directed me into a back room, away from all the pain and blood of the serious casualties. I had been hit with a fragment the size of a musket ball, but it had been rejected by my bone and there was nothing but a deep hole. The heat and impact of the metal had kept the wound from bleeding, and only smaller fragment punctures above my elbow had blood creeping from them. It looked like my uniform had been shredded near the elbow without producing the expected injury beyond the cloth. I was carried on adrenaline and felt nothing more than a dull sustained pain and limited movement. I was tired. I just wanted to get back to Hurricane Point and my empty concrete room. Ameen was having his ears examined. None of us could hear very well. "Mild concussions," said the doctor. "Typical." I remember a low audible static in my head. It seemed like it wasn't in my ears but rather somewhere inside my mind. I tried to remember what the mission was.

Back at Hurricane Point, I stood at the sand-filled weapon-clearing barrels to empty my rifle. I removed the magazine and placed it in my flak vest to free my hands. I could barely move my elbow, so the intuitive task of pulling the charging handle to the rear was strangely difficult. After two humbling attempts, I racked the bolt back, ejecting the bullet I had checked in the chamber that morning. It fell and was consumed by the fine dust at my feet, disappearing like an icicle into deep snow. I found it with my fingers, wiped it clean, and returned it to the top of my magazine. It would remain the first bullet loaded every day until finally it was fired out into Ramadi. By June, it had been on every street in western Ramadi and had been aimed at almost every window at one point or another. A perpetual golden bullet.

During my first tour I had convinced myself that I was invulnerable. I was not careless, but I was unafraid in part because fearlessness was required of me. My Marines assumed that an acceptance of risk was ordinary. We became accustomed to our endangerment. When we took our casualty, we were at a loss to completely believe it and went right back into our ritual of patrols as if nothing had happened. While I was deployed my family worried, all of them keeping their worry from me as much as they could.

My second tour was different. I expected to be killed in Ramadi. After I was wounded it was worse for my wife and parents, the mystery of my situation expanding my peril in their imaginations, my vulnerability exposed. But the belief in immortality and the certainty of doom produced almost the same lack of anxiety in me.

On June 16 we were going south to cross the railroad tracks. It was a routine operation in conjunction with combat engineers conducting a search-and-detonation mission on a tip that there was a cache of explosives hidden near the canal running to the south of Ramadi. The village there was always bizarre, inhabited mostly by fishermen, nets spread out in their yards to be cleaned and repaired by their families. The people didn't seem to mix with the rest of the city that lay a mere two hundred meters away on the other side of the tracks. We never knew who we would find there, the entire settlement sometimes abandoned to children and dogs, sometimes flush with men. We called it Springfield because we thought it had a population of characters to rival that of *The Simpsons*. I accompanied the infantry company led by a captain who had become a friend during the deployment. It was to be a security patrol to do a local census and questionnaire, while engineers located artillery rounds delivered by insurgents to be used against us later in Ramadi. While we patrolled through town, we found it almost empty again, the streets vacant, dogs quiet. To take the edge off, the Captain and I exchanged lines from *Monty Python and the Holy Grail*. One of us would begin:

"You were in great peril."

"I don't think I was."

"Yes, you were. You were in terrible peril."

"Look, let me go back and face the peril."

"No, it's too perilous."

We had a similar sense of humor and were also like-minded about how to approach the embattled city. The day felt long, and we finally got word that the ammunition had been found and charges set. We took cover and two pitched rumbles sent a shudder through the town. Trucks were inbound, and as we rallied near the edge of the tracks on the south side, we began to receive small-arms fire from somewhere on the north, where we were heading. We boarded vehicles and crossed the tracks, relieved to finally be heading back to base after so much sweating. Mortars came in, and an IED erupted ahead of us on the road, with no effect. Enough trouble, though, to steer us onto another road. The convoy changed direction, turning east on a dirt path through a jumble of houses. Moving under sporadic fire, we knew something bad was imminent, and the enemy picked the first vehicle in the convoy, detonating several artillery rounds daisy-chained together around a fuel tank. The blast was so powerful that it blew the up-armored vehicle off the ground. The road ahead went black with smoke, and the company frequency went silent for a moment. The Captain was dead and his gunner missing, crushed beneath the burning vehicle. I would spend the night protecting my friend's smoldering wreckage while we waited for a recovery vehicle to come.

I wrote home:

> . . . There were too many memorial ceremonies this month and I attended them all. Was in attendance. Present.

It is early in the night on the holy day and I can hear the broadcasts from three nearby mosques. Praise with the tone of lament. Voices spread out through an extended exhale of language that I cannot interpret but feel I may understand. Bats fly with a random deliberateness in the gray of incomplete darkness. Blind to the world as we see it but somehow not colliding with it, both of us recognizing what is solid and what is not. It is, then, the same world to men and to bats. They hunt insects that hunt us and hunt each other. Everything is similar. Everyone is hunting. I have moved through the dark, defining the space in the grainy green glow of night-vision goggles. I have been out all day patrolling and sweating and thinking that I wouldn't need them. You always bring all of your gear because you never know how a day will end. You have them strapped to the front of your helmet and their awkward weight pulls your head forward. There is no depth perception and objects appear like energy huddled into familiar forms . . . which they are. You can't see the dust but you know that it is there. Something explodes. Try running through a city like that. The phosphorus burn of tracers flashing too bright for your eyes to adjust to. Gone as fast as they pass. You don't know how long you will have to stay on the roof that you have found yourself on. You have ordered the family of the home into a room beneath you. You are out of water. You hope that the rest of the bats in your unit know that it is you on the roof as they hurl themselves into the area to reinforce. Someone is shooting. Watch the tracers. Keep low. You may be there all night. You may be there for the rest of your life. You watch the alleys and the windows for anyone you don't know. You don't know anyone. Think through the Rules of Engagement. Positive identification of a threat is required before you can fire. Reasonable certainty. You are in the middle of an urban sprawl. Your friend's shattered vehicle is upside down by the road ahead with its tires burning. Extinguishers are all expended and Marines are throwing sand on the wreckage. The tires cannot be smothered. You can smell the smoke. All the while, it isn't your house that you have invaded or guard. The family in the room beneath you is just waiting for you to leave. Someone is still shooting. You are not sure, in the shimmering imagination of night-vision equipment, if you see something moving. It can't be positively identified. You are holding your fire. You are holding your position. Holding your position can be a profession. Three months remain. You don't want to let anyone down.

My golden bullet was gone. Its empty shell casing lay behind a wall in someone's yard. You build a fort . . . and you defend it. But the fort was not ours. We were not defending its occupants. Leaning against the wall behind a Marine was the single AK-47 assault rifle the Iraqi family was allowed to keep for self-defense. We had emptied it and made it safe as we collected these people in their kitchen and guarded them from us, using their house to fight back against their neighborhood. I had found this danger because I had sought it. I had no one but myself to blame for discovering it to be ugly.

The purity of service had been corrupted by the moral ambiguity of political language. Language had been the first casualty of the war. It was not the dirt or the smoke or the smell or the blood. My days were not condemned by the things I had expected. It was the pointlessness and the faces of people who were left to live in the violence we had brought with us or had drawn to us. Our bullets had gone out into other people's lives. We gathered our wreckage and our dead, and someone, who lived there, filled in the holes in the road made by the bombs left for us.

For 215 days, we threw ourselves at the city and washed back into Hurricane Point. At headquarters, one hundred meters away, other Marines read our reports, and the Euphrates passed between without noticing any of us.

In an essay for *Harper's*, finished while I was still in Iraq, my father wrote, "We do not talk about what could happen to Ben. We cannot. . . . We are in our midsixties, and every day is precious to us, but we have talked away a chunk of a year of our lives by ticking off each day of his second tour as one more that hastens him home . . . Perhaps we feel that by slicing another day off our lives, as we wish it away to bring him home, we are spending our lives to buy his."

I returned at the end of September on the day of my daughter's first birthday. She hid behind my wife's legs and sneaked smiles at me. I guessed that she had no idea who I was. I almost forgot why she wouldn't. I had known fathers who were never coming back to their children. I cleaned my rifle and pistol one last time, again, and turned them in to the armory.

Questions

1. According to Busch, why does the fact that a returning soldier "has survived as a witness" to war mean that his country is no longer innocent? (417)

2. Why does Busch say that for the returning soldier, "It is, perhaps, better that his home is deserted"? (417)

3. What is the significance of Busch's losing his "golden bullet"? (421)

4. What is the danger that Busch says he sought, and why does he discover it to be "ugly"? Why does he say that he and his comrades are guarding the Iraqi family "from us"? (421)

5. What does Busch mean when he says, "Language had been the first casualty of the war"? (421)

6. What does Busch mean when he says that he had almost forgotten why his one-year-old daughter would have no idea who he was when he returned home?

Ed Hrivnak

After wounded troops are treated in a field hospital, those in need of additional care are flown out of Iraq or Afghanistan to a larger, more modern medical facility in another country, usually Germany or Spain. In many cases, they are patched up and returned to their units. But if their injuries are more serious, they are sent back to the United States for long-term assistance and rehabilitation. U.S. Air Force Captain Ed Hrivnak (1969–), assigned to the 491st Expeditionary Aeromedical Evacuation Squadron, Air Mobility Command, was a fireman living in Washington State before serving in Operation Iraqi Freedom. Hrivnak was a veteran of the Gulf War in 1991 and had assisted in peacekeeping missions that flew into Rwanda, Somalia, Bosnia, and other countries. But despite all that he had seen as a firefighter and during his previous military deployments, Hrivnak was profoundly moved by the casualties he tended to, most of them young, day after day as part of a medevac crew. The following excerpts, which span from late March to mid-July 2003, are from Hrivnak's journal from this period.

After twenty years of service, Hrivnak retired as a captain and is now a professional fire officer in the Pacific Northwest, where he lives with his wife, a lieutenant colonel, nurse practitioner, and three-tour veteran. Hrivnak has conducted research for the Assistant Surgeon General's Office of the U.S. Air Force on the stress of caring for combat casualties and has lectured widely on this subject. His writings have been published in the *New Yorker* and other periodicals, and his war stories have aired on PBS, *ABC World News*, and National Public Radio. Portions of "Medevac Missions" appeared in the award-winning documentary film *Operation Homecoming* (2007).

MEDEVAC MISSIONS

First Mission

Our patient load is 11-7+2 and a duty passenger. That means eleven litter patients, seven walking wounded, and two attendants. Some can take care of themselves, some need lots of help. All have been waiting for us for a long time and need pain medicine and antibiotics. The patients include: gunshot wound (GSW) to the stomach, partial amputations from a land mine, open fractures secondary to GSW, head injury/struck by a tank, blast injuries, shrapnel injuries, and dislocations. The patients are mainly from the Marines and 101st Airborne (Screaming Eagles). Many were involved in ambushes.

One trooper confides in me that he witnessed some Iraqi children get run over by a convoy. He was in the convoy and they had strict orders not to stop. If a vehicle stops, it is isolated and an inviting target for a rocket-propelled grenade. He tells me that some women and children have been forced out onto the road to break up the convoys so that the Iraqi irregulars can get a clear shot. But the convoys do not stop. He tells me that dealing with that image is worse than the pain of his injury.

Back in Germany, the patients are off-loaded and we clean up our mess. Then a sergeant comes out and declares that we have to sign a paper stating we will not drink and drive in Germany. We look at him with anger. Our mission from start to finish was twenty-nine hours long. Most of us were up twelve hours prior to that, minus catnaps. Forty-one hours later and someone in peaceful Germany is worried we might drink and drive.

The field where we picked up the patients, we find out later, came under rocket attack six times after we left.

Another Mission "Down Range"

I've noticed that the most seriously injured are the youngest. The older, experienced soldiers do a better job of staying alive and avoiding the flying metal. One soldier I'm treating looks like a young boy. We talk for a bit as I assess him. I medicate him for his pain. It is the first of many infusions.

The morphine is not working, but it's the strongest stuff I've got. At some point during these adjustments I accidentally dislodge a Hemovac suction unit from one of his infected wounds. Foul-smelling, reddish-yellow fluid drains from the tube and drips off the litter. I start looking at his bandages to find the other end of the tubing. I open one bandage and find sand fleas where his toes used to be. I try my best to keep a straight face, but the sight nauseates me. Scott, one of my level-headed medics, finds the tubing and resets the suction, then cleans up the mess I made.

We finally get this soldier comfortable. Because we moved him so much, I decide to reassess his extremities. I know there are parts of his leg and thigh missing from reading his medical record, but I can't tell from the thick bandages. The wounds were left open to allow them to drain. The dressings are wet and covered in a light layer of sand. I ask the solder to wiggle the toes he has. On one side his toes move fine; on the other side there is no movement. What is left on that side is cold and hard to the touch. He looks at me and our eyes are locked. His eyes say, "Tell me I'm going to be okay. Tell me that I'm going to be fine, tell me I'm going to be whole again. . . ." These are some of the longest seconds of my life because I know he is counting on what I say to him.

I bend down below the litter to break eye contact. I act like I'm adjusting some of the medical equipment attached to him. My mind is racing. I have always been honest with my patients. Do I lie or tell him the truth? The seconds move so slowly as I fight my internal battle on what is right. I stand straight up and there are his eyes. I'm at the end of the litter and with the noise of the plane there is no way he could hear me speak. We are now communicating solely with our eyes and facial expressions. I'm sure less than two seconds passed before I gave him a big smile and a thumbs-up. Those two seconds felt like an hour. He broke into a big smile of relief and I felt broken for lying to him. He motioned to me and

I walked to the head of the litter. I leaned in so he could yell into my ear over the jet noise. "Why do my feet feel so cold?" he asked. I yelled back, "There is a lot of swelling in your feet and the blood circulation is not so good because of the swelling. It is way too early in the game to tell how well you are going to heal. The swelling is going to affect your senses and ability to move." These were all true statements. I felt reassured with my answer. It is too early to say how the soldier will recover. But I still feel bad about lying.

Easter Day

Some come onto the plane with the thousand-yard stare. Some come on with eyes darting about assessing the new environment, maybe looking for an ambush or a booby trap. Some walk with a nervous jitter, some walk on like zombies. Some have eyes glazed over from a morphine-induced stupor. Once we are at cruising altitude, you can feel the tension drop within the aircraft.

I thought I was doing a decent job at nursing when my medical crew discovered a cure-all on our Easter Day mission. We had collected money at our staging base and bought frozen pizzas and cookie dough. Halfway through the flight we started cooking the pizzas. I walked from patient to patient and asked them if they would like a pizza. There were many looks of disbelief. These boys had seen nothing but MREs (field rations) for over three months. Then the smell of pizza started to drift from our aircraft ovens. (We have five small convection ovens on the plane.)

Our crew passed out the pizza to the faces of eager boys. They did not look like combat veterans anymore. Most of them had gleeful looks like young children at an Easter egg hunt. It was like we just gave them a little taste of home and America. They started to joke and laugh with each other. After the pizza we brought out the fresh-baked cookies (which takes a little skill in a pressurized cabin). The cookies were hot and dripping chocolate. I weaved between the seats and litter stanchions and let the boys grab the gooey cookies. You should have seen the looks on their faces. It was on this mission that I realized that there is more to treating the casualties of war than pushing drugs and dressing wounds.

A Mission to Baghdad

We were in Bravo alert and had been told that not much was going on. A crewmate and I were passing the time in our room watching BBC World News when a news flash came on describing multiple ambushes and fire-fights around Baghdad. Several hours later we were alerted for an urgent mission to that very place. We ended up loading thirty-eight patients, the majority of them combat injuries. The worst patient assigned to me was a Ranger who was nineteen years old, but looked to be about fifteen. He was on the litter prone, facing the two critical patients. His arms dangled over the side of the litter. As I walked by, his left arm reached up and grabbed my calf. He was loaded with morphine and difficult to understand. He was rambling, "Take care of my buddies ... TAKE CARE OF MY BUDDIES, don't worry about me and are they going to be okay? Are they going to live?" The critical patients he was facing were his friends. When we loaded the patients we had no time to take into consideration their relationships to one another. He was looking directly at his buddies while the CCATTs* worked desperately to keep them alive.

As the flight continued, I got bits and pieces of what happened. Five Army Rangers were on patrol when a remote-control homemade bomb was detonated under them. Hidden Iraqi irregulars then sprayed the soldiers with small-arms fire. One Ranger died at the scene, and another died at the field hospital. We got the three survivors. My patient was the only one still conscious. Each time I walked by him, he reached up and grabbed my leg, always asking about his friends. I went over to the CCATT nurse, Brian, and asked him how they were doing. He told me, "I got one guy who is shot through the neck and is paralyzed. The other guy has multiple shrapnel wounds and a severe brain injury. These guys are messed up. I hope they killed the fuckers that did this."

Halfway home, I finally caught up on my other patients. I sat down to jot some notes on a patient's chart and fell asleep for a moment. Instantly I started dreaming and then woke up with a start. I had never felt so

---

* Refers to the critical care air transport team, which treats patients with life-threatening conditions.

exhausted. I looked up to see the prone Ranger waving for help. He was in pain. I gave him a touch of morphine. As I leaned into him, he lamented about his friends again. I told him they were still alive. He then vomited on me. It was the perfect capper to an arduous flight. I have no memory of the patient offloads—I was on autopilot at that point. We got into crew rest midday and I had disturbing dreams.

Faces of War

The Humvee is like the Pinto of the 1970s: it burns quickly when hit by a rocket. One GI told me he saw a Humvee burn down in less than three minutes. You can't get out of the vehicle fast enough when it is hit. I was transporting a medical officer who was stuck in such a situation. He was hauling medical supplies to Iraqi civilian hospitals when they were ambushed by an RPG. He was burned on most of his upper body and face. The tops of his ears were burned off. His arms and hands were covered in heavy bandages and ointment covered his red, peeling face. I sat and talked with him as we waited for an ambulance. This officer was prior enlisted, married, and has three children. He decided to become a medical officer to provide better for his family and to get out of the field. He told his family not to worry about him, because he would be serving in the rear with medical logistics. He would not be fighting on the front lines. (Where are the front lines in Iraq?)

He was not concerned about his burns, but he was worried about what his children were thinking. He said, "I talked to them on the phone yesterday. They didn't understand why I was burned. I promised them I was going to be okay—that I would be safe. The kids don't get it and I'm not sure how to explain it to them." I stared at his face and burns the whole time he was talking. His face was an expressionless mask. I couldn't tell if he was tired like the rest of the patients or if the burns were causing his unvaried, mask-like appearance. The tone of his voice when speaking of his children was his only sign of emotion.

What does the future hold for these men who go home to their families mentally and physically different? And what of the critically injured who have a long future of VA hospitals followed by VA disability? How do they cope? How do they adjust? I feel obligated to stay out here and take care of the wounded. I want to do all I can to help them.

Battle Buddies

These Marines and soldiers are good at waiting. They see we are doing our best and rarely complain. One soldier, trying to be patient, went too long between morphine shots. He tried to gut it out. He did not want to slow the loading of the airplane. We loaded him on the bottom rack and he immediately grabbed onto the litter above him. I looked down at him and saw his knuckles turn white with a death grip on the litter crossbeam. Tears poured down his face but he did not make a sound. I grabbed the primary flight nurse and told him to give this kid some of the good stuff. The nurse said he would get the morphine when we were done loading the rest of the litter patients.

I can't blame this nurse. It was his first real casualty mission in the war. It is easy to lose sight of one patient and get caught up in what is going around you. I told the nurse to toss me a syringe of morphine and I would take care of him myself. When I returned to this GI, a battle buddy was holding his hand and talking softly to him. Their hands were locked like they were ready to arm-wrestle. I quickly pushed the morphine into his vein and apologized for letting his pain get to such a level. I felt like I had failed him. His buddy stayed with him, talking to him, consoling him, until the pain medicine took effect and the soldier's hand relaxed. These two were not in the same unit. They were not wounded in the same part of Iraq. They were brought together and bonded by their wounds. Their injuries made them part of a fraternity, a private brotherhood I felt privileged to witness.

Questions

1. Why does Hrivnak include the trooper's story about women and children run over by a convoy along with his description of his patients' physical injuries?

2. Since Hrivnak says that he had "always been honest" with his patients, why does he mislead the severely wounded soldier about his foot injuries? Do you think he did the right thing? (426)

3. How do Hrivnak's experiences on medevac missions demonstrate his insight that "there is more to treating the casualties of war than pushing drugs and dressing wounds"? (427) How can caretakers learn what kinds of additional care will be helpful?

4. Why does Hrivnak feel "obligated" to stay in Iraq and take care of the wounded troops? (430)

5. What does Hrivnak mean when he describes wounded soldiers as belonging to a "private brotherhood," even if they did not serve in the same unit? (430)

Siobhan Fallon

Two weeks after Siobhan Fallon (1972–) married Major K. C. Evans in 2004, her husband was deployed to Afghanistan for a year-long tour of duty. Two tours of duty in Iraq, each a year in duration, followed between 2006 and 2010.

For the duration of Evans's second and third deployments Fallon lived at Fort Hood, in Texas. It is Fort Hood that provides the setting for "The Last Stand" and "Gold Star," and for the other interconnected stories in Fallon's award-winning debut collection, *You Know When the Men are Gone* (2011).

The Iraq war looms over the collection—overshadowing not only the lives of those deployed to combat zones, but the families who stay behind. During her years at Fort Hood, Fallon led a support network of army spouses (her husband led the corresponding group for the troops in Iraq), and from this experience she gained insight into the wide-ranging concerns faced by military spouses. Many women faced the challenges of frequent moves, long separations, single-parenting, and constant fear for the safety of the absent loved ones.

In these two stories, Fallon explores the ways in which marriages are profoundly affected by war and its consequences. Together, the stories prompt reflection on the complex cross-currents of loyalty, mutual responsibility, and need for individual fulfillment that face spouses as they try to adjust to the changes that result from separation and loss.

YOU KNOW WHEN THE MEN ARE GONE

(selection)

THE LAST STAND

Specialist Kit Murphy entered Abrams Gym slowly, still getting used to the hop and swing of his crutches, the pressure under his armpits, and the jerking motion of his injured foot. Everyone was acting as if this was a normal welcome home ceremony—there were unit banners and flags on the wall as well as a DJ with a red, white, and blue cowboy hat yodeling nonsense into his microphone. But no one was fooled, not with the doctors standing around. Kit could spot medical corps even though they wore their camouflage uniforms: the medics watched the thirteen returning soldiers too closely in that impatient-doctor kind of way, like they were hoping someone would fall over and make their valuable presence worthwhile. And the waiting family members cheered daintily rather than that stomping, raucous, happy-to-be-alive way that crowds usually behaved, all of them trying to keep the horror of the moment to themselves, not sure what to expect or wish for, watching their wounded slowly making their way back to the land of the whole.

Kit wasn't sure what to expect or wish for either as he scanned the crowd for Helena. He hadn't been able to get in touch with her for over a week; lately it was her mom, Linda, who cooed at Kit over the phone as if he were a colicky baby in the throes of a tantrum rather than a husband trying to have a word with his wife. On the bus ride from the airport, he had been dreading this moment of standing alone, of being selected to get a pity-hug from the too-dressed-up FRG leaders or too-dressed-down Red Cross volunteers who greeted the soldiers standing unloved amid the embraces. But behind the loose-necked gaggle of veterans waving their made-in-China American flags, he saw Helena's red hair, the lift of her chin, and the widening recognition in her eyes. Kit felt his cheeks blush hot with embarrassment; he kept his eyes on her hair and wouldn't look around, afraid another soldier would see how relieved he was to find someone waiting for him.

"I didn't know if you got word I was coming back," Kit said from the passenger seat of Helena's rental car. Two months ago his Humvee had been hit on Route Pluto, outside of Sadr City, surprised by a clever little Iranian bomb that had been hidden under the corpse of a skinny dog. Kit had immediately been evacuated to the Ibn Sina Hospital in the Green Zone, then helicoptered to Baghdad International Airport, then flown to the Landstuhl Regional Medical Facility in Germany, though of course he couldn't remember any of that. The doctors in Germany let him call home when the concussion had healed enough for him to string words together. At first Helena wanted to know everything about his injury and they would talk until an orderly came into the room or Kit passed out with the phone pressed up against his ear. But when he got to D.C., to Walter Reed, when the surgeries didn't seem to be doing him any good and nothing was healing the way it was supposed to, when a month had passed and then six, seven, eight weeks, it was harder to get in touch with her.

"I left messages with a nurse; I think her name was Valencia," Helena said, eyes on the road. "Didn't she give them to you?"

Kit shrugged. He knew all the nurses and they had some pretty unusual names, but none of them were called Valencia. It was the nurses who alerted him that something might be wrong, the way they seemed overly excited when handing him one of Helena's phone messages that she had asked them to write down rather than being connected directly to Kit's room, even though he was wide awake in his bed and playing last generation's Nintendo: *Helena called but didn't want to wake you up! Helena hopes you are feeling better! Helena is so happy you are coming home!* Full of exclamation marks with overenthusiastic hearts at the bottom. He would crumple the pink slips into tiny balls of anger. On his flight from D.C., his section of the plane was dotted with fellow battered soldiers leaning forward with sweat on their foreheads, all of them wondering if their wives would be waiting, and if they were, how long they would stick around when they saw the burn scars, the casts, the missing bits and pieces that no amount of *Star Wars* metal limbs could make up for.

"I'm here, aren't I?" Helena asked softly, lifting her right hand from the steering wheel and placing it on his elbow, a pat really, but that touch was everything he needed. Kit took a deep breath and knew just being with Helena again meant he was home.

They pulled into a Padre's Motel parking lot just outside the main gate, a big sign advertising rates of $180 a week, breakfast and HBO included.

"I thought you were going to find an apartment?" he asked.

Helena shook her head. "I just got here last night."

When they opened the motel room door, Kit immediately noticed the twin beds. He looked at Helena, who sat down on the corner of one, bouncing on the edge of the mattress like a kid with an attention deficit disorder.

"I thought two beds would be best for your foot," she said, her voice oddly loud and cheerful. "You know how I toss and turn. You wouldn't want me to roll over on your cast in the middle of the night!"

"Yeah, I would." He sat down on the other bed and stared. He had been away for more than a year, he had almost died, and his wife got a room with *two beds*?

Helena stood up, flipping that waterfall of strawberry-blonde hair over her shoulder the way she always did when she was nervous. She went into the small kitchenette and opened the fridge with a Vanna White motion of her arm, illuminating rows of bottled beer. "You've got to be starving! Let's have a drink and order pizza."

Kit took the bottle she handed him and twisted the cap off so hard it tore little ridges from the skin of his palm.

They watched TV, ate a pepperoni pie, and Kit tried to drink enough Coors to not feel anything at all, wishing for whiskey. Helena, talking nonstop, told him about his old friends at home: how John Roark got a senior in high school pregnant and they married on the due date; how Sunny Shay was making a fortune on her sex toy website but Father Mellon refused to give her communion at Sunday Mass; how Tim Lewski got yet another DUI as he drove home after refereeing a kids' soccer game. Kit didn't speak or even listen, just watched her thin hands as she spoke, the way they fluttered in the air like Fourth of July sparklers.

Helena had been pregnant when he deployed. A lot of wives had been, as if the soldiers started trying to procreate when they got their orders for Baghdad, tried to imprint themselves in a desperate scramble for immortality before ending up in the unknown. She claimed that she was showing when he left but her belly looked just as sweet to him as it always had, a little round, maybe, but he liked that, that her body was so soft compared to his. She lost the baby at the beginning of the second trimester, and by the time Kit got back for midtour leave, she seemed unfazed by the miscarriage and wouldn't give him any details. She made sure to take her birth control pills for the fourteen days that he was there, and she told him that she wanted to move home with her folks, to take classes at the community college, be near her high school friends, and wait tables at the restaurant where she used to work, Grits to Gravy. Kit hadn't objected. He had even helped put all their stuff in storage. He liked the idea of her with her momma. But now he wondered if she had met someone else, a waiter from Grits, a manager at the local Kmart, even her smarmy high school volleyball coach, who always hugged her too long, someone who had stayed while Kit was gone.

When the pizza was finished and the beer bottles emptied, Helena went into the bathroom and came out in a baggy sweatshirt and sweat-pants, her face shiny-clean and her breath minty, gave him a chaste kiss on his cheek, climbed into her own bed, and clicked off her bedside light.

"Sweet dreams," she said lightly, and Kit said absolutely nothing in return.

He woke up a few hours later, his foot throbbing with heat. He imagined the skin swelling around the stitches and narrow steel rods, blood and pus seeping out, sand still flecked around the edges of the wound, as if Iraq would not let him go. He wondered if he'd be able to find his bottle of Vicodin in his duffel, then remembered how the doctor said it was his last refill, from now on he'd have to make do with Tylenol, and he figured he'd better save it.

He glanced over at Helena. She was making that cooing sound she made when she was in a really deep sleep, her hair hanging off the pillow and catching the green light of the alarm clock. Two a.m.

When he was deployed, in his cot at night, in a tent with eleven other guys farting and snoring and jacking off around him, he would make lists in his head to help lull himself to sleep. At first it was the same lists other guys made and swapped while on guard duty or during a long patrol, all those empty, hot desert hours to fill, like listing the five best Steven Seagal movies, or remembering the winners and losers of as many World Series as possible, or all the different sexual positions tried with different women. But the longer Kit was in Iraq, the more specific his lists became. Like *All the Things at Home I Never Thanked My Wife For*, which was his longest. The current absence of all the things on this list perfectly illuminated how much life sucked in Baghdad. Besides the obvious, like how Helena cooked him a hot meal every night rather than served him food from a bag that had waited in a warehouse for a year, then rode on a boat for a few months, then sat on a truck for a few weeks, then was picked over by a disgruntled staff sergeant who took all the decent meals and handed lowly Kit *Chicken, Chunked and Formed, with Grill Marks,* or *Beef Frankfurters* (more commonly referred to as *Five Fingers of Death*).

The things Kit listed in his head, such wonders of Helena's female ingenuity, were: how there was always toilet paper on the roll and a backup within reach, unlike being caught in the shitter at midnight only to realize that the roll of scratchy Chinese toilet paper at his feet had been sitting in a puddle of urine; the mirrors in the bathroom were never covered with catapulted floss gunk or tagged with wannabe army Latino gang slang; there was always something cold to drink (and not just that small swishable amount that guys left behind in the fridge because they were too lazy to throw the carton out); the sheets were fresh instead of oily with old sweat and crinkly with new sand; the towels were dry rather than rolled up and damply soaking his pillow; his socks were matched and paired like little heads of lettuce in his drawer rather than shoved, stiff with days of use, under his cot; there were clean clothes to choose from instead of a pile to sniff through, and those clean clothes smelled like American soap detergent instead of the cheap, astringent cologne that the local national cleaners doused the soldiers' clothes with when they were contracted to do the laundry.

That list could go on for hours, and often did. Of the twelve soldiers crammed into a tent that could comfortably sleep eight (though most of the other tents were jammed with eighteen, all asses and elbows, so no one in Kit's tent was complaining), there was always someone coming and going to guard duty or to take a piss or cursing under his breath in his headlamp as he read letters from home. The sun in Iraq rose at 3:30 a.m. The spiteful light would burst into the tent every time the door opened like a nuclear camera flash that singed the retinas of all the soldiers tossing in their cots. Kit would pull his sheet over his head and think of his list with such fervent desire that the semi-unconscious state of longing was almost as good as being asleep.

And now here she was, everything Kit wanted, the only person who could figure out how to make something good of his situation, and she was there in another bed, as far away as she had been before he stepped onto the plane. Kit tried to sit, feeling around on the bedside table for the TV remote. He either wanted to throw it at Helena's head, as hard as only a Lincoln High MVP pitcher could, or click on the TV. The impulse to remain a functioning part of society won. He turned the volume up, glancing at her every few minutes, wanting her to roll over and blink those eyes, wanting her to smile at him and ask him what was wrong so he could talk to her, so she could tell him that things between them were okay. But she slept on and Kit watched cheetahs hunting on PBS, the twist and somersault as they brought an antelope down and then tore it into bloody bits.

He tapped the remote against his cast, pretending he had an itch, but that didn't wake her either. Kit fell asleep as dawn started to filter through the gaps under the motel curtains. The light of the television flashed over both of them in their separate beds, unheeded like a lightning storm.

They went to a Waffle House for breakfast and Helena drove the rental car, Kit sullen and yawning in the passenger seat.

"We can get your truck out of storage today," she said brightly. He shrugged. He didn't think he'd be able to manipulate his boot enough to drive a stick shift, but he didn't want to say the words aloud.

Inside, he ordered too much food, then watched his wife as she added creamer and sugar to her coffee and would not meet his eyes.

My wife, he thought, and outrage struck his chest as forcefully as a wild baseball. "Who is it?" he let loose, angry at himself for being angry instead of trying to win her back.

She glanced up. "Who what?"

"There's someone else, right?"

She moved her hand to touch his wrist but he quickly lifted his own coffee cup to get out of reach, the black liquid scalding the inside of his mouth.

"There's no one," she whispered.

Kit looked down at his place mat. "Three weeks ago you were telling me that you would find an apartment, that you'd try to transfer your credits to a school in Texas, that you missed me—" He stopped, afraid his voice would crack.

"Look at me," she said, and this time she managed to put her hand on his. Kit lifted his face and took her in. She looked exactly the way she had when she graduated from Lincoln High two years ago, sturdy and confident the way a girl who got straight As and played varsity volleyball since freshman year ought to look. She had always been plain, pale-skinned, with a few freckles on her cheeks, blue eyes so clear you could only see pupils, and a slight underbite that made her chin look stubborn and ready for a fight. Guys looked at her because of her long red hair and then they usually looked away. But when she smiled, her jaw clicked back into its rightful place and anyone who saw her smiling usually kept looking and had no choice but to smile back; she seemed so aware of the people she was with, she seemed to watch them like she could take their pulse with her silvery eyes.

"I love you," she said just as the waitress put down their sunny-side-up eggs and his side of sausage, bacon, and pancakes. When the waitress left Helena leaned forward again. "I love you but I don't think I can do this anymore. I want to be home. I like my college classes and I need to be near my family."

"I'll get out," he said, and it was the first time since he'd seen those two separate motel beds that he felt hope. "I'll work at the lumberyard; my stepbrother's always telling me he'll give me a job. I've got only six months left of my commitment. You can wait that long, can't you? You can stay at home, I don't care. I'll get out."

Helena pushed her fork across her plate, piercing a yolk and watching it bleed across her hash browns. "You can't get out until your foot is better," she said softly. "I've looked it up. You'd get awarded partial disability, about twenty-five percent of your salary, and what's that? Six grand? What could you do at the lumberyard with your foot like that? And we're more than three hours from the closest VA hospital—how would you go back and forth for physical training?"

Kit sat back in the booth. He had forgotten about his foot. "Then I'll stay in. But I won't deploy again." His voice picked up speed. "The army will have to give me some cushy office job. I'll only be working from eight a.m. to five p.m.; it will be like a regular civilian job. I'll be home for dinner every night. You can handle that."

"I'm happy now." Helena shook her head. "I don't want to come back here."

"Happy without me?" Kit wanted to throw up on all the food in front of him, the eggs getting cold and hard with a film of gray grease on top.

She took an envelope from her purse and a breath to steady herself. "I talked to a lawyer." Kit looked over his shoulder to see if he recognized any guys in the booths behind him. "These are the papers for a legal separation. If we separate and don't divorce, you'll still get your housing allowance and extra marriage pay, but you can move into the barracks and save up. I'm making enough money of my own so you don't need to worry about me."

"You don't want to do this."

"I do," she whispered, as if deliberately echoing the words that had once tied them together. "Yes, I do."

The waitress boxed up all the food they couldn't eat even though Kit had told her not to, and he held the foam awkwardly balanced on his lap during the drive back to the motel.

Three months into the deployment, his buddy Blake had opened up a package from home and found divorce papers underneath a bag of melted M&M's. Blake almost choked on his lip of dip, then went on a tirade so long, obscene, and flecked with tobacco spittle that their platoon sergeant, Sergeant Schaeffer, told him to shut up or go talk to the chaplain. But Helena hadn't chosen the easy way out like that, hadn't told him this news in a letter or over the phone; she had flown out to Hood, been waiting, was sitting next to him still. Hell, the thing that had always set Helena apart, from the cheerleaders or ponytailed softball players eager to sit with Kit in the back of the bus, was her kindness. How she volunteered at the animal shelter, spent her Thanksgivings at soup kitchens, waited at the curb at dawn to give Pepsis to the garbagemen. Would someone who voluntarily hosed dog feces out of kennels really leave her busted-up and Purple Hearted soldier husband just days after he returned?

Inside the motel room, Kit decided to change tactics. While Helena was washing her hands at the bathroom sink, he stepped up behind her and put his arms around her waist, nuzzling his chin in the back of her neck. He felt her body stiffen.

"I don't care if there was someone else," he whispered. "It doesn't matter. Things can go back to the way they used to be—"

She turned around so quickly, slipping out of his arms, that he almost fell over.

"I told you there isn't anyone." She paced the narrow passage between the beds and the TV.

"Remember how good we had it?" he asked.

"Good?" She spun toward him, her hands on her hips. "You were always training late on the range and working weekends. Our apartment smelled like vomit and paint thinner from the last tenants. The neighbors had slasher films blasting all night. I was afraid to go outside by myself."

Kit was suddenly very tired. He leaned into the wet sink and tried to take pressure off his injured foot. He stared at his wife. For thirteen months he had dreamed of their home together, the meals she had waiting for him, the hot running water, the refrigerator always full, the steady air-conditioning, and the comfortable couch. Everything in hindsight had seemed like a delirious indulgence, just to have electricity at the end of every switch and lightbulb. He had forgotten that Helena hated that apartment on Trimmier Avenue, how she had to use a pair of pliers to get the dishwasher to work, how the shower leaked water from one end of the bathroom to the other, how she tried to get a dog-walking business going and failed.

"We'll find a nicer place," he said dully. He no longer wanted to have this conversation, he didn't want Helena's version of their life together to ruin the one he held in his mind.

She was pacing again. "I wish I was a better wife." She stopped and looked at her foot, eyes translucent with tears. "I just want to go home and start all over again." Then, so quietly he almost didn't hear her, "Alone."

So he called up some of his single buddies, Crawford and Dupont.

"Who's up for a day of drinking?" he asked, and arranged for them to pick him up.

He left Helena sitting on her bed, her thin arms crossed over her chest.

"Don't you want to get your truck?" she asked. "And your things out of storage? I wanted to get you set up. . . ."

But Kit ignored her, rifling through his duffel bag for that last bottle of Vicodin, swallowing three without any water, not caring that they got caught in his throat. And he didn't take his crutches as he slammed the motel room door behind him.

They went to The Last Stand Bar and Grill. Crawford and Dupont got the usual stares when they walked in together. Crawford wore the white button-up shirts and skinny ties favored by proselytizing Mormons, argued against evolution, and was hooked on comic books. Dupont had the word "Afrika" tattooed across his dark shoulders, boasted about the wartime rap videos he had put on YouTube, and got a manicure once a week. But Crawford, Dupont, and Kit had done basic training at the same time, managed to get sent to I-7 Cav, then spent the deployment together in Iraq. They'd trained, bitched, slept, and pissed together for the past two and a half years: it was the equivalent of knowing each other for about a decade in the civilian world.

The Last Stand was a First Cavalry Division favorite and the walls were studded with memorabilia to prove it. There was a badly drawn poster of the doomed Custer, who had commanded the Seventh Cav Regiment, and newspaper clippings about the raffles and fundraisers that the bar had hosted in order to send packages to the soldiers overseas. There were signs stolen from Fort Hood parking lots, photos of soldiers in Iraq standing with thumbs-up in front of Saddam's palace or pitted desert landscapes, and unit patches that the customers tore off their uniforms and traded in for free drinks. But for a cavalry unit renowned for its long-ago horsemanship and now destined to ride nothing but tanks and Humvees, the shining glory of the bar was the mechanical bull in the corner. Cowboy hats or baseball caps of those who had fallen off hung above the metal animal, nailed to the ceiling in warning.

"Isn't that sweet little wife of yours here?" Dupont asked, buying a round of tequila shots and canned Miller Lite to start.

"She's a bitch," Kit replied, and reached for the small glass of tequila and the yellow oblivion it promised.

"To ditching bitches," Dupont toasted, and the three guys swallowed the tequila and slammed the shot glasses on the bar.

Kit had turned twenty-one in Iraq, his birthday spent guarding Assassins' Gate, one of the checkpoints of the Green Zone, and that day his buddies had toasted him with hot canteen water that tasted faintly of bleach. After the desert, after months of hospitals and strangers, sitting with Crawford and Dupont while drinking beer at a bar felt like the best thing in the world. And they wanted to hear about his foot, all the gory details of his surgeries, the pain he was in, and most of all how many Vicodin he had left and what their value might be in the barracks.

It was "Boom Boom" Dupont who had ripped Kit out of the Humvee after the IED went off, the IED that turned the entire undercarriage of his truck into a fiery wall that consumed the five men inside. Sergeant Schaeffer had been sitting next to Kit and caught most of the molten explosion. His body threw Kit against the side of the Humvee and some-how, miraculously, shielded him from the flame until Dupont, from the truck behind, grabbed Kit by the right arm and pulled him out. Kit had escaped with almost every single bone in his foot pulverized and burns on his face and hands.

Sergeant Schaeffer had not survived.

"To Sergeant Schaeffer," they toasted for round number three, four, and five. The sun was setting outside, the fluorescent lights in the bar starting to glow in the dusk, and a few bottle-blondes in cowboy hats and short denim skirts were two-stepping near the jukebox. Kit felt the floor shifting underneath him.

"Take it easy," Crawford said when Kit stumbled up to the bar to order another round. They had called Crawford "Choirboy" in Iraq because he didn't curse, dip, smoke, or drink coffee. But Kit had once gotten a look in his buddy's TUF box and, under the layer of X-Men and Black Knight comics, the guy had the biggest collection of Jenna Jameson DVDs Kit had ever seen. Crawford continued, "We've had time to get our tolerance back. The first week I was home I would get drunk just twisting the cap off a bottle of Jack."

"I'm okay," Kit said, reaching for his wallet. He wanted to call the motel, to make sure Helena was still there, but he ordered tequila instead.

He looked over and saw Dupont, six-four and darker than the smoke-stained bar walls, undulating to the country music as if it were a ballad by Mariah Carey. The girls at the jukebox smoked their cigarettes and ignored him the way most girls living outside Fort Hood ignored guys with high and tight haircuts. But Dupont had the grace and nonchalance that women inevitably wanted to get close to, and the tallest girl couldn't help but start two-stepping next to his swaying hips. Then he made a motion toward the hibernating mechanical bull. The girls lifted their eyebrows and shrugged, then followed him over to where the hats forlornly covered the ceiling like the scalps of Custer and his massacred men.

Kit sniffed his shot, winced, and downed it. He thought of Helena's life at home. The business classes at community college; nights at the Go-Go Putt with the high school friends she had never strayed from; her boss, Mackey, who called her "my girl" and gave her grotesquely untalented figurines he carved out of walnut shells; her gossip-loving sister who could talk for hours and just had twins; even her mom, Linda, with her big huggable arms and freezer full of everyone's favorite ice cream. Kit hadn't realized the idea of home could pose such a danger. That it could steal Helena away from him so completely. Or that it could never be his own home again.

"Let's ride that bull," Kit said, the warmth of agave in his stomach almost quelling his nausea.

"Don't be a beef-wit." Crawford finished his beer and looked down at Kit's cast.

"Trust me, Choirboy, I don't feel a thing."

Kit watched Dupont and then the blondes, in quick succession, get tossed from the bull, each of them donating something to the sacrificial ceiling. The girls lost their cowboy hats. Dupont left his T-shirt dangling from a lightbulb and, stripped down to his wife-beater and the smudged Louisiana Tiger inked on his right shoulder, was suddenly thin and shy around the ladies.

Something's got to go right for me, Kit thought, assessing the headless, legless creature. When Kit was nine and his mother was splitting up with his second stepfather, he spent the summer in Winnemucca, Nevada, with his mom's folks. Every day his granddad would take him out to a cactus-laden field and put him bareback on a horse, a sullen old mare that would bite a hand rather than take the sugar. Before she got a chance to sink her teeth into Kit's thigh, his granddad would hit her hard on the rump and she would gallop as fast as those old legs let her. Kit would hold on to the matted mane, his heels tight in her belly, and it felt like flying. If he could ride that mare, he could ride this metal thing, and maybe it'd help him get lucky with the blonde girl who flashed him her light blue panties when she did a somersault off the bull. That would show Helena.

The guy manning the mechanical bull looked at Kit's foot. "You sign the release form?"

Kit nodded and he let him through.

Kit got up on the contraption carefully, getting his good foot through the stirrup and pushing the toe of his cast into the other. He grabbed the horn in the center of the saddle and just to act jaunty he lifted his left hand up over his head, rodeo-style. He heard Crawford and Dupont cheer wildly, and even a hoot or two from the hatless blondes.

The bull started to move, slowly at first, letting Kit get the hang of it. It seemed easier the faster it went. And it was like his granddad's nag. He could almost hear her hooves against rock and dirt below, the wind in his ears, and that rhythm, that perfect, beautiful motion of being aligned with another creature, mindless with adrenaline and the pounding. God, he loved this, why didn't he ride more often? What could beat this feeling? Damn, he could do it, he would do it. Blue Panties was his.

Then the bull lurched and started moving in a new direction and the tenuous hold of his cast in the stirrup came loose. He felt himself pitching forward, and if he had been sober he would have tried to tuck and roll like he had learned in Airborne School, but instead he landed hard and the pain that shot up his left foot into his spine forced tears out of his eyes. He stayed like that, flat on his back, until both Crawford and Dupont came running over and helped him up, his leg dangling uselessly behind.

They had to carry him into the motel room. Helena opened the door, her eyes swollen with sleep or tears, wearing one of his army gray T-shirts over a pair of sweatpants.

They put him on his bed.

"You sure you don't want to go to the hospital?" Dupont asked for Helena's benefit, and Kit shook his head. "Call us tomorrow, okay?"

Then they left, heads bowed, and Helena closed the door behind them.

"You smell like you'll have a headache tomorrow," she said, going to the kitchenette sink and pouring him a plastic cup of water.

Kit drank, and when she filled the cup again, he drank that, too.

"I was worried about you," she said.

Kit crushed the cup and tossed it at the wastebasket, missing. "Well, soon enough you won't need to worry, right?"

"I guess not." She turned off the light and he heard the springs of her bed creak. "Is your foot okay?"

"No." He wanted to say that it was never going to be okay, that he couldn't screw it up any more tonight than it already was. His eyes started to get used to the darkness and he could make out her outline by the alarm clock's light, how she sat at the edge of her bed.

Kit tried to arrange the pillows behind his head. He would have to wait until Helena fell asleep and then he could put on the TV. He knew, with the pain, he wouldn't be sleeping tonight.

"Let me do that," Helena whispered, and stood. He lifted himself up and she arranged the pillows under his shoulders, the army T-shirt brushing Kit's face, and he could smell her skin, the warm, new-kitten smell of it, her apricot shampoo and the vanilla drugstore perfume she liked to put on her wrists. He put his hand out, he couldn't help it, and touched the ends of her hair. She hesitated, hovering over him, and then he felt the bed shift and suddenly she was next to him, breathing on his throat in the dark.

"Is this my consolation prize?" Kit asked, feeling an electric surge of cruelty rush through him so strong his hands began to tingle. "You want to make yourself feel better by giving the cripple one last lay before you leave him?"

"You're not a cripple," she whispered, and put her lips on his.

Afterward, she rested her cheek against Kit's chest and he watched the small rise and fall of her head in time with his breath. He could hear a thick saturation in her throat that meant she was trying not to cry, and he tried to think of something to say, something that would stitch her to him forever.

"You haven't asked about the baby," she whispered.

He blinked. "I didn't think you wanted to talk about it."

She didn't reply for so long he was sure she had fallen asleep. "I never told you about the sonogram." She lifted her head and Kit could see her profile, her nose and her tough little chin. "I heard his heart, Kit, his wildly beating heart. So strong. I could see it on the screen, too, like a fist opening and closing. Three days later he was dead."

Kit played with her hair, running his fingers through its length, wondering what she was accusing him of. "I called as soon as I got the Red Cross message—"

"I know you did," she said, and Kit felt a drip of hot water on his bare skin. "I just can't get it out of my mind." She hesitated. "The sound of that heartbeat. I wish you had been there."

"Me too." Then, in the dark, he almost told her about Sergeant Schaeffer, how his body had pinned Kit down, his arms outstretched over him like some Old Testament angel. How he could smell Schaeffer burning and he thought it was his own flesh. How Kit had cried in that Humvee, hearing his friends screaming in the smoke, every intake of breath frying his throat and lungs, tongue and teeth. He had tried to pray but he couldn't, just cried like a child, helpless, until Dupont got him out.

But he couldn't tell her. And he couldn't tell her about his foot either—how he knew he was going to lose it, how he would become one of those guys people glance at with a jolt of pity, trying not to stare. He knew that when they fixed him up with a metal limb he would be out of the infantry, and he needed Helena to know that without her, without the army, he would have nothing.

Instead of speaking, Kit kissed the top of her head and played with her hair until she fell asleep against him. Exhausted, body aching, still half-drunk, Kit fell asleep, too.

He woke up when she opened the dusty motel blinds and let the sun into the room. When the light exploded across his retinas, he thought he was back in his tent in Baghdad, unhurt and whole, but when he put his hand over his eyes he felt every muscle of his body throb from a combination of being thrown by a bull and thrown by tequila, and he realized where he was.

Helena turned toward him, dressed in dark jeans and a tank top, her hands on her hips. "I should have made you drink more water."

Kit glanced around the room and saw her suitcase packed and ready on her unmade bed. He saw his crutches leaning against the far wall.

"Should I leave the rental car?" Helena continued quickly, checking under her bed. "I could take a cab. But the rental place is at the airport so it's really best if I drop it off now. Maybe one of your friends can drive you to the storage unit for your truck?"

Kit tried to sit and agony blossomed up his left foot. "You're not still leaving—"

"I got you a bagel and some Gatorade; that should help with the hangover."

"Helena, sit down. Talk to me." He had meant to tell her about the lists he used to make, how each one of them made him realize how much he needed her, and how could he go back to a life without her now that he had categorized everything that made life with her so good?

She reached for her suitcase. "I really have to go. Call my mom's house when you get your cell phone activated." She took a step toward the door. "The room is paid until tomorrow; I didn't know when you'd want to check out."

Kit leaned over the bedside table and used it to help him stand up, sucking in his breath. "Wait."

But the door was open and Helena stood in the shaft of bright light, looking at him over her shoulder, her hair lit up like flame, her hand still on the knob.

"We'll talk soon," she said, the click of cracked glass shimmering through her voice. "I promise."

Kit made a move toward the door, throwing himself at it, hoping something would catch him before he hit the ground, a bureau, a chair, anything that would get him out that door, anything that would get him near Helena so he could touch her again, kiss that freckle under her eye and put his arms around her and he would not let her go. But the door shut behind her and there was nothing for Kit to hold on to, nothing to break his fall, and as his knees buckled beneath him he knew with certainty that Helena, that everything, was gone.

GOLD STAR

Josie Schaeffer drove around the commissary parking lot looking for a space. She had forgotten it was payday. She *never* shopped on payday—when the biweekly paycheck was automatically deposited into every soldier's account in the United States Army at the same instant, and therefore into the checkbooks of the forty thousand soldiers' families here at Fort Hood. The parking lot was a tangle of women pushing overflowing shopping carts, kids hanging on to the back or skidding around in wheeled sneakers, pickup trucks with their beds weighed down with toilet paper and diapers.

Checking her watch again, she finally pulled into the empty Gold Star Family designated spot in front. She waited a moment, peering at herself in the mirror, composing her face into what she imagined an ordinary face looked like, tugging her mouth into a smile but then giving up. She knew the spouses walking by with their loaded carts were hesitating, trying not to stare into Josie's window, trading lifted eyebrows with the other women passing. As she got out and locked her car, a white-haired veteran paused by his truck in the Purple Heart Recipient space a few feet away. He was wearing a black baseball cap with VIETNAM embroidered in block letters across the front. He stepped across the yellow line between them, his ropey-veined hand outstretched.

"I'm grateful for your sacrifice," he said. "Our country can never thank you enough."

He made it sound as if she had willingly offered Eddie up; Josie shuddered but gave the man her hand. This is why she avoided the Gold Star spot: "Gold Star," with its imagery of schoolchildren receiving As and stickers for a job well done, was the military euphemism for losing a soldier in combat. Family members received a few special privileges like this lousy parking space, but that meant the pity rising from the asphalt singed hotter than any Texas sun. Josie blinked to keep her eyes dry and the vet took a step back, seeing he had inflicted pain. "I'm sorry," he whispered.

Inside, the commissary was even more packed than the parking lot; shoppers inched their carts forward, each aisle a halting four-car pileup. Josie moved through the crush, keeping her oversized sunglasses on, hoping no one would recognize her. She glanced at the shelves and tried to remember how to feed a man. It was easier than she thought it would be—the items that her husband once craved stood out and she carefully filled her basket: a loaf of crusty French bread, a package of Swiss cheese, a wand of salami, half a pound of roast beef, a bag of tortilla chips, a jar of hot Tex-Mex salsa.

A soldier had called her about an hour ago, leaving a nervous, rambling message on her machine. "This is Specialist Murphy, ma'am. You don't know me but I was hoping I could come and see you sometime, if that's convenient with you. It's just, um, you see, I knew your husband." At that point Josie lifted her head from the couch. "Sergeant Schaeffer, your husband, well, I was with him the day the IED went off," the voice continued as she reached for the phone.

"Come over for lunch. Can you do that?" she asked abruptly.

"Ma'am? You mean today?"

Josie nodded into the phone, as if he could see her. "Today, as soon as you can."

"Um, okay—I mean yes, ma'am. I'll be finished with my physical training at thirteen hundred hours. Is that all right?"

Josie looked around the cluttered kitchen with its unwashed dishes, the stacks of newspapers and books covering her dining room table, the laundry she had washed the week before and piled up on her couch, still not folded. She had two hours before one o'clock and no food in the house.

"That would be fine," she said.

Back from the commissary with her groceries, Josie heaved all the rumpled clothes onto her bed and then did the same with the piled books and newspapers. She hesitated in front of the mirror over her bureau. Grief had disfigured her. There were bags under her eyes that never faded even when the crying finally did; her shoulders were curled into themselves as if she were trying to keep something fragile and cracked safe inside her ribs; and the weight she'd lost in the past three months had exacerbated the creases in her forehead and around her mouth. So aged at twenty-six. She brushed her bangs down over her eyebrows, pulled her dark hair into a ponytail, and checked her T-shirt for stains. She couldn't remember if she had showered yesterday, but at least her hair wasn't greasy and her clothes seemed relatively clean.

In the first weeks after Eddie's death, there had been visitors, soldiers who came to her apartment and sat uncomfortably on the edge of her chairs. She almost hated the smooth-faced boys, each one of them alive, able to run their five-mile physical training at dawn, go to a Burger King drive-through, catch a movie, get picked up for a DUI. Able to do anything. They seemed to sense her blame, never accepting her offers of coffee or potato chips, afraid to look her in the eye, rarely speaking to her other than the army requisite "ma'am." But they stayed in her home for hours, waiting to be relieved by another soldier, as if acting on direct orders from their chain of command to keep guard. She knew they were there to ensure that she didn't starve to death or slit her wrists in the shower; they also ensured that she didn't stay in her bedroom with the covers over her head, weeping and compulsively remembering every moment of Eddie that she could. She had to exist because the soldiers sat on her couch and watched Fox News. They had known her husband, how disciplined and focused he was, and so she changed her clothes each day, vacuumed the rugs, wiped cola spills off the countertops.

There were also wives who timidly knocked on her door, first the CARE team led by the chaplain's wife, then wives from the FRG whom she recognized from past military balls and barbecues. But Josie had always kept herself apart, sure that she and Eddie would be out of the army soon and any military friendships would be a waste of time. The wives, too stunned to smile or speak, had stared at Josie, seeing their own worst nightmare. They made up for their silence with food, tons of it, exquisite meals or simple casseroles that Josie couldn't stomach, and they left bereavement cards on her table that Josie wouldn't read. She wanted to tell the women to go home and be kind to their husbands instead of wasting their time with her. *Take care of your man*, she would have liked to say, whispering, *Take care before it's too late.*

But the soldier coming over today was someone she wanted to meet. She wanted him to talk about her husband, to tell her a story so she could picture Eddie again, his wide mouth, his square fingers tapping his knee, his blond hair catching the sun as he tipped his head back in laughter. Already the Eddie in her mind was looking too much like the photos in the apartment, frozen and posed and still.

It was the moments in between that she was the most afraid of forgetting, the moments that were too ordinary for photographs, the small memories, like waking up with him in the morning, how he held his knife and fork when he ate dinner, the concentration in his blue eyes when he did a crossword puzzle, his feet propped up on the coffee table. Or the way he walked in after a week-long training exercise and sat down on the couch to take off his boots. She would climb up into his lap, put her arms around his neck, and press her face into his chest and stay there as he rubbed his stubbled chin over the back of her head. She could smell all the days he had been away in his uniform, the dirt from the field and the burned smokiness of his sweat, the thin smell of gasoline from his Humvee and the oil he used to clean his rifle. He would put his big hands around her back and she felt enclosed in his strength and knew he was hers again, at least for a little while. But now she had forgotten the texture of his uniform under her cheek, the sound of his boots slipping off his feet and hitting the floor, the feel of his fingertips on her back. She was losing him all over again.

"Hello, ma'am," the soldier said. He held a bouquet of carnations and his face didn't know whether to grin or look somber. "I'm Specialist Murphy. Kit Murphy, ma'am."

"Kit, please call me Josie," she said, opening the door farther, taking in the sight of him. He was young, twenty or twenty-one, tall and bony, his uniform loose around the shoulders and waist as if he had not always been so thin. His skin was the grayish white of a wet piece of paper and there were dark smudges under his eyes. It wasn't until he stepped across the threshold that she noticed his limp and peered at his left foot and the black ski-boot contraption. Then she realized who he was. Two months after Eddie's funeral, the army held a memorial service, awarding him the Bronze Star with the "V" for Valor, suddenly claiming he had saved someone's life. Josie didn't go. Eddie's father had flown down from Michigan to accept the decoration, taking it home with him. That was also around the time the soldiers stopped standing guard over Josie and the wives no longer brought food, as if the community had ascertained she was no longer a risk to herself. Without their vigilance, Josie started just stretching out on her couch all day.

"Are those for me?" she asked Kit.

He looked down at the flowers in his right hand as if they didn't belong to him, and his pale cheeks turned red, making him look almost healthy. "Yes, ma'am," he said. "I thought I should bring something . . ."

"They're very nice." Josie took the dangling bouquet from his hand. The smell of the flowers made her think of wet dirt thumping down on the coffin, black high heels that pinched her toes, and the Kleenex that disintegrated into pulp as she rubbed it against her eyes. She had tried to be a dignified widow but was barely able to breathe during "Taps."

Josie found a dusty vase in the kitchen and called out to the soldier, who still stood in her living room. "I hope you like roast beef?"

Kit nodded and walked toward her, pausing in front of all the frames. She had gone through their albums and removed her favorites, putting Eddie wherever she could—on the dining room table, the television set, nailed into the four walls—so that wherever she turned, he would be looking at her.

"Sergeant Schaeffer was the best noncommissioned officer I ever met," he said softly, picking up a photo of Eddie from his Ranger School graduation, forty pounds thinner than he'd been before Ranger School, his cheekbones sharp slabs.

Josie put a plate of sandwiches and a jug of instant iced tea on the table. Her hands were shaking and the tea sloshed against the rim.

"He loved his job, ma'am," Kit continued. "He made other people love their job, including me." He put down the photo and eased into a chair, sitting in front of the sandwiches and taking one before Josie had time to get out the napkins and plates. "He would say things like, 'There is an entire video game industry trying to copy what you men get paid to do every day,' or 'You defend your country, you carry a gun, you blow things up, what do you have to complain about, soldier?'" Kit laughed with his mouth full, his eyes on the photos ahead of him.

Josie poured sweet tea into a tall glass and slid it across the table. This wasn't what she wanted to hear. Eddie had been planning on submitting his exit paperwork when he got home from Baghdad. He could have gotten out of the army the previous year; his commitment was up five months before the deployment to Iraq, and Josie had been jubilant. But then he told her he couldn't leave his platoon right before they went to war—it was as if they had all been training for the state championships and now that the practice was over and the big game was here, he was abandoning them. "It's not a game," Josie had said. But Eddie didn't listen. It had been a fight that raged for days. She threatened to leave him, asked who was he really married to, damn it, her or his men?

That was why they had no kids—she wasn't going to have a child who only saw his daddy every other year. For the five years they'd been together she had used that argument against him, knowing that eventually Eddie would want a kid more than he'd want the army, he would get out, and she would win. And then Eddie was dead a month before coming home to her, and there would never be a child now.

That was what her bargaining had got her.

"I want to hear about the IED," Josie said, sitting down across from Kit, balling up a napkin in her hands. "Nobody would tell me the details."

Kit swallowed his mouthful and took a huge gulp of his tea. Josie wondered when he had eaten last.

"He saved my life," Kit said softly, looking into his glass. There were crumbs on his chin.

"Did he *mean* to save your life?" Josie could feel her voice rise with that edge it had taken on lately when she spoke on the phone with Eddie's father, who seemed proud of his son for dying, for getting blown up thousands of miles from home on a roadside in the middle of nowhere, his blood soaking into another country's sand. "Did he know he was saving you?"

Kit moved uncomfortably in his chair and didn't look at her. "We were trapped in our Humvee and his body protected me from the flame, ma'am. It was almost like he was hugging me to keep me out of the fire."

"Almost like?"

Kit put his glass of tea down carefully. He kept his eyes on the table and blinked, sucking in his cheeks so that he looked even more starved and sickly. Then he lifted his face and his wet eyes finally looked into Josie's. "I don't mean any disrespect, ma'am, but does it matter? I'm alive because of your husband. He was the best soldier I knew and he saved my life."

She hesitated. There were so many arguments in her head, angry words to toss at this man in front of her, denials and recriminations. The first reports Josie had heard said her husband died instantly in the blast. No heroism, just death. But if Eddie had deliberately saved this boy's life, then he had deliberately sacrificed his own; he had been conscious and in agony, and he had known he was leaving her behind.

They sat for a while in silence, Josie holding her napkin. Kit with his hands on the table next to his half-eaten sandwich. He cleared his throat. "I would have been at the memorial service but I was still in the hospital in Germany. I'm real sorry I missed that."

Josie shrugged. "I wasn't there either. The funeral was bad enough."

Kit nodded once, as if he understood pain was something you lived with as best you could.

"Thank you for lunch." He took a piece of paper out of a pocket on his sleeve and handed it to Josie. "Here's my cell phone number. Please call me if there's anything I can do. I'm pretty busted up but I can still take out the garbage and open jars of pasta sauce or whatever it is they say men do better than women." He tried to smile, a half smile that didn't touch his eyes.

"Wait," Josie said, standing. "Don't leave yet." She glanced around the kitchen. "I'll wrap these sandwiches so you can take them with you. I'll never eat all this food." But instead of getting out the tinfoil, she stepped around the table and stood in front of him, her thigh almost touching his bent knees. Kit looked at her, alarmed, as if she might hit him or kick his wounded foot.

Before he could get out of his chair, she sat down in his lap.

"Ma'am, um, I have to be back at Headquarters—"

"Shhhh," Josie whispered, linking her fingers around his neck. She pressed her face into the stiff folds of his uniform and felt the Velcro of his rank against her cheek. She tried to smell her husband, but this uniform was too clean, too new, this soldier too thin and fragile, so rigid in the chair, sucking in his breath. But Josie held on, the camouflage material swimming in front of her eyes, the back of his neck smooth.

After a dazed moment, Specialist Kit Murphy put his arms loosely around her and Josie Schaeffer clung to him, knowing this man was not her husband, that her husband was never coming back, but for now she was as close to him as she could get and she would not let him go.

Questions

1. Why doesn't Kit wake up Helena if he wants to talk to her, rather than hope she wakes up to the noise of the TV or his tapping on his cast?

2. Why does Kit limit his list of things he misses about his wife to concrete, small things related to an orderly home?

3. Should Kit have worked harder to persuade Helena to try to preserve the marriage?

4. Why does Helena tell Kit about the baby the night before she leaves him for good?

5. Are any of the difficulties in Kit and Helena's relationship unique to servicemen and their spouses?

6. Why does Kit go to visit Josie?

7. Why is it important to Josie whether Eddie had meant to save Kit's life?

8. In dealing with grief over the loss of someone in combat, is it beneficial or harmful to know as many of the details of their death as possible?

Brian Humphreys

A platoon commander with the Second Battalion, Seventh Marines, Second Lieutenant Brian Humphreys (1972–) served in the vicinity of Hit, Iraq, for seven months, beginning in February 2004. After surviving his first ambush, Humphreys described his visceral response to the incident once it was over:

> We have been under fire for nearly an hour and a half. We have fired over 2,500 rounds at enemy positions not more than fifty yards from our vehicles. None of my Marines has been hit. None of the vehicles has been hit. Not a broken windshield. Not a dent in an armored panel. Nothing. We have fought for our lives, and can scarcely believe it. *Did that just happen?* I think as we pull out of the traffic circle to the south, our weapons pointed in every direction, our pulses pounding. Another thought enters my mind before I have the chance to shut it out: *That was fucking awesome.*

Humphreys is hardly alone in writing about the initial thrill of being in a war zone. As with previous American conflicts, troops on the front lines frequently wrote in their journals and letters (and now e-mails) about the almost intoxicating rush they experienced during their first days and weeks in-country. And for many combatants, whether they fought in the Civil War, World War II, Korea, Vietnam, Desert Storm, Afghanistan, or Iraq, these feelings often changed over time. They would for Humphreys as well, as reflected in the following personal narrative.

Humphreys left active duty in 2006 and served in the Marine Reserve as a civil affairs officer until 2010. He is now a PhD candidate in political science at Rutgers University, currently doing dissertation research in Amman, Jordan, on the development of the new Iraqi Army and its national identity following the fall of the old regime.

VETERANS

Bang, Bang, Bang. The sheet-metal door amplifies the sound of the large fist striking it. Sergeant Graham is standing in the doorway, silhouetted by the white-hot afternoon sunlight.

"Sir, we have a unit in contact, two friendly KIA. The platoon is getting ready downstairs."

"You've got to be shitting me" is my first response after being woken out of a sound sleep. Death has visited us before, but it is not ubiquitous enough to have lost its shock value. I throw my uniform and flak jacket on, grab my rifle, and head down a flight of stairs. The platoon is already on the vehicles, ready to roll with an ambulance.

"Interrogative, are you still in contact?" I ask by radio as my column of Humvees speeds north.

"Negative," comes the reply. *That guy always has an impeccable bearing even in one word*, I think to myself while watching the sides of the road for wires and triggermen. He is the company executive officer. I am the boot lieutenant. The Marine Corps has yet to beat my slovenly tendencies out of me. Fate, cruel as it is, put us in the same company together.

The palm groves to our east that line the Euphrates River whip by. To the west of the asphalt ribbon are the scorched wadis used by insurgents to stage their attacks. Up ahead I see the telltale cluster of Humvees and Marines. I pull up to the first vehicle and find the patrol leader.

"Where do you want the ambulance?" I ask.

"Just have it pull up, we'll guide it in," he replies, as if we have arrived to help fix a flat tire. The ambulance in the middle of my six-vehicle column pulls forward, and I get out to find where the casualties are.

"What the hell is that?" I ask a Marine. Perhaps the explosion had somehow killed a farm animal of some sort who wandered out on the road. A sheep maybe? Or a cow. No, not big enough. Well, what is that and how did it happen? The Marine gives his buddy's name and asks me to help find his head. *Fuck.*

We do not want the stray dogs that occupy Iraq with us to find our brothers. The corpsmen, with their blue latex gloves and body bags, scour the bushes for the last scraps of human tissue as waves of heat rise from the desert. The Associated Press dutifully reports that three Marines were killed in Al Anbar province in Iraq. Names have not been released by the Defense Department pending notification of next of kin. We will not read the two-sentence notice for several days. The Internet Room is always padlocked while we wait for somebody to get a knock on the door half a world away.

At one point the casualties got so bad that it seemed the room was closed for a week at a time while notifications were made. Iraq is coming apart at the seams. Pictures of flag-draped coffins being unloaded from air force transports surface on the back reaches of the Internet, as if they were a grainy celebrity sex video that decent people should avoid looking at. But I think otherwise. The images of flag-draped coffins show the end of war as we are meant to see it, and as we are meant to believe it. Uniforms, flags, patriotism, honor, sacrifice. In these images we are not street fighters struggling to survive and kill in a distant gangland, but soldiers in the nation's service. They will help the families, I think. They will help us. In our own way, we too, need to believe.

Today, the Marines will have to wait to log on to their chat rooms, HotOrNot.com, MilitarySingles.com, and the online shopping sites. I myself have become something of a spendthrift in Iraq, ordering more books and CDs than I normally would. I have seen death enough times among people who had been indestructibly living only the day before. It is better to go ahead and buy the CD you have been meaning to get. There are reminders wherever you care to look. For instance, the pile of blood-soaked flak jackets sitting in the company's combat operations center, a low-tech jumble of maps and radios. The flak jackets' owners are either dead or in the hospital recovering from their wounds.

The executive officer reminds us that the flak jackets need to be sent back through the Marine Corps's supply chain as soon as possible. Somewhere, somebody will wash them and inspect them for damage, filling out all the necessary paperwork. It is the banality, even more than the carnage, that shocks. Our occupation grinds on. Others will assign meaning to our lives here, noble or otherwise. For us, though, there is a close meanness to the fight. There are no flags, no dress uniforms. We are fighting a rival gang for the same turf, while the neighborhood residents cower and wait to see whose side they should come out on.

Imperceptibly, we are coming to the end of our deployment. Time has stood still for months, with days and nights fusing together in the burning hot air of the desert. But now, our deployment is being measured in finite units of time. It takes getting used to.

Echo Company will remain in our forward operating base as a deterrent to the insurgents, but otherwise will have no dealings with the Iraqi people. Our only other mission is to keep our own supply lines open. One of the lieutenants jokes acidly that he knows a way to shorten our supply lines by fifteen thousand miles. Our forward operating base is still the target of the occasional mortar shell. Sometimes, if we are asleep, we do not even wake up, but death never quite leaves us, still creeping along the highways and wadis as we wear out the days.

Returning from a patrol with my platoon, I find a blue sedan riddled with bullet holes on the side of the highway. There are a few Iraqi soldiers standing around when we find it. We quickly learn the car belonged to Captain Laithe, one of the senior men in the local police force. Connected, calculating, and English-speaking, he had collaborated with the Americans since the fall of Baghdad. I've wondered since I first met him why he cast his lot with us, what calculation he made, and whether we could even understand it—what mix of nobility and venality it contained. His future, however he imagined it, ended with the finality of death in a hail of bullets on the highway less than a mile from our forward operating base.

Not long before we leave, I am awakened out of a sound sleep again, this time at midnight. The company executive officer is at the door. We have another KIA. I feel the same shock I did the first time, only a certain numbness has developed, like a nerve deadened by repeated blows. Our turn had almost passed, and now this. I nod, and begin collecting my gear. One of my fellow platoon commanders is outside in the pitch black. It is the body of one of his Marines that we will go out in the dead of night to recover. I ask him if he is all right. I ask him if his Marines are all right. The worst thing, he says, is that by now they are used to it. It is better and worse at the same time. I realize that we have all come to accept the loss of familiar faces, to live with it, and cross the line of departure again the next morning. It is this acceptance, rather than the thud of hidden bombs, that has finally made us veterans, and will finish the words on the obscure page of history we occupy.

We head off in the pitch black, navigating the highway through the grainy green glow of our night-vision goggles. We move north to a point just north of the place where we lost the two Marines in the bomb explosion months before. One of the Humvees in the patrol struck a land mine a short distance from the Iraqi National Guard post the Marines had been tasked with protecting.

The sun is rising above the river palm groves when the trucks arrive to remove the wrecked vehicle. The dead Marine's remains are loaded in another truck and driven north toward Al Asad Air Base. The remains will be laid in a flag-draped coffin and then secured in the cargo hold of a transport plane to be flown back to the United States. We, too, will soon go to Al Asad. We will then strap ourselves into the cargo hold of an identical plane to begin our own journey home. The scrawled memorials on barracks walls to fallen buddies will stay behind for the troops who replace us. They might read the awkwardly worded poems and epitaphs written in loving memory, and half-wonder who we were.

In the beginning of September 2004, Echo Company is finally packing up to leave, and Humphreys concludes his journal with the following entry.

We are flying out of Iraq tonight, seven months after we arrived to crush the insurgency. We are leaving. The insurgents will remain behind without us. The contents of my pack and seabag are on the floor. To the left and right of me, fifty-five other Marines—privates, sergeants, and officers—have also dumped their worldly belongings onto painted squares for inspection by military police at Al Asad Air Base. Somehow, every transition in the Marine Corps involves dumping your trash on the deck. The first night of boot camp the drill instructors rooted through our measly belongings, the relics of the civilian world we were leaving behind. They used white latex gloves, as if they might catch something from the sticks of beef jerky and playing cards.

The military police just use black leather gloves. They do a perfunctory search for contraband, as defined by the First Marine Division on the "this-means-you" poster plastered to the wall. No lottery tickets or advertisements. No flags of foreign countries not manufactured for sale or distribution. No lizard hides. No sex toys. No rocks of any sort, no matter how sentimental. No shrapnel. No personal effects of enemy soldiers, to include body parts.

The drill instructors guarding the gates of the corps were meant to keep us from bringing the civilian world into the war world. The military police are here to make sure we take nothing from the war world back, except ourselves. Many of the Marines are short-timers, with only a few months left in the corps. They will return home and cross back over to the other side to continue their lives with friends who barely noticed they were gone.

For the rest of us, Iraq will be waiting for our return. We can leave, but the country and its war will remain. The war that began after the president's Mission Accomplished speech is too diffuse for us to make a noticeable mark on it. There is no end to where we are going. There is no Berlin, no Tokyo out there for us to push toward. We are simply part of a larger historical process that unfolds slowly and unpredictably, like rising smoke. How long the fire underneath us will smolder, or what the earth will look like when it has exhausted itself, is impossible to know for those of us who are in it.

The flight attendants on the chartered 747 parked at the edge of Kuwait City International Airport greet us with hand clapping and squealed congratulations. I grunt some type of reply and make for a window seat. Back home, Sunday football kicks off with flags, uniforms, and exhortations to support our brave troops serving overseas, and to remember those who have made the Ultimate Sacrifice. I wonder numbly whether I am expected to bask in the adulation. I am weary. We fought. We survived, but some did not.

I do not need to be told to remember.

Questions

1. According to Humphreys, how do "images of flag-draped coffins show the end of war as we are meant to see it"? (460) Why does he think that these images can help those who have been in combat?

2. Why does the "banality, even more than the carnage" of combat operations shock Humphreys? (460–461)

3. What does the platoon commander mean when he says that getting used to the death of comrades is "better and worse at the same time"? (462) Does serving effectively on the battlefield require becoming used to the loss of life?

4. Why does Humphreys think that the acceptance of the death of comrades "has finally made us veterans"? (462)

5. What does Humphreys mean when he says, about himself and his fellow Marines, "We are simply part of a larger historical process that unfolds slowly and unpredictably"? (463) Is this view of war comforting or disturbing?

Parker Gyokeres

Family members of Staff Sergeant Parker Gyokeres (1973–) served in every major American conflict since, in his words, "the defense of Jamestown in 1609." Gyokeres himself was deployed to Iraq to provide "force protection" for the air base in Tallil from November 2003 through March 2004 with the U.S. Air Force's 332nd Fighter Wing. His younger brother, Zachary, also a staff sergeant in the Air Force, was assigned as a flight engineer on a combat rescue helicopter in Afghanistan shortly before Parker left for Iraq. During his five months in Tallil, Parker Gyokeres wrote hundreds of pages of journals, all of which he e-mailed to his wife, relatives, and other loved ones back home. Gyokeres downplayed the risks he faced, and the majority of his journals detailed the more offbeat and humorous incidents that helped him endure the monotony of life on an air base in the middle of the desert. But there are also moments in his journals when the true nature of war reveals itself in all its cruelty. Perhaps the most serious of his entries is the final one, which, even after he e-mailed it to friends and family months after returning home, he continued to edit. Gyokeres was no longer writing for them. He was writing for himself.

Gyokeres cross-trained into the public affairs career field in 2006 after "a three-year struggle to convince the Air Force that I may be a better writer than bomb loader." He is now a tech sergeant stationed at Joint Base McGuire-Dix-Lakehurst as a photojournalist with the 621st Contingency Response Wing.

THE HARDEST LETTER TO WRITE

Hello all,

This has been, by far, the hardest letter to write. I returned home to the dichotomy of being universally welcomed with open, respectful, grateful arms—by a country that is increasingly against why I was ever in Iraq. I performed my mission well and have great pride in my actions, and those of my peers, but I can also understand why people are questioning if there is any long-term hope for Iraq and its people. The reason we were sent there in the first place will require a lot more study, but that's another book for another person.

The main issue for me has been adjusting to a life without the dear friends I served with and whom I grew to love—and, without whom, I felt lost, alone, and unable to relate to others. I am told this is normal. That did not, however, make it easier. And I know I'm doing better than many for whom I care deeply. They hide it well, but they are struggling.

The world I returned to was disorienting, confusing, and frustrating to me. The racket and clutter of daily life gave me a tremendous headache. I now know why some people choose to simply unplug and move into the woods. Obviously we heard our share of noise in Iraq, some of it sudden and terrifying, but overall it wasn't so incessant. Wherever I walk today I feel like I'm surrounded by a barrage of electronic trash—music blasting everywhere, cell phones ringing, people chatting away and having the most inane conversations, and all of it louder than when I left for Iraq. Over there, we had the comforting simplicity of a routine. There was a purity to our lives. There were life-and-death implications to our actions, but all we had to worry about was our friends and ourselves. I'm not saying that either we or our jobs are any better or worse than anyone else's back here, but just different. I'm slowly acclimating to a civilian world and the speed of modern life, but it has not always been pleasant.

For a while I truly wished I was still in Iraq. As much as I looked forward to leaving, when I got back to the U.S. a part of me wanted to return immediately. My wife was upset to hear me say that, for a while, I preferred a war zone to a home life. Again, I am not alone. Some of my friends and other returning veterans I know have talked about this as well. Departing Tallil was like leaving a family. We also left behind memories, some of them beautiful and some horrific, that left a deep impression on us.

Traumatic, life-changing, or profoundly spiritual events can bond people together in ways that are hard to explain. My friends and I shared all three. I do not want to overstate my own situation or suggest I was in grave danger. I was not. But there are experiences I had and things I saw that were extremely disturbing. The worst, by far, came only two days after we arrived at Tallil, when I had my first opportunity to work in our visitor control center at the base. I had been on duty for only a few hours when a call came over the radio that there was a local ambulance en route to pick up an Iraqi bombing casualty. Moments later an Army Humvee arrived carrying two soldiers who identified themselves as the ones tasked to meet the ambulance. They explained to me that they were there to transfer to the Iraqis a body—the body of an eight-week-old infant killed by a bomb set off by insurgents.

I will never forget the sight of those soldiers reaching into a grossly oversized body bag, folded into quarters, and then removing a package no bigger than a travel pillow. It was anointed in oils and wrapped in ceremonial muslin dressings for a religious burial. Instantly a hush fell over the small group as the child was gently carried from the back of that beaten-down, ugly Humvee and solemnly placed on a nest of blankets inside the Iraqi ambulance. Both vehicles then slowly pulled away, leaving a semicircle of terribly scarred people in its wake. I felt like somebody had punched me hard in the stomach.

You do not forget moments like these.

Just over a week later, a critically wounded man arrived at the base in a gutted Iraqi ambulance with four other men. One of his companions, whom we were told was his brother, whispered into his ear, and held the man's head and smoothed his matted hair, while he rocked back and forth, clearly in great emotional distress. The man's injuries were sickening. His hands were stumps, and all his wounds were terribly infected. His breathing was very slow, increasingly labored, and punctuated with large, gasping heaves. There were black flies everywhere, and he looked sallow, sunken, and transparent, a husk of a man covered in fresh scabs and badly drawn tattoos. I recognized some of the tattoos as those of the infamous Fedayeen, the brutal terror thugs of Saddam's regime. If there was ever a "Bad" guy I would encounter in my life, those tattoos told me all I needed to know. Here was a man who looked fifty but was probably only thirty, and would never see thirty-one. He had lived a hard life and would meet a hard death, and I stood and watched, without remorse.

One of my fellow force protection escorts (who is a medic at Wilford Hall, the AF's largest hospital) did an appraisal. While snapping off her gloves, she said, "This man is going to die whether he's given treatment or not, and there isn't a single thing any hospital can do about it. It's too late." It was a brutal statement, totally lacking in compassion, but it was an honest and logical one that we all at the time readily accepted. There was one among us, however, who felt that even if the man was going to die, he wasn't beyond mercy. As the first medic climbed out of the ambulance, the second one quietly placed gloves on her hands and with grim determination climbed *into* that reeking, fly-infested, and urine-soaked ambulance, alone. She looked at us with cold flint in her eyes, as if *daring* us to do something different, and began waving a small piece of cardboard over the dying man's face to keep the flies away. As we stood there stunned by her compassion, she began to do the unthinkable, as a small, lone female in a vehicle full of hostile, frustrated Muslim men. She began to pray for him.

As I realized what she was up to, I became concerned for her safety—a little at first, and then more so as each second passed. She was female, and if these men became offended it would be very hard to get her out of that ambulance uninjured. As I moved closer to the door of the ambulance to reach in and snatch her out if things went south, I discreetly slid my weapon sling into my hands, behind my back. The men asked our interpreter what she was doing. He said, "Praying." Immediately, they all laughed out loud at her for being so foolish. Our interpreter shot back at them, "No, no, don't laugh, she's doing this because she believes only God can help him. She's trying to help your brother. Where is your faith?"

At that, the men instantly fell silent and looked chastened. The man's brother shakily took off his shoes and knelt inside the tiny ambulance with his forehead against the filthy floor and began to pray for his dying brother. The other three took off their shoes where they stood, amongst at least fifteen armed escorts, medics, and translators, and knelt on the ground in the direction of Mecca and began to pray to Allah. The fearless faith of one person changed the hearts of four angry men with a single silent prayer. Those men were humbled and suddenly very different as they prayed fervently to Allah.

Later, when I asked her how she could do what she did, all alone and oblivious to her safety, she said to me in a strong voice, "I *wasn't alone* in that ambulance."

It took a week of wearing a mask of brittle bravado for me to finally begin talking with my friends about what I had seen. I had been furious with God for allowing so much pain into our world, for allowing people to act like soulless animals and kill infants, for allowing all of this to happen in the first place, and I felt physically sick having witnessed what evils man is capable of. The courage of this extraordinary woman gave me something to cling to.

These are the people I left behind.

Many of us also came to admire and even love some of the Iraqis we met. Yes, there were troops who grew to distrust and hate them, especially as tensions escalated and it was harder to tell the good guys from the bad guys. But a lot of us had very positive experiences with the locals. They genuinely wanted us to remember them as happy, intelligent, fun-loving people and, most importantly, as friends. I have heard many times, "You need to come back years from now and visit us with your family." To be torn from a place that has become so much a part of your own life and where so many intense memories are rooted is much harder than people might imagine.

As difficult as things were when I got home, sitting here now I fully realize how blessed I am—and was over there. Our base in Tallil was relatively safe, far from constant mortar attacks, car bombs, and truly wicked people trying to do desperate, vicious things to us. Others had it much, much worse. They are the true heroes of this war. And they are the ones I think of most as I write this.

One friend of mine at Tallil, who was very full of life and sang in the little church choir we had organized, was temporarily transferred to a base closer to Baghdad and in a considerably more dangerous area. When I saw her again, it was as if only her ghost had returned. She never came back to the church—or to us. She pretty much kept to herself, and it was painful to watch this once gregarious woman become so distant and reserved. Others reached out to her, but to no avail.

I saw her in passing one day, and I finally asked her how she was doing. I was genuinely interested to hear the truth, her truth; for it was obvious that there was a real event, or perhaps many, that had caused her to withdraw. She suddenly grew dark, and a cold expression, like the sudden remembrance of a lost loved one, came across her face. Instantly I knew I had screwed up and had carelessly trampled on an unseen line. I wanted to take it back, but it was too late. The awkward silence was broken by her curt reply, which, in so many words, was not only her answer to the question but an indication that the conversation was over entirely: "I don't want to talk about it." She then turned and walked away.

We never spoke again.

In hindsight, and knowing the subject might still be raw, I should have waited before asking—or given her time to approach me or someone else. Until I came home and watched as other friends wrestled with their emotions, it was the first time I had seen how debilitating weeks of trauma and stress can be. It was a sobering realization, and I wondered how many others like her have we created in these last few years? How many others live with the shocking and barbaric images of war that are seared into one's memory forever? I pray that they will find someone they can confide in and unload this burden so that the pain they carry with them is lessened over time. My writing gave me an outlet while I was over there, and it continues to help me now.

I was fortunate not only because I had it easy compared to so many other troops, but because my wife supported me during my angry, confused, and sleepless times. I cannot thank her enough for this, and she has always been there for me and never stopped loving me. This is all that matters, and I do not want to leave her again or make her go through all the anxieties and worries that she silently endured as well. My wife could not understand how I could become so close to people I had served with for such a relatively short period, and she was upset about my apparent inability to leave it all behind. But it was for my own well-being that she was concerned, and not out of jealousy. Most importantly, she knew when to listen and when to let me work through my emotions.

This is perhaps the most important thing any loved one or friend can do. Those of us coming back from Iraq or Afghanistan are not looking for sympathy. We might be reluctant at first to talk about what we've been through, good or bad, and some troops might never be able to open up, which is certainly their right. There are also things about war that people will never comprehend unless they have experienced them firsthand. But I hope that those who need to will reach out, and it's helpful knowing that there are people who care about us and are at least making an effort to understand.

Your support has made this journey an incredible one for me, and I couldn't have gone through it alone. Thanks for joining me—and thanks, above all, for listening.

Parker

Questions

1. Why is Gyokeres's letter about returning home harder for him to write than the letters he wrote while serving in Iraq?

2. Why does Gyokeres find the world he returns to so "disorienting, confusing, and frustrating"? What does he mean when he says there was a "purity to our lives" in Iraq? (467)

3. Why does the medic say, "I *wasn't alone* in that ambulance"? (470) How do her actions help Gyokeres come to terms with his anger over the human violence he sees around him?

4. When Gyokeres asks his friend who has returned from Baghdad how she is doing, why does her expression make him think he has "carelessly trampled on an unseen line"? (471)

5. Do you think Gyokeres is right when he says that there are "things about war that people will never comprehend unless they have experienced them firsthand"? (472)

6. How can family members and friends help returning warriors cope with missing the people they served with?

Michael Poggi

While some troops adjust relatively easily to postwar life and even express a desire to return to Iraq or Afghanistan, many struggle with everything from flashbacks, frequent nightmares, and aggressive behavior to substance abuse, persistent depression, and thoughts of suicide. Some veterans don't even realize that they are suffering from posttraumatic stress disorder (PTSD) until they have a total breakdown.

As a member of the elite First Reconnaissance Battalion, First Marine Division, Michael Poggi (1975–) fought in Iraq as part of a team of "ambush hunters" whose mission was to seek and destroy enemy forces lying in wait for U.S. convoys. When Poggi came back to the United States in the summer of 2003, he saw many of his friends afflicted by PTSD, and he knew that he, too, was affected by his months of intense combat. Poggi found it cathartic to write about the psychological repercussions of war, and a year after he returned home he wrote the following story, which is based on real events and characters but is not, he emphasizes, purely autobiographical.

Poggi was promoted to sergeant in 2004 and deployed with Operation Enduring Freedom to Afghanistan with Marine Special Operations Command (MARSOC) in 2007. After he returned in 2008, he served as an instructor for individual training and sniper courses before deploying to Afghanistan again in 2011. In 2012, as a gunnery sergeant, he transferred to one of the MARSOC battalions, and in 2013 deployed to Afghanistan for a third time.

Along with his many ongoing work commitments in the Marines, Poggi completed his bachelor's degree in 2010 and, in his own words, "still dabbles in short fiction."

SHALLOW HANDS

I've been drinking steadily since coming back from the war. There's a caustic aftertaste in my mouth aggravating the queasiness in my stomach. Making my way through San Diego traffic to get to the airport, I know I shouldn't be driving like this. I park in the overnight lot and walk to the national terminal to catch a flight to Boston. This trip will be the first time I've been home in a long while.

I hate crowds, maybe because I am hung over, or maybe because they make me a critic of all humankind. I just can't help but think people are spoiled lambs walking around with their heads up their hinds, oblivious to the goings-on in the world. It makes me so damn sad. I look around the terminal and see people bitching and moaning about their flights. I don't know any Iraqi kids who complain about waiting for shit; they dream about not getting shot dead or killed by an explosion. Over there is some woman buying her kid a whole damn armful of candy while she holds her cup of Starbucks in the other hand. Some kid in Afghanistan just got his leg blown off by a land mine, but go ahead and pamper your ankle-biters with more shit they don't need! Half the world is starving! I watched people kill each other for dollar bills, why should you care? Fucking lamb.

I have been back from the war for a month. I spent most of it cruising around Southern California, harassing college girls with my tattoo stories and getting drunk. Thankfully I haven't woken up in a pool of urine lately. Nonetheless, I feel more alive than ever. Everything seems so different, so colorful. The sky is so vividly blue and white now, sunsets are beautifully orange, and the ocean a glimmering pool of I don't even know what. I don't ever recall noticing things this much. It's funny what being shot at does to a man. Yet, for some reason I can't stand to be in the presence of people anymore. Little inconveniences rub me raw, those polite phony smiles make me want to rip someone's face off when they say "excuse me" in that perky inaudible voice.

I eye everyone in the terminal as a potential threat, every nook and cranny an ambush. I want to stand in the center of the concourse and scream at the top of my lungs. So loud they burst, so loud all the cigarettes will purge themselves from my body. But I'm too damn tired to stand on a soapbox today; besides, it's a quiet anger, a pearled soreness beneath the breastbone that drives me insane, sore with every breath and with every swallow like the feeling of vomit in your throat. I don't know why I feel the way I do. It's not the booze. I know that for certain. It's something else, something that will have to wait until later. I hand over my ticket and board the plane. As I jostle into my seat, I quickly turn my head toward the window and try to think of other things.

Being there was pure, in the dust storms and blazing heat, the children looking up at you like you were God himself come to deliver them. Things were simple. The enemy is everywhere, hiding in every building, every palm grove, waiting to pounce on you when you let your guard down. The children, tugging at your leg, look up with desperate eyes. They will be slaughtered when they go home for collaborating with us. Still they hang on to the hope that for that brief moment we're there we will save them. Sometimes it is almost a nuisance when they'd crowd the vehicle and follow the patrols. I can't help but pity them; I'd give all I had to them if I could. Instead, it seems we're always leaving them when they need us most.

I landed at Logan International five hours later and took a cab to Bukowski's just off Boylston Avenue, by the Prudential Center. I love that place. No one knows it's there really, its windows naturally blend into the urban foliage, and you can watch the people wandering about on Boylston, oblivious to your observation. A great place for a thought or two, and getting drunk of course. I got smashed there that night. I was supposed to meet this girl I dated for drinks, but she never showed. I ended up calling my brother and my buddy Tim. We proceeded to get drunk. I kicked over a mailbox in front of a cop and began my "lamb" speech to everyone on the road. The cop just gave my brother the old "get him the fuck out of here" look. I nearly fought a few people on the way to the train station. I felt bad that my brother and Tim had to struggle with me to cooperate, but that passed quickly.

A few months before the war, I went to a palm reader. I don't know why, but I thought she might shed some light on things; curiosity, I suppose. I don't remember how she looked, although I remember she wasn't some quack fat lady wearing purple. I do remember how she took my hand, how relaxing it felt when I gave it to her. Holding it gently, brushing the lines with the tips of her fingers, plying it ever so slowly, she told me things about my character I knew were true. Ever since, I look at my hands in a different light. I realize how soft and shallow the lines are, and how odd it is that someone you don't know could shake your hand and tell you when you're going to die; it was all so fascinating. Even if it was all bullshit.

They say the line running from your index finger that follows the fleshy tissue down around your thumb to the midpoint of your palm is the lifeline. It's supposed to tell you how long you'll live. I noticed mine stops halfway. I know a lot of guys in my unit with hands like rocks, deep crevices in them like they've been chapped or windburned for ages. It's supposed to be long. But mine isn't.

After days of drinking, I was strewn out on the floor of my brother's apartment in a bloody mess. When I finally came to in the morning, I felt like killing myself. Not because I was depressed, or regretful, but because I was hallucinating and delirious. I thought I was going crazy. Spiraling down into the void, I stumbled around the apartment, completely disoriented and confused, slamming down water and vitamins, hoping that the delirium would pass, and it did not. I started to scream, first in my head, where the battle was, then out loud. So loud my brother came running down from his bedroom to see what was going on. I can only imagine what he was thinking when he saw me balled up in the corner, quivering and weeping assurances to myself.

It took me two days to get over the breakdown. I just walked around in a trance and sat watching television on the couch. My brother came home from work one afternoon and put an end to it. He sat next to me and told me that our dad had called and wanted to see me. He wanted me to go as soon as possible. I had been waiting for this to happen. I was ashamed to look and feel this way in front of my father.

He had always been proud of my service. He served with the army in Vietnam, and he's seen his share. He was of the old school that seems withering today, one that preaches conservative compassion mixed with blue-collar sense of duty. He taught me about nature, from back when I was a little boy in the car seat pointing at the hawks circling the highways, to the days as a teen when we took long walks in the woods and talked philosophy. The musty pictures of a bearded adventurer line a desk stacked with nature guides and animal skulls, a living tribute to the man. I would spend lots of time at his desk as a kid, picking up and staring at the skulls, reading the guides, and playing with the samurai swords he'd bought so many years ago in Southeast Asia.

Now I was supposed to put myself before his expecting eyes and hide the shame and booze. It was almost too much to bear as I stood on his porch and rang the bell after minutes of hesitation. He opened the door, hugged me in a powerful embrace, and then led me in.

The living room was as I'd remembered it, but the fireplace mantel had been transformed into a shrine to me, and I winced. We moved to the kitchen and sat down for coffee. He could barely contain his excitement, but I could see his intuition told him something was wrong.

"You look good, Tommy," he said, grabbing my shoulder. I thanked him and sipped my coffee, but I knew he was lying. I looked like shit and felt like the sewer.

"So you've been back for a few days I hear. Staying with your brother . . . How's your head?" he asked with a smirk.

"It's doing fine now, Pop," I replied quietly.

"Good, just go easy, Tom, you know you get out of hand with that stuff."

"I know, Pop. I know," I said. *He had no idea.*

"So did you . . . you know."

"Kill anyone?" I answered.

He nodded.

"Yes," I said blankly. Truthfully, it hadn't bothered me that I had killed someone, or more than one for that matter. It was us or them and the fact that it was them means I am here drinking coffee with my dad and not buried in the sand thousands of miles from here and that's that.

"You did the right thing, boy." He sighed. "If you ever want to talk about it, I know where you are coming from. I had to do the same in my day."

"Thanks," I said. The room went quiet, and I could hear someone raking leaves two houses down. It made me smile for a moment. I always liked this time of year. The smells and sounds seemed more alive in autumn, even as the leaves were dying; another paradox to ponder.

We talked about the family for a long while, and then I looked at my watch.

"It's getting late, Dad, I think I better get going," I said, standing up. "I'll be back tomorrow."

Dad grabbed me on both shoulders and forced me to look him in the eye. I noticed the calloused old hands; I noticed the grooves in them as they reached for me, deep and wise . . . unlike mine.

"Not everyone is going to understand what you've done, Tommy. It's your job to be patient. You've got to understand that most people in this country have never left it. They never will. But you, you have seen what's out there. It's up to you to make them understand. So take it easy with the booze. Relax and clear your head out." He patted me on the shoulder as I stepped out. I waved goodbye and started the two-mile walk to my brother's apartment in the moonless cool night.

Most of the trees were bare now, and I couldn't avoid the childlike draw of kicking through the coating of dry leaves on the streets as I walked down the neighborhood's narrow roads, my hands shoved deep in my pockets. I traced the shallow lifeline of my right palm over and over again with my fingers, and I couldn't shake off the thought of mortality that it caused. I remember the palm reader told me to "live every day to its fullest" and to "enjoy every moment"—the kind of shit you tell to someone with terminal cancer. I couldn't help thinking that I wasn't meant to live for long, and my life was a void of nothing, except the anger and frustration of not knowing what I was doing with it. I felt contempt for everyone around me, and I knew it; I carried it like a loaded pistol just aching to pull the trigger.

I began drinking heavily again. I tried to escape. I spent a night in jail. How it happened I couldn't recall in truth. All I know is what patchwork memories I can muster through the inebriated haze and what they tell me about when I did pull that trigger. I guess I had taken too many shots too fast and assaulted the barroom in a tirade. My friends had called the police. Can't blame them, but I'll never go back to that shit hole again.

My brother bailed me out to take me to the hospital, then left since he had to get to work early. The doctor in the emergency room looked at my hand, then back up at me with a disappointed look. "It's definitely broken, my friend. There appear to be several hairline fractures spider-webbing off of the major point of impact. Luckily there are only minor contusions on the outer edges and on your palm where you obviously braced a fall." He sighed and injected more Novocain into my wrist as he swabbed the cuts with Betadine solution. I tried to look away, but out of some grisly curiosity I watched as he cleaned the wounds, cutting and peeling the skin back. I wanted to see what had become of the hand that told so much. It wasn't telling shit now. It was wrapped up and numb.

I stumbled out of the emergency room at 4 a.m. and hailed a cab, my hand in a splint, arm in a sling. Fuck if I'd go back to my brother's place. He'd been pretty cool with everything, I owed him that, but he didn't need my baggage. I checked my wallet to make sure I had enough funds, and told the cabbie to take me to the Adams Inn in Quincy. It's an old motel down by the Neponset. I could get a room facing the river and watch the muddy water and highway traffic.

I went back to my brother's apartment later that day, after some sleep and some Percocets. I grabbed all my bags and penned a note telling him where to reach me. I found a message from my dad. He wanted to see me today. I tossed it in the trash on the way out the door. There was no way I could see him like this. There was no way I could face anybody like this.

I did end up in a room overlooking the river. I set up my laptop on a nightstand, and with my good hand began typing furiously. I imagined my hand blown off in the war. The thought made me laugh out loud at the irony. I hadn't been wounded in combat, yet here I was at home, hand split open and broken.

Everything I typed was angry. I thought that after I had the opportunity to vent a little, it would end—it would stop—but it did not. It kept going; from the lambs in the airport and their spoiled children to my mom's death, to my brother's success and my failure, to my credit card bills and my high car insurance. Everything was fucked up. I wrote page after page and stopped only when I had to urinate or refill my whiskey-coke. On the way back from the bathroom, I paused to read the last page of what I'd written:

> Fuck it. Fuck it all. Fuck the lady bitching at the line in the DMV . . . a few hours out of your life isn't going to kill you. Fuck my ex-girlfriend and all her boring ass phone calls about her brother and friends and backaches and fucking cramps. Fuck that wannabe businessman yacking on his cell phone like he is somebody. It's all just so amazing to me. All of them, heads stuck so far up their asses they can't see daylight. I hate them for their ignorance; their bliss . . . yet I am amazed that in our country, we can have a war with a thousand casualties, and nobody hardly notices. I FUCKING NOTICE. I notice the kid in the wheelchair rolling through the mall with his dad proudly pushing and his mom tearing up. I notice the guy with the fake leg at the bar who I used to serve with and buy his beers and recall old times. I notice the ones without the scars and prostheses, the ones with the eyes that stab right into you, the eyes that see through you. I notice because I have them too . . . and every time I notice one of them, I notice ten mindless ignorant people; people who talk about birthday parties and dry cleaning, and meetings at work. People who go home to sit down for dinner and ask their kids how school was, and never once consider that their kid could be in Iraq in a year and that chair would be empty forever. You can't talk to them about the horror of a dead child's lifeless mutilated body staring back at you from the void, knowing you took part in that end, or laugh at the humor and terror in your weapon jamming in a firefight where every crack and pop of the incoming rounds has you shaking and ducking for cover. You know they don't even know what you really do in the military in the first place, so when you talk about the chow and the bullets and the asshole Gunny, they just look at you and nod. So you just sit there and smile politely, thank them for their homecoming, and try to get out of there as soon as you can, before the bitterness and anger seep through. I'm bitter at

their weakness and their ingratitude. I'm bitter at their fucking lives and their petty complications. I'm bitter I couldn't be ignorant as well. FUCK IT ALL.

It was amazing how it flowed from my fingertips, and into this. Though "this" wasn't anything. I knew I'd delete it tomorrow when I woke up, but I was shocked at how true it was to me. I turned to the bureau mirror and stared into the face of the man looking back at me. I saw an animal—a predator no doubt—but I saw a pathetic excuse for a man first.

I looked at the bottle of whiskey I'd emptied while I typed, and, in a moment of clarity, realized—I am an alcoholic. The thought bothered me more than anything I could have ever imagined. A wound a thousand times deeper and more painful than any shrapnel or bullet graze, it was a wound to the heart. I started to weep apologetically to my reflection, seeking some response but getting none. The people we killed, the shit that went down. It all rushed back to me in a moment. I questioned some of the kills. I thought of the civilians caught in the crossfire. I wept more. I looked down to my iodine-stained wrappings, I envisioned the lifeline's shallow groove tainted brown, and I wondered again why it was so weak. Maybe the palm reader was right to say I should live life to its fullest. I won't live long this way at all.

Questions

1. While Tom is at the airport in San Diego, why does he see people around him as "spoiled lambs"? (475)

2. Why does Tom think of his time in Iraq as "pure" and "simple"? (476)

3. Why doesn't Tom talk to his father about his war experiences, even though his father invites him to?

4. Why does Tom, after reading the last page he had written, say, "I knew I'd delete it tomorrow when I woke up"? (482)

5. Is Tom justified in feeling anger toward people who seem oblivious to the war?

6. When and how is expressing anger destructive and when is it helpful? How can writing about anger be helpful in dealing with it?

John McCary

At some point during their deployment, many servicemen and servicewomen understandably become overwhelmed by the unrelenting strain of living in a combat zone. Twenty-seven-year-old U.S. Army Sergeant John McCary (1976–) was serving on a human intelligence team attached to Task Force 1-34 Armor, First Infantry Division, in Al Anbar province in Iraq. In late January 2004, after a month of heavy casualties in his unit, several of whom were friends, McCary vented in an e-mail to his family back in North Carolina about the increasing ruthlessness of the insurgents and the random, horrific violence claiming the lives of his fellow soldiers. But despite his palpable sense of anger and frustration, McCary emphasized that he knew more than ever what he was fighting for amidst the chaos of war. McCary himself survived his tour of duty and returned home in September 2004. He was honorably discharged from the army in April 2005.

After leaving the army, McCary worked for the Defense Advanced Research Projects Agency where he developed a military software suite. He went on to receive a master's degree in international security from the Georgetown University School of Foreign Service and wrote for the *Wall Street Journal* for a year. He was accepted into the State Department's Foreign Service and served as a Foreign Service Officer from 2010 to 2012 in Port-au-Prince, Haiti, where he covered human rights and security through presidential elections, riots, and the return of former dictator Jean-Claude Duvalier. Currently he lives with his wife in the Pacific Northwest and has finished a novel based on his experiences in Iraq.

TO THE FALLEN

Dear all,

We are dying. Not in some philosophical, chronological, "the end comes for all of us sooner or later" sense. Just dying. Sure, it's an occupational hazard, and yeah, you can get killed walking down the street in Anytown, USA. But not like this. Not car bombs that leave craters in the road, not jeering crowds that celebrate your destruction. We thought we had turned the tide, turned the corner, beaten the defensive rush and were headed upfield, striding into the home stretch. But they are still here. They still strive for our demise. It's never been a fair fight, and we haven't always played nice.

But not like this. No one leaves the gate looking to kill, or looking to die. No one wakes up in the morning and says, "I sure hope blowing up a whole group of Iraqis goes well today." You may be worn out, hounded by hours on end of patrols, investigations, emergency responses, guard shifts, but you never wake up and think, today's the day we'll kill a whole bunch of 'em. There's no "kill 'em all let God sort 'em out." That's for suckers and cowards, people afraid to delve into the melee and fight it out, to sort it out like soldiers.

They've killed my friends. And not in some heroic fight to defend sovereign territory, not on some suicide mission to extract a prisoner or save a family in distress. Just standing out directing traffic. Just driving downtown to a meeting. Just going to work. All I can think is, "Those poor bastards. Those poor, poor bastards."

And the opposition, they've damned anyone with the gall to actually leave their homes in the morning, because they've killed their own, too. "Indiscriminate" is one word. "Callous" does not even suffice. What battle cry says "Damn the eight-year-old boy and his little sister if they're in the area! Damn them all!"? What do you say to your men after you've scraped up the scalps of an entire Iraqi family off the road, right next to the shattered bodies of your soldiers, held together only by their shoe-laces, body armor, or helmets? "We're fighting the good fight"? I don't think so. We're just fighting. And now we're dying.

It's nothing new, not really. I know what that look is now, the one on the faces of WWII soldiers coming back from a patrol, Vietnam vets standing at the Wall. But now it's us. You know the little blurb from Connie Chung that says "two coalition soldiers were killed at a check-point today after a car bomb exploded while waiting in line"? And you think, "Ah, just two. At least it wasn't like thirty. At least it wasn't in a movie theater, or the town square."

Yeah ... I changed my mind about that one. When you sit at the memorial service, gazing down at the display: a pair of laced tan combat boots, a hastily printed 8″×10″ photo, their service rifle, barrel down, their Kevlar helmet set on top of the buttstock, and you hear their friends say, "He talked about his son every night. He's two. He can hardly talk but his dad just knew he would be a great linebacker." Or, "His wife is currently commanding a platoon elsewhere in Iraq. She will accompany the body home but has chosen to return to her own flock, to see them home safely though her husband will not join her. Our thoughts go out to their families." WHAT THOUGHTS?! What do you think? What good will you do knowing this? What help will you be, blubbering in the stands, snot drizzling from your nose, wishing you could have known before-hand, wishing you could have stopped it, pleading to God you could have taken their place, taken the suffering for them?

What do you say to the fathers of the men responsible, when you find them relaxing in their homes the next day, preparing for a meal? Should you simply strike them down for having birthed such an abomination? Or has the teeth-shattering, punch-in-the-face crunch of seeing a fallen comrade laid to rest sated your lust for blood and revenge?

Resolve, resolute, resolution, resoluteness. You feel ... compelled, to respond. To what? On whom? Why? Will your children someday say, "I'm sure glad Dad died to make Iraq safer"? No. They died standing with their friends, doing their jobs, fulfilling some far-flung nearly nonexis-tent notion called duty. They died because their friends could've died just as easily, and knowing that ... they would never shirk their duties, never call in sick, never give in to fear, never let down. When you've held a conversation with a man, briefed him on his mission, his objective, and reminded him of the potential consequences during the actioning of it, only to hear he never returned, and did not die gracefully, though blessedly quickly, prayerfully painlessly . . . you do not breathe the same ever after. Breath is sweet. Sleep is sweeter. Friends are priceless. And you cry. There's no point, no gain, no benefit but you are human and you must mourn. It is your nature.

It is also now undeniable, irrevocable, that you will see your mission through. You will strive every day, you will live, though you are not ever again sure why. Ideals . . . are so . . . far, far away from the burnt stink of charred metal. I, we, must see it through to the end. They have seen every instant, every mission, every chore, every day through, not to its end but to theirs. How can you ever deny, degrade, desecrate their sacrifice and loss with anything less than all you have? Their lives are lost, whether as a gift, laid down at the feet of their friends, or a pointless discard of precious life . . . I doubt I'll ever know.

I'm OK, Mom. I'm just a little . . . shaken, a little sad. I know this isn't any Divine mission. No God, Allah, Jesus, Buddha, or other divinity ever decreed, "Go get your body ripped to shreds, it's for the better." This is Man's doing. This is Man's War. And War it is. It is not fair, nor right, nor simple . . . nor is it over. I wish the presence of those responsible only to dissipate, to transform into average citizens, fathers, sons, and brothers. I don't care about bloodlust, justice, or revenge. But they . . . they . . . will not rest until our souls are wiped from this plane of existence, until we no longer exist in their world. Nothing less suffices. And so we will fight. I will not waver, nor falter. Many of my fellows will cry for no mercy, no compassion. For those responsible, for those whose goal is destruction purely for effect, death only as a message, for whom killing is a means of communication, I cannot promise we, or I, will give pardon. With all, we will be harsh, and strict, but not unjust, not indiscriminate. And we will not give up. We cannot. Our lives are forever tied to those lost, and we cannot leave them now, as we might have were they still living.

We have . . . so little time . . . to mourn, so little time to sigh, to breathe, to laugh, to remember. To forget. Every day awaits us, impatient,

Questions

1. Why does McCary say that a "kill 'em all let God sort 'em out" attitude is for "suckers and cowards"? (485) What does he mean when he talks about sorting it out like soldiers?

2. Why does McCary call duty a "far-flung nearly nonexistent notion"? (486)

3. Why does McCary see continuing to fight as a "tribute to the Fallen"? (488)

4. Is it necessary to believe you are fighting "the good fight" to serve well?

5. How do you draw the line between behaving harshly toward the enemy that you hold responsible for killing your comrades and behaving unjustly toward that enemy?

6. What is the best tribute a veteran can offer to his or her comrades who were killed in action?

Glossary of Military Acronyms

AF: Air Force; Armed Forces

APC: armored personnel carrier

ARVN: Army of the Republic of Vietnam

CCATT: Critical Care Air Transport Team

COP: command operations post

DEROS: date eligible for return from overseas

EFP: explosively formed penetrator

FOB: forward operating base

FRG: Family Readiness Group

GSW: gunshot wound

HMMWV: high-mobility multipurpose wheeled vehicle

IED: improvised explosive device

KIA: killed in action

MOS: military occupational specialty

MP: military police

MRE: meal ready to eat

NCO: noncommissioned officer

NVA: North Vietnamese Army

PFC: private first class

POW: prisoner of war

PTSD: posttraumatic stress disorder

PX: Post Exchange

RPG: rocket-propelled grenade

R&R: rest and recuperation; rest and recreation

VA: Veterans Administration

VC: Vietcong

Acknowledgments

All possible care has been taken to trace ownership and secure permission for each selection in this anthology. The Great Books Foundation wishes to thank the following authors, publishers, and representatives for permission to reproduce copyrighted material:

Selection from ILIAD, by Homer, translated by Stanley Lombardo. Copyright © 1997 by Hackett Publishing Company, Inc. Reproduced by permission of Hackett Publishing Company, Inc.

The Melian Dialogue, from THUCYDIDES: THE HISTORY OF THE PELOPONNESIAN WAR, edited in translation by Sir R. W. Livingstone (1960). Reproduced by permission of Oxford University Press, USA.

On Discipline in Democratic Armies, from DEMOCRACY IN AMERICA, by Alexis de Tocqueville, translated by Harvey C. Mansfield and Delba Winthrop. Copyright © 2000 by The University of Chicago Press. Reproduced by permission of The University of Chicago Press.

Selection from WAR AND PEACE: NORTON CRITICAL EDITION SECOND EDITION, by Leo Tolstoy, edited by George Gibian, translated by Aylmer Maude. Copyright © 1996, 1966 by W. W. Norton & Company, Inc. Reproduced by permission of W. W. Norton & Company, Inc.

Why War? from COLLECTED PAPERS, VOLUME 5, by Sigmund Freud. Reproduced by permission of Perseus Books Group and by permission of the Marsh Agency, Ltd., on behalf of Sigmund Freud Copyrights.

Italian Ordeal Surpises Congress, by Anne O'Hare McCormick. From the *New York Times*, December 23, 1944. Copyright © 1944 by the *New York Times*. Reproduced by permission of the *New York Times*.

Poems, from THE COLLECTED POEMS OF WILFRED OWEN, by Wilfred Owen. Copyright © 1963 by Chatto and Windus, Ltd. Reproduced by permission of New Directions Publishing Corp.

To a Conscript of 1940, from COLLECTED POEMS, by Herbert Read. Reproduced by permission of David Higham Associates, Ltd.

Soldier's Home, from THE SHORT STORIES OF ERNEST HEMINGWAY, by Ernest Hemingway. Copyright © 1938 by Ernest Hemingway; copyright © 1966 by Mary Hemingway. Reproduced by permission of Scribner, a division of Simon and Schuster, Inc.